Mary
for
Earth and Heaven

To the memory of so many, known and unknown,
who have furthered understanding
of the Blessed Virgin Mary
through the work of the
Ecumenical Society of the Blessed Virgin Mary

Mary
for
Earth and Heaven

Papers on Mary and Ecumenism
given at International Congresses of the
Ecumenical Society of the Blessed Virgin Mary
at Leeds (1998) and Oxford (2000)
and Conferences at Woldingham (1997)
and Maynooth (2001)

edited by

William M. McLoughlin OSM
and
Jill Pinnock

with a Foreword by

Cardinal Cassidy

First published in 2002

Gracewing
2 Southern Avenue, Leominster
Herefordshire HR6 0QF

ISBN 0 85244 556 3

Typeset by Action Publishing Technology Ltd,
Gloucester GL1 5SR

Printed in England by
MPG Books Ltd,
Bodmin PL31 1EG

Contents

Acknowledgements

The poem 'Mary, my child's lovely', by Frances Young, was first published in *Face to Face* by T. & T. Clark and is used here with permission.

The paper 'Mary and the saints in early Scottish poetry' by John Macquarrie was first published in the festschrift in honour of the eightieth birthday of Eamon Carroll OCarm, entitled *Mother Behold Your Son*, published by the Carmelite Institute, Washington DC, 2001.

The Editors wish to express their appreciation for editorial assistance from Fr Edward Yarnold SJ and Mr David Carter.

The poem 'The Women in the Matthean Genealogy', reproduced in the Homily by Dr Edward D. Garten, is used with the permission of SPCK.

The statue of Our Lady and Child shown on the front cover was presented to Chichester Cathedral to mark the Seventh International Congress of the Ecumenical Society of the Blessed Virgin Mary held in Chichester in 1986. It is reproduced here by kind permission of the Dean and Chapter.

Notes on Contributors

Janet Barcroft, a graduate student at the Centre for Jewish–Christian Relations in Cambridge, was the winner of the Millennium Essay Prize for her essay examining the place of Jewish–Christian Relations in the Northern Ireland conflict. She is the Church of Ireland representative on the Assembly of the Council of Churches for Britain and Ireland.

Sr Mary Cecily Boulding OP MA BD PhD, a Roman Catholic member of ARCIC II, was until recently lecturer in theology at St Cuthbert's College, Ushaw, Durham, specializing in ecclesiology, Reformation issues, and ecumenism.

The Most Reverend Dr Philip Boyce, a member of the Discalced Carmelites, taught spirituality and dogmatic theology at the Pontifical Theological Faculty of the Carmelites (the Teresianum) in Rome. In 1974 he received his doctorate for his dissertation on the spirituality of John Henry Newman. He is (Roman Catholic) Bishop of Raphoe, Co. Donegal, and a member of the Congregation for Divine Worship and the Discipline of the Sacraments.

The Reverend Fr Walter T. Brennan, of the Order of the Friar Servants of Mary (OSM), solemnly professed friar and priest of the United States of America Province, had served as the Prior-Provincial of the former Eastern Province of the United States from 1988 to 1991 and was Director of the Marian Center until his death on 8 March 2001, aged 65. He taught for many years at Chicago Theological Union and lectured often and widely on Theology and the BVM, including summer sessions at the International Marian Research Institute, Ohio.

The Revd Fr Eamon R. Carroll OCarm DD, formerly of Loyola University, Chicago, is a noted Marian scholar, and was recently presented with a *Festschrift*, in honour of his eightieth birthday, entitled *Mother Behold Your Son*.

David Carter MA MLitt was formerly Head of Religious Studies at Wilson's School, Wallington, Surrey, and is Chairman of the London branch of ESBVM; he is a Methodist member of the Roman Catholic–Methodist Theological Dialogue in England and Wales and of the British Methodist–Roman Catholic committee which produced *Mary, Mother of* *the Lord: sign of grace, faith and holiness.* He is a tutor with the Open University.

The Right Reverend Richard Clarke studied at Trinity College Dublin and King's College London, and was appointed (Church of Ireland) Bishop of Meath and Kildare in 1996. He is the author of a book on faith entitled *And Is It True?*

The Very Reverend Ireneu Craciun DD (Maynooth), who comes from Romania, is the parish priest of the Greek Orthodox community in Dublin.

His Eminence Cardinal Cahal B. Daly is Archbishop Emeritus of Armagh. He was an Observer at the 1988 Lambeth Conference.

Sr Marie Farrell RSM is senior lecturer in Systematic Theology and Spirituality at the Catholic Institute of Sydney, Australia.

The Reverend Dr Edward D. Garten, an American Methodist, is Dean of Libraries at the University of Dayton, Ohio.

The Reverend Fr Michael Hurley SJ, founder and first Director of the Irish School of Ecumenics, and founder of the Columbanus Community of Reconciliation, is the author of *Christian Unity: An Ecumenical Second Spring?*

The Right Reverend Edward Knapp-Fisher MA (Oxon) MA (Cantab), was a member of ARCIC I. Formerly Principal of Cuddesdon Theological College, Oxford, he was (Anglican) Bishop of Pretoria 1960–75, and subsequently SubDean of Westminster; he is presently Custos of St Mary's Hospital, Chichester.

Neville Kyrke-Smith MA studied Theology at Worcester College, Oxford and was an Anglican minister for eight years. His marriage to Jean – a Russian graduate – sparked an interest in Eastern Europe and after following her into the Catholic Church in 1990, he became National Director of the Catholic charity Aid to the Church in Need. He travels widely promoting its charitable work, including Ukraine, Belarus, Russia, Siberia and China.

The Reverend Brendan Leahy is lecturer in the Mater Dei Institute, Dublin, and author of *The Marian Profile in the Ecclesiology of Hans Urs von Balthasar*.

The Reverend Dr John Macquarrie was Lady Margaret Professor of Divinity and Canon of Christ Church, Oxford, 1970–86. He is the author of numerous important works on spirituality, theology and philosophy, including *Mary for All Christians*.

The Very Reverend Canon John McHugh DD, formerly Lecturer on New Testament at Ushaw College and Durham University, and English member of the Pontifical Biblical Commission, is author of *The Mother of Jesus in the New Testament* (1978), and is presently engaged in research on St John's Gospel.

The Reverend Fr Peter McVerry SJ lives in the Ballymun community and works with the Centre for Faith and Justice. He single-handedly established Ireland's first hostel for homeless children in Dublin in 1979; since then he has set up three other hostels for homeless young people, and has recently opened a drug detox centre in Co. Meath.

The Right Reverend Samuel Poyntz MA BD PhD Hon DLitt was (Anglican) Bishop of Cork, Cloyne and Ross 1978–87 and Bishop of Connor 1987–95. He represented Ireland at the Toronto Conference of Anglican and Catholic Bishops. He was formerly chairman of the Church Unity Committee of the General Synod of the Church of Ireland, and of the Irish Council of Churches, Co-chairman of the Irish InterChurch Meeting and Vice-President of the British Council of Churches.

The Reverend Keith G. Riglin MA BEd MTh is Minister of St Columba's United Reformed Church, Cambridge, and Church of Scotland Chaplain to the University of Cambridge.

Josephine Robinson MA, married and mother of three, is chairman of the Association of Catholic Women and author of *The Inner Goddess: Feminist Theology in the Light of Catholic Teaching*. She works as a volunteer with the charities Christian Aid, the Order of Christian Unity, and Life, as speaker, counsellor and fundraiser.

The Reverend Jeremy P. Sheehy MA DPhil, sometime Dean of Divinity, Fellow and Chaplain of New College, Oxford, is Principal of St Stephen's House, Oxford.

Mar Bawai Soro, Bishop in Western California of the Assyrian Church of the East, was born in Iraq, ordained in Chicago, gained his Master's in Theology at the Catholic University of America in Washington DC, and received his STD at the Pontifical University of St Thomas (Angelicum) in Rome. A distinguished member of a range of international ecumenical commissions, he was privileged to be involved in the signing ceremony at the Vatican on 11 November 1994 of the **Common Christological Declaration** between Mar Dinkha IV, Patriarch of the Assyrian Church of the East and Pope John Paul II, which resolved a 1500-year disagreement and helped promote the various dialogues in which he participated and to foster the growth in unity of these two churches.

The Revd Fr Alberic Stacpoole OSB MC MA DPhil FRHistS is a monk of Ampleforth, and formerly Senior Tutor at St Benet's Hall, Oxford. He is the author of *Vatican II by Those Who Were There;* he was General Secretary of ESBVM from 1980 to 1994, and has often contributed to the published writings of the Society.

The Reverend Fr Norman Tanner SJ is University Research Lecturer at the University of Oxford, and editor of *Decrees of the Ecumenical Councils*, 2 vols. (1990).

Sr Benedicta Ward SLG MA DPhil is Reader in the History of Christian Spirituality in the University of Oxford. Her published works include *Miracles and the Medieval Mind* (1982).

The Right Reverend Kallistos Ware is Bishop of Diokleia and assistant bishop in the Orthodox Archdiocese of Thyateira and Great Britain. During 1966–2001 he was Spalding Lecturer in Eastern Orthodox Studies in the University of Oxford, and had pastoral charge of the Greek parish in Oxford.

The Reverend Fr Edward Yarnold SJ DD is University Research Lecturer and Tutor in Theology at the University of Oxford, and formerly Master of Campion Hall, Oxford. He is internationally renowned as a writer and speaker, and has served the ESBVM both as Associate General Secretary and, since 1994, as Hon. General Secretary. He was a member of ARCIC I and II from 1970 to 1991.

The Reverend Professor Frances M. Young OBE BA MA PhD HonDD, a Methodist minister, is Edward Cadbury Professor of Theology and Pro-Vice Chancellor of the University of Birmingham. Her published works include *From Nicaea to Chalcedon*, and *The Making of the Creeds*. She is married with three sons, the eldest of whom was born with severe mental disabilities. Her theological exploration of this experience is found in *Face to Face: A narrative essay in the theology of suffering.*

Foreword

The forthcoming publication of a further Collection of the Papers of the Ecumenical Society of the Blessed Virgin Mary, at the beginning of this new Christian Millennium, is indeed an important contribution to the ongoing search for greater communion within the Christian community.

The Millennium that we have now left behind was a disastrous time for the unity of Christians. Firstly, East and West were divided and then at the halfway stage of the millennium, the Western Church suffered a whole series of divisions. Doctrinal arguments all too often led to violence and war.

There was no difference of understanding or doctrine regarding the place of Mary in the Church at the time of the schism between the East and the West. On the contrary, however, Mary was unfortunately to figure prominently in the disputations of the Reform in the Western Church.

As Christians during the twentieth century set out on the path of mutual reconciliation, it was logical that in the West the role of Mary in the Church would become a matter for serious consideration. This was particularly true with respect to the Church of Rome and the Churches coming out of the Reformation. The Church of England and the Church of Rome were divided on this matter not so much on the basic doctrine in respect of Mary, as on the devotional practice within the Roman Catholic Church and the Marian dogmas of the Assumption and the Immaculate Conception.

But even within the Reformation Churches, the question of Mary was related at first more to what was seen as exaggerated devotion to Mary, rather than to dissent about the place she should have in Christian self-understanding. Luther reacted vigorously to what he saw as 'terrible papist proportions' in Marian devotion at that time. Yet in his last sermon, on 17 January 1546, when death was in the offing, he said: 'Is Christ alone to be adored? Or is the holy Mother of God rather not to be honoured? This the woman who crushed the serpent's head. Hear us. For your Son denies you nothing.'

In recent years, various dialogues in which the Roman Church is engaged have taken up the question of Mary. ARCIC II is presently engaged in such dialogue. Already we can say that greater understanding with regard to the place of Mary in the Church has resulted.

The Ecumenical Society of the Blessed Virgin Mary has helped considerably in creating an atmosphere for such ongoing dialogue, and the present series of papers, published under the title **Mary for Earth and Heaven**, is an example of the value of the work that the Society is doing.

Of all the women that have a place in the Bible, Mary without doubt has the place of honour. While Christians can learn much from the outstanding female heroes of the Hebrew Scriptures, they see Mary as one of themselves – yet one who is chosen by God to be the mother of Jesus, the Son of God and Second person of the Most Holy Trinity. She was the first Christian and we can learn from her obedience to God's plans for us in this world in which we seek to make his presence known. With Mary, we are children of a loving Father, and like her we can say: *The Almighty has done great things for me, Holy is his name* (Luke 1.49). As we observe her in the Scriptures going about her daily tasks, we find inspiration for being ourselves bearers of Christ and of his love to those in special need of that loving presence.

The Papers published in this Collection look at Mary as she appears in the Scriptures, in Systematic Theology, in spirituality and in the Great Councils of the Church, and then speak of her role in the search for Christian Unity, in relation to the place of women in the Church, and in promoting justice, in the writings of the Fathers of the Church, and in literature.

I feel sure that any reader of these Papers will find there ample matter for thought and I would hope that at the end will agree with me that after all Mary should not be a source of division, but rather a powerful force for communion among these who acknowledge her Son Jesus Christ as Lord and Saviour.

Edward Idris Cardinal Cassidy
Rome, 21 February 2002.

Preface

It is always possible to make heavy weather of a task. Thirty-five years ago an inspiration took hold of a group of Christians who sought to make light what many thought to be not only a heavy task but one doomed to failure. They undertook a move away from what have since been called the frozen hearts and narrow minds of the 1950s that had held sway for generations and to try to overcome the mutual suspicions of Christians expressed in regard to differing attitudes to understanding the role of the Blessed Virgin Mary. Centuries of the habit of defending respective outlooks against the unknown other of strangers has tried to give way to an effort to know others, perhaps to test them and their sincerity, but ultimately to commit to a renewed friendship in Christ because of a new awareness of his Mother and her place in the life of his followers.

The principle of Cardinal Mercier and the Malines Conferences has constantly motivated the society in seeing there is no virtue in the cynicism of saying our divisions in this regard are inevitable and insurmountable, when in fact suspicion of what others believe and think is not infrequently based on ignorance. In order to follow the Master's command to love one another, the task of first knowing one another is an imperative in order to remedy the suspicion founded on ignorance which is the reason for all divisions. To eradicate suspicion, the need was and is to transform ignorance through a sound knowledge, and not allow false assumptions about and erroneous preconceptions as to what others truly understand and hold to prevent us from seeking one mind and heart. The risk-takers among us want to let the Spirit of Truth show us that if our ways are right we may help others to see; and if our ways are wrong that the Spirit may help us to see.

As a society, the Ecumenical Society of the Blessed Virgin Mary readily recognizes the significant ecumenical advances that have been achieved, but equally is conscious with many others that the same enthusiasm that was evident in the early stages has seemingly weakened. The cynic might ask whether many were ever really on board the ecumenical ride, or say that too many had thought there might be a reunion among the Christian traditions not without a change of heart indeed, but without a fundamental change of mind on any body's part. Seminal ecumenical influences both within the Society and in the wider Christian world long for the retention of what is best, while discarding what is unworthy in all the Christian traditions. To achieve this, there are many things we still need to learn from one another. In *Ut unum sint*, the Pope proposes among other things a dialogue on the Marian topic between the Christian traditions, Reformed and Catholic alike. His Holiness Pope John Paul II insists on the ecumenical imperative, but does so at the same time as insisting on certainty in truth and clarity of meaning in matters of doctrine.

As the Ecumenical Society of the Blessed Virgin Mary marked thirty years of effort dedicated to the fostering of the declared aims of the Society, in that very same year, though without any seeming awareness of the contribution of the ESBVM, as a response to that overture of the Pope there appeared the Marian document *Mary in the Plan of God and in the Communion of Saints* prepared by the Groupe des Dombes. The latter was composed of theologians from different Christian confessions, who published an ecumenical text at Dombes in 1997, hoping to overcome the very real differences in theology and practice (especially in worship) that trouble and divide the Christian traditions by suggesting the quiet growth of the Marian dimension which is inherent in the Christian religion. Ten years earlier, in 1987, the ESBVM published a collection of papers, in which a key contributor to the ecumenical exchange on Mary, the Revd Dr J. A. Ross Mackenzie, then Minister of the First Presbyterian Church, Florida, had reminded us of the Jacob Lipschitz statue that stands in the cloisters of St Mary's Abbey, Iona, with its remarkable inscription, 'I have made this Virgin for a better understanding to spread among all people'. An important meeting between Anglican and Roman Catholic bishops took place in Mississauga, Canada, in May 2000 under the presidency of Cardinal Cassidy, then President of the Pontifical Council for Promoting Christian Unity, and Dr George Carey, Archbishop of Canterbury. In response to a specific recommendation from this meeting, ARCIC carried forward its discussion on Mary in the life and doctrine of the Church, a topic to which it had given preliminary consideration in 1999 as a matter outstanding from its original mandate, and these deliberations continue. ESBVM Congresses (Leeds in 1998 and Oriel, Oxford, in 2000) and Conferences (Woldingham in 1997 and Maynooth, Dublin in 2001), together with regional conferences and wide-ranging efforts of individual members of the Society have pursued the task of dialogue on the Marian topic, resulting in the material collected in this latest volume of papers. A forthcoming Fourteenth International Congress to be held in Chester in 2002 plans a continuation of the same exchange.

In 1978, His Holiness Pope John Paul II, visiting Constantinople, spoke of his millennium dream that the year 2000 'may find us standing side by side in full communion'. To hope is to look to the future with real confidence, and is not merely wishful thinking. It is to imagine the real. As we slipped into the third millennium, with that goal unachieved, are we to give up this hope? The power of the Spirit is the help of Christian hope. Jesus promises the Spirit for his followers whose own resources are inadequate. The coincidence of the transferred Solemnity of the Annunication occurring again at the time of this Preface being written reminds us that the Holy Spirit has come upon Mary (Luke 1.35) and she waits with the believing community for the outpouring of the Spirit on all (Acts 1.14). The inadequacy of the followers of Jesus persists. Our times powerfully demonstrate the reality that Christians are often fallible and ever disappointing in their weakness, yet always potentially glorious human beings. In light of this, cannot the ESBVM help by pondering Mary as the follower in whom that potential is realized?

The focus of the ESBVM on the Blessed Virgin Mary's importance in the efforts of Ecumenism so resonates with new developments in the dialogue at this stage, that it seems evident that the work of the Society is far from over. The frozen hearts of bygone times are warmed by pondering with the Virgin on all these things in her heart. The fact that the Society currently enjoys the patronage of key leaders from nearly all the major Christian traditions suggests a continuing responsibility, and the significance it has come to hold expressed in the renewal of the Canterbury link with the Society in 1997 by Dr Carey when he said: 'The ESBVM has had an important place in the ecumenical landscape for many years and has made a significant contribution to the unity of God's Church'. May the service of the Society continue with courage and well-founded hope!

8 April 2002
Solemnity of the Most Holy Annunciation of the Lord
W. M. McLoughlin OSM
Sts Peter and Paul, Combe Down, Bath

Mary
in
Scripture

1

The Wedding at Cana
(John 2.1–11)

John McHugh

'On the third day there was a wedding at Cana in Galilee' (John 2.1). Many commentators see here a reference to the resurrection-day, and I must confess that for many years I too followed this opinion, seeing in the first manifestation of Jesus' glory (2.11) a foreshadowing of the glory of the resurrection. It is interesting to notice now that I made no use of the idea in my book on *The Mother of Jesus in the New Testament*. The parallel with the resurrection was clearly of no help at all for understanding the Cana story.

There is, however, another possible interpretation. John 1.19–51 presents its story in four consecutive days. After verse 19, verses 29, 35, 43 read 'on the next day', to which the phrase in 2.1 'on the third day' adds two more. The narrative is thereby set in the framework of a 'First Week' in Jesus' ministry. The six days are marked out as follows:

Day 1	vv. 19–28	John's witness about himself
Day 2	vv. 29–34	John's witness about Jesus
Day 3	vv. 35–42	Three of John's followers join Jesus
Day 4	vv. 43–51	Philip and Nathanael join Jesus
Day 6	ch. 2.1–12	The Wedding at Cana

The emphatic phrase 'on the third day' will therefore indicate the sixth day of the First Week of Jesus' ministry.

'The mother of Jesus said to him, They have no wine' (2.3). Several writers, ancient and modern, have understood these words to imply that Jesus' mother was pleading for a miracle, which he was unwilling to perform at that time. Augustine expressly states that Jesus here refuses to perform a miracle at his mother's request, and Chrysostom even sees, in the words which follow, a reprimand to Mary for wanting to parade herself as the mother of a son who could work miracles.

Thomas Aquinas is more subtle. In explaining the role of Mary in this text, he writes that we need only place our needs before God, without inquiring how he may help; and that is why Mary simply mentioned to

Jesus the shortage of wine. John Calvin, too, doubted whether Mary 'hoped for, or asked for, anything, since he had so far performed no miracle'. Perhaps the most gentle interpretation is that of Bengel (1687–1752): Mary wished politely to suggest that Jesus, and the others too, should leave before the poverty of the newly-weds was, to their embarrassment, exposed.

Mary's words do not of themselves imply that she is hinting that Jesus should intervene, much less that he should perform a miracle. But, when one considers the context, it certainly looks as if it was in the hope or expectation that Jesus would do something to relieve the embarrassment of the newly-wed couple.

The various renderings of verse 4 in the main English-language versions illustrate both the broad measure of agreement about the sense of the phrase in John 2.4a, and the difficulty of catching the idiom in English.[1] Literally, it means 'What is that to me and to you?' It is an idiomatic expression found in both the Old and New Testaments, and 'used to deprecate interference or, more strongly, to reject overtures of any kind. The shade of meaning can be deduced only from the context' (Jerusalem Bible).

Many have taken these words (however translated) to be a merely rhetorical question. For example, 'What is that to me and to you?': answer, 'Nothing!' It certainly appears, at first, that Jesus by this reply is declining to act as his mother might wish. Yet she does not take his words as a rebuff (2.5), and indeed Jesus immediately provides a solution to the problem. Hence the most satisfactory interpretation of these apparently inconsistent verses is to take the phrase as a serious question, and to look for a serious answer. I suggest that in the context at Cana the best translation is 'What relationship is there between you and me?' But it is too simple to answer 'None'. Jesus is rather questioning the relationship that has up to this point bound him to his mother, and implying that he can no longer remain part of the Nazareth family. It is John's equivalent of Luke 2.49 and 4.16–30.

The introduction of the term 'Woman' supports this interpretation. Apart from the two occurrences at Cana and Calvary in John 2.3 and 19.26, there is no text in the Bible or in rabbinical writings where a son addresses his mother as 'Woman'. The choice of this unusual form of address thus confirms the view that in these two texts the evangelist wished to draw attention away from Mary's blood-relationship with Jesus, in order to intimate that she was to have, in the gospel story, a role very different from that of being Jesus' physical mother.

The second half of verse 4 may be translated either as a statement or as a question. If the words are a statement, they give the reason why Jesus refuses to intervene, namely, because 'My hour is not yet come'.

On the other hand, if the words are not a statement, but a question, their meaning is reversed, and the sense becomes 'Is not my hour now come?' This second interpretation (which is that of Augustine) has been steadily gathering adherents over the twentieth century. If the text be construed as a question, Jesus meets his mother's anxiety about the dearth of wine by indicating that it is time for him to leave the family home and to begin his Father's work. The two parts of verse 4 are really declaring two aspects of the same truth, and are best put into English by combining the two sentences into one. 'What relationship is there, woman, between you and me, now that my hour is approaching?' The story can continue, but in a direction different from what the reader might have expected. Jesus' mother, unperturbed, simply remarks, 'Do whatever he tells you'.

From this point onwards, the story is familiar, but to understand it, we need to ask why the evangelist has chosen to mark the climax of the First Week of the public ministry with the account of this wedding.

It was Hosea, around 735–725 BC, who first introduced into the heart of Israel's religion the language of marital love. His own love for the wife who deserted him unveiled to him the depth of God's unconditional and unchanging love for faithless Israel (chapters 1–2, especially 2.19–20; 11.1–4). Later prophets began to speak of the Covenant of Sinai as the moment when God had wedded himself to Israel (Jer. 2.2), and to look forward to an era when Yahweh and Israel would once again be united as bridegroom and bride, in faithfulness and everlasting love (Isa. 54.1–8; 61.10; 62.4–5). The New Covenant promised in Jer. 31.31–4 and Ezek. 37.26–8 would take effect when the exiles of Judah 'returned' to Yahweh with their whole heart (Jer. 24.5–7), saying 'Let us join ourselves to Yahweh in an everlasting covenant which will never be forgotten' (50.5). The image reached its high point in the allegorical interpretation of the Song of Songs, which made possible the acceptance of this poem into the canon of Hebrew Scripture. In the Old Testament, the bridegroom and bride are always Yahweh and his Chosen Poeple, Israel, never once the Messiah. In the words of Isa. 54.5, cited in that same rabbinical text, 'Your Maker is your husband: Yahweh Sabaoth is his name'.

In the New Testament too, the wedding-feast is a symbol of the coming of salvation, of the fulfilment of time. It features three times in the parables, in the parables of the King's Son (Matt. 22.1–14), of the Ten Virgins (Matt. 25.1–13), and of the Waiting Servants (Luke 12.35–6). Further, with only two possible exceptions, here at John 2.9 and at Rev. 18.23, in the New Testament the word for 'bridegroom' always refers to Jesus Christ. References to the Church as the bride of Christ clearly imply that Christ was regarded as the heavenly bridegroom (2 Cor. 11.2; Eph. 5.25; Rev. 19.7; 21.9), and Rev. 19.9 speaks of the wedding feast of the Lamb. In short, by the time John's Gospel came to be written, Jesus of Nazareth was for all his followers the bridegroom, the King's Son.

So at the beginning of the Gospel, in the Cana story, the evangelist presents the Word made flesh as the bridegroom standing at the threshold, come to claim his bride (compare Rev. 3.20). Not that Jesus is the bridegroom-in-the-Cana-story, whom he saves from embarrassment; but in another sense, it *is* Jesus who is the true bridegroom, for it is he who has been keeping the best wine till the last.

'He manifested his glory.' What are we to make of the water that became wine? There is nothing quite like this narrative anywhere else in the Gospels. Many Christians understand it as a historical record of the fact that Jesus once changed water into wine, physically, but others would regard that interpretation as a trivializing of divine omnipotence. They seek a more easily credible interpretation, and we may observe that the Gospel does not state that the water was *changed* into wine. The verb *changed* does not occur in the Gospel. John 2.9 refers simply to the 'water *become* wine', and 4.46 'where he *made* the water wine'.

Augustine is a good guide to start with. His first homily on this text begins by observing that every year rain-water is turned into wine, and on a far grander scale, yet nobody marvels, simply because it happens all the time. Augustine then writes: 'excepto miraculo, aliquid in ipso facto mysterii et sacramenti latet' (*Tract.* 8.3), a sentence which may be translated as 'setting aside the miracle, some hidden, some secret and symbolic meaning lies concealed in what was actually done'. He expounds this meaning in the following homily, beginning with the principle 'Christ kept the best wine until now – that is, his Gospel' (*Tract.* 9.2). The writings of the Old Testament, read without Christian understanding, were like water (2 Cor. 3.14–16), but when interpreted by the risen Lord (Luke 24.13–47) became like wine. 'Our Lord Jesus Christ changed the water into wine, and what previously had no taste began to have a taste, what before did not intoxicate became intoxicating' (*Tract.* 9.5). Augustine then begins to search for hidden meanings in the details of the story, seeing in the six water-jars the six ages of the world, and we need not follow him in this. But we can safely accept his principle, that the Cana story is like a parable, teaching the reader to see (or, rather, to taste) in the religion of the Old Testament something which, when transformed by Jesus Christ, is intoxicating. The Cana story cannot be understood except in the light of the Old Testament background.

It was in fact only natural that as the Church developed, the metaphor of drinking the water of wisdom should be applied to the teaching of Jesus, as it had formerly been applied to the teaching of the Old Covenant (Sir. 15.3). In the Fourth Gospel, the first explicit hint of this application occurs in the private conversation at John 4.13–14, the public proclamation at 7.37–8. The same theme recurs in the Book of Revelation, where we read of drinking from 'the springs of the water of life' (Rev. 7.17; 21.6; 22.1, 17). The metaphor was early established in Christian catechesis (1 Cor. 10.4), and the idea of drinking from the wellsprings of Jesus' wisdom developed quite naturally (compare Isa. 12.3; Ps. 36.8–9).

A wedding feast would normally take seven days, and as always in the Mediterranean, wine would be in plentiful supply. Abundance of wine was also a blessing promised for, and characteristic of, the Day of Yahweh, the end of time, as we read at the conclusion of Hosea (14.7) and of Amos (9.13–14); compare Jer. 31.12; Zech. 10.7. However, the abundance of wine described in the Old Testament does not signify only a liberal supply of alcoholic drink. In the Old Testament, wine is sometimes (admittedly rarely) a symbol of God's holy wisdom, divine revelation. So in Isa. 55.1 we read, 'Come, buy wine and milk without money', and in Prov. 9.4–6, 'Eat of the bread and drink of the wine that I have mixed for you'. Here wine signifies wisdom, teaching that is precious and valued. Both water and wine are in Jewish thought symbols of heavenly wisdom.

Can this story of the wedding at Cana have been in any way based on historical recollection, or was it simply made up for kerygmatic or for catechetical purposes?

Only three miles west of Cana is a little village called Kaukab. We know that beween AD 150 and 200 there were some Christians living there who were rightly proud of the fact that they could trace their family tree back to Jesus of Nazareth.[2] It is not absurd to suggest that their family could recall that Jesus had once attended a wedding at Cana at which the wine had run out; that at his suggestion, water had been served in place of the wine; and that the steward in charge of the feast, when he tasted this water, said, perhaps as a witticism, perhaps as a sagacious comment, 'You have kept the best wine until now'. Could not the family recollection of some event like this lie at the origin of the gospel story?

The canonical text contains some evidence that it was intended to have a symbolic meaning. The first indication is to be found in the way the central fact of the narrative, the discovery that water has become wine, is presented. The chief steward alone tastes the water, and one sip leads him to utter his remark. Further, it is only when the drink is tasted that it is found to have been turned into wine; was there no visible change in colour, no fragrance of a bouquet? Lastly there is no hint that anyone other than the chief steward touched the drink; and the text clearly reads: 'when he had tasted *the water* (become wine)'.

I argued at the beginning that the wedding was deliberately placed on the sixth day of the First Week of Jesus' ministry. Now, though the Gospel does not say that Jesus gave any teaching on this occasion, presumably he was not entirely silent, and it is not far-fetched to suggest that, if he spoke, he said something about the wedding. In that case, might he not have spoken about the institution of marriage (Gen. 1–2), about Hosea's profound meditation on marriage as a symbol of God's love, and about God's promise to restore the broken bonds of love even with Samaria and her daughters (Hos. 14.4–7; Ezek. 16.53–5)?

The evangelist is therefore declaring that Jesus on this occasion at Cana spoke in a manner which was, in comparison with the most wholesome water of wisdom found in Jewish teaching, even more attractive, the choicest wine. That is to say, Jesus at Cana began to instruct his disciples in the understanding of Holy Scripture. At his first visit to Cana, Jesus 'brings us joy ... and gives us to drink of the wine that proceeds from His power, which was water when it was drawn, but became wine when Jesus transformed it. And truly before Jesus the Scripture was water, but from the time of Jesus it has become wine to us' (Origen).[3]

If this is the message of the story about the first sign at Cana, that Jesus taught his disciples how to comprehend and to interpret the Old Testament, then Mary's role in the story becomes clearer, and easier to understand. She was already there. She is presented as the mother of Jesus, that is, as the one by whose motherhood he is entitled to call himself an Israelite, a Jew, and the one who had brought him up in the ways of the Law, teaching him to observe all the commandments of Moses. It is she who now says to him 'They have no wine', words which may indicate (especially after the Fall of Jerusalem in AD 70) that the people of Israel are no longer able to celebrate worthily and joyfully their marriage to their God. And Jesus turns the life-giving water of the Old Testament into wine.

To this Jesus replies that the daughter of Zion who was his physical mother has now fulfilled her role of bearing him and rearing him. So has Judaism. Jesus, on the sixth day of the First Week of his ministry, leaves family and home to undertake his Father's work. But on the sixth day of the Final Week of his life (cf. John 12.1), when all is accomplished, 'the mother of Jesus', this same Daughter[4] of Zion, will be honoured and graced with a new role, as will Jesus' Jewish disciples, representatives of the faithful remnant of the old Israel (19.25–7). On that day there will be another wedding, its bride a new Jerusalem, the wedding of the Lamb (Rev. 19.6–9; 21.1–4).

Notes

1   AV=KJV=RV, 'Woman, what have I to do with thee?'; RSV, 'O woman, what

have you to do with me?'; NRSV, 'Woman, what concern is that to you and to me?'; NEB, 'Your concern, mother, is not mine'; REB, 'That is no concern of mine' [*sic*]; JB, 'Woman, why turn to me?'; NJB, 'Woman, what do you want from me?'; NIV, 'Dear woman, why do you involve me?'; NAB, 'Woman, how does your concern affect me?'

2   According to Julius Africanus, an officer in the army of Septimius Severus, and a friend of Origen: *floruit* AD 195–240. The text is in Julius' *Letter to Aristides*, in Eusebius, *History of the Church* I.vii.14.

3   Cited in C. H. Dodd, *The Interpretation of the Fourth Gospel*, Cambridge 1953, p. 299, fn. 2.

4   Note the upper case initial.

(This paper was given at the ESBVM Woldingham
Conference in June 1997)

2
Homily given at Maynooth by Cardinal Cahal B. Daly 14 June 2001

I am glad to be back with the Ecumenical Society of the Blessed Virgin Mary at their first residential conference in Ireland. I recall expressing, at a Conference in Milltown Institute, Dublin, in the 1970s, a hope that an Irish Branch of the ESBVM might be established. That Irish Branch has been set up and is actively promoting interchurch study and discussion of the place of Mary, Mother of Jesus, in Christian faith and theology and in ecumenical dialogue. I am confident that its work will flourish in both parts of the island. You have held a conference in Dromantine once, and I hope that you will return to the north sometime in the future.

Catholic devotion to Mary, the Mother of God, *Theotokos*, has been held to be a great obstacle to Christian unity, a major stumbling block to ecumenical dialogue. There is now, thanks in part to the work of your Society, a greater realization that Christians in the Reformed tradition have historically tended to neglect the role of Mary in the Bible and in the earliest history of the Christian Church, and that they can rediscover Mary without compromise of Protestant principle, and indeed, by returning to some of the writings of the founding fathers of the Reformation. The Protestant theologian, Hans Ansmussen, a half-century ago, wrote that one cannot take Jesus Christ seriously without considering his mother; for, without Mary, Jesus would not have come into the world. Karl Barth, reflecting on 'The Mystery and Miracle of Christmas', in his *Dogmatics in Outline*, declared that the conception of Jesus was realized, not sexually, but 'rather by way of the ears of Mary, which heard the Word of God'. He goes on:

> 'Born of the Virgin Mary'. From the human standpoint, the male is excluded here. The male has nothing to do with this birth ... To what is to begin here, man is to contribute nothing by his action and initiative. Man is not simply excluded, for the Virgin is there. But the male ... must now retire into the background ... Here the woman stands absolutely in the foreground, more-over the *Virgo*, the Virgin Mary. God [chose] ... the human creature who can

confront God only with the words, 'Behold the handmaid of the Lord; be it done to me according to as Thou hast said' ... That Mary does so, and that thereby the creature says 'Yes' to God, is a part of the great acceptance which comes to man from God.

(*Dogmatics in Outline*, pp. 99–100.)

Barth concluded that every time people want to flee from this miracle, a theology is at work, which tries to 'conjure away the mystery of the unity of God and man in Jesus Christ, the mystery of God's free grace'.

Barth's reflection surely leaves an opening for giving Mary her place in the story of salvation, without any compromise to the Protestant affirmations of 'grace alone' and 'faith alone' and 'one Mediator alone', Jesus Christ. The initiative always comes from Jesus Christ. All Christian action is response to God's grace and to his all-powerful Word. As St Thérèse of Lisieux put it, 'everything is grace'.

The Eucharist

I wish today to reflect with you particularly on another mystery and miracle of God's dealing with humanity, namely the Eucharist; for this is the time when the Catholic Church celebrates the Feast of Corpus Christi, the real presence of the body of Christ in the Eucharist. This, too, the great Sacrament of Unity, has often sadly been and continues to be a matter of controversy and division between Christians. In the ecumenical dialogue, it is, I believe, always better to begin with what is common to our various Christian traditions, rather than what divides; and to turn to what divides, not primarily to refute, but to seek to understand why our brother and sister Christians believe as they do and worship as they do. That approach can serve both to deepen our own faith, enriched by the faith experience of others, and to set the differences in a wider context. It is not a question of disregarding or minimizing the differences, but of trying to understand the differences, and to understand one another, in our differences, better.

Pope John Paul II, in his most developed statement of the Catholic approach to ecumenical dialogue, says that, in other than Catholic communities, 'certain features of the Christian mystery have at times been more effectively emphasized'. He goes on: 'Ecumenism is directed precisely to making the partial communion existing between Christians grow towards full communion in truth and charity' (op. cit. p. 19).

The Catholic position on, for example, the real presence of the Body and Blood of the Lord in the Eucharist, and particularly the use of the term 'transubstantiation', have been seen, to use Barth's terms, as an attempt to 'conjure away the mystery', to explain the 'how' of the real, objective presence of Christ; whereas Catholics see it as a strong affirmation of the reality and objectivity of the presence, an affirmation of the 'that' of the presence, and certainly not as an explanation of 'how'. The 'how' of the presence remains a mystery, before which we bow in reverence, not a problem which we have solved by a theory or a theology. Indeed, for all Christians, it remains a mystery how it can be true that the body and blood of Jesus are present when we celebrate the Eucharist 'in memory of him'.

I suggest that the Eucharist must be seen in the context of the total Paschal mystery of Jesus Christ, his passion, death, resurrection and ascension into heaven and sending of the Holy Spirit. In Holy Week we recall the passion and death of Jesus. At Easter we celebrate his resurrection. Since Easter we have celebrated the feasts of the Ascension and of the coming of the Spirit at Pentecost and the feast of the Most Holy Trinity. The Feast of Corpus Christi is closely linked in time and in significance with all of these feasts and the mysteries they celebrate. Jesus had told his disciples, according to St John, that he was leaving them in order to send down the Holy Spirit, and that then, in the power of his Spirit, they would be his witnesses to the ends of the earth and to the end of time, until he would come again to take them to himself so as to share the glory which was his before the world began, in the heart of the Most Holy Trinity.

Christ himself, in the Gospel of St John, links the Eucharist directly with the ascension. The structure of the great eucharistic discourse in John 6 clearly reflects the eucharistic liturgy of the apostolic Church, as we find this in the Apostolic Fathers and in the *Tradition of Hippolytus*. As in John 6, the eucharistic assembly always begins with the reading of the Scriptures, which is followed by a celebration of the Supper of the Lord itself; we Catholics now speak of this as the Liturgy of the Word and the Liturgy of the Eucharist respectively. These two are inseparable from one another: Scripture evokes faith and is the necessary preparation for the celebration of the 'mystery of faith', which is the Eucharist. Each of these in St John's Gospel, is centred on bread: there is a transition in chapter 6 from the bread of life, the bread which comes from heaven, the bread of God's Word, and the new bread which Christ gives, which is the very flesh of God's Word made flesh. The same word *sarx* is used here as was used in the prologue of St John's gospel, where we are told that 'The Word was made flesh'. The two sections in chapter 6 are so closely linked that it is difficult to pinpoint the exact verse where Jesus passes from the one to the other. The link between them is faith, that faith which brings us to the Father through Jesus Christ, 'the one who comes from God'.

The literalness of the language used in the verses from 51 to 58 is very striking: *trogein* for 'eat', or 'chew', and *sarx* for flesh. The language shocked even the followers of Jesus to the point that they protested: 'This is a hard saying', or 'This is intolerable language'. How could anyone accept it? In reply Jesus says: 'Does this upset you? What if you should see the Son of Man ascend up to where he was before?' Then he goes on to say: 'It is the spirit that gives life; the flesh has nothing to offer'. These words lead some to say that Jesus has abandoned the literalness of his earlier words, and that he is now substituting a spiritual sense for the literal sense of the words 'flesh' and 'eat'.

The words 'spirit' and 'life', however, clearly parallel Paul's words for the mortal Jesus of flesh and the risen Jesus, raised up to the glory of the Father. The 'second Adam', Paul tells us, has become 'a life-giving spirit' (1 Cor. 15.45). Indeed, since the Resurrection, Jesus has become 'son of God in all his power ... in the order of the spirit' (Rom. 1.4), and we now know Christ, not as the Christ of flesh, but as the Christ of spirit. St Paul says: 'even if we did once know Christ in the flesh, that is not how we know him now' (2 Cor. 5. 16). This does not mean that the risen Jesus is no longer bodily. Jesus does not withdraw the literal sense of his words in John's sixth chapter. This is indicated by the fact that, even after his explanation of body in terms of spirit, many of his disciples 'left him and stopped going with him'. Jesus allows them to leave, and says, even to the twelve: 'Do you want to go away too?'

The words of Jesus in John 6 clearly parallel the words spoken by Jesus to Mary in the garden as she wept outside the tomb where she had expected to find the dead body of Jesus, but instead found the tomb empty. Jesus appeared to her, but she did not recognize him. Recognition came only when Jesus called her by her name, 'Mary'. Impetuously, she ran to him, clasped him tightly, clung to him possessively, determined that no one should ever take him away from her again. Gently but firmly Jesus disengages her hands, saying 'Do not cling to me, because I am not yet ascended to the Father. Go and find the brothers and tell them that I am ascending to my father and your father, to my God and to your God.' (John 20.11–18.)

And yet the resurrection appearances in John, and also in Luke, show that the risen and ascended Lord retains a corporeal reality. He is able to be seen and touched and felt in bodily form. He is not a disembodied spirit: to the disciples, he says: 'Touch me and see for yourselves; a ghost has no flesh and bones as you can see I have' (Luke 24.39); and, to Thomas: 'Put your finger here ... Give me your hand: put it into my side.' (John 20.27.) But the body is now transformed, transfigured. A feature that occurs in very many of the resurrection appearances in all the gospels is that the risen Jesus is so transformed as to be at first unrecognizable; and yet he is still real and bodily.

Mary can be assured that there is no need to cling to Jesus with her physical hands; there is another kind of touching and clinging which is still more immediate and intimate, more dependable and objective, than the touch of hands: it is the touching of faith, founded on God's word. And this new kind of touching is given to the other disciples too, and they will have this same real and touchable Lord, the Lord of transfigured and Spirit-filled flesh, with them as they set out to preach the word of God to all nations and hand it on to all generations until the end of time.

The mysteries of the resurrection and ascension and the mystery of the Eucharist are, therefore, closely linked. By his resurrection and ascension, Jesus is raised above all temporal and spatial constraints. He is set free from the limits and limitations of space and time and is therefore given power over all material creation and can override the laws of matter and motion. Because the Lord is risen and ascended and has therefore been given power over all things and can draw all to himself, (cf. John 12.32 and 17.2) he can take possession of material bread and wine, and change them into his body and blood, our 'bread come down from heaven, his flesh for the life of the world' (John 6.51) and our 'spiritual drink'. We speak of Jesus as 'coming down' on our altars under the signs of bread and wine. We could equally speak of Jesus as 'lifting up' the bread and wine into oneness with his own body, his crucified but now risen and ascended body in heavenly glory, his flesh, now transfigured into life-giving spirit.

The mystery of the ascension is very well expressed by the late and great Archbishop William Temple of Canterbury, in his book, *Fellowship with God*. Archbishop Temple wrote:

> The ascension of Christ is his liberation from all restrictions of time and space. It does not represent his removal from the earth, but his constant presence everywhere on earth.
>
> During his earthly ministry he could only be in one place at one time. If he was in Jerusalem he was not in Capernaum; if he was in Capernaum he was not in Jerusalem. But now he is united with God, he is present wherever God is present; and that is everywhere. Because he is in heaven, he is everywhere on earth; because he is ascended, he is here now. In the person of the Holy Spirit he dwells in his Church, and issues forth from the deepest depth of the souls of his disciples, to bear witness to his sovereignty.

Holy Spirit and Eucharist

The Eucharist is closely linked also to the sending of the Holy Spirit by the ascended Lord. Jesus reassured his disciples that it was for their own good that he should go away from them in his mortal presence and return to the Father, because 'if I do not go away, the Spirit will not come to you, but, if I go, I will send Him to you'. Only then, he said, would the Spirit come: 'There was no spirit as yet', John comments, 'because Jesus had not yet been glorified.' (John 7.39.) The Spirit showed himself in power in the glorification of Jesus by his resurrection and ascension. The Spirit is equally present in power in the Eucharist. We have seen this already in the gospel passages I referred to, particularly in St John.

The liturgy of the Eucharist follows Scripture closely in this regard. At two points in particular, the presence and action of the Spirit are highlighted: before the words of institution and before the Holy Communion. Just before what we Catholics call the consecration, the celebrant extends his hands over the elements and invokes the Holy Spirit. In the ancient liturgy and in the Eastern Churches, this is called the *epiclesis*. This is the ancient biblical sign of the calling down of the Spirit. Its place in the Eucharist is clearly brought out in our Eucharistic Prayers: number III, for example, says:

> And so, Father, we bring you these gifts.
> We ask you to make them holy by the power of your Spirit,
> that they may become the body and blood
> of your Son, Our Lord Jesus Christ,
> at whose command we celebrate this Eucharist.

A second time the Holy Spirit is invoked, and this time it is to change the whole assembly into the body of Christ, by incorporating them more closely into Christ through making them more and more living and active members of his Church. In the same Eucharistic Prayer III, we pray:

> Grant that we, who are nourished by [Christ's] body and blood,
> may be filled with his Holy Spirit, and become one body, one
> spirit, in Christ.

In Eucharistic Prayer II we pray:

> May all of us who share in the body and blood of Christ,
> be brought together in unity by the Holy Spirit.

Eucharist and Church are, therefore, very closely linked. The first fruit of the Eucharist, St Thomas Aquinas said, is the building up of Christ's body, the Church, in unity and charity. Cardinal de Lubac has shown that the term 'mystical body' was used first of the Eucharist, and only later of the Church. Our incorporation into Christ is also our incorporation into Christ's Church, which is his body. In Eucharistic Prayer III we pray:

> May he [the Holy Spirit] make us an everlasting gift to you
> and enable us to share in the inheritance of your saints.

This aspect of the Eucharist is, unfortunately, sometimes neglected. Wherever Christ is, there too is his Spirit. St Augustine adds: 'Wherever the Church is, there is the Spirit'. All of these realities come together in the Eucharist. It is the total paschal mystery which is made present for us in the Eucharist: the passion, the resurrection, the ascension, and descending of the Spirit, and the Church. Cardinal de Lubac pointed out that, in the third part of the Creed, in which we express our belief in the Holy Spirit, we say that we believe in the Holy Spirit, the Holy Catholic Church, the communion of Saints, etc. But these, he points out, are not separate articles of faith; instead, they are a spelling-out of the implications of our faith in the one Holy Spirit. Indeed, the original text of the Creed made one single, unpunctuated phrase of the words: 'We believe in the Holy Spirit in the Holy Catholic Church'. Our Eucharistic Prayer I, after the Consecration, prays:

> Father, we celebrate the memory of Christ, your Son.
> We, your people and your ministers,
> recall his passion,
> his resurrection from the dead,
> and his ascension into glory.

In an Apostolic Letter, entitled *Dies Domini*, 'keeping the Lord's Day Holy', Pope John Paul says that the Sunday Eucharist is 'a synthesis of the Christian life and a condition for living it well'. He goes on:

> It is crucially important that all the faithful should be convinced that they cannot live their faith or share fully in the life of the Christian Community unless they take part regularly in the Sunday Eucharistic assembly. The Eucharist is the full realization of the worship which humanity owes to God, and it cannot be compared to any other religious experience ...

Sunday is the day of joy and the day of rest, precisely because it is 'the Lord's Day', the day of the 'Risen Lord'. (*Dies Domini*, 81.)

The late Austin Farrer once said: 'We come to Mass to have the Resurrection all over again'. Edward Norman, of York Minster, expresses these aspects of the Eucharist very beautifully, when he writes:

> The Christian life is centred in the Holy Eucharist. It is also called the Mass, or *Missa*, to indicate that the followers of Christ are being sent out to teach his truth. The Eucharist is thus the authority of the mission of the people of God, a personal and collective participation in the death of Jesus and the mystery of redemption. It is only secondarily, and by contingence, an affair of human

fellowship, where believers share bread and wine as a kind of love-feast memorial of Christ – though that is an aspect of Eucharist that many Christians today emphasize. The truth and authenticity of Christianity, however, do not depend on the experience of faith among believers but on the succession of teaching derived from those who stand in the tradition of the Apostles. The Apostles had themselves first received the Body of the Lord and handed on the knowledge of his objective presence in the Eucharist.

The Eucharist purchased our Redemption and authorizes our truth. We, shamefully, are forever inclined to reduce this priceless gift to mere personal consolation, a means of self-understanding, individual therapy, a celebration of human camaraderie, a beautiful experience. But the message of Jesus is blood and nails, ripping flesh and the execration of the multitude. The Eucharist is not a piece of sentimental drama; it is the actual presence of Christ amongst those he came to save. 'Happy are those who are called to such a feast.'

Happy are we who today are called to the wedding feast of the Lamb, who is the risen and ascended Lord Jesus Christ, present among us in his real and crucified and risen and ascended and living body and blood, in the power of the Holy Spirit; and who is present in order to transform us into his body, a people made one in the unity of the Father and the Son and the Holy Spirit. Amen.

Mary
in
systematic
theology

3

The Word made Flesh and the Blessed Virgin Mary through the theology of the New Creation

Walter T. Brennan OSM

Belief in the incarnation of the Second Person of the Blessed Trinity through the hypostatic union is shared by all Christians. A reflection on this mystery as it portrays the beauty of Christ and of all creatures in this 'new creation' can intensify the union among Christian churches. The 'beauty' of the mother of Jesus, Mary, is part of this reflection. It is hoped that her role in this approach will also intensify this quest for unity.

The mystery of the incarnation is the beginning of something 'new' for Christians: a new covenant, a new law, a new human nature, a new self, and new being. Everything is seen as new (see Rev. 21.5). The effect of this stupendous mystery was seen in early Christianity as a 'new creation' (2 Cor. 5.17; Gal. 6.15; Eph. 2.15, etc.).

The incarnation is a mystery. It is, as Rudolf Otto described a religious mystery, at once *tremendum* and *fascinosum*. It is *tremendum* because it claims a truth that is almost beyond belief. It is a greater marvel than creation. God even 'more wondrously', as the Liturgy of the Roman Catholic Western Church prays, recreated and renewed creation in this action of the Trinity.[1] If the praying people of God use the word 'wonder' in the recitation of many psalms to talk of the great deeds of God, then the incarnation has to be seen with the eyes of faith as an even more wonderful deed of God. God, in the Second Person of the Trinity, took human nature on. And God the Creator planned this from the beginning (Col. 1; John 1). This is a wonder of faith. It fills the believer with awe.

This mystery is also *fascinosum*. It involves all of creation which is now fulfilled in the Christ, the Lord of the Cosmos. As St Athanasius said: God became human so that humans could become God. Nature and person are changed wonderfully when the Word becomes flesh and dwells among us. This mystery gives a new beauty and dignity to all of creation. It gives hope and light to the believer – the humble and poor in spirit. It is attractive and full of delight. The celebration of Christmas is always a happy feast for Christians, because it celebrates this mystery inclusively for those with faith. (It includes the conception of Christ for most Christians on a popular level.)

In this 'new creation' Jesus is the true image of God, the new Adam (Heb. 1) without sin or ugliness.[2] Jesus took all sin and ugliness to the cross and his death, giving victory and resurrection and beauty in a wondrous exchange. As image of the source of beauty and being, Jesus in his human nature shows us what divine beauty is in himself and gives that beauty to all creatures, especially the baptized who are clothed with Christ, children of the beautiful light of the Creator. Persons and nature are beautiful with the beauty of Christ in the new creation. And among persons, the baptized have more of this beauty as they are conformed more and more to Christ by the Holy Spirit. And among the baptized the mother of the Lord, the vertex of all creation, the face that most resembles Christ (Dante), manifests most the beauty of her Son, the Creator, and of God the Creator.

The approach to Mary in our attempts to understand her Son has been twofold in our history as Christians, both East and West. Edward Hutton remembers[3] that Fr Vincent McNabb OP once described the traditional approaches of the Church to God by saying there were two gates into the Church of God: the gate of Wisdom and the gate of Beauty. This is how Christians of the East and the West have approached God and the mother of Jesus in God's plan of redemption. The *via pulchritudinis* is an old approach to Mary. We will use this approach to see her beauty and understand her place in the mystery of the incarnation, the new creation.

An approach to all of theology as a theology of the new creation is somewhat new, at least as a 'scientific' or 'methodological' approach. In recent times in Roman Catholic theology the new creation is acknowledged in the Dogmatic Constitution on the Church of Vatican II (*Lumen Gentium* 7), and some theologians acknowledge the new creation.[4] An approach to Mary, mother of the Lord, through the theology of the new creation is a new endeavour. To consider Mary in the new creation through the 'way of beauty' is a new approach with roots in the past. The approach to Mary through the 'way of beauty' is not new.[5] Putting the new creation and the way of beauty together is new or regained today. I think this is what St Augustine meant when he wrote in *The Confessions* 'O Beauty so ancient and ever so new'. This approach, though new today, belongs nevertheless to Christian tradition.

Our reflection will be organized into four parts:

1. Natural religion and beauty
2. Hebrew religion
3. The Christian new creation
4. The Mother of Jesus and the Incarnation in the new creation.

1. Natural Religion and Beauty

For all people who have not received God's revelation in the Hebrew religion or in the Christian religion, the primordial time of 'the beginning' is, as Mircea Eliade has shown, a 'theophany'. Being in creatures as desirable [beauty] is an effect of the supreme source of existence. The source of beauty is the cause of being. The beauty and being of creatures comes from 'the beginning', the creator(s). As all being is a gift to the people, so is beauty. This gift shows that all being is enjoyable and appetible. The existents in life demonstrate the beauty put in creatures by the creator(s). This 'ontophany' shows the reception or participation of the effect in whatever the cause has to give – reality, being, goodness, and beauty. The most beautiful being participates the most in the beauty of the Source, the gods. A leader or a king is seen as beautiful or majestic, representing the gods. All religions see that beauty is a gift given by the creator(s), and showing that the creator(s) has/have this characteristic, too. The effect demonstrates something about the nature of the cause. The creator leaves footprints in creatures.

2. Hebrew Religion

Creation is a free gift to creatures of being and of beauty. It is a covenant and call for the Hebrew people. God 'sees that it is good', an image of God's own being, beauty, and goodness.[6] Created beauty shows the beauty of the Creator ('the heavens declare the glory of God'; 'the skies proclaim God's justice, all peoples see God's glory'. Psalms 97 etc.). Creation is one of the 'mighty deeds' of God. God gave human beings freedom amid the beauty of Creation (Gen. 2.9). God in merciful love promised that people would be remade and redeemed from the sin and ugliness they made of creation.

The most beautiful creatures became a sign of God's own beauty and sublimity. The best that human beings can make, such as beautiful garments for the royal family, became symbols of the beauty and majesty of God. Light and glory became symbols for the other-worldly beauty of God. Splendour belongs to God who made splendid things that speak of God's own beauty and splendour. The aniconic tradition tells us that the chosen people had the obligation to see that effects of God, as beautiful as they might be, were not the supreme beauty of the Creator and should not be confused with God's creating beauty and power. All beautiful signs of God's presence and gifts were, like the temple, signs of a goodness that people could only approach with holiness and justice. Holy men and women shine with the light of God. They are innocent in their original beauty like the virgin earth. God's warmth and love for God's own people become something the non-Jewish people can see. They reflect the moral beauty of God to us. God is the Source of all goodness and beauty. Human beings are made in God's image. Freedom can lead to sin, the lack of justice, not doing what we hear God saying we should do. Then moral beauty is turned into ugliness. To regain the beauty and innocence God gave at the beginning, God gives the help of prophets and holy people who shine with the beauty and goodness of God. These holy people help other people to see the beauty that is theirs by creation as images of God. Eventually God promised to take on the ugliness people made in the world and to redeem God's own people through a suffering servant of God, who would show that the beauty and holiness of God were unique.[7]

3. The Christian New Creation

Christians believe that God shared God's own unique holiness and beauty with all creation in a new creation through Christ the Son, planned from the beginning by God's foreknowledge that people would need the help of God to attain this end.

> In these last days [God] has spoken to us by a Son, whom he appointed heir of all things, through whom he also created the worlds. He is the reflection of God's glory and the exact imprint of God's very being, and he sustains all things by his powerful word. When he had made purification for sins, he sat down at the right hand of the Majesty on high, having become as much superior to angels as the name he has inherited is more excellent that theirs. (Heb. 1.3–4, New RSV).

> He is the image of the invisible God, the firstborn of all creation; for in him all things in heaven and on earth were created, things visible and invisible, whether thrones or dominions or rulers or powers – all things have been created through him and for him. He himself is before all things and in him all things hold together. He is the head of the body, the church; he is the beginning, the firstborn from the dead, so that he might come to have first place in everything. For in him all the fullness of God was pleased to dwell, and through him God was pleased to reconcile to himself all things, whether on earth or in heaven, by making peace through the blood of his cross. (Col. 1.15–20).

> Blessed be the God and Father of our Lord Jesus Christ, who has blessed us in Christ ... before the foundation of the world to be holy and blameless before him in love. He destined us for adoption as his children through Jesus Christ, according to the good pleasure of his will, to the praise of his glorious grace that he freely bestowed on us in the Beloved. In him we have redemption through his blood, the forgiveness of our trespasses, according to the riches of

his grace that he lavished on us. With all wisdom and insight he has made known to us the mystery of his will, according to his good pleasure that he set forth in Christ, as a plan for the fullness of time, to gather up all things in him, things in heaven and things on earth. In Christ we have also obtained an inheritance, having been destined according to the purpose of him who accomplishes all things according to his counsel and will, so that we, who were the first to set our hope on Christ, might live for the praise of his glory. In him you also, when you had heard the word of truth, the gospel of your salvation, and had believed in him, were marked with the seal of the promised Holy Spirit; this is the pledge of our inheritance toward redemption as God's own people, to the praise of his glory. (Eph. 1.3–15).

While these poetic creations, or hymns, were from the late period of formation of the New Testament, and showed the belief of Christians as it developed from earlier times, the belief that Christian life is a new creation in the new Adam, planned from the beginning and sealed in the Holy Spirit, was an earlier statement of this truth. This belief in the meaning of the Incarnation in its comprehensive sense, as a new creation in the fullness of time, planned by the Creator, was a part of gospel faith since the time of St Paul (cf. 2 Cor. 5.17; Gal. 6.15; Rom. 5.14 and 8.19–24, 29–30; 1 Cor. 15.45, 47; *et alibi.*).

As the 'true image' of the invisible God, to whom we are conformed by the Holy Spirit, Jesus the Christ reflected the beauty of God and gave this beauty to all creation. (Heb. 1.3; Rom. 1.20–3 and 8.18–25). The Christ is Lord of the Cosmos by the intent of the Creator, who planned the incarnation in its comprehensive sense. Christ gave beauty to all things and to all people.

Just as the incarnation of the Word of God was an ineffable wonder, so was the resurrection of Jesus, the Word made flesh. Both were part of the Creator's plan. The incarnation was 'decreed' (as the popes who defined the immaculate conception and the assumption put it) in its comprehensive sense. The effect then of the comprehensive incarnation of the Word was an effect on 'all things'. As St Paul wrote in Romans, chapter 8: 'creation itself ... will obtain the freedom of the glory of the children of God'. 'Glory' means the beauty of God, divinization, grace.[8]

In Western speculative theology in recent years the neo-scholastics spoke of the cosmic role of Christ, the incarnate and resurrected Son of God. But they spoke more of types of causality than of beauty.[9] Even physical scientists spoke, and speak today, of the harmony in the design of the universe, and how the Creator ('God' Albert Einstein says) showed wisdom in the things of nature. But of 'beauty' there is hardly a mention.[10] This began to change recently. Perhaps it started with Teilhard de Chardin's attempt to describe a 'third nature', with creation, that God took on hypostatically. Recently the Servants of Mary advocated the 'way of beauty' to understand God and the mother of Jesus.[11] The French journal of the Dominicans, *Nouveaux Cahiers Mariales*, recently published an issue dedicated to 'beauty' as an approach to God and to the mother of Jesus.[12] The Italian journal of the Servites, *Monte Senario*, also recently published an issue on 'La Via della Bellezza'.[13] The statement of Dostoevsky that the world will be saved by 'beauty' has been quoted much in recent years. Putting 'beauty' together with 'the new creation' is a theological venture that is new and called for today.

In Eastern Christianity there has always been an emphasis on the beauty of divinization and the role of the *Theotokos*. The tradition is there. Perhaps a new language from concerted scholars of East and West will make that tradition more available, especially in the West. There is a marked interest today in 'ikons' in the West, which is a sign that this is started.

4. The Mother of Jesus and the incarnation in the new creation

God the Creator, from all eternity, planned that all persons be conformed to the image of Christ, the New Adam and the true image of God. The Holy Spirit does this conformation. Then people are baptized (formally or 'by desire') into Christ and given the power of the Spirit to become holy in their daily lives. They are 'divinized', becoming participators in the divine nature as children of God and heirs with Christ of all he would inherit. In the fullness of time this plan of God came into existence with the incarnation of Jesus, the Son of God.

The incarnation of the Son had as its intended end the purpose of this plan of the Creator. The preaching and actions, sufferings, death and resurrection of Christ were included in the incarnation.

In this fullness of time the incarnation began with the annunciation of God's messenger to Mary, the servant of God. According to the Creator's plan she was called, foreknown, and united with Christ from all eternity. In what St Peter's first letter (3.3–6) calls 'the lasting beauty of a gentle and quiet spirit ... precious in God's sight' her 'yes' from her inner self started the reality of the new creation. She was 'all holy', 'full of grace', united with the Trinity in this plan of the Creator–Trinity. She said 'yes' for all. As 'divinized' by the power of the Holy Spirit who overshadowed her, she became a model for all that this plan of God could work. She said 'yes', no matter how much she understood, to the attainment of divine beauty, union with Christ, for all people. And she exemplified this reality as a servant of God united in holiness to the beauty of God the Creator (Father) and to the beauty of the Son now conceived within her as human, and to the beauty of the empowering Holy Spirit who overshadowed her, like the glory and beauty of God overshadowing the people chosen in the old creation for this moment. The new creation began with the beauty of God and of human beings and of all which rejoiced in the song of the heavenly angels at his birth. (See *Lumen Gentium* 56, where the splendours of the grace of Mary as a new creature are remarked.)

St Augustine remarks that it was a greater grace for Mary to be called to be a disciple of the Lord than to be the mother of the Lord. She conceived Christ *prius in ventre quam in mente*. As a disciple of Christ Mary grew in understanding and faith the closer she became to Christ. From her ignorance at the meaning of the twelve-year-old Christ's words in the temple (Luke 2.50), through her persevering presence in the public life of Jesus, to the cross, her 'conformity' to her Son grew. She always heard the word of God in Jesus and did it. As a servant of God, and now of Jesus her Son, she anticipated the new covenant, so that at Cana (John 4) she could, in view of the 'hour' of Jesus yet to come, ask Jesus to give new wine to those at the wedding feast. As a holy and therefore beautiful person, resplendent with the beauty of God and of Jesus, she is made mother of all who serve in love when the 'hour' does arrive (John 19). At Pentecost the Holy Spirit again empowers her, just as the Spirit did at the annunciation, this time to be the mother of the Body of Christ, servant of Jesus. As a mother who has served and loved she becomes the model for all who serve and love Christ. She has been conformed more and more by the Spirit to the image of Jesus who brought into being the new creation as a new covenant. She has become most like Christ, on whose face shines the beauty and glory of God (2 Cor. 4.6). Her face most resembles the face of Christ, as Dante wrote. She participates uniquely in the 'glory' and 'beauty' of the resurrection.

If all creation groaned for this 'new being' and new conformity to the Creator in Christ, this 'splendour' and 'glory' and 'light', she who was first in the new creation in time as well as in her growth of faith, she who was 'full of grace' and became mother and model for all in this new life of union with God through Christ, shone with this special beauty as a creature in first place after Christ in the new creation.

For this reason tradition has regarded her splendour and dignity as unique. She is the new Eve. She is the *Theotokos*. To her is ascribed by Christians the words about holiness and beauty in the Hebrew Scriptures which they saw as referring to Christ.[14] In sermons and prayers early Christians praised her, 'the fair ewe', mother of the paschal lamb of God (Melito of Sardis *c.* 190). 'Lovers of spiritual beauty', as St Augustine described followers of his rule, acknowledged her spiritual beauty. She was regarded as the 'ikon' of divine beauty in the East. St Gregory Palamas wrote that God through the Holy Spirit 'wanting to create the image of absolute beauty and manifest to angels and to mortals the power of his art . . . truly made Mary totally beautiful. In her he brought together the individual beauty distributed among other creatures and set her up as the adornment of all beings, visible and invisible.'[15] The Liturgy and bishops of the past and present sang and spoke of her beauty. In the Middle Ages, Blessed Amadeus of Lausanne (d. 1159) wrote that Jesus called Mary 'beautiful in the virginal conception, beautiful in your divine maternity, etc.'[16] The recent *Collectio Missarum, I*[17] offers for prayer the Preface of the Mass of Mary, Mother of Fairest Love. This work is a truly poetic liturgical creation of praise to the beauty of the first disciple of Jesus: 'Beauty was hers in her virginal motherhood: she brought forth her Son, the radiance of your glory, as the Saviour and brother of us all.'

To follow the Way of Beauty is to see Mary in her graced beauty pointing to the absolute beauty of Christ the Creator. It is contemplative. It is liturgical. It is a way that is open to all people. To see that this way has been followed in Christian history is to be comforted with the insight that God is the Creator of a beauty-filled order and not just a harmony knowable only to scientists. To acknowledge her beauty as our sister is an inspiration to follow Christ who is all-beautiful. To know that this is the beauty of our mother can lead us to see the beauty which our brother, Jesus, gives us even in afflictions. To see that all things have a new and beautiful being in the new creation is to be grounded in the absolute beauty of the Creator and the divine love shown to us by Christ who saves and beautifies us.[18]

Notes

1 The Liturgy of the Roman Church, previous to 1968, prayed at the washing of hands of the celebrant: 'Deus qui mirabiliter condidisti et mirabilius reformasti . . .'

2 All being is good in classical theology in the West. Sin or evil is a lack of being or goodness. It is ugliness, as Fr Walter Farrell OP describes the view of Aquinas in *A Companion to the Summa*, II (Sheed & Ward, New York 1938).

3 *Catholicism and English Literature* (Muller, London 1942), p. 146.

4 So E. Schillebeeckx, in *Christ, the Experience of Jesus as Lord*, tr. J. Bowden (Seabury Press, New York 1980), pp. 468–73, only briefly mentions the new creation.

5 *Lumen Gentium* 56 mentions Mary as a 'new creature'. See W. Brennan OSM, 'Rethinking Marian Theology: the New Creation', in *Milltown Studies* 35 (1995) pp. 113–29. The Servites in their 208th General Chapter, 1983, published a Marian document that has become well known, *Do Whatever He Tells You* (Curia OSM, Rome 1983). That General Chapter called, in that document, pp. 70–7, for an approach to Mary through the Way of Beauty. This document shows that the approach to Mary by the 'way of beauty' is not new. Pope John Paul II has mentioned this approach to Mary. The Pontifical

Council for Culture talks about the 'beauty' of culture (23 May 1999) in the document *Toward a Pastoral Approach to Culture*. Articles on Mary and Art have been published in many journals in this century. The concrete material of this approach has always been a part of Eastern Christianity, and of Western Christianity since early times.

6 See *Do Whatever He Tells You*, 208th Chapter of the Servants of Mary (General Curia OSM, Rome 1983), p. 70, 'beautiful and good'.

7 See A. Colin Day, *Roget's Thesaurus of the Bible* (Harper, San Francisco 1992), pp. 587–8 for a list of the usage of the word 'beauty' in the Bible.

8 See B. Antonini, 'Fede e bellezza', in *Monte Senario* II, 6 (1998), *La Via della Bellezza*, 21, for brief statements on Hans Urs von Balthasar and on St Thomas Aquinas on this topic.

9 See, for example, the incisive, but dated, work of the Scotist Jean-François Bonnefoy OFM, *Christ and the Cosmos*, trans. M. Meilach OFM.

10 In Fall, 2000 the magazine *Loyola* (Chicago, Illinois) was dedicated to traces of harmony in the universe. The topic of interest was about how science and religion come together. There was not a mention of 'beauty' in the articles, although 'awe', 'wonder', 'rationality', and 'intelligence' were mentioned.

11 The document *Do Whatever He Tells You*, already mentioned.

12 *Nouveaux Cahiers Mariales*, 'Marie, Chemin de Beauté' (Lyon 2000).

13 See note 8 above.

14 For a partial list of these pericopes see *Do Whatever He Tells You*, p. 71.

15 This quotation from his homily on the Dormition is quoted in *Do Whatever He Tells You*, p. 71.

16 See the quotation in *Do Whatever He Tells You*, p. 77.

17 *Collection of Masses of the Blessed Virgin Mary* (Liturgical Press, Collegeville, MN 1992), I, p. 772.

18 See Ilia Delio OSF, 'Mystics and the Cosmic Nature of Christ', in *New Theology Review* 13, 3 (August 2000) pp. 45–55.

(This paper was given at the ESBVM Oxford Congress
in August 2000)

4

What are they saying about Mary today?
A review of current literature

Eamon R. Carroll OCarm

In a paper he presented at an international symposium held in Rome, October, 1994, on 'The Theological Image of Mary: Faith and Culture', Johann Roten, a Swiss, who is the head of the International Marian Research Institute at the Dayton, Ohio, Marian Library, reviewed recent writings on the Blessed Virgin in the German language. He had many stimulating comments on his sweeping, pointillistic, survey – e.g. 'kneeling constitutes the litmus test of mariological discourse and its genuine inculturation'. The American Jesuit Avery Dulles, in a paper for the twenty-fifth anniversary of the conciliar Decree on Ecumenism (1964 – 1989), called attention to the heart of that document with its hopeful title, *Unitatis Redintegratio*, issued on the same date as the pastoral Constitution on the Church with a similarly encouraging name, *Lumen Gentium*. The Council said: 'The reconciliation of all Christians in the unity of the one and only Church of Christ transcends human powers and gifts (24) … Therefore we place our hope entirely in the prayer of Christ for the Church.' The 'soul of the whole ecumenical movement' is a call to 'change of heart and holiness of life, along with public and private prayer for the unity of Christians'. Dulles commented: 'Theologians must do their work but they must direct their hopes elsewhere.' In spite of persisting differences, such obvious examples as the Roman dogmatic Marian definitions of the immaculate conception and the assumption, and perhaps above all, more than anything else, papal primacy of jurisdiction, Dulles expressed this strong hope: 'The churches can gain a more accurate understanding of each other's true positions and a deeper respect for their shared commitment to the gospel. They can achieve a large measure of common witness, common worship, and common service to the world.'

The American Lutheran veteran, Jaroslav Pelikan, recently retired from a half-century of teaching, has commented similarly, that 'worship is the metabolism of Christian life'. To return to Fr Roten's October 1994 review of German language studies on our Lady, he commented on the almost exponential growth of mariological activity in the short span of just twenty years, from timid retrieval in 1973 to 1993, and we could renumber that to 1998.

In the post-conciliar confusion, Karl Rahner once commented 'Some of our Catholic doctrines are in danger of being silenced to death'. That phrase, 'silence to death', was the Nazi approach to Christianity. Somehow the ESBVM continued to grow, even to thrive, during that winter time.

The recent article by Donal Flanagan in *The Furrow*, 'A New Marian Dogma', makes the perceptive comment that Pope Paul VI's 'beautifully written and long awaited Apostolic Exhortation, *Marialis Cultus*', (February 1974) built on ideas proposed in *Lumen Gentium* and indicated future lines of development for Marian doctrine and devotion, yet did not make the hoped-for impact. Indeed, says Flanagan, 'it signally failed to overcome the Marian apathy consequent on the Council'. I would add the further comment that it seems to have received a warmer welcome, a more ready acceptance, in the wider Christian world than among Catholics. Though there were some perceptive Catholic scholars who prized highly Paul VI's Marian efforts, among them the exegete Raymond Brown:

> I am not a prophet but I think that, when this century is finished, this Pope, maligned because he was so subtle, may prove to have been the most adept interpreter of Vatican II. I do not know [*Brown was speaking in December 1981*] if Paul VI read modern biblical criticism; but if I had to phrase where it leads to in relation to Mary, I could not have phrased it better.

He then quoted *Marialis Cultus*: 'The Virgin Mary has always been proposed to the faithful by the Church as an example to be imitated, not precisely in the type of life she led, and much less for the socio-cultural background in which she lived and which scarcely today exists anywhere.' (*Menlo Papers: Mary*. Symposium, December 1981. St Patrick's Seminary, Menlo, CA: the occasion was the 450th anniversary of Guadalupe.) After commenting on the disappointing immediate results of *Marialis Cultus*, Flanagan continued: 'It was left to the persuasive vigour and the persevering tenacity of Pope John Paul II to recall the Church effectively to its Marian heritage'.

The exuberant revival of Marian and mariological writings in the German language described by Fr Roten can be matched in other language groupings as well as among religious orders and congregations, especially those bearing a Marian designation; I am thinking of my own Carmelite family.

So you [my readers] can appreciate the problem of selection with my assigned topic: What are they Saying about Mary Today? – A Review of

Current Literature. Here is how I am tackling it: for many years, since 1967, right after the Vatican Council, I have done a 'Survey of Recent Mariology' at the annual convention of the Mariological Society of America (founded half a century ago and meeting every year since), subsequently printed in the Society's proceedings, *Marian Studies*. Here I have dipped into half a dozen of the most recent Surveys to answer the question that is my title: 'What are they Saying about Mary Today?'

A splendid example of the rebirth of interest in Mary, both doctrinally and devotionally, is the periodical, *The Month*, the January issue of 1998, devoted to the Blessed Virgin, with the lead article by James Hanvey SJ, of Heythrop College, followed by Gerard MacCarthy, looking to the New World, on 'The Virgin of Guadalupe', then an article by Anne Winston-Allen on the theme of her recent book, *Rosarium revisited: the name of the prayer*, and finally a book review of *Toward a Theology of the Body*, by Sr M. T. Prokes, of which more later in this paper.

If my presentation seems a potpourri, even a patchwork, I beg your indulgence to regard my choices as a sort of literary smorgasbord of the many great things being said today about the all-holy Virgin, *Theotokos*, blessed Mother of Jesus the Saviour and Redeemer.

Following the format of my annual surveys, I will begin with three items of special interest, and then run rapidly through a set of rubrics from magisterial documents through scripture and tradition, doctrine, liturgy and devotion, and ecumenism.

The opening trio are first from Scotland, then two from America. First is the title *Iona: the Earliest Poetry of a Celtic Monastery*, edited by Gilbert Markus and Thomas Owen Clancy, from the University of Edinburgh. The preface is significantly dated for the feastday of St Columba (9 June 1994), who, as he said, 'wishing to be a pilgrim for Christ', left his native Ireland in 563 to settle on tiny Iona in the Hebrides. Both the British and Irish postal services issued a stamp to commemorate the anniversary of his death, 597 – 1997. (Don't confuse him with a man with a very similar name, who was also a traveller, Christopher Columbus – a mix-up I have seen in some continental publications.) The book gives seven poems, in Latin and in English translation, from the zenith of Iona's influence, 563 to 704. A review in *The Tablet* brought the book to my notice; the reviewer was Esther de Waal, who wrote, 'This is a book for serious reading. But it is also a book for praying with and singing with.' She paid particular notice to the eighth-century *Cantemus in omni die*, on Mary the God-bearer at the heart of the mystery of the incarnation. The hymn begins 'Let us sing every day, harmonizing in turns, together proclaiming to God a hymn worthy of holy Mary'. Also: 'The mother of God made a tunic of seamless weave; Christ's death accomplished, it remained thus by the casting of lots.' Also 'Truly, truly, we implore by the merits of the Child-bearer, that the flame of the dread fire not be able to ensnare us.' Reviewer de Waal published recently *Carmina Gadelica: The Celtic Vision*, an anthology from the Hebridean Islands (Doubleday, 1997). A year ago I heard Ross Mackenzie, a member of ESBVM whom many of you have met (and read), Scottish-born, refer to the praise of holy Mary in the *Carmina Gadelica*. A selection of these ancient songs and poems is also in the book by J. Philip Newell, who has served as Warden of Iona Abbey, succeeding the fabled George Macleod, *Listening for the Heartbeat of God* (Paulist, Mahwah NJ, 1997) especially chapter 3, *Listening for God in All Things: Carmina Gadelica*, on the songs recorded a century ago by Alexander Carmichael (1832–1912). These traditional compositions, passed down from parents to children, in spite of slaps and scoldings of schoolmasters and ministers, praise the goodness of creation. Deeply christological, they are filled with the memory of Mary his Mother. One example only: a prayer said at the deathbed of a loved one:

> Sleep this night in the breast of thy Mother.
> Sleep, thou beloved, while she herself soothes thee;
> sleep thou this night on the Virgin's arm,
> sleep, thou beloved, while she herself kisses thee.

The second introductory item is by the American Lutheran Jaroslav Pelikan (who recently joined the Greek Orthodox Church in America). Concluding a half-century of teaching, he delivered at Yale University in the autumn of 1995 the lectures which make up the book *Mary Through the Centuries: Her Place in the History of Culture* (Yale University Press, 1996). It was a complement to his prize-winning *Jesus Through the Centuries: His Place in the History of Culture*. Over the years Pelikan has often written about the Blessed Virgin; in this book he brings together many earlier studies, in a rough chronological sequence, starting with the Scriptures: 'Throughout history the attention to the person of Jesus Christ was . . . closely linked to his Mother', beginning with the Epistle to the Galatians. One chapter takes its title from Dante: 'The Face that Most Resembles Christ's'. I found especially valuable Pelikan's comments on Mary as the obedient and faithful new Eve, to which he devotes chapter 3: 'The Second Eve and the Guarantee of Christ's True Humanity'. Against a-historical attempts to reject the 'New Eve' tradition as hopelessly anti-woman, he argues for fairness, writing that one need not defend stereotypes, yet 'historical justice demands that both sides of the dialectic be included'. The very same authors who are castigated as irremediably 'patriarchal' offered a strong counterpoise, he writes, 'in their even more extensive interpretations of woman as embodied in Mary, the

"Woman of Valour", *mulier fortis,* who as descendant and vindicator of the First Eve, crushed the head of the serpent and vanquished the devil'. Back in the fifties, as a young scholar, Pelikan was called upon, by way of 'damage control', to replace earlier articles on the Virgin Mary in the *Encyclopedia Britannica,* particularly the very unecumenical judgemental entry in the classic Eleventh Edition (1910). With characteristic fairness Pelikan's *Britannica* piece concludes as follows:

> Even those non-Roman churches which have most vigorously criticized the 'Mariolatry' they claimed to find in the dogmas of the immaculate conception and the assumption have frequently addressed praises to her in their hymnody, that they would have hesitated to express in the prose of their dogmatic theology. Thus, in ways she could never have anticipated, all generations have called her blessed.

My third initial entry is also from the United States: the title *Mary: Glimpses of the Mother of Jesus* (University of South Carolina Press, 1995) by the Protestant scholar, professor at Princeton Theological Seminary, Beverly Roberts Gaventa. She uses literary analysis to explore the picture of Mary in four early Christian narratives: the Gospel of Matthew; Luke in his Gospel and Acts; John's Gospel; and the second-century 'First Gospel of James', the *Protoevangelium Jacobi.* To her four sources Dr Gaventa puts such questions as these: What does Mary say and do? How do others speak to her or about her? In what ways does she change as the story develops? Though conversant with modern biblical criticism which investigates the background of the narratives, and respectful of the sense of the Church's subsequent interpretations, hers is a 'literary quest' rather than historical or theological. The author's perceptive insights are remarkable assessments of what she describes as just 'glimpses'. The Mary of St Matthew is both 'threatened and threatening'. For Luke, in both Gospel and Acts, she is 'disciple, prophet and mother'. In John she is glimpsed at Cana and Calvary. The 'First Gospel of James' is assessed as a second-century picture of Mary, and Dr Gaventa does the reader the great service of a full translation. In a subsequent address at an ecumenical gathering at Princeton (30 September 1996), she pursued the line of her book: 'When poor and imperilled Christians turn to Mary as the Mother of Sorrows, consciously or not, they touch a thread in Matthew's Gospel'. On the same occasion she said, à propos of Luke's portrait of Mary as mother, prophet, disciple:

> If we can say that Mary is a disciple, even the first disciple of Jesus, then we have taken an important step together. And if we can say that Mary is a disciple, then is it not a Protestant sort of thing to affirm that Mary is, symbolically speaking, the Mother of Disciples, even the Mother of Believers?

Now to offer some briefer references across a spectrum of rubrics, starting with magisterial statements. As Dulles said in a lecture entitled 'Mary at the Dawn of the New Millennium',

> For John Paul II, Mary is the primary patroness of the advent of the new millennium. As the Mother of Christ, she is pre-eminently an advent figure – the morning star announcing the rising of the Sun of Righteousness. Like the moon at the dawn of a new day, she is wholly bathed in the glory of the sun that is to come after her. Her beauty is a reflection of his.

It would take volumes adequately to report on this pope's addresses and letters, even more reaching back into his episcopal documents, and recalling the Polish Marian family piety of young Karol Wojtyla. His coat of arms (whatever the rules of heraldry) shows simply a bare cross and, in its shadow, the monogram of Mary, along with words from St Louis Grignion de Montfort (d. 1716), 'Totus tuus'; I am entirely yours. The same St Louis Grignion de Montfort would be even more centrally marked by the slogan 'Deus solus': God alone. Between September 1995 and November 1997, John Paul II devoted his Wednesday audiences to an extended catechesis on Marian doctrine and devotion, concluding with a topic very close to his heart, Christian unity. This set of seventy instructions [*then currently in press*] shows the pontiff as a pastoral teacher.

The almost inexhaustible treasure of patristic writings is being increasingly studied and published in English translation. Some years back Kathleen McVey produced many of the hymns of St Ephrem, translated from Syriac, and filled with the thought of the Blessed Virgin. I am in the habit of quoting at every conceivable opportunity a short extract from St Ephrem, by way of Robert Murray SJ, linking Eden, the Exodus, the Eucharist, the new Eve, Mother of the Saviour, and the Church.

> The Church gave us the living bread
> for that unleavened bread which Egypt gave.
> Mary gave us the bread of refreshment
> for the bread of weariness which Eve gave.

Fr Murray's explanation opens up its riches:

> In this complex typological parallel, the Eucharist in the Church is the antitype of the Passover bread in Egypt, and this is then paralleled by Mary's relationship to Eve, also expressed in terms of bread. This is now rather a metaphor suggested by Gen. 3.15 ('in the sweat of your brow shall you eat bread'), but it cannot fail to suggest Christ's body itself, born of Mary; since the Eucharist is Christ's body under another form, the Church and Mary are implicitly thrown into the closest relationship.

The American Jesuit Brian Daley has recently published *On the Dormition of Mary: Early Patristic Homilies* (St Vladimir's Press, Crestwood, NY). Along with a dozen homilies Daley, who does both a splendid introduction and the translations, offers John Damascene's canon for the feast of the Dormition. Readers of *The Tablet* may recall the Christmas number of 1992, where Fr Daley wrote a strong article in defence of the virginal conception, in answer to the denials of the American Bishop Spong and the British theologian G. Parrinder.

Moving into the broad field we call the Middle Ages, I recall a number of publications. The journal *Cistercian Studies* ran a series of articles on Aelred, his sermons on the birth of Mary, her purification, and the assumption, and then a number entirely on 'Our Lady of Citeaux'.

Often attributed to St Bernard, but in fact by Ogier of Locedio (d.1214) is the widely circulated medieval lament, 'Quis dabit capiti meo et oculi meis aquam' (Who will give tears to my head and my eyes). The Latin, and an English translation, are given in the 1996 title: *Texts of the Passion: Latin Devotional Literature and Medieval Society* by Thomas H. Bestul. The conclusion of this lament, in praise of John the disciple, captures its charm and appeal:

> O happy and blessed John: the Lord has committed to you a treasure of great privilege. The Lord will repay to you a reward for love, a reward for the affection which you always had toward his mother who was commended to you. You are blessed by Christ, and blessed by his mother whom you loved with a pure heart. May all who love her be blessed by her. And above all, blessed be her Son, our Lord, who with the Father and the Holy Spirit, lives and reigns for ever and ever.

A final medieval reference: the 1997 second edition of *Medieval Latin*, a textbook from the University of Chicago, edited by K. P. Harrington, revised by Joseph Pucci, gives as initial item in the section 'Varieties of medieval Latin, part 5 (1100 to 1350)', St Anselm's famous third prayer to Mary, 'when the mind is troubled by fear'. Here is another occasion of which I always take advantage – to recommend one of the great books and book bargains of recent years, still fortunately back in print, the Penguin paperback by Sr Benedicta Ward, *Prayers and Meditations of St Anselm*. I recall with equal enthusiasm the writings of Sir Richard Southern on St Anselm, also on Anselm's Saxon secretary, the monk Eadmer, early defender of the immaculate conception, a view not held by Anselm himself. You may share my sense of recognition in this quotation from Eadmer, from Southern's *St Anselm: A Portrait in a Landscape*. Eadmer is speaking to his monks at Glastonbury in 1121 after his return from an unsuccessful bid for a Scottish bishopric. He is urging them to restrain the forwardness and insolence of those young men who open their mouths solely that they may appear to know, and who give free rein to whatever their loquacity [at expense of lucidity?] may suggest, thinking themselves great when others in their simplicity will listen to them. I know there have been people like this – perhaps I was one of them – so I can easily believe that now there are men such as I formerly was. But now I am an old man with white hair, and many things which in my youth I thought important, I now hold of no account.

Under the heading 'liturgy and devotion' there are a fair number of possible entries. Mgr James D. Crichton's book (it is the seventeenth from this liturgical pioneer) is *Our Lady in the Liturgy*, co-published in Ireland and the US. Along with the major Marian feasts in the Roman calendar, he takes up the lesser commemorations, and has also two final helpful chapters, 'Some Marian Chants and Prayers', and 'The Psalms in Marian Feasts'. The Liturgical Press from St John's Abbey, Collegeville, MN, the American publisher of Crichton, also devoted its Winter 1997 issue of the journal *Liturgical Ministry* entirely to our Lady; among the contributors is David Butler, English Methodist. The French Franciscan expert on the prayers of the early church, A. Hamman OFM, urged students to concentrate on the place of Mary especially in her major liturgical feasts (art. in 1990 *Marianum*). In 1987 a set of forty-six new votive Masses of our Lady was issued by the Holy See. The general introduction is valuable, as are the forewords to the individual entries, explaining the ancient origins of the prayers. The Spanish Discalced Carmelite J. Castellano Cervera wrote in 1996 of the unique liturgical presence of the Blessed Virgin, in accord with the conciliar statement (*Sacrosanctum Concilium* 103) that the Mother of Jesus is inseparably linked to her Son's saving work. Another Spaniard, this time Ignatius Calabuig, president of Marianum, the Servite Roman University, wrote of the prayers attached to the psalms in early centuries, with the goal of applying these psalms from the Hebrew Bible to contemporary needs and Christian circumstances. As those know who are conversant with the old breviary, now called *The Prayer of Christians*, this is still done. I offer one striking example, of which much more could be made. Some years back the Lutheran Jaroslav Pelikan told an audience of American Catholic liturgists that Ps. 44(45) reflects the ancient sense of the bond between Mary and the Church. From early days that psalm was used in the Office of Virgins, then extended to the Church and to Blessed Mary. In the iconography illustrating the Mary–Church bond Psalm 44(45) has been sometimes incorporated as one of the texts, along with lines from the Song of Songs. Ps. 44(45) verse 10: 'On your right stands the queen in gold of Ophir'. The glorified Christ is depicted as crowning his Mother, figure/archetype of the Church. A prime example is the apse of S. Maria in Trastevere (Rome). The artist Pietro Cavallini (1290) did the mosaics on the Life of the Blessed Virgin Mary. Recently Regent Records in England released a new recording from the choir of Lincoln College, Oxford – *Magnificat: The Life of the Blessed Virgin Mary in Music*, great choral and organ works by nearly twenty composers, Palestrina, Tavener, Britten, Rachmaninov, Gorecki, to name just five. The booklet accompanying the CD and cassette is illustrated with the Cavallini mosaics. A recent Italian book studies these works of art and their theological background.

Sponsa Verbi, 'spouse/bride of the Word', is the dominant theme in our Lady's coronation. The Risen Christ embraces his mother, a scroll in the Lord's left hand reads, 'Come, my chosen one', the other scroll, 'O that his left hand were under my head', and this is the gesture with which the glorified Saviour summons and embraces his Church: you may recall the final chapter on the Blessed Virgin in de Lubac's *Splendour of the Church*. I return to Psalm 44(45). It occurs in the current breviary a number of times, regularly in vespers of the second week, under the title 'The marriage of the king'. (It is also used on 2 February and for virgins and holy women). The introductory antiphon throughout the year is 'The bridegroom is here: go out and welcome him'. In the Easter season it is 'Blessed are they who are called to the wedding feast of the Lamb, Alleluia'. We recall the opening words of the actual psalm: 'My heart overflows with noble words. To the king I must speak the song I have made, my tongue as nimble as the pen of a scribe'. In the *Prayer of Christians* in use in the US, this prayer occurs after the psalm, in perfect accord with the liturgical understanding of many centuries past:

> When you took on flesh, Lord Jesus, you made a marriage of mankind with God. Help us to be faithful to your word and endure our exile bravely, until we are called to the heavenly marriage feast to which the Virgin Mary, exemplar of your Church, has preceded us.

So far as I have been able to discover, this is taken from the French; it is not found in the Office prayers in other languages.

It has been said that the Second Vatican Council recovered the image of the Church as the 'people of God', succeeding the strong emphasis from the twenties, illustrated *par excellence* in the 1943 encyclical on the Church as the 'mystical body of Christ'. No single image exhausts the almost infinite riches of the Church in relation to Christ, so there is scope for a revival in depth of the biblical and patristic depiction of the Church as bride of Christ, an extremely important heritage that is under some attack of late. The Second Vatican Council came closest to the understanding of the Church as bride of Christ the Bridegroom, at the end of the final chapter of the Dogmatic Constitution on the Church, in terms of the Virgin Mother of God, glorified archetype of the Church:

> In the bodily and spiritual glory which she possesses in heaven, the Mother of Jesus continues in this present world as the image and first flowering of the Church as she is to be perfected in the world to come. Likewise, Mary shines forth on earth, until the day of the Lord shall come, as a sign of sure hope and solace for the pilgrim people of God. (*Lumen Gentium* 68).

Under the heading of 'devotion and devotions', again the problem is one of choice. There is an enormous popular interest among Catholics in claims that the Blessed Virgin has appeared in one or another place. Official positions are very reserved, and this field is so vast that I have not gotten into it, although it is the type of thing that I am asked about, sometimes by phone. When I tell the reporter I have no personal experience of the alleged claim and/or site but am willing to set forth the criteria by which church authorities (starting with the local bishop) make their judgements, the inquirer usually signs off.

Roman Catholic devotion to the Rosary of Mary is well-known. A professor at Notre Dame University in the US, Fr Nicholas Ayo, in 1994, did an excellent book *The Hail Mary: A Verbal Ikon of Mary*, and I find fascinating the two chapters on the Rosary in the book by the distinguished Anglican theologian, the late Austin Farrer (d.1968). I quote from the expanded American edition of 1989. According to Farrer, the will of Mary is a handle to lay hold of the will of God. He also noted that 'no dogma deserves a place unless it is prayable, and no Christian deserves his dogmas who does not pray them.' Of the Rosary he comments that there was a time when he would have characterized as 'vain repetition' the 'fingering of beads'. He has learned better: 'But now if I wished to name a special sort of private devotion most likely to be of general profit, prayer on the beads is what I should name'. His previous censure, he adds, was from ignorance, his present view from experience. I limit myself to a few quotations: the Rosary 'supplies us with a chain of scenes ... so well chosen that everything in heaven and earth crowds into them ...' 'The difficulty of meditative prayer is to keep hold of the thread and not to stray; and it seems almost too good to be true, that I can have an unbreakable thread, not the gossamer of my ideas but jeweller's beads and wire between my finger and my thumb.' Through Mary we live the joyful mysteries, the sorrowful mysteries (the middle chapters of Mary's history), and the glorious mysteries.

> For the joyful mysteries have cemented a unique bond of love between her Son and her, and we desire to follow it to the end; not only through Easter

and Pentecost but open into Mary's death and glory. For he who did not abhor her womb took her to himself in her death, and crowned her with glory in heaven.

By way of conclusion: In the January 1997 number of *The Month*, there is a review of the book *Toward a New Theology of the Body* by the Canadian Sr Mary Timothy Prokes FSE (Franciscan Sisters of the Eucharist). Reflecting growing interest in 'body theology' as rooted in the core mysteries of the Christian faith, this title continues earlier writings, reaching back to her doctoral dissertation at St Michael's College of Toronto University (1976), 'The Flesh was Made Word', and her 1993 book *Mutuality: The Human Image of Trinitarian Love*. She took part in the workshop held at the Josephinum School of Theology, Columbus, Ohio, January 1982, on the theme 'The Implications of Mariology for a Theology of the Body'. There were eight participants (one was Fr John McHugh, of our ESBVM) meeting under the sponsorship of the Institute for Theological Encounter with Science and Technology (centred in St Louis). The director of the Institute, Fr Robert Brungs SJ, posed this challenge: 'The whole meaning of redemption, and, therefore, of the New Kingdom, is contained in the union of the God–man and a woman; in other words, the meaning of God's final union with his creation is to be found in a masculine–feminine union'. And he then put the question to the panel: 'Is this a too radical statement? Can it be otherwise, namely, that the relationship or union between Christ and Mary does not contain and express the meaning of God's relationship to his creation?'

Sr Prokes' contribution to the session was published in *Communio* 2 (Summer 1984) pp. 157–76, 'The Nuptial Meaning of Body in Light of Mary's Assumption'. Most of the other papers were also published: F. M. Jelly OP, in *Marian Studies* 34 (1983) – he organized it with Fr Brungs – 'Towards a Theology of the Body Through Mariology'. My own offering appeared in *Carmelus* 31 (1984), pp. 6–23, 'Mary as the New Eve: Notes on a Theme'.

Sr Prokes' writings are filled with insights about the bond between Mary and her Son. Jesus and his Mother show interpersonal relationships as magnified and maximized. She writes (in *Mutuality*);

> Deeper bonding comes through hearing the word of God and keeping it through doing the will of God. The limited but cogent references to Mary in the gospels are precisely in this vein. 'Let what you have said be done to me' is the hallmark of Mary's self-gift in response to divine self-gift ... Through his own Mother ... he broke open what it means to be mother, sister and brother.

There is even greater significance to the bridegroom approach. Quoting

Fr Brungs, Sr Prokes notes that *una caro* (the 'one flesh' of the Bible for marriage) applied to Jesus and Mary is not simply a spousal image, but also maternal and eucharistic. I was reminded of the great eucharistic motet. 'Ave verum corpus natum ex Maria Virgine'. In *Toward a Theology* ... chapter 11 is on 'Human Suffering', and there are good lines on Mary as

> the first, most intimate sharer in Jesus' afflictions. She would not be spared from the anguished grappling with the mystery of suffering. The limited number of Gospel passages that refer to Mary consistently speak of her unique call to mature co-suffering with Christ

– from the presentation to Calvary. She 'knew an embodied suffering that was a share in Christ's salvific suffering.' (pp. 148–9).

(This paper was given at the ESBVM Leeds Congress
in August 1998)

5

Theotokos in a Trinitarian perspective

Ireneu Craciun

From an Orthodox perspective, it is appropriate that this Twelfth International Ecumenical Congress of the Ecumenical Society of the Blessed Virgin Mary should take place during August. This particular month is set apart for us as a month dedicated to the Mother of God. During its first fourteen days, the faithful gather in churches to chant the profoundly moving *Paraklesis* to the Mother of God. This preparatory period is followed then by the Great Feast of the Dormition itself, and its continuous celebration during the subsequent octave.

'*The same, yet different*' was the verdict given by a Westerner, upon listening to the presentation made by an Easterner, at a Conference on Christology which was held in Dublin some years ago.

Similarly, we definitely have an almost '*the same*' discourse on Mary's person and mission, grounded on our common East–West mariological tradition of the first millennium, which is '*yet different*' basically, with respect to our approach to the Marian mystery.

More precisely, in Orthodox understanding the Marian topic is situated at a level different from that of any other theological topic, namely one more existential, experiential, and typological. In other words, when everything in church life speaks of, or points to, the *Theotokos* in an appropriate liturgical and iconographic language, any 'scholastic' approach, we believe, becomes superfluous and inadequate to deal with such an immediate Christian experience.[1] Nevertheless, when in church both liturgy and specially iconography, using a superior *symbolic* language, unfold the Marian mystery to the faithful and point to her elevated place as being *next to Christ*,[2] it remains to us, theologians and committed lay people in the field of mariology, to translate this glory in academic theological discourse. It is here that we meet some apparent deficiencies in our Eastern theology. For contemporary Orthodox theologians, in general, do not perceive Mary as a subject of critical analysis[3] but rather theologically speak of her either as an 'appendix' to christology, or as an 'extension' to ecclesiology.

I believe that neither of the two qualifications does justice to what the faithful experience *in church* in connection with the *Theotokos*.

Consequently, I believe that theologically speaking, the mystery of the Mother of God rightly unfolds itself in a Trinitarian perspective. It is in her unprecedented and forever unequalled personal relationship with the Father, Son, and Holy Spirit, our Triune God, that the greatness of this human being, one of our own, resides. When seen in a Trinitarian light, we are able to grasp, as far as humanly possible, her glory as the Elected One of the Father, as Mother of the Whole Christ, and as Bearer of the Holy Spirit, his icon. We are also able to understand how in her passing away, the Mother of God became *Typus Ecclesiae* in that she is the first fruit of the resurrection, experiencing now, by anticipation, the eschatological fulfilment of the age to come.

Relying on liturgy and iconography as well as on patristics and contemporary Orthodox theological thinking, specially Romanian, I would like to reflect on the Marian mystery looked upon within a Trinitarian framework. As I intend to do so, I become aware of the existence of two 'parallel' East–West Triadological developments, not necessarily grounded in opposition,[4] with their own particularities, such as the *Ousia–Energeia* distinction and the *Filioque* clause.

'When I say God,' says St Gregory of Nazianzus, 'I mean Father, Son, and Holy Spirit.'[5] 'Three Divine Persons, possessing the one *Ousia* (Substance) in a distinct manner as Unoriginate, Begotten, and Proceeding; Three Divine Persons, Who by virtue of perpetual movement of reciprocal love, engage in an eternal ontic dialogue in Three.'[6] Such is the concrete and dynamic approach of Eastern thought to the mystery of the Trinity.

Bearing in mind the complete otherness as well as the absolute transcendence of the Deity, that a human being, Mary of Nazareth, has reached such a level of personal contact and has established such an unparalleled relationship with the Triune God is absolutely remarkable.

This finds an expression in a medieval statue, *La Vierge Ouvrante*, found at the Musée de Cluny in Paris, which daringly shows the Virgin 'containing' the Trinity. Equally, an icon in the East, painted under Western influence, depicts the Virgin kneeling, while the Father and the Son, in the presence of the Holy Spirit, place a crown of glory upon her head. In both cases, art is bearing testimony to the Virgin's uniqueness.

She is the Elected One of the Father, *Theonymphē*, the Bride of God.

The annunciation scheme in Luke 1.26–38, is definitive in appreciating Mary's relation to the Father. This scheme may not be a diary of the day of the annunciation. It contains, nevertheless, the communication of a unique message, which was then articulated in a post-resurrectional language. Here, *He Who Is* (Exod. 3.14) communicates his message to Mary of Nazareth, one of ours, who belongs to a certain historical time, geographical space, and has a definite civil status.[7] This biblical revelation finds a powerful and most dramatic expression in the matinal canon for the Feast of the Annunciation. Its implications are evident.

Firstly, a very positive and optimistic view of man. Even in his fallen state, man is never completely cut off from God, but could develop his natural tendency towards good and thus continue a tenuous dialogue with his personal God. Mary, in relation to the Father, appears as the one who consciously developed this tendency to the utmost of which any human being is capable. She thus became the summit of all Old Testament sanctity. She thus

> moved God to take pity on men, overbalanced the wickedness of the entire race, showed humankind worthy to receive God in its midst, and the earth worthy to have God dwell on it,

as Cabasilas says.[8]

Secondly, a re-evaluation of human freedom, willing love, and personal dignity. In her twofold capacity, as divinely elected and also as a representative of all mankind, Mary responded to the message of the annunciation with conscious, joyful consent. She was free to choose. She could have refused, and if she had refused, God would have respected her free will. We reverence her not only because God chose her, but also because she herself made the right choice. The divine initiative was met here, in the annunciation scheme, with a positive human response. And, as soon as Mary pronounced her *Fiat*, the re-creation started. This crucially important moment became the source and inspiration for an entire corpus of patristic literature. It is summed up by Evdokimov when he says:

> The Fiat of the Creator is answered by the Fiat of the creature: '*Ecce Ancilla Domini*'. In the response of the Virgin there bursts forth the pure flame of her who gives herself and thereby is ready to receive.[9]

In addition, there is also a mystical dimension of Mary's relation to the Father as pointed out by Theophanes, a fourteenth-century Archbishop of Nicaea. He holds that Christ's twofold co-essentiality
– with the Father – according to His Godhead, and
– with His mother – according to His humanity,
gives Mary a very special place in relation to the Father. It is Christ's *viscera* (totality of personal feelings and emotions) that establishes an 'intimacy' between the Father and Mary, because this *viscera* is a treasure which belongs to both.[10]

The patristic and extensively used liturgical Marian title *Theonymphē*, (Bride of God), which is also important in defining Mary's relation to the Father, finds expression in Mother Teodosia's poem 'The Engagement'.[11] After making a majestic presentation of the atmosphere in the Temple on the day of Mary's engagement to Joseph, Mother Teodosia says:

> Something of this glory lets me understand
> That not old Joseph is the bridegroom
> >   of the Most Holy One.
> For, beyond the youthful assembly of the virgins
> >   Gathered in the Temple
> I behold, in spirit, the Deity
> >   in majesty appearing
> To sanctify Anne's daughter to become
> >   The Bride of God.

In essence, by her free, conscious, and reverential personal response to the Father's initiative, Mary became the workshop of the Trinity in bringing about the incarnation.

She is Mother of the Son, the *Theotokos*. In fact, she is mother of the whole Christ, Head and mystical body. In other words she is *Mater Domini* and *Mater Ecclesiae*.

Every faithful person, upon entering an Orthodox church, is met by two icons of the Mother of God in particular which communicate this Marian double role – Christological and ecclesiological – most vividly: the icon of *Panagia Odigetria*, on the icon screen, and *Panagia Platitera*, in the sanctuary apse.

The first icon, known also as the icon of the incarnation, depicts the Mother of God holding her Divine Son on her left arm, while with her right hand she is gently pointing towards Christ, who is the Way (John 14.6). The second icon, in the sanctuary apse, shows a solemn depiction of the Mother of God enthroned, while her Divine Son is resting upon her lap. The Mother of God here is usually being attended either by archangels or by hierarchies of the Church. She is representing here the whole Church 'containing' the Uncontainable.

Mary's relation to the Son may be compared, by analogy, with the Son's relation to the Father. Thus she is related to Christ's humanity, just as the Father is related to the Son in his divinity. As God, the Son is begotten of his Father alone, just as he is born – as man – of his mother alone. This comparison underlines the fullness of the two natures hypostatically united in Christ. As man, Christ does not derive his humanity from two parents; he is not the blend of two parents possessing, as it were, composite character-istics. This points to an unparalleled, and most profound intimacy between the mother and her Divine Son. In fact, this unique relationship was qualified by the two universally-binding pronouncements *de fide*: *Theotokos* (Ephesus 431) and *Aeiparthenos* (Constantinople 553). Both defi-nitions are christological with evident Marian implications.

Mother Teodosia Latcu chose one such moment of untold intimacy between Mother and her Divine Son, namely the hour of glorification on Golgotha, to pour out her soul in a poem simply named 'The Mother'.

> When He was toilingly ascending to Golgotha
> You followed Him, forgotten by the crowds.
> No one knew that two lives were being torn apart
> for the salvation of all.
> And no one saw that four palms,
> Were being stretched on the wood
> to be transfixed with nails.
> And that there were two foreheads
> crowned with thorns at Pilate's court.
> And the mind does not comprehend
> That in fact the soldier, at once,
> two bodies has pierced.
> No one ever dared write about
> The great wonder of eternal love,
> For behold, on the same wooden Cross,
> Mystically speaking, two crucifixions
> had been taking place.

This idea of utmost intimacy between Mother and her Divine Son is also taken up in another poem of exquisite mystical beauty called 'The Two':

> Looking up at her tortured, dying Son,
> Mother, too, felt all-consuming pain.
> For it was at that moment
> That the prophecy was fulfilled
> about the sword piercing her heart.
> For her untainted body knew brokenness
> When she intimately participated
> in His crucifixion.
> And, my soul, broken as well with so much sorrow
> Is wondering: is it, Lord, Your sorrow,
> Much greater than that of Your Mother?

The poem continues by affirming that it was as a result of her all-consuming and immediate participation that the Mother of God became also Mother of the Church, that is, Mother of the whole Christ. For, at the foot of the cross, St John the Evangelist was representing the community of the faithful when he heard the Lord uttering: 'Behold your Mother'. (John 19.27). Mother Teodosia concludes:

> From the Cross, You gave a new kind of kinship
> When You entrusted us, to Your Mother,
>   at Your Holy Crucifixion.

Here we see that Mary did not became *Mater Ecclesiae* on account of some privilege, or even due to natural affiliation, but precisely because of her personal participation, and within the context of the new type of kinship, – spiritual not physical – which now links all members of the Mystical Body, that is, the Church. The primacy of spiritual relationships over the physical ones, in the Church, finds biblical expression in the incident recorded by St Mark (3.31–5) when our Lord, pointing at his listeners, says: 'Anyone who does the will of God, that person is my brother, and sister and mother'. It is precisely here that the true glory of the Mother of God lies. She is, above all, the one who *listens* and *does* the will of God. Not accidentally her recorded words are: '*Do* whatever He tells you' (John 2.5).

Thus, she is setting before us the criteria of Christian discipleship: to *listen* and *do* the will of God.

In addition, her direct involvement in the life of the Church is that of perpetual intercession on behalf of her spiritual family. Is it not that precisely mutual prayer which is the very essence of the Church? Her prayer for us is all-encompassing. After the example set out in Cana (John 2.1–11), we confidently believe that no need of ours is ever overlooked by her. But, does this Marian mediation obscure in any way Christ's own mediation? Definitely not, because Mary's is *human* mediation, while Christ's is *divine* mediation. These are two essentially different things, as clearly expressed in the original Greek by the use of *eis* in qualifying Christ as the one Mediator. (1 Tim. 2.5)[12]

Furthermore, in her dormition or assumption, she who is *Mater Ecclesiae*, became also *Typus Ecclesiae* in her new status as *Maria Glorificata*. In her dormition, the *Theotokos* passed beyond the final resurrection. Along with her Risen Son, she is now the first-fruit of the eschatological harvest. She is *Typus Ecclesiae*, because she is experiencing now what the whole Church will experience after the *Parousia*, namely the fulfilment of the Eschaton. In other words, through Mary, who has now crossed to the other side of resurrection, the Church catches a glimpse of what it will be, in the age to come.

At a personal level, she is the personal *typus* of our expectations for the future, their personal guarantee. Immortality in the age to come, of which Mary stands as concrete evidence, can be cogently argued, as Prof. Staniloaie does, on the grounds of the indestructibility of the human person which is required by the indestructibility of God and man's relationship.[13]

What she is now, we believe we all shall be in the age to come, namely wholly spiritual, and wholly transparent with the grace of the Holy Spirit.

She is a Spirit-bearer, *Pneumatophoros*; The Holy Spirit's Icon.

The two descents of the Holy Spirit upon Mary, at the annunciation and on Pentecost Sunday, together define her relation with the Divine Person of the Holy Spirit.

At the annunciation, Mary acted as our representative. The Holy Spirit prepared her, in view of the incarnation, by a process of *katharsis* (purification). St Gregory of Nazianzus uses the term *prokatharsis* (pre-purification).[14] This process points to Mary as a true descendant of Adam, sharing in the consequences of the Fall. The work of the Holy Spirit in Mary, consisted in forming and vivifying the body, taken from the substance provided by her. This created body was then indwelt and personalized by the Divine Logos. There is a striking similarity in theological reflection regarding the Spirit's power of creativity and his work in Mary, between the Byzantine theologian Leontius and Prof. Staniloaie.[15]

It is important to note that Christ is truly Adam's descendant precisely because he has a complete human nature created by the Spirit not *ex nihilo*, but from the Virgin. Thus, Christ is *Totus in nostris,* as Pope Leo says in his dogmatic letter *Ad Flavianum,* precisely because he is Son of the Virgin.

The Orthodox icon of Pentecost either deliberately leaves an empty space at the core of the Apostolic College, or places the Book of the Gospels there to represent Christ. Some other icons depict, in this central place, the Mother of God, to underline that she herself became a *Pneumatophoros,* a Spirit-bearer, in the outpouring descent of the Holy Spirit.

A Spirit-bearer person, as Mary tells us by her own example, is a person open and transparent to, and more importantly co-operative with, the action of the Holy Spirit who dwells within. This idea finds expression in Mother Teodosia's poem called 'The Annunciation':

> The Archangel's greeting makes you wonder,
> You lift towards him your questioning eyes,
> And an involuntary movement of your hand

Is meant to keep afar his
                        blessed Good tidings . . .
Your person, Mary, is the unwritten scroll
In which, at your Fiat, the Holy Spirit wrote
The eternal Logos, at His Incarnation.

And this leads us to a consideration of Mary as an icon of the Holy Spirit himself.

There must be a very intimate relation between him whom we call *Panagion*, and her whom Easterners love to address as *Panagia*. Evdokimov, developing this theme in particular, observes that the Spirit always points to Christ (John 16.13–14), and that consequently, the third Person of the Trinity is in some measure hidden, anonymous, elusive. He is speaking to us not about himself, but always about another. While the Son is the image of the Father, and the Spirit is the image of the Son, the Holy Spirit himself has no image within the Holy Trinity.[16] Indeed, in his personal coming, the Holy Spirit does not manifest his Person; he does not have his image in another Person of the Trinity. The Spirit, as a Person, remains unmanifested, 'concealing Himself', as Lossky says, 'in His very appearing.'[17]

The Holy Spirit appeared in the form of fiery tongues at Pentecost, and he appeared as a turtle-dove, (in the feminine – Greek: *Peristera*), at Christ's baptism in the Jordan. If, therefore, the Holy Spirit expresses in some mysterious but distinctive way the feminine aspect of God, the maternal principle in the Deity, have we not here a special reason why Mary should serve as an icon of the Paraclete?

Mary of Nazareth, the pride of humanity, became the workshop of our Triune God. Her unique relationship with the Deity, materialized in her positive, creative, and vitally important participation in the incarnation, is best summed up by Cabasilas[18] as follows:

> The Incarnation of the Word was not only the work of the Father, Son and Spirit, the First consenting, the Second descending, the Third overshadowing, but also the work of the will and the faith of the Virgin. Without the Three Divine Persons this design could not have been carried into effect; nor yet without the consent and faith of the All-pure Virgin. Only after teaching and persuading her does God make her His Mother and receives from her the flesh that she consciously wills to offer Him. Just as He was conceived by His own free choice, so in the same way she became His Mother voluntarily and with her free consent.

It is in this Trinitarian light that the multitude of dispersed aspects of her glory come together, as do small brilliant pieces, to form theologically a mosaic of the Ever-Virgin Mother of God.

Yet, no matter how skilful this mosaic is, the Marian mystery will remain for ever just that: a Mystery of Faith. This is so eloquently expressed in the *Paraklesis*[19] when the Mother of God is called *Akatanoiton Thauma*, the Inexplicable Wonder. For can we ever explain how Mary of Nazareth nursed her Creator?

When confronted with her presence, of paramount importance in the spiritual life of the faithful, do we not remain as the *Akathistos* says – just like 'orators most eloquent who become mute as fish before the Theotokos' (Ikos 17)?

I do not find a more appropriate way of concluding, than quoting from another treasure of Mother Teodosia's, entitled 'Rosa Mystica':

> You Mary, All Holy, sweetest of all names,
> Rose born in the mystery of the world
> > beyond the horizon,
> Pour out the grace of your holy purity,
> As there was none before, or after you.
> Over our world stifling in smoke,
> You, Empress, wave the hem of your
> > perfumed garment.
> And, over our misery of bitter taste
> Wave the sweet fragrance of your outworldly roses
> Granting us, even for a second, to experience
> Your grace, O Lady, you, the Mystical Rose.

Notes

1 Nikos Nissiotis, 'Mary in Orthodox Theology', in *Concilium* 168 (1983) pp. 25–6.

2 Identical view on the place of the Mother of God is being expressed *iconographically* in the Orthodox Church just as Vatican II's *Dogmatic Constitution on the Church* expresses it *in writing* in its Art. 54. (Cf. *Vatican Council II*, Austin Flannery's 1981 edition, pp. 414–15).

3 Bishop Kallistos of Diokleia, 'The Sanctity and Glory of the Mother of God: Orthodox Approaches', in *The Way* 51 (1984), pp. 79–96.

4 M. A. Fahey SJ and J. Meyendorff, *Trinitarian Theology of East and West* (Brookline 1977), p. 18.

5 *Oratio 23 PG* 35: 1161. The West replaces this dynamic conception with a more static approach that starts with the one substance and then says that it subsists in three Persons. Cf. W. Kasper, *The God of Jesus Christ* (London 1983), p. 259.

6 Prof. Dumitru Staniloaie, 'Relatiile intertrinitare si viata Bisericii' in *Ortodoxia* 1/1965 p. 720 ff. See also *Teologia Dogmatica Ortodoxa* (Bucuresti 1978), vol. 1, pp. 306–20.

7 It is vital to stress the complete humanity of Mary in order to preclude any

idea of her as a goddess. Since Jesus' existence can be established through definite reference points, his birth in the year 7 or 6 BC and his violent death on 7 April 30, (3 April 33), (cf. Xavier Léon Dufour, *Dictionary of the New Testament* (London 1980), p. 246) we can date Mary's historical existence between about 22 BC and AD 30–70 (cf. G. Ashe, *The Virgin*, London 1976, p. 78).

8 Nikolaou Kabasila, *Hē Theometor – Treis Theometorikes Omilies* (Athens 1968), p. 124.

9 P. Evdomikov, 'La Nouveauté de L'Ésprit', *Spiritualité orientale* 20 (Bellefontaine 1977), pp. 142–3.

10 Bishop Theophanes Nicaenus, 'Sermo in Sanctissimam Deiparam', in *Lateranum* I/1 (Romae 1935), p. 22.

11 Mother Teodosia Zorica Latcu (1917–90), University Professor, Linguist, professed nun at Vladimiresti Monastery (Eastern Romania) in 1948, theologian, prolific poet, in the spirit and manner of St Simeon the New Theologian (d.1022). Expelled by the Communists along with her Abbess, Mother Veronica, and all three hundred and fifty nuns following the brutal closure of the monastery in February 1955. Between 1955 and 1990 she lived in internal exile, experiencing the whole spectrum of secret police barbarity, from prison to house arrest, to endless interrogation and unspeakable abuse, to confiscation of her entire work and its subsequent destruction. All of this she suffered on account of her steadfastness in the Faith and her blatant refusal to co-operate with the political system. The quoted theological poems, along with about two hundred others, were personally and secretly dictated to me in the summers of 1975–9, when I was a theology student. After the Revolution, in February 1990, she was among the first to return to her re-opened monastery, after thirty-five years of exile. According to her cell attendant, she beheld the Mother of God in glory, in the blessed hour of her departure, on 9 August 1990. Mother Teodosia Latcu was my spiritual mother.

12 See also *The Analytical Greek Lexicon* (London 1973), pp. 119 and 272.

13 Prof. Dumitru Staniloaie, *Teologia Dogmatica Orthodoxa*, Bucuresti 1978, vol. 3, pp. 209 ff.

14 *PG* 35: 325B, 633C.

15 *Contra Nest. et Eutych.*, *PG* 86: 1343A. also *Teologia Dogmatica Ortodoxa* (Bucuresti 1978), vol. 2, p. 83.

16 P. Evdokimov, op. cit. p. 262.

17 Vladimir Lossky, *The Mystical Theology of the Eastern Church* (London 1957), pp. 159 ff.

18 *On the Annunciation* cited by Evdokimov, op. cit. pp. 141–2.

19 Beside the *Akathistos Hymnos*, there are two Intercessory Canons, *Paraklesis*, to the Most Holy *Theotokos*. These unequalled Byzantine marvels, which combine theological precision with exquisite artistic beauty, form an important part of both communal prayer in church, and prayer of the domestic church, at home. The *Great Paraklesis* has an imperial origin, being the work of Theodore I Doukas Lascaris (1204–22), an emperor in exile, who reigned at Nicaea during the Latin occupation of Constantinople. The *Little Paraklesis*

has most probably an Athonite origin, being composed by Monk Theostriktos (or Theophanios). An English translation of these Canons is offered by Holy Transfiguration Monastery in *A Prayer Book for Orthodox Christians* (Boston, Mass. 1987), pp. 249–300.

(This paper was given at the ESBVM Leeds Congress
in August 1998)

6

Mary Mother of the Church and the dimensions of Catholicity

Edward Knapp-Fisher

Introduction

This Congress [Leeds 1998] is taking place in the period preparatory to what John Paul II correctly and invariably refers to as the Great Jubilee of the Third Millennium. This is a necessary reminder that the celebration for which we are preparing is primarily a religious and distinctively Christian occasion. Its primary purpose should be the celebration of the mighty works of God, and only secondarily of the achievements which he has enabled men to accomplish.

A jubilee is 'an occasion of emancipation and restoration' (OED). The Coming Great Jubilee commemorates the 2000th anniversary of the birth of the Saviour of the World, by whom alone humanity can be emancipated from bondage to evil, sin and death. Redemption he offers to all through his Church, in which he is ever present and active through the Holy Spirit. The impact of the Church upon the world is, however, disastrously blunted by the scandal of our divisions in blatant disobedience to our Lord and his reiterated prayer for all his members that *they may all be one*, as he is in the Father and the Father in him. Nor can a divided Church claim to be an effective channel and instrument of the Holy Spirit. It was not such a fragmented community, with its often conflicting claims, but a Church united according to his will, that Christ promised that he would lead into all truth (John 16.13). The visible unity in faith and love of all who claim to be Christ's must surely be our most urgent objective as we stand on the threshold of the Third Millennium. Without it we cannot with conviction or credibility proclaim the gospel of reconciliation to a world in conflict.

It is a demonstration of the devil's insidious subtlety that he, the great deceiver, has succeeded in making the Church and our Lady two of the focal points of dissension and disagreement between Christians. It was, therefore, the vision of the founder of our Society, and is its abiding vocation, 'to study at various levels the place of the Blessed Virgin Mary in the Church under Christ and related theological questions; AND IN THE

LIGHT OF SUCH STUDY TO PROMOTE ECUMENICAL DEVOTION'. (The Constitution of the Society.) It is our hope and prayer that through this Congress we may have been made more faithful, informed and effective in promoting its objects thus defined in our Constitution.

Mary, Mother of the Church

It is well known that, at the first session of Vatican II in 1962, the Theological Commission presented a draft of a separate document on the Blessed Virgin Mary. This was rejected by the Council Fathers on the grounds that it would be a serious obstacle to ecumenical progress to deal with mariology in isolation. In consequence a chapter on Mary was incorporated into the Dogmatic Constitution on the Church (*Lumen Gentium*). As Fr Avery Dulles SJ has commented: '[This] chapter, as finally adopted, goes considerably beyond the mere discussion of her relation to the Church, but this theme is sufficiently central to justify the inclusion of the chapter in this Constitution'. (*Documents of Vatican II*, Abbott, p. 13.) This point is emphasized by significant words in the concluding paragraph of the Constitution which describe the Blessed Virgin Mary as 'exalted above all the saints . . . [she] aided the beginning of the Church by her prayers'. (*LG* 69.)

It can surely be taken for granted that there is now general agreement that mariology cannot be considered in isolation. 'Mariology is but a chapter in the treatise of the incarnation, never to be extended into an independent treatise.' (Mary Anne deTrana, paper to the ESBVM Congress, 1991.) Gordon Wakefield makes the same point: 'Any devotion to Mary must follow from her relation to Christ and the mystery of the incarnation'. (*Mary is for Everyone*, 'The Blessed Virgin Mary in some modern poets', p. 303.)

In 1963 Paul VI, anxious to expedite the proceedings of the Council, declared Mary to be *Mother of the Church*. This title evoked surprise and some criticism both at the time and subsequently. It was considered and rejected by the conciliar Theological Commission on the ground that it appeared to locate Mary *outside* the Church. Four years later the Holy Father responded by planning to build a new church in Rome dedicated to 'Our Lady, Mother of the Church, of which she is the first, blessed and privileged child'. (Hebblethwaite, *Paul VI*, p. 368.) If this is paradoxical it is no more so than the affirmations that God is One and God is Three: that Christ is also his Mother's Saviour; that Mary is Mother of God and Bride of God. Recall, too, the first verse of Dante's 'Hymn to our Lady' (trans. R. A. Knox):

Maiden yet a Mother,
Daughter of thy Son,
High beyond all other
Lowlier is none.

Divine mysteries which defy precise definition can only be described in terms of paradox – as Eastern Christians are perhaps readier to recognize than we are in the West.

Orthodox Christians, like Anglicans, are reluctant to define divine mysteries. 'Apophaticism ... constitutes the fundamental characteristic of the whole theological tradition of the Eastern Church'. (Vladimir Lossky, *Mystical Theology of the Eastern Church*, p. 26.) It is significant that in his lecture [*see pp. 42–52*] Fr Craciun consistently spoke of 'the Marian mystery'. Nor, in the Eastern tradition, is a sharp distinction drawn between mysticism and theology. (Lossky, *Mystical Theology*, p. 8.) It is interesting to note, in passing, that a Protestant, Max Thurian, makes a similar point. He states that the term 'spirituality' is rarely used by Protestants because it is not distinguished in isolation from 'theology'. (M. Villain, *Unity*, p. 112.)

Reluctance to define does not, however, signify that the Orthodox dissent from certain divine truths which Western Catholics seek more precisely to define: that of the *assumption (dormition)* is a case in point.

The dogma of the *immaculate conception*, however, creates problems for Eastern Christians because, as Fr Craciun observed, their understanding of *original sin* is rather different from that of their Western brethren. This dogma, writes Lossky, 'is foreign to the Eastern tradition ... She [Mary] was not holy in virtue of a privilege, of an exemption from the destiny common to all humanity, but because she has been kept from all taint of [actual] sin, though without impairment of her liberty' (*Mystical Theology*, p. 140). With this not only Anglicans would concur. The distinguished Methodist theologian, Dr Gordon Wakefield, writes: 'Mary's is also a human story'. (*Mary is for Everyone*, p. 303.)

The reluctance of Anglicans and others, as well as of the Orthodox, to attempt further definitions of mysteries is a warning that the promulgation of any new dogmatic definitions would constitute a serious obstacle to ecumenical progress. More recently, the proclamation of Mary as 'Mother of the Church' has been criticized by Fr Georges Tavard on the grounds that it is not traditional and has triumphal overtones. This view does not appear to be widely shared (cf. *The Catechism of the Catholic Church* (ET), p. 220). Dr John Macquarrie comments: 'Fr Tavard seems to have found this title maximalist. As an Anglican I would not have thought so. In relating Mary to the Church one is acknowledging her creaturely status much more clearly than is the case with the title

"Mother of God".' (ESBVM *Newsletter*, January 1997.)

There are many Anglicans and others who would agree. I would add that 'Mother of God' is likely to be more acceptable to non-Catholics and less liable to be misunderstood by them than such titles as 'Mediatrix' and 'Co-redemptrix'. Such designations do indeed tend to obscure her humanity. It is because she is one of us that she is 'a sign of hope for all the faithful' (*LG* 53). We are inspired and encouraged by her freely-given obedience through which, in the words of Irenaeus, 'she became the cause of salvation both for herself and for the whole human race' (quoted in *LG* 56). The aptitude and propriety of Paul VI's inspired declaration that Mary is Mother of the Church is endorsed some sixteen centuries earlier by St Augustine of Hippo, who emphatically stated that Mary is 'clearly the Mother of all Christ's members' (*LG* 53).

The Church and the dimensions of catholicity

It is all too easy to think of the Church in limited and restricted terms. If our God is often too small, our ecclesiology is frequently too narrow. When we think or speak of the Church, our thoughts rarely encompass more than the local church building and its congregation, and perhaps also our diocese or district. Even when we widen our ecclesial horizons we often fail to look beyond the bounds of the Church Militant here on earth, the shortcomings of whose members are only too apparent. We forget that the members of the Church now in this world are but an infinitesimal part of the totality of the Holy Catholic Church.

Here again the devil is always ready to exploit the discouragement, even despair, which such a limited understanding of the Church's catholicity tends to breed, as C. S. Lewis reminds us. Recall the advice given by Screwtape in one of his letters to his nephew.

> One of our great allies at present is the Church itself; I do not mean the Church as we see her spread out through all time and space and rooted in eternity. That, I confess, is a spectacle which makes our boldest tempters uneasy. But fortunately it is quite invisible to these humans. All your patient sees is the half-finished, sham Gothic erection on the new housing estate. When he goes inside he sees the local grocer with rather an oily expression on his face bustling up to offer him one shiny little book containing a liturgy which neither of them understands, and one shabby little book containing corrupt texts of a number of religious lyrics, mostly bad, and in very small print. When he gets to his pew ... he sees just that selection of his neighbours whom he has hitherto avoided ... It matters very little, of course, what kind of people that next pew really contains. Make his mind flit to and fro between an expression like 'the body of Christ' and the actual faces in the next pew ...
>
> (*The Screwtape Letters*: Letter II).

The differing views of the Church held by separated Christians are reflected in their ecclesiologies, in their understanding of ministry, and in their worship.

Protestantism, particularly in the Reformed churches, has tended to emphasize the local aspect of the Church as the *gathered community*. This limited conception of the Church is also emphasized by the unwillingness of the Reformers to acknowledge the existence of any intermediate state on our pilgrimage from earth to heaven. John Bunyan's 'Christian' passes immediately from this world to heavenly bliss. In 1644 John Vicars gives a quaint and outspoken account of changes imposed upon Westminster Abbey during the Commonwealth period: it illustrates not only the Puritans' restricted and narrow ecclesiology, but also their suspicion of sacraments and their abhorrence of ecclesiastical ornaments in general and of holy statues and pictures in particular. The Shrine of Our Lady of Pew was demolished with especial violence and venom. Vicars writes:

> There is a most rare and strange alteration in the face of things in the Cathedral [*sic*] Church of Westminster. Namely that whereas there was wont to be heard nothing almost but roaring boys and squeaking organ pipes, and the Cathedral catches of Morley and I know not what trash; now the popish altar is quite taken away, the bellowing organs are demolished ... There is now set up a most blessed orthodox preaching ministry ... and of godly ministers appointed thereunto, and for the gaudy, guilded crucifixes and rotten rabble of dumb idols, popish saints and pictures, set up and painted thereabout ... now a most sweet assembly and thick throng of God's pious people, and well-affected living and teachable saints, is constantly and most comfortably every morning to be seen at the services.
>
> (*House of Kings*, 1966)

In their doctrine of ministry stress is laid on the *parity of ministries* and the *priesthood of all believers*. Public worship is predominantly congregational and unstructured, with the emphasis generally rather on the Word than the Sacraments. The worship of the churches of the Reformation has during the past fifty years been considerably influenced by the Liturgical Movement. *Ex tempore* prayers are increasingly being replaced by set forms, except in the case of 'charismatic' congregations.

In Anglicanism, as always, theology and practice are characterized by diversity and are sometimes divergent. Article XIX, 'Of the Church' was in its formulation influenced by the continental Reformers. In consequence it concentrates attention on the local, limited aspect of the Church: 'The visible Church of Christ is a congregation of faithful men, in which the pure Word of God is preached and the Sacraments duly ministered according to Christ's ordinance ...'

In Catholicism, formularies and practice provide frequent reminders of the dimensions of the universal Church. The Church is the 'Body of Christ', the 'extension of the Incarnation', the 'universal sacrament of Salvation' (*LG*), 'the People of God'. *The Catechism of the Catholic Church*, after describing our Lady as 'Mother of Christ, Mother of the Church', summarizes the authentic catholicity of the Church in a paragraph entitled 'The Three States of the Church': 'We believe in all the faithful of Christ, those who are pilgrims on earth, the dead who are being purified, and the blessed in heaven, all together forming one Church.' (ET pp. 218–20.)

Within the context of the Catholic Church the ordained ministry is hierarchically structured in consistency with its historical roots which the doctrine of Apostolic Succession is designed to secure. The unity of the three states of the Church is expressed by its liturgy, in which the present is embraced by the eternal. This is most gloriously expressed in the Liturgy of the Eastern Orthodox – and of Eastern Catholics – with their genius for preserving and promoting that sense of mystery which is the essence of worship, and which is enhanced and expressed in the ikonostasis. This is the most striking symbol of the Communion of Saints, with whom in the Eucharist all Christ's members, throughout all ages, are in him and by him most intimately united.

There is a further fact which we who have been baptized into Christ and recognize the dimensions of the Church's catholicity should acknowledge and recall. This is our continuity with our Jewish forebears, the People of God under the Old Covenant. We, the People of God under the New Covenant, implicitly acknowledge and express our indebtedness to them by, for example, the place given in our worship to the Psalms and Old Testament lections, and by the portrayal in our churches of Old Testament patriarchs as well as of Christian saints. Of the continuity between the old and the new, Christ, Israel's long-expected Messiah, is the sacrament and his Mother the symbol. A true daughter of Israel, as the Magnificat proclaims, cousin of the Baptist the forerunner, together with Simeon and Anna, Mary supremely represented the faithful remnant through whose obedience and devotion God performs his mighty works. She who confidently looked for the coming of the Messiah became his Mother, linking the ancient people of God with the Church re-born at Pentecost.

When we recognize the dimensions of the Church and its catholicity our understanding of Mary as Mother of the Church is also enlarged. Upon earth our Lady shared with us the suffering which all members of a crucified Saviour must, on their earthly pilgrimage, be prepared to endure.

Sing we, too of Mary's sorrows,
Of the sword that pierced her through,
When beneath the Cross of Jesus
She His weight of suffering knew.
(G. B. Timms, *New English Hymnal*, no. 185)

But unique in vocation, obedient to God's will at whatever cost, Mary could be spared experience of the second state of the Church, the stage of purification, and be immediately translated to the fullness of eternal beatitude in heaven. Supreme among the saints, she may properly be also acclaimed as Queen of Heaven.

Heaven with transcendent joys her entrance graced,
Next to His throne her Son His Mother placed;
And here below, now she's of heaven possest,
All generations are to call her blest.
(Bishop Ken, *New English Hymnal*, no. 182)

Christ is King, who reigns in glory; he is the Head of his Body the Church; he is the only Mediator between God and Man, through whom his Mother, with the rest of us, is redeemed. Second only to her Son, she is the Mother of the Church and holds the primacy in the Communion of Saints. Since, while we are still *in via*, she has reached journey's end, she is a sign of hope for all the faithful.

Conclusion

We are frequently tempted to worry about the future of the Church. For such pessimism there are many grounds, of which the most obvious are the average age of our congregations and their steady decline in numbers. There is nothing novel about this situation.

The sea of faith
Was once, too, at the full, and round earth's shore
Lay like the folds of a bright girdle furl'd;
But now I only hear
Its melancholy long withdrawing roar.
(Matthew Arnold, 'Dover Beach')

So wrote an English poet a century and a half ago. This gloomy prognostication was expressed more prosaically by his father, Thomas Arnold: 'The Church as it now stands no human power can save'. (1832).

A salutary corrective to such a frame of mind is constantly to call to mind the authentic dimensions of the Church and its catholicity as enunciated in its three states: to see the Church, its nature and its mission *sub specie aeternitatis*. At the present time we members of the Church *Militant* are pilgrims *in via*, still far from our goal. There must be no evasion of our present responsibilities, no escapism, no nettle left ungrasped. The sacramentality of each moment with its demands and challenges is to be our watchword. Like all travellers we must take every step along the way seriously, yet never lose sight of our destination, however remote it may still be.

Death will mark the end of this preliminary stage of our long journey. All with a grain of self-knowledge will acknowledge that when they come to die they still have far to go. As we have noted, the rejection of any idea of an intermediate state was characteristic of the Reformers. This was probably due less to antipathy to the doctrine itself than to their reaction against certain medieval practices associated with it (e.g. private masses, and the trade in indulgences). This seems to be confirmed by the wording of the Anglican Article XXII, 'Of Purgatory', upon which Puritan influence is plainly discernible. 'The Romish doctrine concerning Purgatory, Pardons, Worshipping and Adoration, as well as Images, Relics and also Invocation of Saints, is a vain thing, fondly invented ...' It is significant that it is 'the Romish doctrine', not the conception of purgatory itself, which is rejected. The second, intermediate state is a necessity for all except our Lady and a select few known only to God. For the rest of us the immediate vision of God in the plenitude of his glory would be excruciating torture, more than we could bear. This second state, the Church *Expectant*, will include the purging of our still-surviving sinfulness but will also, surely, have its positive aspect – our continuing growth towards holiness. Our Lord's words to the penitent thief are significant: 'Truly, I say to you, today you will be with me in Paradise'. (Luke 23.43 RSV). 'Paradise' means 'garden', a place where things grow. We still have far to grow before we become full-grown sons and daughters of our Heavenly Father.

Finally, we shall, through the mediation of our Lord and Saviour and by his never-failing grace, at last be ready for that vision of God which is our destination and our destiny. A sign of hope, our Lady directs our attention towards our goal, which she has already attained.

> Hail, O star that pointest
> Towards the port of heaven,
> Thou to whom as maiden
> God for Son was given.
>
> (*Ave Maris Stella*, ninth century)

We who are still far from home, are inspired by her example and supported by her prayers, as we persevere in our long pilgrimage until we share with her and all the saints the fullness of eternal life. This is the Church *Triumphant*.

Our awareness of the true catholicity of the Church, militant, expectant and triumphant, transcending the boundaries of space and time, is our great reassurance. This is the reality of the Communion of Saints into which we have been baptized. Still far from our heavenly home, our Father's house, yet we are inspired by our Lord and Saviour, empowered by his living presence through the Holy Spirit. And at all times and in every circumstance we are thankful for our fellowship in and through Christ, with his Mother and all the saints; we are encouraged by their examples and supported by their prayers.

Charles Wesley's reference to only the first and third states of the Church do not, I believe, imply that he would have doubted or denied the reality and necessity of the second state. In spite of this apparent hiatus the frequent repetition of his well-known hymn illuminates the nature of the Church and helps us to preserve our perspective:

> Let saints on earth in concert sing
> With those whose work is done:
> For all the servants of our King
> In earth and heaven are one.
> One family we dwell in Him,
> One Church, above, beneath:
> Though now divided by the stream,
> The narrow stream of death.

But it is the Eucharist which is the supreme act of worship and the characteristic activity of the *whole* Church. Here Christ and *all* his members through time and eternity are most intimately united with him and one another. Here indeed and in truth we have both a foretaste of and a share in the worship of heaven, as

> with angels and archangels
> AND WITH ALL THE COMPANY OF HEAVEN
> We laud and magnify God's Holy Name
> Evermore praising him, and saying,
> > Holy, Holy, Holy, Lord God of Hosts,
> > Heaven and earth are full of thy glory,
> > Glory be to Thee, O Lord, most high.

*(This paper was given at the ESBVM Leeds Congress
in August 1998)*

7

The saints' everlasting rest –
the Reformed position

Keith G. Riglin

A brief version of this paper was first presented to the London districts' meeting of the Methodist Sacramental Fellowship on 2 November 1996 – the commemoration of All Souls – and it was the Fellowship who gave me the title.

'The saints' everlasting rest – the Reformed position.' I suppose a quick answer would be, horizontal and underground like everyone else, but I presumed that a fuller answer was and is anticipated.

'The saints' everlasting rest' – which I understand to mean the beatific state enjoyed by those who have departed this life in the faith of Christ and whom the Church, in her tradition, has affirmed of being of especial virtue and example. Most obviously amongst whom would be blessed Mary, mother of our Lord and daughter of grace,[1] and apostles such as James, remembered by the Church on 25 July, but also others, such as Columba of Iona, 'abbot and missionary', recalled on 9 June, and the patron of my own congregation in Cambridge.

'The Reformed position' – which I understand to mean that tradition in which I stand as a member of and an ordained minister in the United Reformed Church. The Reformed tradition is one of the branches of Christendom which emerged from the Reformation in the sixteenth and seventeenth centuries CE. Like the other emerging traditions – notably Lutheranism and Roman Catholicism (the post-Tridentine Church of Rome surely bears many of the marks of a denomination if not a sect) – the Reformed regards itself as no more and no less than part (at times in our history, the only true part) of the catholic Church. 'We conduct our life together ... in forms which we believe contain the essential elements of the church's life, both catholic and reformed.'[2]

Nonetheless, the historical roots of this tradition can be traced to the life and work of the sixteenth-century French reformer John Calvin (1509–64) who made such an impact on the city of Geneva that the Reformed tradition has, erroneously, sometimes been termed Calvinism. Yet we reject such 'isms' and 'ologies' – borrowing the words of another of our spiritual forebears, Richard Baxter (1615–91), the presbyter ejected in 1662, along with 2000 other ordained ministers, from the conformist episcopal body in England – we would perhaps prefer to describe ourselves as 'mere catholics'. We, like Martin Luther (1483–1546), the father of the Reformation, are content to be called Protestant – although the term occurs in no official statements – for we protest *for* the catholic faith against what were then perceived to be the medieval errors of the Church of Rome.

The Reformed tradition has always laid heavy stress on the need for a coherent theology. In the sixteenth and seventeenth centuries this was seen in the production of numerous formularies, notably, in the English-speaking world, *The Westminster Confession*, approved by the English Parliament in 1648. This confession was produced to unite the established churches of England and Scotland, and remains to this day the subordinate standard of the Church of Scotland.[3]

Incidentally, it is not so for the successors of the divines of England, who simply include it in the statement: 'We acknowledge the declarations made in our own tradition by Congregationalists [and] Presbyterians ... in which they stated the faith and sought to make its implications clear.'[4]

An attempt to produce a coherent theology is seen in the work of systematic theologians such as John Calvin, in *The Institutes of the Christian Religion* and, in the twentieth century, Karl Barth (1886–1968), in *Church Dogmatics*. Such theologians have sought to be both biblical and realistic. The conservative evangelicalism which emerged in the nineteenth century is thus no part of the Reformed tradition. 'The highest authority for what we believe and do is God's word in the Bible, alive for [God's] people today through the help of the Spirit.'[5] No biblical literalism here, rather a realistic attempt to hear the word of God, not equated with holy Scripture but contained therein, in the context of the community of the baptized (the Church), and relying on the guidance of God's assured presence, even the Spirit in our midst.

This rather lengthy introduction sets the scene for an examination of our subject. What is the Reformed position on blessed Mary and the other saints? Is there a clear hagiology in the kirk?

To find an answer to this I intend, briefly, to consider some of the writings of the two Reformed theologians already mentioned, Calvin and Barth, together with the British divine Peter Taylor Forsyth (1848–1921) – sometimes called the pre-Barthian Barth – in whom I have a particular interest. This is followed by some personal reflections on the journey of faith, and then some conclusions.

In chapter 20 of book III of *The Institutes* of 1559 John Calvin discusses the life of prayer. In a section dealing with the prayers of the departed, he states: 'In regard to the saints who having died in the body live in

Christ, if we attribute prayer to them, let us not imagine that they have any other way of supplicating God than through Christ who alone is the way, or that their prayers are accepted by God in any other name.'[6]

Calvin here is attacking the practice – still the case, as he puts it, 'wherever popery prevails' – of obtaining access to God through any other name. It is 'the extreme of stupidity, not to say madness, to attempt to obtain access by means of others, so as to be drawn away from him [Christ] without whom access cannot be obtained.'[7] Why pray to St Gertrude of Nivelles, the hospitable abbess of the seventh century, about one's garden or one's problems with mice and rats, or the fourth-century St Nicholas about one's encounter with a sailor – I refer to the traditional patronages of these two blessed folk – when, as the Scripture states, 'there is one God; there is also one mediator between God and humankind, Christ Jesus, himself human'.[8] Or, to quote St Ambrose, the fourth-century doctor of the church, as does Calvin the patristic scholar: 'He is our mouth by which we speak to the Father; our eye by which we see the Father; our right hand by which we offer ourselves to the Father. Save by his intercession neither we nor any saints have any intercourse with God.'[9]

Calvin proceeds to describe the context of his objection to the invocation of saints. He believes it to be because the Christian believers have become 'filled with anxiety, as if they supposed that Christ were insufficient or too rigorous'. Yet, why fear God, asks Calvin, in the sense of being afraid? 'At the same time they reject the kindness of God in manifesting himself to them as a Father, for he is not their Father if they do not recognize Christ as their brother.'[10]

As well as illustrating the Reformed understanding of all Christian theology ultimately being christology, Calvin makes clear his objection. To pray to or through any other, not to make all our petitions and intercessions 'through Jesus Christ our Lord', is to deny the graciousness of the God whom we know in this same Christ Jesus.

It would appear to be the case that, just as mariolatry (the worship of Mary) seems to have emerged in the Church in reaction to an hierarchical and patriarchal view of God, so the medieval cult of the saints emerged – an intercessor becomes needed to plead with the friend of the mother of the mediator to ask her to ask him to pray to his distant heavenly Father on behalf of the miserable offenders we are, 'and there is no health in us'. As the satirical *Not the Church Times* of 1981 so delicately put it in its published prayer to the legendary St Anne, mother of the blessed Mary, 'holy Annie, God's granny, *ora pro nobis*'![11]

Nonetheless, it is also the case that, just as a proper mariology (a doctrine of Mary) which honours the one who is blessed among women[12] is far removed from the medieval cult of the Virgin, and as the distant other-worldly patriarchy is from 'our Father in heaven' taught by Jesus,[13] so there may be, even in Calvin, a proper hagiology which is not cultic, idolatrous or a denial of the one mediator.

What if one was to ask the departed saints, to whom, Calvin does admit, we can attribute prayer, to pray for and with us without imagining, to use Calvin's phrase, 'they have any other way of supplicating God than through Christ'? What if such communion with the saints was affirmed in the context of being together 'in Christ'? To quote the apostle Paul: 'We do not live to ourselves, and we do not die to ourselves. If we live, we live to the Lord, and if we die, we die to the Lord: so then, whether we live or whether we die, we are the Lord's.'[14] John Wesley, certainly no disciple of John Calvin but, as an Anglican, in the Reformed tradition,[15] wrote in a letter of 9 May 1773, of the saints in paradise – it is 'not improbable [that] their fellowship with us is far more sensible than ours with them ... They no doubt clearly discern all our words and actions, if not all our thoughts too'.[16] We shall return to this reassessment of Calvin shortly.

In volume 4 of *Church Dogmatics*, entitled 'The Doctrine of Reconciliation',[17] Karl Barth discusses the holy one, who is Christ, and the saints. For Barth the saints are a people of holy ones fashioned by God, 'those who in spite of their sin have the freedom ... to represent him among all other men and to serve him in what they are and do and suffer.'[18] Barth's study of Scripture leads him to conclude: 'The saints of the New Testament exist only in plurality. Sanctity belongs to them, but only in their common life, not as individuals. In this plurality they are, of course, identical with the Christian community ... The holy one constitutes the saints.'[19] He cites biblical phrases such as 'the church of the saints'[20] and 'ministry to the saints'.[21]

As such, according to Barth, any merit the saints may have is not theirs at all but belongs with, originates from, is attributed to, the one holy one who is Christ. As the historic context is different, Barth has no cult of the saints against which to react, at least not in his own communion, although, as one would expect, he shares Calvin's concern for affirming the sole mediation of Christ and would be wary of any practice or belief, no matter how well-intentioned, which would or could lead to a departure from this.[22]

Finally, a word from P. T. Forsyth, an ordained minister in the then Congregational Union of England and Wales.[23] In his volume *The Soul of Prayer* (1916) Forsyth writes of the work of the Spirit. 'When we speak to God it is really the God who lives in us speaking through us to himself. His Spirit returns to him who gave it; and returns not void, but bearing our souls with him.'[24] Prayer is thus, for the Christian, communion with the risen Lord, life in the Spirit, an end in itself, what one has called 'the end in which the believer eschatologically shares'.[25] This belief in prayer as an end in itself stems from Forsyth's belief in the supremacy of the grace of God which, for him, extends beyond death – the power of God's persuasive love not limited by human finitude – 'In Christ we cannot be cut off from our dead nor they from us wherever they be'.[26] Thus, in *This Life and the Next* (1918), Forsyth argues both for prayers for the dead –

> I venture to say ... that the instinct and custom of praying for our dearest dead, or our noblest, should be encouraged and sanctified as a new bond for practical life between the seen and the unseen, where we have bonds all too few ... It would never have been lost but for ... the commerce which the church made of magical influence on another world[27] –

and, perhaps most significantly, for a Protestant reappraisal of purgatory – 'We threw away too much when we threw purgatory clean out of doors ... There are more conversions on the other side than on this'.[28] With Forsyth the Reformed tradition has indeed moved on from the seventeenth century, when Richard Baxter, in *The Saints' Everlasting Rest*, could write of the dead:

> The harvest is gathered, the weeds burned and the work done. The unregenerate will be beyond hope, the saints beyond fear for ever ... as the memory of the wicked will eternally torment them, as they look back on the pleasures they enjoyed, the sin committed, the grace refused, Christ neglected and time lost, so will the memory of the saints for ever bring them joy.[29]

We thus have seen, in this all-too-brief survey, a number of themes. From Calvin, a concern to avoid an unhealthy hagiolatry which denigrates the work of Christ and our prayers offered through him. From Barth, a stress on the plurality of sainthood, the holy ones whose holiness is corporate and stems from their incorporation 'in Christ', an expression whose true meaning is the whole community of the baptized. Such a communal incorporation is itself thoroughly biblical and is foreshadowed in the apocalyptic vision in the Book of Daniel, where the blessings bestowed on 'the holy ones of the Most High' parallel and flow from those bestowed on the 'one like a son of man', the messianic figure presented to 'the Ancient of Days'.[30] From Forsyth, a belief in prayer as having an end in itself, both affected by and giving further effect to our sharing in the dynamic life of God, again 'in Christ', in whom both the quick and the dead are one.

With these three themes, can a case be made today for the Reformed pastor to celebrate in the daily prayer of the church, as in the eucharist, not only 'with angels and archangels' but also 'with all the company of heaven', with the saints, both living and departed, not only praying for them, as Forsyth himself argues, but with them? If such a case can be made, then the experience and reasoning of God's people today are part of that case, so now one turns to autobiography.

Although my baptism was in St Paul's Church, Hammersmith (the church of my mother and of her parents before her), my Christian upbringing revolved almost entirely around Kenton Baptist Church – the Nonconformist chapel in Harrow whose Sunday school readily received me, whose Boys' Brigade gladly instructed me, and amongst whom a first public profession of faith in Christ was made. I can still recall the religious instruction I received there – 'It is appointed for men to die once, and after that comes judgement'[31] (it was always men in those days!). I feared the judgement, yet Jesus was my saviour and I felt secure. No room here for the invocation of the saints. Indeed, the only lasting memory of the concept is of the hymn by Lesbia Scott (1898–1986), 'I sing a song of the saints of God' – 'And one was a shepherdess on the green . . . and one was a doctor, and one was a queen.'[32]

Four years were spent as a student teacher at what was then the College of All Saints, Tottenham, an Anglican college of higher education. There I discovered chapel, with the habit of daily prayer and weekly eucharist. I learnt catholic sacramental theology and devotion from my tutor, a priest in the Oratory of the Good Shepherd, and liberal theology (certainly so to a youthful evangelicalism) from my Methodist lecturer. All Saints' Day was, of course, a high day. I still recall the grandness of the occasion, the order of the liturgy, the chaplain's rich vestments, and William How's great hymn: 'But lo, there breaks a yet more glorious day; the saints triumphant rise in bright array: the King of glory passes on his way: Alleluia!'[33] Yet for me at that point this was all they did. They are with the Lord, but they are dead, awaiting that great triumph, when 'the Lord himself, with a cry of command, with the archangel's call and with the sound of God's trumpet, will descend from heaven, and the dead in Christ will rise.'[34]

When a vocation to the ordained ministry came it was inevitable that it should be expressed in the Baptist community. All Saints' was thus followed by three years at Regent's Park College, Oxford, after which came ordination within 'the churches of the Baptist faith and order',[35] although a faith and order which tutors at Oxford had taught belonged firmly within the Reformed tradition, the only distinctiveness being a peculiar baptismal practice. Since ordination in 1983 four years have been served as an associate minister and university chaplain in Bath, two years in theological education in Jamaica, and seven years as minister of an ecumenical congregation in Amersham.[36] In January of 1997 I was inducted to the pastorate of St Columba's United Reformed Church, Cambridge, where I also serve as Church of Scotland chaplain to the university. The denomination may have changed, but the attachment to the Reformed tradition remains, indeed, is stronger. So why now, continuing as a Reformed pastor, is a different position held on the saints' everlasting rest, and what is that position?

A number of factors contribute. One is the experience of differing religious traditions. The first two years of ordained ministry included postgraduate study at Heythrop College, London – a Jesuit institution. In Jamaica, teaching was alongside and for Roman Catholics and even Ethiopian Orthodox, as well as the more familiar Anglicans, Baptists, Congregationalists, Methodists and Presbyterians. There have been more personal experiences. I recall Fr Peter Ball CGA, sometime Bishop of Lewes, speaking at an ordinands' conference of how, as he enjoyed the beauty of the Sussex countryside, he would often speak to St Francis – you were right about God's good creation. What could possibly be wrong with this? I recall attending the ordination of a Jesuit friend in New England – after which I had my first and so far only experience of concelebrating at mass with a Catholic priest – not only did the service not seem to be the 'blasphemous fable and dangerous deceit' described in the Anglican formulary,[37] the invocations sung in the intercessions – 'holy St Gregory pray for us, holy St Lucy pray for us . . .' – sounded, if not familiar to Reformed ears, certainly not wrong.

A second factor is a love of history and especially of hagiography. At the united evening services of the covenanted churches of Amersham-on-the-Hill the habit was developed of telling the stories of those saints whose feast days fall nearest to the Sunday in question, a habit I am continuing in Cambridge. Together with biblical saints, we considered Agnes, Alban, Antony of Egypt, Bernard of Clairvaux, Charles and John Wesley, Ignatius of Antioch, John Bunyan, Martin of Tours, Nicholas, Paulinus of York, Polycarp of Smyrna and Valentine (both of them). As well as reminding the average Protestant that there was a church between the apostles and the Reformation, the communion of the saints was affirmed.

Thirdly, the death of loved ones. By the grace of God I have only known the death of three close to me – my father in his sixties, my sister-in-law in her thirties, my good friend Mary in her eighties. Their deaths not only remind me of my own mortality: new devotion has been encouraged. Upon viewing a church or cathedral with votive candles it has become the tradition of my family to stop, light candles and say a prayer. When the responsibility has been mine I now light three candles. My partner once asked me why. One for each of the three people I have mentioned, was my reply. How strange, she remarked, for she without fail lit candles for the living, I always for the dead.

A final and increasingly important factor is an understanding of the

Christian faith as journey not as arrival. There seems great poignancy in the description of the first Christians as followers of the Way,[38] and of the Johannine descriptions of Christ in the 'I am' sayings, mostly to do with movement and dynamism rather than a static state – the door through whom to enter, the good shepherd to guide, the light of the world to follow, the way, the truth and the life.[39] This understanding of faith as a journey is well expressed in the prayerful words from *A Wee Worship Book* (1989) of the Iona Community. 'You did not say you were the answer, you said you were the way; you did not ask us to succeed, you asked us to be faithful; you did not promise us paradise tomorrow, you said you would be with us to the end of the world.'[40] This rediscovery of faith as pilgrimage seems to have flourished especially in the Reformed tradition, which may account for the fact that two of the most dynamic religious communities of this century emerged within it – Iona in Scotland[41] and Taizé in France.[42]

Faith as a journey leads some, many, to believe that the Christian's walk with God in Christ continues beyond death – Forsyth's reaffirmation of purgatory. There is a familiar verse at the end of the writer's description of the heroes of faith in the Letter to the Hebrews. 'Therefore, since we are surrounded by so great a cloud of witnesses, let us lay aside every weight and the sin that clings so closely, and let us run with perseverance the race that is set before us, looking to Jesus the pioneer and perfecter of our faith.'[43] For some of its history the Reformed tradition has, especially when touched by evangelical revival, stressed 'the sin that clings so closely', but not the witnesses before or the race afterwards.

If faith is a journey, a race, although a race in which none may be a loser, and if it continues with God in the dynamism and community of God, then why abandon those witnesses who are beyond death and are, to continue the metaphor, closest to the finishing line? The security and assurance of evangelical faith has never left me, but it has been joined by the delight and occasionally the pain of the voyage with others.

So we return to the themes of Calvin, Barth and Forsyth. If Christians are taught, especially when young in the faith, to ask those who have moved on from milk to solid food to pray for them,[44] could not a case be made for asking for the prayers of the one whom 'all generations will call blessed'?[45] And not only her, but others who have gone before us? Only, of course, because of Jesus Christ, not instead of him; only because we are all one 'in Christ'; and only because our prayers are an end in themselves, as we enjoy communion together in and journeying with the Lord. To quote the hymn: 'And it's from the old I travel to the new; keep me travelling along with you.'[46]

There is a story in 2 Maccabees, a book which was canonical for the

Greek-speaking synagogues and Christian communities in the Jewish diaspora at the turn of the era. It is a story of Judas Maccabeus, who discovered the bodies of some of his fellow Jews who had died, with foreign idols under their tunics. This accounted, he believed, for their deaths – 'they all blessed the ways of the Lord, the righteous judge, who reveals the things that are hidden'.[47] Perhaps here Judas' understanding of the divine economy is weak, but he is surely strong in what follows.

> The noble Judas took up a collection, man by man, to the amount of two thousand drachmas of silver, and sent it to Jerusalem to provide for a sin-offering. In doing this he acted very well and honourably, taking account of the resurrection. For if he were not expecting that those who had fallen would rise again, it would have been superfluous and foolish to pray for the dead. But if he was looking to the splendid reward that is laid up for those who fall asleep in godliness, it was a holy and pious thought.[48]

Such acting well and honourably by remembering the dead in prayer seems appropriate for all those who share in the Christian conviction, as is said in the *Service Book* of my own church, 'death is not the end but a new beginning'.[49]

This is not to pray for a change in the spiritual state of any who have died: it is not the offering of masses for the dead; indeed, it is not praying *for* anything. No sacrifice in Jerusalem or Rome or even in Geneva is necessary, for Christ has died and is risen. But what in the *Book of Common Order* (1994) of the Church of Scotland is called 'Commemoration of the Faithful Departed', those who, as 2 Maccabees states, 'fall asleep in godliness', now has its proper place in the liturgies of the Reformed tradition.

The motto of the Reformed tradition is *Ecclesia reformata semper reformanda* – 'the church (having been) reformed stands always in need of reform (or needs always to be reformed)'. It means that what was very meet, right and the bounden duty of one generation of Christians may not be so for another. Not because truth is relative, but because the incarnate One who is the Truth is dynamic. The following is reported of the Congregationalist minister John Robinson (*c.* 1575–1625) as he stood before those of his congregation at Leyden to sail with the Pilgrim Fathers in the *Mayflower* of 1620.

> He charged us, before God and his blessed angels, to follow him no further than he followed Christ; and if God should reveal anything to us by any other instrument of his to be as ready to receive it as ever we were to receive any truth by his ministry. For he was very confident that the Lord had more truth and light yet to break forth out of his holy word.[50]

The word of God whose servants we are is not a dry printed page but a living saviour who speaks afresh to each new generation and community.

This Reformed pastor is also a companion of the Society of St Francis. In *Celebrating Common Prayer* (1992) there is a Franciscan ending to the office which no Christian in the Reformed tradition, with a Christ-centred faith, a strong conviction that there is but one mediator between God and humankind, a knowledge that we are all one in Christ, and that prayer is an end in itself, should have any problem in offering. 'May our blessed Lady pray for us. May all the saints of God pray for us. May the angels of God befriend us and watch around us to protect us. May the Lord Jesus give us his blessing of peace.'[51]

I conclude with a story of Oliver Cromwell (1599–1658) who, as a Congregationalist, did much, at least in England – Ireland is another story – to champion religious liberty. He stood before the General Assembly of the Church of Scotland, whose understanding of the Reformed tradition, then as now, was too connexional and presbyterian for the Baptists and Independents amongst Cromwell's supporters – surely a meeting between what Americans call a rock and a hard place. And Cromwell said, 'I entreat you, in the bowels of Christ, consider that you may be wrong'. I believe that in our history the Reformed tradition has been wrong, or at least as misguided as other traditions against whom it has protested, and that we now should affirm, as did Forsyth eighty years ago, 'There is nothing apostolic or evangelical that forbids prayer for [the dead] in a communion of saints which death does not rend. It is an impulse of nature which is strengthened by all we know of the movement of grace'.[52]

On the saints' everlasting rest there is today no one Reformed position, but this Reformed pastor has, I hope, gone some way, through a little history, a little theology, a little Bible and a little more autobiography, towards presenting his own.

I was once leading worship in Scotland in a beautiful chapel in the countryside outwith Edinburgh. As is proper I was dressed in black cassock, preaching gown, bands and academic hood. I read my prayers in the tradition of common order and the faithful departed were commemorated. One member of the congregation kept his eye on me throughout. Afterwards this man who, I discovered, was a minister of the Free Church of Scotland, the so-called 'wee frees', came up to me – 'Minister, you may look like a Presbyterian but you sound like a Jesuit'. I hope that in this presentation, whatever I may have sounded like to you, or indeed, looked like, you have seen and heard only me ... and a case made from within a particular Christian tradition, and from personal reflection and spiritual journey, for unbroken fellowship with our dead in Christ.

Notes

1 'Mary is to be seen as the daughter of grace, not as the mother of grace: for she too is saved only by the loving-kindness of the Word.' R. Mackenzie, *ESBVM*, May 1997.

2 *The Nature, Faith and Order of the United Reformed Church*, as approved by the General Assembly (1990).

3 'The Church of Scotland holds as its subordinate standard the Westminster Confession of Faith, recognizing liberty of opinion on such points of doctrine as do not enter into the substance of the faith, and claiming the right, in dependence on the promised guidance of the Holy Spirit, to formulate, interpret or modify its subordinate standards.' Preamble to the Order for the Ordination and Admission of Elders, *Book of Common Order*, Church of Scotland (Edinburgh 1994), p. 337.

4 *United Reformed Church*, op. cit.

5 ibid. See also the *Declaration of Principle* of the Baptist Union of Great Britain – 'Christ ... is the sole and absolute authority in all matters pertaining to faith and practice, as revealed in the holy scriptures.'

6 Para 21. *Institutes of the Christian Religion*, translated by Henry Beveridge (1845), one-volume edition (Grand Rapids 1989).

7 ibid.

8 1 Timothy 2.5. Scripture quotations from *New Revised Standard Version* (1989) Anglicized edition (Oxford 1995).

9 Quoted by John Calvin, op. cit.

10 ibid.

11 *Not the Church Times* (London, 22 September 1981), p. 6.

12 Luke 1.28.

13 Matthew 6.9.

14 Romans 14.7–8.

15 Despite the arguments of John Henry Newman in his famous *Tract 90* of 1841 – in its *Thirty-Nine Articles* (1562) and *Book of Common Prayer* (1662) Anglicanism stands, at least with one foot, in this common tradition, catholic and reformed.

16 Quoted in Michael J. Townsend, *Our Friends in Light: Praise and Prayer in the Communion of Saints*, (Methodist Sacramental Fellowship 1993), p. 9.

17 *Church Dogmatics*, vol. 4, 2 'The Doctrine of Reconciliation', translated by G. W. Bromiley (Edinburgh 1958).

18 Karl Barth, op. cit. p. 511.

19 op. cit. p. 513.

20 1 Corinthians 14.33.

21 2 Corinthians 8.4.

22 Cf. Alasdair I. C. Heron, *Agreement and Disagreement: The Common Ground and Major Differences between the Church of Scotland and the Roman Catholic Church*, 2nd edition (Edinburgh 1984). 'The Church of Scotland ... does not believe that others, however holy, are more approachable than Christ or in any way closer to us than he ... Accordingly it holds that Christian faith and hope and worship must be grounded and focused upon Christ himself, and not

diverted in any other direction. Any such diversion, however well-intentioned, is not consistent with a proper recognition of this unique centrality.' p. 28.

23 In 1966 the churches of the Union covenanted together as the Congregational Church in England and Wales. In 1972 the greater part of this body united with the Presbyterian Church of England to form the United Reformed Church.

24 P. T. Forsyth, *The Soul of Prayer* (1916) fourth impression (London 1960), p. 32.

25 J. H. Rodgers, *The Theology of P. T. Forsyth* (London 1965), p. 186.

26 *This Life and the Next* (1918, reprinted 1946) p. 34.

27 op. cit. p. 36.

28 op. cit. cf. 'Never too late for God' in *P. T. Forsyth and the Cure of Souls*, an appraisement and anthology by Harry Escott (London 1948), p. 92.

29 *The Saints' Everlasting Rest* (1650) edited by Christopher Pipe (London 1994), pp. 51–52, 68.

30 Cf. Daniel 7.18 with 7.13–14.

31 Hebrews 9.27.

32 *The Baptist Hymn Book* (London 1962) no. 259.

33 William Walsham How (1823–97). *The BBC Hymn Book* (London 1951) no. 227.

34 1 Thessalonians 5.16.

35 See *Orders and Prayers for Church Worship*, Baptist Union of Great Britain and Ireland (London 1960).

36 In 1908 a 'fellowship of believers' was formed. In 1924 the church joined the Baptist and Congregational unions, and in 1965 became a congregation of the Presbyterian Church of England. The church is now part of the Baptist Union of Great Britain and the United Reformed Church and, since 1995, has been in covenant with the local Anglican and Methodist churches.

37 No. 31 of the *Thirty-Nine Articles* (1562) of the established Church of England.

38 Cf. Acts 9.2 and 22.4.

39 John 10.9; 10.14; 8.12 and 14.6.

40 'Morning Liturgy 2', *A Wee Worship Book* (Glasgow 1989), p. 9.

41 Founded in 1938 by the Revd Dr George MacLeod, officially recognized by the General Assembly of the Church of Scotland in 1951, and now an ecumenical community.

42 Founded in 1940 by Br Roger, an ordained minister of the Reformed Church of France.

43 Hebrews 12.1–2.

44 1 Corinthians 3.2.

45 Luke 1.48.

46 'One more step along the world I go' by Sydney Carter (1915–). No. 549 in *Rejoice and Sing*, URC (Oxford 1991).

47 2 Maccabees 12.41.

48 2 Maccabees 12.43–end.

49 'The Funeral', *Service Book*, United Reformed Church (Oxford 1989), p. 68.

50 From the notes of Edward Winslow, probably taken at the time. Quoted in

The Baptist Hymn Book Companion, revised edition (London 1967), p. 217.
51 *Celebrating Common Prayer*, Society of St Francis (London 1992), p. 269.
52 op. cit. p. 38. Forsyth adds, 'The arguments against it are apt to be more theologically pedantic than spiritually proficient.'

*(This paper was given at the ESBVM Woldingham Conference
in June 1997)*

8

The Holy Spirit,
our Lady and the Church

Jeremy Sheehy

Perhaps the best way in which I can begin this paper is to try and explain some of the lines of thought which mean that this subject which I have taken as my title was in my mind when Fr McLoughlin first approached me about writing a paper for the Congress.

First, I was of course aware that Pope John Paul II, in his programme for the preparatory period to the celebration of the opening of the third millennium of the years of the incarnation, had asked that this year be the year of the Spirit. That theme has been picked up by the conference in its title 'The Holy Spirit and the Blessed Virgin Mary' and in its devotional theme of 'the presence of the Virgin in the Church as the woman open to the voice of the Spirit, the woman of hope who, like Abraham, accepted God's will hoping against hope'. And Mary as the one overshadowed by and filled with the Spirit has been one of the themes of worship and devotion at Walsingham this year, where I am proud to be one of the Guardians of the Anglican Shrine, and where the National Roman Catholic Shrine of Our Lady at the Slipper Chapel has been celebrating its centenary.

But, secondly, I have also been for the last couple of years a member of the Church of England's Faith and Order Advisory Group. Amongst all the concern that ecumenical strategists and tacticians sometimes have for arranging structures for mutual recognition of baptism, eucharist, and the ordained ministry, amongst all the concern for conferences and special services and bilateral and multilateral dialogues, it is important that we are reminded that one condition for growing unity is the common confession of the apostolic faith, and one element in visible unity is the continuing and common confession of the apostolic faith. In 1982 the Commission on Faith and Order of the World Council of Churches (on which Commission churches which are not full members of the World Council of Churches have nonetheless appointed members, such that in that sense the Commission is more ecumenically representative than the Council itself) initiated a theological programme to draw up an agreed expression of the meaning of the Nicene Creed today. The aim of the project was emphatically not to draw up a new modern ecumenical creed, but rather to help the churches reappropriate their apostolic faith by arriving at a common explication of the apostolic faith as proclaimed in what we usually call the Nicene Creed. In 1990 after a series of meetings, consultations, study guides and reports the Commission published its document *Confessing the One Faith.*[1] I want to quote from Fr Jean-Marie Tillard, the French Canadian Dominican, Vice-Moderator of the Commission on Faith and Order and Moderator of the Apostolic Faith Steering Group, who writes in his introduction:

> The coming together of all Christians in an authentic communion of faith, evangelical life and mission requires the common confession of the apostolic faith. As many of the responses to the Lima document on *Baptism, Eucharist and Ministry* have shown, Christians cannot be truly united unless they recognize in each other the same apostolic faith, which is witnessed in word and life. The document *Confessing the One Faith* is an instrument to draw the churches to a common understanding of this faith, which has to be confessed, especially in the celebration of baptism and eucharist, and proclaimed though the missionary work of all Christian communities.[2]

As Fr Tillard reminds us in his introduction, the confession of a common faith is one of the signs of communion, that key concept in modern ecclesiology. This enables us to see elements of communion where full communion is lacking. But it also works the other way round. Sometimes the consciousness of the confession of a common faith may be an element in communion which is under threat. As an Anglican I can point this out, without the difficulty which some of you might feel pointing it out to me. It seems to me that it is a good thing for an ecumenical congress such as this one to look and see what the document *Confessing the One Faith* has to say about some of the matters which this society particularly discusses, and I do not think that the document *Confessing the One Faith* has yet had the attention I have come to think it deserves. And I noted when I first read the document that the section that dealt with the birth of Jesus from the Blessed Virgin Mary (ss. 121–124) makes frequent mention of the Holy Spirit. We say 'by the power of the Holy Spirit he became incarnate from the Virgin Mary'. The Greek text expresses more of a parallelism between the work of the Holy Spirit and the participation of the Virgin Mary. Literally, it seems to say 'from the Holy Spirit and Mary the Virgin'. As the document says, 'When the Creed brings together the phrases "by the Holy Spirit" and "from the Virgin Mary", it is confessing that Jesus Christ is both God and man.'[3] Perhaps we have not always given full weight to that affirmation of the work of the Spirit (although I expect some Orthodox brothers and sisters would argue that this has been more a problem in the West than amongst the Christians of the East). Noting this was a second line of thought which made me want to write something about this theme.

And then there is a third line of thought which brings me to this theme. Over the last year, I have had several pupils writing extended essays or dissertations which have required them to explore some of the theological writing of the twentieth century which I remember exciting me when I read it first in the 1970s.[4] I am thinking of some of the works which set out a sort of rediscovery of the doctrine of the Church, and in particular, of the Church as the Mystical Body of Christ. I read people like Eric Mascall, and they introduced me to names like Lionel Thornton and Henri de Lubac and Yves Congar. And I loved and still love reading them, and I think that rediscovery of the doctrine of the Church as the Mystical Body, the work which laid the groundwork for this appearing in the 1930s and which then blossomed in the 1950s and 1960s, was very significant.

But introducing these works to a number of students recently I have also realized how weak the treatment of the person and work of the Holy Spirit is in many of them. It is, at times, almost as though their delight in uncovering and expounding the significance of the incarnation for the way in which we think of the Church had blinded them to the significance of the work of the Holy Spirit for the way in which we think of the Church. And so this subject has been in my mind recently because it results from a line of thought which has come to me whilst re-reading some of these works and thinking about them with a criticism in mind which at one stage I do not think would have occurred to me. I summed it up when talking to one student about the book by Yves Congar, *Christ, Our Lady, and the Church*.[5] We talked about it, and the student made some interesting comments and asked about some interesting points. I got out my copy, which I bought in 1978 and which I clearly read soon after. I underlined some passages and made notes in the margin. Talking to this student I said that it clearly had not struck me at the time, because there is no such marginal comment, but what struck me now was how relatively absent the Holy Spirit is from Congar's discussion. There are, inevitably, a handful of references to the Holy Spirit in the index, but none of them guides the reader to a sustained discussion of the role and work of the Spirit or of the relevance of thought about the role and work of the Spirit in understanding the relationship between Mary and the Church. I said to the student that I thought my main criticism of Congar's book could now be summed up by saying that it did need to be completed by a second volume entitled 'The Holy Spirit, Our Lady, and the Church'.

Now, of course, more recently Fr Congar himself did, before he died in

1995, write a three-volume work *I Believe in the Holy Spirit*,[6] although I would suggest that in that work the place of the work of the Spirit in explaining the interrelationships between the figure of Mary and the life of the Church is under-explored.

But it is the criticism that they do not properly allow for the work of the Holy Spirit that I would now want to make of many of the works of that period, which is the third line of thought that caused me to take my present title. There is an imbalance in those works, I now feel, no doubt understandably due to the enthusiasm with which the writers made their points and underlined their rediscoveries. But we, when we read them, need to seek to redress the balance. By entitling this paper 'The Holy Spirit, our Lady, and the Church', I seek at least to make that criticism and to assert the need for that balance to be redressed. I would not claim that I am here going to summarize what that second volume might have said. I am simply going to argue that there needed to be a second volume and to suggest some dangers we can fall into when we do not have that second volume. I am going to organize my comments in three sections: first of all, introducing some of the ideas in Congar's book *Christ, Our Lady, and the Church*, highlighting where we might now want to introduce acknowledgment of the work and place of the Holy Spirit, secondly, examining the section on our credal proclamation of the incarnation 'by the Holy Spirit and from the Virgin Mary' in the document *Confessing the One Faith*, and noting how the ideas in this section might furnish us with material for reflection on the ecclesiological significance of the relationship between the Holy Spirit and our Lady, and, thirdly, noting, by way of conclusion, some of the tensions and difficulties that can creep into our exposition of the life of the Church when the place of the Holy Spirit is not given its proper significance. I shall suggest that a proper attention to the significance of the Blessed Virgin ought to be a corrective, but has not always functioned as it should have done.

Christ, Our Lady and the Church, was published in French in 1952 to celebrate the fifteenth centenary of the Council of Chalcedon and was published in English in 1957. It attempts to identify the differences in christology which cause Christians to be unable to agree about the Church and the Virgin Mary. It begins by discussing the differences in ecclesiology between Christians, and especially between Christians of the continental Reformation traditions and Roman Catholic Christians. Congar identifies as typical of the continental Reformation traditions a 'notion of vertical ecclesiology'[7] according to which 'that which unites us to the fountain-head of salvation is not in the last resort churchly and visible; it is an act of God which, as such, is beyond the power of human calculation'.[8] Congar notes that Barth frequently compared the Church to John the Baptist,[9] whose task was to point to Christ, and comments:

'St John's ministry is to be the herald of the gift, he is the last link in the line of prophecy. Our Lady's ministry is to bring the gift itself, to be the first link in the lifeline which is Christ's Mystical Body.'[10] And what, one surely wants to ask, is the place of the Holy Spirit in this work? How is the work of the Holy Spirit in John different from the work of the Spirit in Mary? Here is a prime example of the surprising lack of attention to the Holy Spirit in this work of Congar's. Barth frequently commented that one reason for his hostility to devotion to the Blessed Virgin was that it summed up the Catholic confidence that there was a need for human co-operation with God's saving work,[11] but he also said, when talking of Schleiermacher, that he thought that if a theology which seemed to him to place too much stress on human initiative and human resources was to be made acceptable (as he would see it), it would come about as a result of its presentation as a doctrine of the Holy Spirit.[12] I think this may be a useful clue for those who try to explain the significance of the Blessed Virgin to those who have tended to be hostile to such ideas. Congar writes of our Lady and the Church: 'each ... represents the part that human instrumentality is given in the work of salvation through the Incarnation; the one brings it about, the other communicates it to men and permeates the world with its effects'.[13]

But Congar now seeks to investigate the christological dimension of this divergence between the Catholic and the Protestant. He comments 'in Christology as well as in ecclesiology and Mariology the crux of the argument is the part played by mankind, the scope and extent of creaturely co-operation with the Creator.'[14] The Protestant approach here, Congar argues, is a sort of Monophysitism. Luther, he says, can attach no positive value to the principle of the Chalcedonian Definition. 'The sacred Humanity united to the Divinity without confusion or division is the instrument of our salvation, and the means by which all grace is communicated to us.'[15] The first part of the book concludes with Congar expressing the wish that Christian communions which hold to Chalcedon would be able to see how the position defined there has conclusions throughout the field of Christian theology and devotion:

> We could wish that they would set themselves to draw out carefully the conclusions, involved in the statements of Chalcedon, concerning the economy of our salvation, with its three sub-divisions closely bound up one with the other; the part played by the sacred Humanity of Christ, the instrument of divinity, by which grace and truth have come and still come to us; the part played by our Lady, through whom the sacred Humanity is one with ours; the part played by the Church, the society whose framework is the means by which the fullness of grace and truth flow down from the wounds of the crucified, the Word made flesh, into the human souls from which he wills his Mystical Body to be built up.[16]

Having examined the christological roots of ecclesiological and mariological divergence, Congar now turns to examine the christological
presuppositions of Roman Catholic piety. He believes that while 'a
tendency, which has been the cause successively of the heresy of
Apollinarius, and later of its half-tones, Monoenergism and
Monothelism (*sic*), appears frequently as an outcrop in the Christian
consciousness',[17] the modern devotions to the Sacred Heart and to
Christ the King are effective antidotes because of their emphasis on the
sacred humanity of Jesus Christ. The tendency is there, nonetheless, and
it is dangerous. He goes on to suggest that Roman Catholic devotion to
the Church has very often been expressed in statements with a 'distinct
Monophysite tinge'[18] and writes that the 'mischief done by this attitude
may be compared to that which we have to be on our guard against in
Christology, caused by inability to see in Christ anything more than God
at work in the world under the appearance of human nature. The true
humanity of Christ, together with that of the Church, is insufficiently
emphasized.'[19] And, I would also want to add, it is important that we
remember God at work in the world through the activity of the Holy
Spirit, which will also help to correct our ecclesiology. And Congar goes
on to show that such a 'tinge' can also be found in devotional statements
focusing on the Blessed Virgin, and collects a formidable catena of illus-
trations. He comments, of his collection of quotations:

> It is not difficult to see the proper perspective in which these passages should
> be read in order to give them a full catholic sense; we do not read them in any
> other sense, as those who wrote them did not. We do, however, see in the
> justifications they put forward the shadow cast by a view of Christ which
> appears by no means always in accord with the words of the New Testament
> and the faith of Chalcedon.[20]

Again, I think one might suggest that attention to the Holy Spirit by such
writers and in our reflection on them might help us to set them in a more
acceptable perspective.

Having argued that there is less attention than we might want to the
work of the Holy Spirit in Congar's work of 1952, I now want to look at
the short section on the incarnation 'by the Holy Spirit and from the
Virgin Mary' in the 1990 document *Confessing the One Faith* of the World
Council of Churches, and to highlight the welcome strength of its reference to the Holy Spirit. The section begins by noting:

> the Scripture commonly associates the Holy Spirit with the work of creation
> and new creation. The eschatological completion of humankind and of all
> creation, inaugurated in the resurrection of Jesus Christ, the new Adam, is
> penetrated by the pressure of the life-giving Spirit. And so when Christ came

to redeem and renew humankind, his very conception was the work of the same Spirit that animated humankind at its first creation.[21]

And so the overshadowing of Mary at her conception is rightly related to the raising of Jesus from the dead. And the stress on the place and work of the Spirit is one of the ways in which the document demonstrates the unity of God's saving action:

> Moreover, it is the same Spirit who will bring about the transfiguration of all creation to share in the glory of God. When the Creed attributes to the power of the Holy Spirit the incarnation of the One through whom all things are made, it relates this event to the whole world, its renewal and its consummation.[22]

The document then notes the affirmation of the Council of Ephesus that our Lady can rightly be called '*Theotokos*', 'Mother of God', and, bearing in mind how equivocal some churches in the Protestant traditions have sometimes been about the definition of the Council of Ephesus in the past, I think the explicit note here of the Council of Ephesus is valuable: we read 'all Christians share in the confession affirmed by the Council of Ephesus (431) that *Mary* is "*Theotokos*", the mother of him who is also God, through the creative work of the Spirit of God'.[23] I point out that the work here of the Holy Spirit is again noted.

And the document then points out that Mary's maternity is a guarantee of the fullness of the human nature taken by God and of the reality of the union of the incarnation. 'In referring to the motherhood of Mary, the Creed shows the Son of God to be a human being like us, one who shares our experience in being born and loved by a mother, and nurtured by parental care.'[24]

But Mary, the mother of Christ, is also the model disciple, and another reference is made to the Holy Spirit in explicating this. 'In her obedience to God, and her utter dependence on the Holy Spirit, Mary is the example *par excellence* of our discipleship. Since the first centuries, she has been seen as representing the daughter of Sion, waiting for the accomplishment of the messianic promises and of the coming kingdom.'[25] And it is because of this that Mary is Mother and type of the Church: 'In her complete reliance on God, her active response to faith and her expectation of the kingdom, Mary has been seen as a figure of and an example for the Church. Like Mary, the Church cannot exist on its own; it can only rely on God; it is the vigilant servant waiting for the return of the Master.'[26]

This short section of the document seems to be rich in comment despite its brevity, and particularly notable, as I have said, for the way in which it sets forth the place of Mary as a type not merely of the disciple, not merely of the Church, but of the overshadowing work of the Spirit of God. Mary, the Spirit-filled woman, is a type of the work of the Spirit. Mary is model for the Church precisely because of her relationship to the Holy Spirit of God, which arises from her *Fiat*, her 'Yes' to God.

Now, it has often been pointed out that in the West, the doctrine of the Church has been overly christological in the sense that it has sometimes been insufficiently pneumatological. Congar himself in his much later trilogy *I believe in the Holy Spirit* says this, and points out what he calls the 'forgetting' of the Holy Spirit in works such as Karl Adam's *The Spirit of Catholicism*.[27] Congar also suggests that there has been a tendency in Western Catholicism for the place and role of the Holy Spirit to be taken over so that the Holy Spirit's function is overshadowed by either the sacrament of the eucharist, or by the papal office, or by the figure of the Virgin Mary. I would suggest that one of the reasons why that has been possible is that the accounts given of the place and role of the sacrament of the eucharist, of the papal office, and of the figure of the Virgin Mary have each, in their own way, been insufficiently clearly dependent on and illustrative of the work of the Holy Spirit. And I would go on to add that the same thing has at times been true of the place of the Bible in Protestant Christianity. The Holy Spirit's function has been overshadowed, and this has come about at least in part because the role of the Holy Spirit in Scripture has been insufficiently clearly explicated. Vladimir Lossky in *In the Image and Likeness of God*[28] has this to say:

> To desire to base ecclesiology solely on the Incarnation, to see in the Church solely 'an extension of the Incarnation', a continuation of the work of Christ, as is so often stated, is to forget Pentecost and to reduce the work of the Holy Spirit to a subordinate role, that of an emissary of Christ, a liaison between the Head and the members of the Body. But the work of the Holy Spirit, although inseparable from the work of Christ, is distinct from it. This is why St Irenaeus, speaking of the Son and of the Spirit, calls them 'the two hands of the Father' at work in the world. The Pneumatological element of the Church must not be underestimated, but fully accepted on an equal footing with the Christological if the true foundation of the catholicity of the Church is to be found.[29]

We have been very concerned in this century to rediscover the doctrine of the Church as the Mystical Body and to explicate the consequences of the incarnation for the life of the Church. As the twentieth century, which has been called 'the century of the Church', draws to its close, we do well to listen to those who remind us that the Church is the work of the Spirit, as of the Son. Too great an emphasis on the christo-

logical element in the Church can lead to overly institutional and juris-
dictional accounts of life in the Church, too great a concern with the official and the visible and the controlled. It seems to me that one corrective,
given the 'deep bond that exists between the Virgin Mary and the
Spirit',[30] and given also the role of Mary as model and type of the
Church, is to draw those two pairs of relationships together and to
reflect further on the Holy Spirit, our Lady, and the Church. This has, as
I have claimed, not happened as much as one might think. The Apostolic
Exhortation of Pope Paul VI, *Marialis Cultus*, commented:

> It seems to us useful to add to this mention of the Christological orientation
> of devotion to the Blessed Virgin a reminder of the fittingness of giving
> prominence in this devotion to one of the essential facts of the faith: the
> Person and the work of the Holy Spirit. Theological reflection and the liturgy
> have in fact noted how the sanctifying intervention of the Spirit in the Virgin
> of Nazareth was a culminating moment of the Spirit's action in the history of
> salvation … It is sometimes said that many spiritual writings today do not
> sufficiently reflect the whole doctrine concerning the Holy Spirit. It is the task
> of specialists to verify and weigh the truth of this assertion, but it is our task
> to exhort everyone, especially those in the pastoral ministry and also theolo-
> gians, to meditate more deeply on the working of the Holy Spirit in the
> history of salvation, and to ensure that Christian spiritual writings give due
> prominence to his life-giving action. Such a study will bring out in particular
> the hidden relationship between the Spirit of God and the Virgin of Nazareth,
> and show the influence they exert on the Church.[31]

Many writers remind us that thinking about Mary, mariology as the
theologians call it, must always be a chapter in the treatise on the incarnation. That is, I am sure, a proper reminder, but I think it, on its own,
also holds dangers, unless we also are reminded that our thinking about
Mary, our mariology, is also a chapter in the treatise on the Holy Spirit,
and because of that a chapter in the treatise on the Church.

Notes

1 Faith and Order Paper No. 153, WCC Publications, (Geneva 1991).
2 Tillard, *Confessing the One Faith*, viii.
3 ibid. s. 124 (p. 54).
4 I was reading Eric Mascall, *Christ, the Christian and the Church*, 2nd edn,
   (Longmans, Green & Co., London 1955) and *The Recovery of Unity*
   (Longmans, Green & Co., London 1958), and Louis Bouyer, *Life and Liturgy*
   (Sheed & Ward, London 1956).
5 Longmans, Green & Co., (London 1957).
6 Chapman (London 1983).
7 Congar, *Christ, Our Lady and the Church*, p. 10.

8 ibid.
9 ibid. pp. 12f.
10 ibid. p. 14.
11 ibid. p. 17. See *Church Dogmatics*, 1/2, pp. 139ff.
12 *Protestant Theology in the Nineteenth Century* (SCM, London 1972), pp. 460, 471; *The Theology of Schleiermacher* (Eerdmans, Grand Rapids 1982), pp. 277ff.
13 Congar, op. cit. p. 15.
14 ibid. p. 25.
15 ibid. p. 31.
16 ibid. pp. 38f.
17 ibid. p. 45.
18 ibid. p. 59.
19 ibid. p. 69.
20 ibid. p. 76.
21 *Confessing the One Faith* (WCC, Geneva 1990), s. 121, p. 53.
22 ibid.
23 ibid.
24 ibid.
25 ibid.
26 ibid.
27 Congar, *I Believe in the Holy Spirit*, vol. 1, p. 159, commenting on Karl Adam, *The Spirit of Catholicism* (Sheed & Ward, London 1929).
28 V. Lossky, *In the Image and Likeness of God* (Mowbrays, Oxford 1975).
29 Lossky, op. cit. p. 177.
30 *I Believe in the Holy Spirit*, vol. 1, p. 163.
31 *Marialis Cultus*, 26, 27.

(This paper was given at the ESBVM Leeds Congress in August 1998)

Mary
and
Spirituality

9

John Henry Newman and the Immaculate Mother of the Incarnate Word

Philip Boyce OCD

It is surprising to find a significant contribution to Catholic mariology in the life and writings of an author who was born into the Anglican Church in the nineteenth century. John Henry Newman, the man in question, who was ordained for ministry in 1825, was soon to find himself at the heart of all that was noblest and best both in the Church of England and in the University milieu of Oxford. He was forty-four years of age before he was received into the Roman Catholic Church, having travelled a conversion journey that in the estimation of Pope Paul VI was 'the most toilsome, but also the greatest, the most meaningful, the most conclusive, that human thought ever travelled during the last [nine-teenth] century'.[1] It was only as that journey ended that he felt free to make his own all Roman Catholic practices, especially devotional and invocatory, of Marian piety.

Newman's Anglican difficulties

Like many Anglicans, however, Newman had serious difficulties at first with what he considered to be Rome's errors concerning the Blessed Virgin and the manifold devotions that had accumulated in it over the centuries.

In fact, extreme devotional manifestations in the honour paid by Catholics to our Lady had been, as Newman himself confesses in the *Apologia*, his 'great *crux* as regards Catholicism'.[2] They were the sponta-neous expression of popular feelings towards the Blessed Virgin, and were produced by a particular cultural and historical context. Newman thought that they had received the wholehearted approval of the highest ecclesiastical authorities in Rome and were meant to be imposed univer-sally. They formed part of what Anglicans considered to be the 'Mariolatry' of the Roman Church. Even during the period of the Oxford Movement, at least up until 1839, he considered the honours paid by Catholics to the saints, and in particular to Saint Mary, to be the very 'essence' of Rome's corruption and theological error.

In 1836, Newman wrote a whole Tract (no. 71) which was to be a manual for use in Anglican controversy with Roman Catholics. He pointed out what he then considered to be the weak points and some errors in certain Catholic beliefs. The honour paid to our Lady was one point particularly condemned. He quoted from some Catholic authors who ascribe a certain 'omnipotence' to the Blessed Virgin. On account of her office as Mother of God, she is said to be able 'to command' her divine Son with a mother's authority. Moreover, certain Catholic writers claimed that Mary's Son never refuses her any request, so that she could be said to have the same power as Christ himself, 'she being by her omnipotent Son made herself omnipotent'.[3]

Some expressions taken literally from the authors he quotes are certainly misleading and indeed imprudent. No wonder that it was popular opinion among Anglicans that Catholics (especially in Latin countries) 'worship the Virgin as a goddess'.[4] In fact, the place held by our Lady in Catholic beliefs and devotions was not simply Newman's *crux* with Catholicism: it lay at the heart of many an Anglican's suspicion and fear. It was also a stumbling-block for Pusey, as he states in his *Eirenicon:* 'that vast system as to the Blessed Virgin, which to all of us has been the special "crux" of the Roman system ... her intercession is held to be co-extensive with His'.[5]

In short, for Anglicans, the Roman practice seemed to eclipse the honour due to our Lord and to interfere with his role as the unique Mediator. Newman was convinced all his life that the divine glory was essentially incommunicable. Consequently, Christ's feelings of devotion towards his mother, just as his special love for St John, the beloved disciple, are not revealed in detail in the New Testament. It would be dangerous and could not be done 'without a risk lest the honour which those Saints received through grace should eclipse in our minds the honour of Him who honoured them'.[6]

Apart from the charge of putting honour and devotion to Christ in the shade, Newman as an Anglican, at least up to the writing of the *Via Media,* held that some Marian doctrines and many devotional practices in the Church of Rome were not to be found in the early church. An 'undue veneration' had sprung up towards our Lady and the saints. It was a typical example of that 'intolerable offence of having added to the Faith',[7] which made Anglicans so sure of their disapproval of Catholic practices. To them it seemed like a form of idolatry and was often referred to as 'Mariolatry'. Those who judged Catholic forms of worship from what appeared to a public onlooker, without understanding the real meaning of these mysteries of faith, simply thought, as Newman himself said in 1841, that the Roman system 'goes very far indeed to substitute another Gospel for the true one. Instead of setting before the soul the Holy Trinity, and heaven and hell; it does seem to me, as a popular system, to preach the Blessed Virgin and the Saints, and Purgatory.'[8]

The veneration due to the Blessed Virgin

Despite these premises we cannot deny a surprising presence of the Virgin Mary in the life and writings of the Anglican Newman. That may seem surprising, yet if we recall the place of Mary in the New Testament and in the writing of the Fathers of the Church, is it after all so surprising? It is true that devotions change from one culture and time to another, but the significant role of Mary in the life of the Incarnate Word, and hence of his followers, cannot be gainsaid.

To a certain extent, Newman's struggle with the place of Mary in his own life and in the life of the Church marks his gradual acceptance of Roman Catholicism. In the *Apologia* he tells us that, in one of his boyhood copybooks, he drew what seemed to him to be a rosary, beads with a little cross attached.[9] It may have foreboded a fierce struggle in the years that lay ahead. A significant obstacle was invocation of Mary and the saints, which was forbidden by Anglicanism. There was also the devotion from which his taste and sentiment recoiled. And then there was Antiquity, the early Church of the Fathers, on which he took his stand and which he thought had no trace of what he regarded as the additions and corruptions of Rome.

Yet there was also the presence of a mother's hand in his life which he could not evade. In 1848, in a letter to Henry Wilberforce, a former pupil and also a convert, he gives a summary of that presence of our Lady in his life:

> I have ever been under her shadow, if I may say it. My College was St Mary's, and my Church; and when I went to Littlemore, there, by my own previous disposition, our Blessed Lady was waiting for me. Nor did she do nothing for me in that low habitation, of which I always think with pleasure.[10]

Newman's study of the Church Fathers gradually enlightened him. In his *Essay on the Development of Christian Doctrine*, it became clear that the conclusions he took from his stand on Antiquity had been failing him for some time. The additions to Roman doctrine were not corruptions but harmonious developments of what was handed down from the beginning. Although all the glory a creature can receive is given to Mary in the Roman Catholic tradition, it remains essentially different from the worship given to Christ and is not detrimental to it. Newman accepted what he saw to be the truth. By August 1845 he even wore a miraculous medal round his neck. On the front of this medal there is engraved an image of Mary, the Mother of God, encircled by the prayer: 'O Mary, conceived without sin, pray for us who have recourse to thee'. There we have two stumbling blocks for an Anglican – the immaculate conception, and direct invocation of our Lady. On this medal, Mary stands on a globe of the world, with a twisted serpent of evil at her feet struggling to get the upper hand. However, she is triumphant thanks to the victory won by her Incarnate Son in his redemptive death and resurrection.

Two months later, the great Newman bowed his head to a humble Passionist missionary from Italy and asked to be received into the Roman Catholic fold. And on the morning of 9 October, in the recitation of the Divine Office, he and his companions no longer omitted the 'Hail, Holy Queen' (the *Salve Regina*), and Antiphons where direct invocation was made, nor did they substitute *Oret pro nobis* (May she pray for us) for the invocatory *Ora pro nobis* (Pray for us).[11] He had then fully realized that the Catholic Church allows 'no saint, not even the Blessed Virgin herself, to come between the soul and its Creator'.[12]

A noteworthy sermon

One of the most complete expositions of Newman's thought about the Blessed Virgin during his Anglican period is to be found in the sermon 'The Reverence due to the Virgin Mary'.[13] It was preached for the Feast of the Annunciation, 1832. He makes much of the words of the Archangel Gabriel to Mary. These same words form the scriptural foundation of the Church's teaching on the divine motherhood, the perpetual virginity and immaculate conception of Mary.

While summing up the reasons why the Virgin Mary is called blessed in Scripture, Newman touches on most of his Anglican thought about her. The first reason for this blessedness arises from Mary's parallel role to Eve in the history of salvation, a point which would become a distinctive feature of Newman's mariology. First of all, in Mary, 'the curse pronounced on Eve was changed to a blessing'.[14] God did not decide to destroy his sinful children who transgressed his original purpose, but he proposed to forgive and save them. Hence he sent his only Son, born of a woman (cf. Gal. 4.4), to redeem them and initiate a new creation from what had become old and corrupt.

Moreover, woman's subjection to man, subsequent on Eve's initial disobedience and most evident in the pagan world, was rectified through Mary's obedience. Christ vindicated the rights and honour of his mother and, through her, of all women according to God's eternal plan for creation. The original dignity of marriage was restored, its spiritual value and symbolism were reinstated. If Newman were alive today he would surely enlarge on this passage of the inspired text in order to shed light on the contemporary discussion on women's rights which is being brought to extremes by certain feminist groups. It is interesting to note that Pope John Paul II, in his teaching on the dignity of women, refers to the Virgin Mary in her role as the second Eve at the annunciation. In her, the Pope contemplates the role which God, at the beginning of creation, originally intended for women. 'Mary is "the new beginning" of the dignity and vocation of women, of each and every woman.' And her words: 'He who is mighty has done great things for me' (Luke 1.49), while referring basically to her divine motherhood, also signify 'the discovery of all the richness and personal resources of femininity, all the eternal originality of the "woman", just as God wanted her to be, a person for her own sake, who discovers herself "by means of a sincere gift of self"'.[15]

Another ground for Mary's blessedness is connected with her holiness, which sprang from her nearness to Christ, the incarnate Son of God. Indeed this relation of hers to Christ and to the mystery of the incarnation lies at the heart of Newman's teaching on Mary. From this basic dogma of the incarnation all the theology of the redemption takes its meaning. Christ was 'truly God and truly Man, One Person, – as we are soul and body, yet one man, so truly God and man are not two, but One Christ'.[16] The nature of the Church, the power of the sacraments, the dignity of man rests on the reality of the incarnation. In Christmas sermons and in those dealing with the Passion, Newman frequently returns to this doctrine in order to illustrate the deepest significance of the birth and sufferings of Christ.

From the truth of the incarnation, as revealed in Scripture, it follows that Mary is the mother of Jesus. The eternal Son of God became a true man, with a human nature like ours, but without sin. He derived 'His manhood from the substance of the Virgin Mary; as it is expressed in the articles of the Creed, "conceived by the Holy Ghost, born of the Virgin Mary"'.[17] Thus he was truly God and truly man. In this Anglican sermon, from which we quote, Newman calls Mary the mother of Christ.

Newman the Anglican has no doubt then about calling Mary the mother of Jesus. However, in this very same sermon he seems to hesitate to call her the Mother of God. In fact, a few lines after he had referred to her as 'His (Christ's) Mother', he says: 'Thus He came into this world, not in the clouds of heaven, but born into it, born of a woman; He, the Son of Mary, and she (if it may be said), the mother of God.'[18]

The hesitancy, culled from the parenthesis, would seem to arise from Newman's desire in his Anglican milieu not to go beyond the plain words of Scripture in their reference to Mary. Since the inspired word consistently calls her the mother of Jesus, he refrained from making an unqualified use of the title 'Mother of God' which could be falsely understood by his hearers. But there does not seem to be any doubt in Newman's mind; there are in fact other instances previous to and following on this date (December 1834) where he explicitly calls Mary the Mother of God.

For example, in a sermon for Christmas Day, nine years before that date, namely in 1825, he had written: 'A daughter of man became the Mother of God – to her, indeed, an unspeakable gift of grace; but in Him, what condescension!'[19] Later, in 1838, he would claim that the Blessed Virgin was holy in soul and body on account of her nearness to God, and in this context, he declares that 'all but heretics have ever called [her] the Mother of God'.[20]

It is clear then that Newman while still an Anglican had the highest regard for Mary, whose holiness he admired and which he considered to come from her proximity in body and spirit to the Incarnate Word of the eternal Father.

The Immaculate Mother

Members of the Church of England in the nineteenth century thought at times that the doctrine of the immaculate conception was the one that offered Catholics greatest difficulty. Newman, as a Roman Catholic, had no intrinsic difficulty with the dogma as such. He saw it intimately harmonizing with the body of dogmatic truths recognized by the Church. The faithful had come to accept it long before it was declared a dogma. Led by an instinct of faith and guided by the Holy Spirit, they accepted it with enthusiasm and almost demanded that the highest church authority declare it to be a definitive point of their faith. In no way was it 'a burden' to Catholic believers. Even in his Anglican life Newman was on one occasion accused of secretly holding this doctrine. The passage occurred in the remarkable sermon on the Virgin Mary, to which we have already referred:

> Who can estimate the holiness and perfection of her, who was chosen to be the Mother of Christ? If to him that hath, more is given, and holiness and Divine favour go together (and this we are expressly told), what must have been the transcendent purity of her, whom the Creator Spirit condescended to overshadow with His miraculous presence? ... This contemplation runs to a higher subject, did we dare follow it; for what, think you, was the sanctified state of that human nature, of which God formed His sinless Son; knowing as we do, 'that which is born of the flesh is flesh', and that 'none can bring a clean thing out of an unclean?'

In these last lines, he appeared to his listeners to imply that Mary's human nature had always been in a sanctified state of grace, hence always without sin. It would seem that he saw his way to accept it privately but he did not say so explicitly until he became a Catholic. Of course, it was not as yet proclaimed to be a dogma. At any rate, the premises were there in Newman's writings and in his patristic readings. When his controversial sermon was published in 1835, three years after he preached it, his only defence to those who accused him of believing in the immaculate conception, was that 'there was nothing against the doctrine in the Thirty-Nine Articles'.[21]

In his Catholic years, Newman had no difficulty with the doctrine of the immaculate conception. On reflection, he even admitted that it never had been a difficulty for him, even as an Anglican.[22] In some ways, it was a pivotal point in his teaching on our Lady: it touched on many points of his mariology. He contemplated it as a logical consequence of Mary being the second Eve. It was a fitting preparation for her who was to be the Mother of God Incarnate, and from her divine motherhood flow all her other privileges.

The point that seemed to Newman 'to be conclusive'[23] in proving the immaculate conception of Mary was that it flows as an immediate inference from that other doctrine (already taught by the Fathers and universally accepted in the Christian tradition) of Mary being the second Eve. This argument has a strong ecumenical weight as well. All agree that Eve was sinless and endowed with grace. It is an open question, whether our first parents were created in a state that enjoyed nothing more than the qualities of their untainted human nature and at a later moment elevated to the state of grace, or whether, as is more likely, that they were elevated beyond nature to the state of grace from the very first instant of their existence. The question was not decided by the Council of Trent. Newman simply states that Adam received the gift of grace before Eve, 'at the very time (it is commonly held) of his original formation'.[24] What is certain is that they were not created in a state of sin or enmity with God. Adam and Eve were sinless from the beginning of their existence.

This suffices for Newman, who regards Mary as the counterpart of Eve: as the latter collaborated with Adam in our fall from grace, Mary co-operated with Christ in restoring our lost privileges. The Virgin Mary, who had a vital role to play in the work of redemption as the Mother of the Saviour, conquered the tempter by obeying in faith, thus undoing the harm of Eve's transgression and failure. Consequently, Newman argues, she must have been endowed at least as highly as Eve was. She too must have been sinless from the beginning of her existence: otherwise the parallel with Eve would be definitely faulty. Both of them were placed by Providence at a critical junction of human history: with Mary a new and better creation dawned for the human race.

> Is it any violent inference, that she, who was to co-operate in the redemption of the world, at least was not less endowed with power from on high, than she who, given as a help-mate to her husband, did in the event but co-operate with him for its ruin? If Eve was raised above human nature by that indwelling moral gift which we call grace, is it rash to say that Mary had even a greater grace? ... And if Eve had this supernatural inward gift given to her from the first moment of her personal existence, is it possible to deny that Mary too had this gift from the very first moment of her personal existence? I do not know how to resist this inference: – well, this is simply and literally the doctrine of the Immaculate Conception.[25]

Newman of course makes reference here simply to the supernatural gift of grace. He does not mean that Mary was given the so-called 'preternatural' gifts of immortality, knowledge and immunity from suffering that our first parents possessed before the Fall. Like her Son, she advanced in knowledge and age, she suffered even more keenly than others owing to her extreme purity and innocence, and she ended her days on earth passing through the doors of death (as is commonly held) to be glorified, however, in soul and body: 'Mary came into a fallen world, and resigned herself to its laws; she, as also the Son she bore, was exposed to pain of soul and body, she was subjected to death; but she was not put under the power of sin'.[26]

The immaculate conception seems to Newman to be also included in the fact that the Blessed Virgin never committed any venial sin. 'Her personal sanctity' leads Catholics on to 'the doctrine of the Immaculate Conception'.[27] Those who come near God, the All-Holy Creator and source of all sanctity, must also be holy. No one came as near to him as the mother of his Incarnate Son, who was to be the living tabernacle of Christ, carrying him in her womb and accompanying him from his birth to his death on Calvary. 'An instinctive sentiment has led Christians jealously to put the Blessed Mary aside when sin comes into discussion.'[28] To profess in the fullest sense Mary's personal sinlessness is the equivalent of stating that she was conceived immaculately: 'Indeed, it is almost saying what has been said in other words, for if no venial sin, *must* there not be Immaculate Conception?'[29]

The theological argumentation is exact. In fact, would it be possible for her to commit a venial sin at all? Considering her position and privileges, her freedom from those wounds that original sin leaves on our nature, attracting us strongly to sinful pleasures, darkening our mind and weakening our will, would not any transgression in her case be very serious – just as the personal sin committed by Eve and Adam was extremely grave? Cardinal Ratzinger says that preservation from original sin does not mean any exceptional proficiency or achievement on our Lady's part, but that it 'signifies that Mary reserves no area of being, life, and will for herself as a private possession' and that she lives 'a total dispossession of self, in giving herself to God'.[30] In such a selfless life there is no room for sin.

Indeed, the Church also teaches the Blessed Virgin's absolute freedom from even the slightest personal sin. The Council of Trent, excluding the case of our Lady from its treatment of original sin, declared that it was the faith of the Church that she was kept free from all venial sin through a special privilege granted by God.[31] Pius IX, in his Bull *Ineffabilis Deus* for the dogmatic definition of the immaculate conception, repeated this thought which he had culled from the Fathers of the Church, saying that Mary was 'always free from every stain of sin, all fair and perfect, a virgin undefiled, immaculate, ever blessed, and free from all contagion of sin, from which was formed the new Adam, a reproachless, most sweet paradise of innocence'.

Newman, however, does not simply base his conviction on theological argumentation. As always, his surest foundation is Sacred Scripture. He reads it in the light of the interpretation given to the pertinent texts by the Fathers of the Church. Thus he recalls the words of Genesis 3.15 and defends the Vulgate reading: '*She* shall bruise thy head' – the same procedure used by Pope Pius IX in the Bull *Ineffabilis Deus*. He adds that the parallel Eve–Mary shows up the full content of the Archangel's words to Mary: 'full of grace'. Newman's exposition is completely in harmony with the mind of the Church and is a fine specimen of theological writing.

Moreover, he draws on another passage from Scripture that speaks of an enduring war between the serpent and the woman. It is the famous vision of St John in the Apocalypse (ch. 20) where the serpent is called Satan, the Evil Spirit. The woman with child is understood by Newman as referring to Mary with Christ. The parallels with the passage in Genesis 3.15 are obvious: the vision of a woman in both texts; she is with a 'seed' in Genesis, and with a 'child' in the Apocalypse; present in both cases is the serpent and the enmity between them. Newman cannot help but conclude that 'the woman is Mary in the third [chapter] of Genesis'. The parallel Eve–Mary becomes still clearer. And the implications for the doctrine of the immaculate conception are evident: the enmity between them is understandable 'if she had nothing to do with sin – for, so far as any one sins, he has an alliance with the Evil One'.[32]

Our Lady's immaculate conception is also closely connected with her divine maternity. In fact, it is this unique privilege of being the Mother of God, a privilege that is evident from the Gospels, that gives even greater force to the texts already mentioned in support of the immaculate conception. God himself is infinitely holy and it was fitting that He should prepare an immaculate mother for his Incarnate Son. Even in the order of nature, the honour or dishonour of a mother is reflected in her son. Therefore, an intuition of faith enables us to see how 'convenient' or appropriate it was that the Word made flesh should do what his almighty power enabled him to do, namely, to preserve his mother free from all sin. 'The divine maternity, then, if attentively considered, postulates the privilege of the Immaculate Conception.'[33]

Thus Newman's teaching on the immaculate conception is theologically very rich in content and is linked with many other aspects of his Marian doctrine and theological thought. In this light it is understandable that he had a particular devotion to this mystery and to the Immaculate Virgin. He had the principal liturgical celebration of the Oratory changed from the Assumption to the Conception and in 1851 (three years before the definition) dedicated the Birmingham Oratory Church to the Immaculate Conception. He was very pleased that his was one of the Congregations that had got permission to have the word *immaculata* inserted in the Preface of the Mass after the word *conceptione*.[34]

There were many misconceptions concerning this doctrine in Newman's day. A popular error was to think it had to do with the conception of Christ in Mary's womb instead of our Lady's own passive conception in her mother's womb. Some people thought the privilege referred not to Mary but to her mother, St Anne. Others understood it to mean that Mary did not need to be redeemed, and that she was an exception to the universal effect of Christ's saving sacrifice. Finally, there arose misconceptions from the different ways of regarding the nature of original sin, so that some thought it postulated a different nature altogether in Mary, one that was strong and in no need of grace. Newman was at pains on many occasions to rectify these erroneous opinions.[35]

The Mother of the Word Incarnate

Steeped as he was in the Scripture and in the writings of the ancient Fathers of the Church, Newman was firmly convinced of the Blessed Virgin's highest prerogative – her divine maternity. That Mary is the Mother of God (*Theotokos* from the Greek or *Deipara* from the Latin) is 'an integral portion of the Faith, fixed by Ecumenical Council'.[36] This is her fundamental dignity.

Newman delves once more into his knowledge of patristic literature in order to show how the title *Theotokos* was deeply rooted in the apostolic tradition. The doctrine was clear from the beginning; when devotion began to extend and false developments of a heretical kind made their appearance, the Church reacted in solemn Council, and formulated with dogmatic precision what it had always believed. The third Ecumenical Council of the Church in 431 ended controversy, proclaimed that in Christ there was only one Person – a divine One – and accordingly declared Mary to be the *Theotokos*, the Mother of God, and not merely the mother of the humanity of Christ.[37]

It is evident from Newman's writings that he remains in profound admiration of this exaltation of a mere creature. So much so that in his meditations he asks himself in wonderment which mystery is most astounding – that God should become man without ceasing to be God, or that Mary, a mere creature, should become the Mother of God.[38]

It is truly an awe-inspiring title, indicating the origin of her greatness, and making it extremely fitting that she should be adorned with countless other privileges of grace. For this title is no extravagant expression of human admiration for the mother of the promised Messiah: 'it intends to express that God is her Son, as truly as any one of us is the son of his own mother'.[39]

Consequently Newman states that no honour, compatible with the nature of a creature, is too exalted for her, no praise too great. Accordingly, it is understandable, almost to be expected, that when this truth of faith finds its expression in devotion, it gives rise to an exalted and exuberant form of language. The poets and scholars of the Eastern Churches in particular vied with each other in their panegyrics, adding metaphor to metaphor, in their efforts to extol the greatness of a Virgin Mother, whose only Son was the only-begotten of the Father. Newman defends this development: 'No wonder if their language should become unmeasured, when so great a term as "Mother of God" had been formally set down as the safe limit of it'.[40]

Coming back to theological sobriety as distinct from the exuberant expressions of filial devotion, Newman makes the penetrating remark that the truth of the divine motherhood of Mary is a safeguard for the very doctrine of the Incarnation. This intuition was part of Newman's faith from his early Anglican days. He expressed it, as we saw, in a sermon preached in 1832 and it would remain a constant conviction of faith throughout his entire life. He repeats it in his *Essay on the Development of Christian Doctrine* in 1844–5: 'it protects the doctrine of the Incarnation and preserves the faith of Catholics from a specious Humanitarianism'.[41]

For there is no more unequivocal way of declaring that God became incarnate than to say that he was born in our flesh and had a mother. Thus the confession that Mary is the Mother of God safeguards what St

John the Evangelist states so clearly: 'The Word was made flesh and dwelt among us' (John 1.14).

> It declares that He [Christ] is God; it implies that He is man; it suggests to us that He is God still, though He has become man, and that He is true man though He is God. By witnessing to the *process* of the union, it secures the reality of the two *subjects* of the union, of the divinity and of the manhood. If Mary is the Mother of God, Christ must be literally Emmanuel, God with us.[42]

We should not be surprised that Newman made so much of this point, for the doctrine of the Incarnation was central to his entire religious and theological thought.

Conclusion

Even from these brief pages, we perceive that Newman admired the Blessed Virgin Mary and loved her tenderly. He wrote elegant, even lyrical pages about her. He took 'Mary' as his Confirmation name. In writing to Pope Pius IX about his Oratorian training he signed himself 'Giovanni M. Newman', the 'M' indicating 'Mary'.[43] Because immaculate and personally sinless, she is a human model of all beauty: 'Nothing so beautiful in the supernatural [world] as Mary'.[44] He contemplated her as an exemplar of virtue and a bulwark against sin in an impure age. She is God's greatest work and cannot obscure her Son. Above all creatures, she is the dearest to God.

Newman's veneration for our Lady is not simply a speculative grasp of her greatness and holiness. It also descends to practical, daily life where he displays unwavering trust in her powerful intercession or 'great, prevailing gift of prayer'. He is fully aware that in her we all have 'a friend in court' and need not fear. 'While she defends the Church, neither height nor depth, neither men nor evil spirits, neither great monarchs, nor craft of man, nor popular violence, can avail to harm us; for human life is short, but Mary reigns above, a Queen for ever.'[45]

Notes

1 *Acta Apostolicae Sedis* 55 (1963), 1025.
2 *Apologia pro Vita Sua*, (London 1908), p. 195.
3 Cf. *Tracts for the Times*. By Members of the University of Oxford (London, 1834–41), vol. 3, pp. 19, 24–5; also published in *The Via Media of the Anglican Church* (London 1908, 1911), vol. 2, pp. 122, 129–30.
4 *Loss and Gain. The Story of a Convert* (London 1911), p. 176.
5 E. B. Pusey, *The Church of England a portion of Christ's one holy Catholic Church,*

*and a means of restoring visible unity. An Eirenicon, in a Letter to the Author of
'The Christian Year.'* (London, Oxford and Cambridge 1865), p. 101.

6   *Parochial and Plain Sermons* (London 1907–11), vol. 2, p. 133.

7   *Apologia*, p. 107; cf. p. 53.

8   *A Letter addressed to the Rev. R. W. Jelf, D.D.*, published in *The Via Media of the
    Anglican Church*, vol. 2, pp. 367–93; cf. p. 369.

9   *Apologia pro Vita Sua*, p. 13.

10 *The Letters and Diaries of John Henry Newman* (London 1961), sq., vol. 12, pp.
    153–4.

11 Cf. Henry Tristram, Cong.Orat., 'Dr Russell and Newman's Conversion', *The
    Irish Ecclesiastical Record* 66 (1945), p. 198.

12 *Apologia pro Vita Sua*, p. 195.

13 *Parochial and Plain Sermons*, vol. 2, pp.127–38.

14 ibid. p. 129.

15 Apostolic Letter, *On the Dignity and Vocation of Women on the Occasion of the
    Marian Year, Mulieris Dignitatem* (Vatican City 1988), no. 11.

16 *Parochial and Plain Sermons*, vol. 2, p. 32.

17 *Parochial and Plain Sermons*, vol. 2, p. 31.

18 ibid. p. 32.

19 *Parochial and Plain Sermons*, vol. 8, p. 252.

20 *Discussions and Arguments on various Subjects* (London 1911), p. 223.

21 The *Letters and Diaries of John Henry Newman*, vol. 19, pp. 346–7. Cf. *Parochial
    and Plain Sermons*, vol. 2, pp. 131–2.

22 Cf. *Meditations and Devotions of the late Cardinal Newman* (London 1911), p. 80.

23 *Certain Difficulties felt by Anglicans in Catholic Teaching* (London 1910), vol. 2,
    p. 49.

24 ibid. pp. 44, 45.

25 ibid. pp. 45, 46.

26 *Discourses Addressed to Mixed Congregations* (London 1909), p. 354.

27 *The Letters and Diaries of John Henry Newman*, vol. 12, p. 334.

28 *Difficulties of Anglicans*, vol. 2, pp. 49–50; cf. p. 136.

29 *Sermon Notes of John Henry Cardinal Newman 1849–1878* (London 1914), p. 106.
    The only real objection which Newman knows against the doctrine was the
    fact that some eminent Fathers of the fourth century, such as Origen,
    Tertullian, St Basil, St Chrysostom and St Cyril of Alexandria, thought that
    our Lady did become a victim to some of the infirmities of our nature by
    committing slight imperfections or venial sins (such as initial doubt) at the
    moment of the annunciation and under the cross. Consequently, Newman
    added a lengthy examination of these texts in the published volume of his
    Letter to Pusey. He shows that these were mere personal opinions of individ-
    ual Fathers and not indications of a living and widespread tradition in the
    Church (cf. *Difficulties of Anglicans*, vol. 2, Note 3, pp. 128–52).

30 *Daughter Zion. Meditations on the Church's Marian Belief* (San Francisco 1983),
    p. 70.

31 Cf. Canon 23 of the *Decree on Justification* (Denzinger-Schönmetzer, No.
    1573).

32 *Meditations and Devotions*, p. 84. The mariological interpretation of this text

from the Apocalypse (ch. 20) is admittedly not the one commonly used by the Fathers of the Church and theologians of former centuries. Neither is it used by Pius IX in his Bull of promulgation of the dogma of the immaculate conception (*Ineffabilis Deus*), nor by Pius XII in his Marian Encyclical *Fulgens Corona*, nor by the Fathers of Vatican II. The usual interpretation is ecclesial. However, Pope Paul VI in his Exhortation *Signum magnum* in 1967 does give it a mariological interpretation. Moreover, it has come to be recognized by some eminent exegetes and theological scholars of the present time as containing first of all a reference to the Church, but one which also has a mariological content. The Church and Mary appear from this text of the Apocalypse (12.1–6) as closely conjoined in the struggle against Satan and in the victory over the powers of evil (cf. Domenico Bertetto, *Maria la Serva del Signore* (Napoli 1988), pp. 289–92).

33 Martino Jugie, *L'Immaculée Conception dans l'Écriture sainte et dans la Tradition Orientale* (Roma 1952), p. 51.

34 *The Letters and Diaries of John Henry Newman* (London 1963), vol. 13, p. 82.

35 Cf. *Meditations and Devotions*, pp. 78–87; *The Letters and Diaries of John Henry Newman*, vol. 19, pp. 361–70; 437–8.

36 *Difficulties of Anglicans*, vol. 2, p. 62.

37 Cf. *Select Treatises of St Athanasius in Controversy with the Arians* (London 1903). Two volumes. vol. 2. pp. 210–15; *Difficulties of Anglicans*, vol. 2, pp. 61–7.

38 Cf. *Meditations and Devotions*, p. 40.

39 *Difficulties of Anglicans*, vol. 2, p. 62.

40 ibid. pp. 65–6.

41 Cf. *An Essay on the Development of Christian Doctrine*. Longmans, Green & Co., (London 1909), p. 426. 'Humanitarianism' in the theological sense of Christ being simply a man.

42 *Mixed Congregations*, pp. 347–8; cf. *Sermon Notes*, p. 23.

43 Cf. *The Letters and Diaries of John Henry Newman*, vol. 12, p. 87.

44 *Sermon Notes*, p. 78.

45 *Meditations and Devotions*, p. 71.

(This paper was given at the ESBVM Oxford Congress
in August 2000)

10

The imperative of charity:
Catholics working with Orthodox
in Russia today

Neville Kyrke-Smith

Introduction

With the Russian Parliament passing a Bill omitting religious freedom, and with the Patriarch questioning the activities of Catholics in Russia, it may seem rather optimistic a view to say that there is a light in the east. Perhaps this is not the bright light, the headline-making movement towards church unity which we all look for, but quietly and assuredly one charity, and a few others as well, are hoping to build bridges of trust between Catholics and Orthodox in Russia. It could seem at times that the bridges, as soon as they are built, are blown up, but it is as the Pope has said, 'an imperative of charity' (*Ut Unum Sint*) that we help our brothers and sisters in Christ in Russia at this time. The Pope wrote in his apostolic letter *Orientale Lumen*, paragraph 23:

> To extend gestures of common charity to one another and jointly to those in need will appear as an act with immediate impact. The Lord's call is to work in every way to ensure that all believers in Christ will witness together.

Hopefully, prayerfully and carefully Aid to the Church in Need is trying to extend such gestures of common charity to the Orthodox. For as Father Werenfried van Straaten, our founder, has said, our organization is established to help the Church 'wherever she is persecuted, threatened, undermined or destroyed and suffers need as a result' – put simply, ACN helps 'through prayer, sacrifice, conversion, information and active charity to heal the wounds inflicted by atheism'.

Russia today: a spiritual wasteland?

The spiritual wasteland of Eastern Europe is one where there are new signs of hope to be seen. Like seeds bringing new life, so the blood of the martyrs, both Orthodox and Catholic, seems to be resulting in new life in the Church, not just in the thousands of baptisms that have taken place and the many hundreds of people still being baptized, but also in numbers of young men and women interested in the Faith. It is as though there is a searching not just for the Russian soul but for a spiritual way forward as western materialism and consumerism take over, with the worst excesses of pornography, lack of morality and corruption stirred into a devastating Molotov Cocktail.

In case you think that this spiritual hunger is something that I am exaggerating, let me tell you that at one stage we were receiving 3,000 requests every day from the former Soviet Union for Russian Child's Bibles after our radio broadcasts there. We still simply cannot keep up with demand for these little Bibles and our work through the Spiritual Library in Moscow and in ecumenical broadcasting in Moscow itself shows that there is a great interest in the spiritual. Indeed people may sometimes ask, 'What about the sects in Russia at this time?' and most of the sects are actually home-brewed Russian sects. I remember on Russian television not long ago, seeing a witch called Anna in a discussion programme with an Orthodox priest. I think that the programme was a bit biased because this rather attractive witch, dressed in pseudo-Orthodox black clothes with traditional Orthodox cross and her flowing auburn locks, had her telephone number flashed up on the screen, so that you could telephone 'Anna the Witch'. But this poor Orthodox priest who was debating with her, feeling his prayer beads, had no such luck. His number was not flashed up on the screen and I am not sure how you were meant to contact him!

The very fact that such witches exist, and that such sects have been developed, shows that there is a great spiritual thirst, – that the Russian soul is uneasy. Father Werenfried himself has recognized the particular need that exists. He wrote 'Now it is clear that seventy-plus years of Communist indoctrination have not disappeared without trace over the Russian people and its leaders. Instead, it has inflicted almost incurable psychological, spiritual and moral wounds which will continue to fester for years. Like a sort of Original Sin, it has been passed down from one generation to the next and its current victims could be saved from it only by the intervention of God, and so we must place our trust in God alone.' Aid to the Church in Need, not just on a wing and a prayer, has been trying to build bridges of love and trust by not just talking about charity and love but by actually *doing something* for the Orthodox in Russia at this time. We have not just sat about discussing the *Filioque* and problems, but we have actually tried to help our Orthodox fellow Christians in Russia.

We have been involved in detailed discussions in Rome concerning this, and there have been two constructive meetings with the Patriarch. The aid assigned to help the Orthodox is being used according to the judgement of their bishops to answer the basic material needs of the priests, for pastoral purposes, and to help the poor. We have now supported priests and pastoral projects through Russian Orthodox bishops in twenty-five dioceses; that is, one-third of all the dioceses in Russia. To get this in perspective, some further statistics may help. In Russia today there are approximately 148 million people, of whom 60 million claim to be Orthodox and 300,000 (0.2%) are Roman Catholic. So in our aid we are trying to support the conversion of Russia through the religion which is rooted in the Russian soil, and rooted in soil which has been fed by the blood of the Russian Orthodox martyrs as well as Catholic. Recent statistics from the Russian government estimated that more than 200,000 Orthodox priests died in the purges of the 1920s and 1930s, and surely the least we can do as Catholics is to help rebuild a Church so devastated by atheistic totalitarian rule.

Projects of love

Let me now give you some examples of some our projects, from a visit I made in September 1996.

1. Nizhny Novgorod

Amidst the difficulties of life in Russia today, a small ACN team witnessed a tale of heroism and unbounded generosity among both Catholics and Orthodox in one Russian town. Let me tell you about an eye-opening day in Nizhny Novgorod.

You may know Nizhny Novgorod as Gorky, the third largest city in Russia. When we arrived there the city was celebrating the 775th anniversary of its foundation. Overlooking the city is the ancient Russian Orthodox monastery which also houses the seminary. The newly-appointed young, dynamic Abbot Kyrill told us there were fifteen monks in his monastery – and ninety-five seminarians. Little by little, parts of the monastery are being returned, having been taken over by the Communists following the Bolshevik Revolution of 1917. The seminarians are crammed fourteen or more at a time into small dormitories. They asked us why we, Catholics, were helping them, Russian Orthodox? One of us answered that the Orthodox are our brothers and sisters in Christ and that as the Byzantine tradition was the norm in this area, it was only natural that we should support that and help them to re-evangelize their country. ACN has now contributed £40,000 to this seminary in Nizhny Novgorod.

Abbot Kyrill hopes that further parts of the building will be returned to the monastery next year, and he would like to open an academy to train lay people too. And it is not just boys who have flocked to the seminary. Many girls have offered themselves to the service of the

Gospel and the Church. In the same town there is a school which prepares young ladies to be catechists, choirmistresses – so important for the beautiful Russian liturgy – and seamstresses. As the priests are kept so busy offering the divine Liturgy and administering the sacraments, these young women will play an important part in animating the parishes. The school is run despite a chronic shortage of space and funds. We visited some of the young girls undergoing their vestment-making course in the sacristy of a small local church. Others were practising heart-lifting sacred chants in the church itself.

We also visited the hostel where they live, on the other side of town. It was originally an Orthodox academy until the communists turned it into a sports faculty for a local college. The young ladies have only the ground floor to sleep and work in. From overhead comes the constant noise of various sports being played! So crowded is the small hostel that this year's intake of new girls had to be delayed a month while the director, Irene, searched for more beds and space in which to put them! The Russian army gave her some old bunkbeds. Now they are piled into the small dormitories three-high. Comfortable? Perhaps. Safe? Who knows! ACN has again tried to help in some small way – with a gift of £3,000 for these women of God.

Along with Abbot Kyrill, Irene joined us for Catholic weekday Mass in the Catholic church for this city, which is a stable presently being converted into a chapel. Fr Mario Beverarti offered up this Mass at a makeshift brick altar in this windowless stable. It was the first time Irene had ever attended a Catholic service. Seeing the poverty of the Catholic parish both of our Orthodox friends expressed their amazement that Catholics should still help their Orthodox brethren. At a friendly dinner offered by the Abbot in his monastery that evening, Irene proposed a toast: that the Orthodox might drop their suspicion of the Catholics and that the Catholics might lose their arrogance. 'We know that we have nothing and need to be trained again in the Faith after decades of enforced atheism,' she said. 'But we are still brothers and sisters in the Faith. May we continue on the road of mutual love and co-operation – in order to witness to Christ to the Russian people.'

We all echoed her sentiments. For Russia has truly given many, many martyrs for the Faith this century. Now these young men leave home and family to give their lives to Christ. They have nothing – the seminary does not even have the material to make them seminarians' cassocks – except a burning faith. These young girls have left everything to live in a strange city, crammed into dormitories more primitive than any army barracks. Yet their gently harmonious spirits know how to bring order and beauty, a holy picture here, a few flowers there, to make their hostel a dignified dwelling.

Our Orthodox friends took us, along with Father Mario, to meet the local Orthodox Bishop, Metropolitan Nikolai. At the end of our encounter he said he had something to give to the Catholic priests: 'I think these belong to you,' he said as he passed on two chalices to a delighted Father Mario. These two old chalices had been confiscated at the time of the Revolution and the authorities had just returned some artefacts to the Bishop, including these Latin-rite vessels. Such a moment is almost a sacramental sign – a true exchange of love.

2. Moscow

Another example of what is possible was to be found in an apartment block in a Moscow suburb. For from a second floor apartment a young Belgian, Jean-François Thierry, and his Russian colleagues carry out a vital part of Aid to the Church in Need's apostolate. After seventy years of State-enforced atheism, there is – as I have said – a devouring hunger for all things spiritual among much of the population of Russia and the former Soviet Union. There is also a chronic shortage of solid Christian books in the Russian language.

Thanks to the generosity of its benefactors, ACN is helping to print and distribute Catholic literature in Russian. We subsidized the translation of the Universal Catechism and this has been requested by, and sent to, Orthodox seminaries. We have also distributed thousands of our famous little Child's Bible. For countless people throughout the world, this is their first contact with the Christian Truth. (In all, we will have distributed thirty million copies by the end of this year in one hundred languages.) Through their children many have been introduced to the Good News of Christ and Christianity. In many parts of the former Soviet Union it is the first Christian book to be seen by younger generations. A priest recently wrote to us to thank us for the Child's Bibles we had sent to orphans. He wrote: 'Your Charity seems to be one of a few which understands the spiritual needs which exist, for the people cry out for food for the soul as well as for the body.'

Most people by now know of the acute social problems in Russia; how a small group has forged ahead economically, and the 'Mafiaization' of the business world. We asked Jean-François if this had any effect on our work of importing and distributing Christian literature? 'The Mafia did pay a visit to our warehouse,' he told us. 'They arrived in their Mercedes car, dark glasses, big suits, the works. "What's all this, then?" they demanded. You know, many many enterprises have to pay "protection money" just to survive. We were nervous to say the least. One of our colleagues, a young Russian lady, told them that what we had here was the Word of God. They slashed open one box. The young lady told them that they were welcome to have a Bible. They dropped it and left in silence. Since then, thank God, we have had no problems with the Mafia.'

At first, Jean-François and our team in Moscow sent out Bibles and other Christian literature free of charge to people who wrote in after hearing our Christian radio broadcasts. These broadcasts are now also being heard in St Petersburg, with Catholic programmes being put out by Orthodox there. Now we are able to ask a participation in the cost from the recipients of our books, who are only too happy to pay. But they cannot afford much. Poverty is rife and inflation rampant in Russia today. We still have to subsidize the printing of such books. A typical letter recently received at our radio station summed up the importance of this apsotolate funded by our benefactors. The writer, a young lady called Tamara, wrote:

> Your broadcasts and discussions are indispensable. They explain simply and clearly the Christian Faith which for so long they hid from us and wanted to eradicate from our souls. I want to ask it if would be at all possible for you to kindly send me a biblical commentary and the prayers to Our Lady, We Fly to Thy Patronage. I only have one other Christian book and would be grateful for any recommendations for further reading which you could give to a new Christian.

In other parts of Russia, in poor Orthodox parishes and monasteries, we also saw our Child's Bibles being used. In one Catholic parish the priest asked us if we had any with us. We gave him the only two we had left. He wanted to use them in his catechetical classes. Would it not be better if each child could have one of these little Bibles though? Catholics and Orthodox are working together in our media and book apostolate in Russia. There is hope. We must not let them down.

3. Some examples of ACN's aid and priorities for the Russian Orthodox

In all in the year 1996, Aid to the Church in Need gave £440,000 to specifically Orthodox projects; £940,000 to joint ecumenical projects; and £750,000 to Catholic projects. Let me highlight a few of the Orthodox projects which we have supported up to now:

- Theological Seminary in Samara: £11,000
- Theological Seminary in Tomsk: £6,500
- Theological Seminary in Kolomna: £6,800
- Theological Seminary in Smolensk: £10,500

- Diocese of Petrazovodsk and Karelia: Restoration of the Vazheozerskej Convent: £10,000
- Diocese of Arkhangelisk and Kholmogorsk new diocesan centre: £15,100
- Proposed project: A Theological School in Kazan: about £11,500 for equipment (computers, printer, photocopier, etc.) Before the Revolution, there was a theological academy in Kazan (one of the four in the Russian Empire). Part of the former library of this academy has been returned to the diocese, and these books will form the core of the new library. Archbishop Anastasii of Kazan and Tatarstan has built a three-storey building for this Theological School.

ACN priorities include:

- Christian Channel
- Blagovest Info
- La Pensée Russe
- Moscow Theological Academy
- St Petersburg Theological Academy
- Theological seminaries and schools – including Jaroslavl, Lolimna Kokstroma, Pskov, and Vjatka
- Theological Colleges and Universities
- Edition of Theological Literature
- Moscow Theological Academy (Sergei Posad)
- Library for Foreign Literature (Moscow)
- Education and advanced training for priests and laity
- Mass media
- Religious literature
- Catechization.

Fr Theodore van der Voort summed up the needs which we are trying to respond to – and the hopes that exist – when he told a meeting of our benefactors last year:

> We dare not ask in what state a church is, because windows are missing, floors are with puddles of water and there are no ceilings. Rain is coming straight in when it rains. But what is so interesting in Russia today is to see that there are many people who are coming as volunteers to the church and offering their help. The people lovingly restore the church building and help resume the church services. The fact that there are so many young people in the church is very hopeful. The older generation praise these people. The Gospel is being preached. Services are celebrated. Some pastoral aid is reaching people. It will get better in Russia in spite of all the difficulties which still

remain. I am very glad that this work is done by Aid to the Church in Need. I am sure it will also enable a better mutual understanding between the Roman Catholic Church and the Russian Orthodox Church, for as a consequence of Soviet rule there are still many people also within the Church who are so suspicious and do not think that everything will end in a positive way. We should not forget that the situation in the seminaries and in these theological schools is quite disastrous because there is a lack of everything – except of students. Only with the help of God will we overcome such problems.

The historical challenge to unity

May I add that the situation in Russia is far from simple; we have to be realistic about the problems that are being faced at the time within the Catholic–Orthodox discussions. I think it could be helpful to sum up the situation at the time of this paper. The fear on the side of the Orthodox is I hope unjustified, but we have to attempt to understand why Metropolitan Kyrill (responsible for the foreign relations of the Russian Orthodox Chuch) recently restated the doctrine of territoriality. At least we have not heard a re-echo of Patriarch Maxim of Bulgaria who last September called on the Pope to return to the bosom of Orthodoxy!

There is much misunderstanding and a lot of historical baggage which means that the path to unity will be a long one. Even if areas of co-operation can continue, I think it is fair enough to say that at times Catholics have been unsympathetic to the traumas and difficulties facing the Orthodox. We fail to look seriously at the territorial under-standings of the Orthodox. We must try to understand Holy Mother Russia and perhaps learn of the protection of our Lady over this Holy Mother Russia. One Orthodox priest commented that it would be helpful if the West contained their arrogance in suggesting answers for the problems faced in Russia today.

It is not easy to help the Russian Orthodox Church. The situation in Russia is different from that in Western Europe; there is ignorance, there is distrust, there is suspicion and, of course, one of the first tasks is to overcome this negative phenomenon. Seventy years of atheist govern-ment and the isolation of the Russian people meant that the Russian Orthodox Church was not able to follow the developments in other Christian Churches. So their idea of the Roman Catholic Church, if any, is close to that they had about the Roman Catholic Church before the Russian Revolution and the First World War. The fact that so much has changed within the Roman Catholic Church is normally unknown to them. Priests do not know the actual state of the Roman Catholic Church.

In case we somehow think that Catholics have no real historical right to be present in Russia, it is worth reminding ourselves of some historical facts. Russia is first of all 'Orthodox Rus'. However, down through the ages, alongside our Orthodox brothers, there have lived representatives of various confessions of faith, and among them Christians – Catholics, Lutherans, Anglicans – as well as Muslims and Buddhists. The Baptism of Russia in 988, when there was as yet no division into Catholic and Orthodox, marked the beginning of Christianization of Russia. The emergence of ecclesial structures in the Roman Catholic Church dates from 1783, when Pope Pius VI established the largest metropolitanate in the world, the Mogliyov Metropolitanate, which stretched from the shores of the Baltic to the Sea of Japan. There is historical data, however, about the existence of a Catholic community in Smolensk already in the twelfth century.

In 1917, before the Bolshevik Revolution, in the present-day borders of the Russian Federation, a territory of four million square kilometres, there were 150 Catholic parishes, a half million Catholics of various nationalities – basically Polish, German, Lithuanian and likewise Russian. Among the Russian Catholics were individuals from such famous families as the Gargarins, Sheremyetyevs, Volkonskys, Galitsyns, Abrikosovs et al. There are now 300 Catholic parishes in Russia, established in order to meet the pastoral needs of existing Catholics; but half of these do not have Church buildings and 95% of priests in Kazahstan and Russia are foreigners.

Archbishop Thaddeus Kondrusiewicz, the Apostolic Administrator in Moscow, told a meeting of our benefactors in London in May 1995: 'We understand and share the concerns of the society and of the Orthodox Church over the practically uncontrolled spread and activities of new sects in Russia, but we fear that as the saying goes that others don't "throw the baby out with the bath water", that is, that the Catholic Church is not viewed as just another sect.' He referred in hope to the appeal of President Boris Yeltsin in his letter to the Federal Council of 16 February 1995, where he stressed that: 'A citizen of the Russian Federation, regardless of nationality and religious conviction, has the right to participate peacefully and confidently in any region of the country'.

Unfortunately, this statement has now come to be threatened once again by legislation awaiting the President's signature at the time of this lecture. Yet this does not mean that mutual co-operation and practical help is impossible.

The papal vision

Pope John Paul II has a special vision of unity: of a Church breathing with both lungs. It has sometimes been suggested that his outlook and

understanding are underpinned by a nineteenth-century Polish romantic view of the world. It is worth trying to understand his particular
ecumenical vision of Europe, which Pope John Paul II stated once again
in his message to Cardinal Cassidy for the Second European Ecumenical
Assembly in Graz, Austria, dated 20 June 1997:

> Europe has a very special responsibility with regard to ecumenism. It is in
> Europe that the major divisions between East and West and within the West
> have arisen. However, it is also in Europe that serious efforts directed
> towards Christian reconciliation and the search for full visible unity have
> taken place.
>
> At another level, the European continent yearns today for the reconcilia-
> tion of its peoples and the elimination of divisive social conditions. A more
> positive relationship has emerged between East and West following the
> decline of communist regimes. However, new problems and new tensions
> have also arisen, sometimes expressing themselves violently in open conflict.
> Christians have a special responsibility in these struggles, for their very spir-
> itual inheritance embodies the spirit of forgiveness and peace.
>
> In a Europe which is seeking not only economic but also political and
> social cohesion, Christians of the East and West can offer a common yet
> distinct contribution to the spiritual dimension of the continent. We must
> neither forget nor mislay the values which Christianity has conferred on the
> history of Europe. As followers of Christ we must all be deeply convinced
> that we have a common responsibility for promoting respect for human
> rights, for justice and peace, and for what pertains to the sacredness of life. In
> particular, in the midst of increasing indifferentism and secularization, we
> are called to bear witness to the values of life and to faith in the Resurrection
> which embodies the entire Christian message.

It is true that John Paul II has a first-hand awareness of the difficult relations between the Roman Catholic and Orthodox Churches. His knowledge of Russian and Ukrainian has helped him understand the Eastern
rite, and by being in Krakow – as student, priest and bishop, – he has a
particular Central European overview of the situation. In 1995 the
Pope's important apostolic letter, *Orientale Lumen*, was published, and
this was followed by *Ut Unum Sint*, the first ever papal encyclical
devoted to ecumenism. Then in November 1995 the Pope wrote another
apostolic letter to mark the fourth centenary of the Union of Brest-
Litovsk. The tone was strongly ecumenical. He declared that, in respect
of the twentieth-century developments in the eastern half of the continent, 'the churches of Europe' were bound together by a heritage of
persecution and martyrdom; the 'real, if imperfect communion, already
present between Catholics and Orthodox in their ecclesiastical life'
could take only added sustenance from the remembrance of martyrs
'whether victims of the ideologies of the East or of the West'.

So we must view what Pope John Paul II says as coming very much from his own heart – and the disappointment of not achieving a meeting with Patriarch Alexis will run deep.

The Patriarch's fears

The official text of the Holy Synod was as follows: 'With regret we have to state that at this moment the meeting between the first hierarchs of the two churches have not sufficiently been prepared, and that a whole series of conditions is lacking, which could make such a meeting fruitful.' Thus a proposed meeting between Patriarch Alexis and Pope John Paul was postponed a few weeks before this lecture: and it is true that the immediate difficulties are going to be hard to resolve.

In addition to this, the recent legislation at the time of writing awaiting President Yeltsin's signature illustrates the nationalistic mood of many Russians. The Duma (Russian Parliament) has voted to pass the second reading of legislation restricting religious freedom in Russia. A Duma staff specialist said that local government officials would have to confirm the church's or the organization's past existence. The communist-dominated committee's proposal violates the 1993 Russian constitution's guarantees of religious freedom for all by creating a new category of so-called 'religious groups' which would enjoy far fewer rights than fully-fledged, registered 'religious organizations'. The Bill also sets up a special procedure for registering foreign religious organizations, contradicting President Yeltsin's letter to the Duma in November 1996 stating that such separate rules for foreigners violate the constitutional principle of equal rights for all religious believers.

I can only attempt to look behind some of the obstacles which must be in the mind of the Patriarch. Patriarch Alexis said in his speech in Graz in June 1997 that he had enjoyed 'truly fraternal co-operation' with Cardinal Martini, but he then went on to refer to 'a massive proselytic activity' and an 'invasion' of Russia. 'This "invasion" means that the notion of ecumenism in the consciousness of the majority of our Church people has now come to signify something dangerous and utterly unacceptable.' He also referred to the territories from which the invasion had been launched.

Perhaps I can make a couple of points about such comments. Firstly, nationalism is not just to be found in so-called reactionary 'right-wing' monasteries, for it has been fuelled by the appalling economic circumstances that most people face. In the same address at Graz the Patriarch said that the Iron Curtain had been replaced by a Silver Curtain: and this curtain is an incredibly damaging and illusory one. Secondly, the mentality of the Cold War is still present, even in the use of the term 'invasion', or Metropolitan Kyrill's talk of 'territoriality'. Some Bishops were caught up in providing information to the KGB and there is obviously a political sphere to the role they perceive for themselves in a State Church. It is no wonder the Russian Orthodox feel threatened by Western culture, with our insensitivity to Holy Russia, and it is no surprise if Catholicism is tarred with the same brush as Protestant sects. Catholics – and Protestants alike – have to earn respect.

Let me add that I am not judging anyone in this situation, but simply trying to point the way to a clearer understanding of some of the sensitive issues involved.

The imperative of charity

Perhaps I may come towards a close by quoting Archbishop Kodrusiewicz once again:

> We shall do all that is possible to spiritually revive Russia so that no one should ever speak or think about her again as an atheistic country, but rather, that in the eyes of all and before God she will be *Svyataya Rus*, Holy Russia: giving glory (although in different rites) to one and the same God, and venerating the same Mother of God, who in difficult times was the hope of Russia, and who asked of her Son, our Saviour, Jesus Christ, the grace of conversion.

The next perspective is that of the Jubilee of the Year 2000. Pope John Paul II says that we have to do everything 'so that in the great Jubilee we can stand before if not as one, at least a great deal closer to the overcoming of division of the second millennium' (*Tertio Millenio Adveniente*, n. 34). We intend to offer the Orthodox Church further aid and I pray that Aid to the Church in Need will be able to build a bridge with the Orthodox – even if quite quietly – in this vital work.

I leave you with the comment of a prophet, for that is how I like to see our undaunted founder, Father Werenfried van Straaten. He began a recent letter by saying 'Easter is over, but Good Friday remains'. In the work of ACN it is always the case that we are stuck on Good Friday – where persecution, oppression and ignorance have seemingly triumphed. However, out of the ashes there are new signs of life. Tertullian's often quoted phrase still rings true – *Sanguis Martyrorum, semen Christianorum* – the blood of the martyrs is the seed of the Church, of all Christians. Perhaps this comes as a bit of a shock to us here in the West, but as a priest in the East said: 'It is only through the flow of blood and tears that this new life has come to the Church'.

And so I end with one example from Russia: Aid to the Church in Need is helping the Orthodox Bishop of Omsk (Siberia) in building a convent with a church, pilgrims' guest house and orphanage. This place of pilgrimage, prayer and atonement is now being constructed on the former extermination camp at Achajir where hundreds of thousands of people of different nationalities were murdered. Until recently the site was almost a barren wasteland with only a few bushes that had sprung up. Yet these bushes came from the seeds the dying had held in their hands as they were shot. New life out of death. The suffering, passion and death of our Lord ... and only thereby the Resurrection. Perhaps this example of our work in Eastern Europe can summarize the hope that exists amidst the politically explosive turmoil that continues in Russia and the regions of the former Soviet Union.

(This paper was given at the ESBVM Woldingham Conference in June 1997)

11

Reason, relics and romance: aspects of devotion to the Blessed Virgin Mary in the twelfth century

Benedicta Ward SLG

I will begin with a poem which seems to me doubly appropriate to this time and place [Oriel College, Oxford, on the Solemnity of the Assumption of the Blessed Virgin Mary]: it is Gerard Manley Hopkins' poem 'Duns Scotus' Oxford', in which he evoked an older, more rural city and then praised the thirteenth-century Oxford theologian, John Duns Scotus (c. 1265–1308), as his chief master and as the first major theologian to defend the doctrine of the immaculate conception of the Blessed Virgin Mary,[1] for which he was known as 'Doctor Marianus':

> Towery city and branchy between towers;
> Cuckoo-echoing, bell-swarmèd, lark-charmèd, rook-racked,
>   river-rounded;
> The dapple-eared lily below thee; that country and town did
> Once encounter in, here coped and poisèd powers;
>
> Thou hast a base and brickish skirt there, sours
> That neighbour-nature thy grey beauty is grounded
> Best in; graceless growth, thou hast confounded
> Rural rural keeping – folk, flocks, and flowers.
>
> Yet ah! this air I gather and I release
> He lived on; these weeds and waters, these walls are what
> He haunted who of all men most sways my spirits to peace;
>
> Of realty the rarest-veinèd unraveller; a not
> Rivalled insight, be rival Italy or Greece;
> Who fired France for Mary without spot.[2]

This well-known, well-loved poem is a pre-eminent example of the unity I wish to demonstrate between theology and beauty: John Duns Scotus, who has been seen by some as the most abstruse of theologians, taught in Oxford in the thirteenth century. By the sixteenth century new theologians had come to think him so supreme an example of the obscure, rarified theology they deplored that his name became a byword for ignorance, being reduced to 'dunce'. Yet for the nineteenth-century Hopkins, that poet of poets, Scotus was the source of his deepest inspiration, one who explained most clearly what Hopkins knew by intuition. When in 1872 Hopkins returned to Oxford as a Jesuit, having deliberately written no poetry for seven years, he wrote to Coventry Patmore that he was 'flush with a new stroke of enthusiasm ... when I took in any inscape of the sky or sea I thought of Scotus'.[3] Hopkins' distinctive use of 'instress' and 'inscape' in his poetry was based on Scotus' principle of individuation, the *haecceitas*, the 'thisness' of things. In this poem he calls Scotus an 'unraveller', one who makes things clear and lucid, and especially relates this to his treatise on the immaculate conception of Mary – he who 'won France for Mary without spot' – where Scotus had applied this theory to most effect. This union of beauty in poetry with discernment in theology is not unusual, though by the sixteenth century there were enough examples of a division between reason and emotion, especially in the cult of the saints, to alarm a good Catholic like Erasmus as well as a good Protestant like Calvin. But at its best in the tumult of new energy and ideas in the eleventh and twelfth centuries, there was no division of the theology of incarnation from the popular piety that related to Mary; the same people were involved in both without a sense of discomfort. This unity of heart and head is in fact a special mark of medieval devotion to St Mary. Non-scholastic writers and scholastics alike both wrote about Mary's place in theology, and also collected miracle-stories about her. Like Honorius of Autun, Rupert of Deutz, a formidable biblical scholar in the twelfth century, interpreted the Song of Songs exclusively of Mary, and in his commentary on St John's Gospel described her as the mother of the salvation of all: 'In the passion of the only-begotten Son the blessed Virgin brought forth the salvation of us all, she is clearly the mother of us all'.[4] Theology and miracles issued from the monastic tradition and the emerging university tradition alike: on the one hand, Rupert, Bernard of Clairvaux, and Peter Damian, and on the other, Abelard, Hermann of Tournai, Peter of Celle, and the Victorines; the list could go on. I should like to illustrate this unity by referring to three instances of it in the eleventh and twelfth centuries: first at Bec, then Laon, then in Paris.

First of all, I refer to Anselm of Canterbury (1033–1109), the greatest philosopher of the Middle Ages, an oustanding scholar on any scale, one of the great minds of the world. He wrote no treatise about Mary but theologized about her in two ways; first, he mentioned very briefly her place in redemption in his treatise *On the Virgin Birth*, in which he referred back to his earlier treatment of this in his major theological work on redemption *Cur Deus Homo*: 'It is absolutely true that the Son of

God was conceived of a most pure Virgin ... it was fitting that the virgin should be radiant with a purity so great that a greater purity cannot be conceived'.[5]

The rest of both these treatises then deal with different aspects of incarnation and redemption. It seems as if for Anselm a philosophical and logical examination of doctrine was not the appropriate vehicle for his thoughts about Mary, and for his sustained theology of Mary it is necessary to turn to his poetry, that is, to three long meditative prayers he wrote addressed to Mary, and which he constantly worked to perfect.[6] The three form a group, each one containing one of the three aspects of devotion which shaped every one of the eighteen prayers and three meditations of St Anselm: that is, first, a recognition of the human state of alienation from God; secondly, repentance for it and a request for help; and thirdly, longing for love and life and praise. This pattern of prayer is divided between the three long prayers to Mary:

Mary 1: when the mind is weighted down with heaviness;
Mary 2: when the mind is anxious with fear;
Mary 3; to ask for her and Christ's love.

Anselm's prayers were immensely popular and frequently used and copied. But later his precise and theologically accurate thought was not always reproduced exactly. His highly emotive and personal language could be misunderstood, and this was so especially in his second prayer to Mary:

> God who was made the son of a woman out of mercy
> woman who was out of mercy made the mother of God;
> have mercy upon this wretch
> you Jesus forgiving, you Mary interceding.[7]

That is entirely both accurate theology and deep devotion, but a less sophisticated reading led to a simplistic sense later that mercy belonged to Mary, judgement to Christ: and that therefore Mary was more easily accessible and would ask her Son to be less severe. That is of course a deplorable theology which diminished Christ's full humanity in an alarming way. Anselm had no such idea in his prayers to Mary, and this is made plain in his Prayer to St Paul where he underlines the fact that mercy belongs to Christ, whom he sees under the image of mother as well as father: Christ, he says, is both father and mother towards Christians, and, using the image of Luke 13.34, he wrote:

> And you, Jesus, are you not also a mother?
> Are you not a mother who like a hen gathers her chickens under her wings?
> and you my soul, run under the wings of Jesus your mother

and lament your griefs under his feathers ...
Christ my mother gather your chickens under your wings ...
for by your gentleness the terrified are comforted ...
for from you flows consolation for sinners.[8]

There is no sense there that Mary is mercy and Christ is judgement: Jesus
Christ is both the judgement and the mercy of God, and Anselm used
the daring imagery of mother as well as father to make this plain. For
him, Mary was the first saint, the human being who gave flesh to her
Son, and therefore the clearest instance of his mercy, a human aspect of
the mercy of Christ, not an alternative to his judgement and righteousness.

In his *Third Prayer to St Mary* Anselm reached ecstatic heights of
praise, which were nevertheless theologically exact and filled with the
phrases of Scripture, especially of the Song of Songs:

O woman full and overflowing with grace
  plenty flows from you
  to make all creatures green again.

O virgin blessed and ever blessed
  whose blessing is upon all nature,
  not only is the creature blessed by the Creator,
  but the Creator is blessed by the creature too.

O highly exalted,
  when the love of my heart tries to follow you,
  whither do you escape the keenness of my sight?

O beautiful to gaze upon,
  lovely to contemplate, delightful to love
  whither do you go to evade the breadth of my heart?

Lady, wait for the weakness of him who follows you,
  do not hide yourself
  seeing the littleness of the soul that seeks you!

Have mercy, Lady
  upon the soul that pants after you with longing.

A thing to be wondered at
  at what a height do I behold the place of Mary!

Nothing equals Mary
  nothing but God is greater than Mary.

God gave his own Son, who alone from his heart
    was born equal to him, loved as he loves himself, to Mary,
    – and of Mary was then born a Son
    not another but the same one
that naturally one might be the Son of God and of Mary.

All nature is created by God and God is born of Mary.
    God created all things, and Mary gave birth to God.

God who made all things made himself of Mary
    and thus he refashioned everything he had made.

He who was able to make all things out of nothing
    refused to remake it by force
    but first became the Son of Mary.

So God is the Father of all created things
    and Mary is the mother of all re-created things.

God is the Father of all that is established
    and Mary is the mother of all that is re-established.

For God gave birth to him by whom all things were made
    and Mary brought forth him by whom all are saved.

God brought forth him without whom nothing is.[9]

Alongside this paean of praise for Mary as the second Eve, the mother of all the living, as the first of saints, the queen of heaven, it is illuminating to read also Anselm's reaction to her place at the foot of the cross. In his *Prayer to Christ* Anselm's emotion towards the crucifixion achieved an extraordinary depth, in which he lamented that he had not been present at the foot of the cross to share visibly in the sufferings of Christ; this remarkable prayer revealed a new dimension of his understanding of Mary as he lamented the fact that he was not able to see her sorrow:

    alas for me that I was not able to see
    the Lord of Angels humbled to converse with men;

    Why, O my soul, were you not there
    to be pierced with a sword of bitter sorrow ...

    Why did you not share
    the sufferings of the most pure virgin
    his worthy mother and your gentle lady?

My most merciful Lady,
    what can I say about the fountains
    that flowed from your most pure eyes
    when you saw your only Son before you
    bound, beaten and hurt?[10]

Here Anselm made a vital link between salvation by the cross of Christ and Mary, the first of the saved. Always underpinning medieval exuberance in praise of Mary there is the double reason for her place in salvation history: she is the mother of Christ who emptied himself and became man; and the mother of the crucified man who emptied himself on the cross. Here Anselm gave new life to meditation on this central theological truth, by this description of Mary at the cross as the mother of sorrows, which became one of the dominant images of the next century. It was a supremely influential evocation, foreshadowing the great strains of the *Stabat Mater Dolorosa*.

Anselm applied faith seeking understanding in his view of Marian doctrine and gave it life through his passionate prayers; but he also was in contact with the relics of the Virgin. Now it seems unlikely that there would be relics of either Christ or the Virgin, both of whom were taken up into heaven bodily at their deaths. But human nature needs the material, the visible, to help it into glory, and there were many claims about relics of both the Lord and of his mother. The justification for this was that at the deaths of Christ and of Mary, what was taken up to heaven was the body that had actually died; anything else that had left the body before the moment of death might remain on earth, so there were relics of the teeth of Christ, his blood, his tears – anything relating to his sufferings or to his birth. Similarly, for Mary there was her shift, her slipper, her milk, which remained and were available; and also there were her hairs. The theory was an example of a lack of perspective typical of the early Middle Ages; everything was 'now' and 'for me'; so it was felt that, like any mother of the eleventh century whose son was dying, Mary would weep and cry and beat her breast and tear out her hair at the foot of the cross; and likewise John, the beloved disciple into whose care she was given, would gather up and preserve those hairs, placing them in a casket in Jerusalem like any responsible eleventh-century young man. It was while Anselm was at Rouen in 1106 that he encountered the hairs of the Virgin. There he met an old friend and former pupil, Ilgor Bigod, a knight and crusader, just returned from the Holy Land. Eadmer, Anselm's inquisitive and talkative secretary, described their conversation:

> he [Ilgor Bigod] prided himself especially on some hairs of Mary the blessed Mother of God of which he said that some of them had been given to him by the patriarch of Antioch, saying 'The bishop of Antioch gave me twelve of them altogether declaring that according to what, as he assserted, he found written in the records of ancient writings ... these hairs had been torn out by our Lady herself when, standing beside the cross of her son, a sword had pierced her soul'.

Eadmer says that Anselm was filled with joy over these relics and recommended their disposal: some were sent to Rouen cathedral, four were given to the abbey of Bec, some arrived at Laon, while Anselm accepted two. He did not however keep them personally, and indeed his interest seems to have been short-lived. He placed them in the care of Eadmer who wrote:

> What others feel about them I do not know, but for myself I know quite certainly that my lord and revered father Anselm always regarded them with great reverence, and that I myself by holy and sublime experience have felt that there is about them something great, and a mark of holiness which should be embraced by the whole world.[11]

It is noteworthy that the pre-eminent philosopher and theologian in no way scorned the relics as mere 'popular' devotion; like miracle stories, appreciation of them was current in the circles in which he lived and taught. But while Anselm regarded them with respect – and that is in line with the fact that as a young monk he had longed to share the visible grief of the Virgin in his prayers – it was not he who kept these visible relics. He gave them to his young and impressionable disciple Eadmer, who later wrote one of the earliest treatises on the doctrine of the Immaculate Conception, a feast which among all the great Marian feasts came to be most associated with England through the legend of Elsinus.[12] Anselm listened to and enjoyed stories of miracles of our Lady and appreciated her relics; they circulated freely in his group of friends and disciples, but it was the lesser scholar Eadmer who wrote a treatise on the Virgin Mary, and it was the more mundane thinker, Anselm's namesake and nephew, the abbot of Bury St Edmunds,who collected her miracles.

A second example of theology combined with devotion to our Lady follows from the history of these relics. Some of these hairs found their way to the relic collection of the cathedral of Laon. Now Laon is not far from Paris, and the two initiators of the movement later called scholasticism were born there: the brothers Anselm and Ralph. They taught mostly in Paris but it was from Laon that they came and it was by that name that they were known.[13] It was to Anselm of Laon that the young

Abelard first went, and it was he who produced the basic method and textbook of the schools. His pupils were many and his theological influence wide. Some of the pupils of Anselm and Ralph came from England, and when they returned home they remained friends with their fellow-students from Laon and invited them to England. This invitation was accepted and used in connection with the relics of the cathedral in 1112. The cathedral of St Mary at Laon was damaged by fire in 1112 and Bishop Bartholomew launched a campaign to raise money to rebuild it. He sent some of his clergy on fund-raising tours, carrying the relics of the church, most notably the relic of the hairs of the Virgin Mary; 'with us we took the feretory of Our Lady ... to receive the offerings of the faithful'.[14] From Pentecost 1112 till 21 September they toured northern France, stopping in various towns so that the relics could be venerated and offerings made; the party returned with considerable funds, and the next year, from Palm Sunday 1113, the relics went on a second pilgrimage to the south of England, which was thought to be particularly prosperous under Henry I, the son of William the Conqueror. Invited by their academic friends, the canons could expect a welcome in Canterbury, Exeter, Salisbury, and Cornwall – which underlines, incidentally, the widespread influence of pupils of the Paris masters, returning home to apply what they had learnt.

Moreover, such a tour had been undertaken before. Between 1086 and 1087 the relics of St Ouen had been carried to England to collect money for rebuilding the church at Rouen; and in England itself, the relics of St Cuthbert were renowned, both for the miracles they occasioned when they were carried about during the Danish invasions, and for more recent tours they made for the collection of funds for rebuilding the church in Durham. For this English tour from Laon, the members of the party were not identical with those on the first tour. They included Boso, the leader, and his nephew Robert, the canons Boniface and 'Amisardus clericus', who all went again; to them was added Robert the Englishman, Ralph, John, and Helinand, who were said be proficient in learning and chanting. No list is given of laymen, but one was certainly there, the boy Hugellinus, who provoked a fight in Cornwall on the subject of King Arthur, when he claimed that the real 'Arthur's Seat' was not in the West Country but in France. The party set out on Palm Sunday, 1113, and returned on the Feast of the Nativity of the Virgin in September of the same year. This time, more details were given in the account of the relics which were the focus for the miracles. The feretory contained the relics of the church of Laon among which, in a special container, were the relics of the hairs of the Virgin. Canon Herman, who wrote the account, made it clear that it was by no means an easy journey, and he recorded some remarkable adventures: for instance, when crossing the Channel they met a fire-breathing dragon; when they went among the Devon men, they found that they defended with their fists their right to own King Arthur against these foreigners, and they also narrowly escaped from slave-traders in Bristol, who nearly kidnapped the canons. The blatant fund-raising purpose of the trip, for which the relics of the Virgin themselves went on pilgrimage, in no way troubled the thinking of the canons themselves. In fact, they recorded many miracles which showed Mary's favour on the tour. The theme of the judgement and indeed punishments sent by Mary upon those who threatened her canons was notable, as well as the cures of the sick at the places where the shrine rested. However dubious one might think this whole process to have been from the point of view of theology, it appealed widely to devotion. The canons returned home in September with 120 marks; the pilgrimage of the relics was a financial success. The great church of Laon continued to rise, a focus for reverence for the Blessed Virgin and her relics, along-side and in no sense in conflict with the severities of the new scholasticism of Anselm and Ralph of Laon and their pupils.

Thirdly, the relics of the Virgin provided another focus for devotion in a place also associated with the new theology. While Chartres was not in any sense the centre of a special school of scholastic thought, and the connection of some names once thought to be associated with learning there have been revealed as spurious, yet it is fair to say that Chartres like Laon was close to Paris, and therefore not immune from the new excitement of the emerging universities, with both scholars and masters involved in the new enterprises of the intellect. Earlier in the eleventh century, Fulbert of Chartres preached a sermon for the feast of the Nativity of Mary emphasizing her power as an intercessor: 'whatever the just ask of Christ they receive more speedily through the intercession of his mother'.[15] Fulbert began the building of the cathedral in her honour, and it was another relic of the Virgin which formed the centre of that church and the focus for the other theme connected with Mary, that of romance. This relic was the *sancta camisia*, 'the most holy shift which the Virgin wore when she was carrying the Son of God in her womb'. The collection of miracles includes a story of how this relic had been used at the siege of Chartres in 911 as a temporary rallying point for the French against the Normans: 'The alarmed citizens trusted neither in courage nor arms or walls, but implored the help of blessed Mary and the shift of the most glorious Virgin which had been brought from Constantinople by someone for Charlemagne; they put it on a spear and displayed it like a banner.'[16]

Whether or not this rather vague legend is of an early date, establishing the presence of the relic at Chartres by the beginning of the tenth century, it does not appear that the shift was continuously used for veneration until the end of the eleventh century. Only then was it invested with its full devotional significance. The shift was a particularly intimate and emotive relic of the Virgin associated with the birth of Jesus, and was used as such. The preface to the miracles described the building as a fitting church to house this relic of the Virgin, which was produced unharmed from the fire. The veneration of such a relic of the Virgin combined with the theme of 'salvation for all through Mary' to trigger the personal enthusiasm of the people of Chartres to rebuild the church which would house this precious relic. The ensuing miracles were connected with the actual physical rebuilding, with carts of wood, stone, staves etc. being brought to the site from the countryside, on which were also conveyed the sick who came there to ask for cures of physical illness. 'We have seen the deaf hear, the blind see, the dumb speak again, the lame walk, and we have beheld many cured of illnesses, weaknesses, and various infirmities.' An atmosphere also of repentance for sins was a theme of these pilgrimages, giving the miracle a background highly charged with emotion which was expressed in the accounts of these miracles by descriptions of prayers and exclamations, groans, tears, sighs.

To this account of the search for healing both physical and spiritual, which could be paralleled at any shrine of any saint of the times, were added longer, more detailed stories which emphasized the theme of the unlooked-for salvation of those whose only merit was that they were to some extent devotees of the Virgin. These stories flowered in the language of the new world of romance and courtly love. Besides the country people from the district around Chartres, there were other recipients of miracles, people who belonged to a different world, that which was being formed just at this time – formed by tales of chivalry and romance: here there were not only peasants but a knight from Sourday; a young and noble husband, a noble lady from Sully-sur-Loire, a knight from Aquitaine, a young scholar from England, always young people, sometimes even children. The stories connected with Our Lady of Chartres gained colour and vitality, and were connected with the overwhelming power of the Virgin which would always be extended to her lovers, however small their contact with her. In one story a knight was observed making love to a girl in a pleasure garden; he cut out the tongue of a child who might betray him: but the boy was healed by the intervention of the Virgin, and the lovers rebuked not for their adultery but for their fear. A young man, on his way home with a present for his betrothed, stopped at Chartres: after a vision of Mary there, he chose her as his mistress and abandoned his girl friend – a story contrasting the themes of sacred and profane love. A knight touched his armour with her shift, and was protected in battle. A clerk who was so ignorant that he knew only one mass, that of our Lady, was especially protected by her from ridicule. Walter of Birbeck, on his way to a tournament, stopped to hear the mass of the Virgin at a wayside chapel; he found that he was then too late for the tournament: but when he met his friends who were returning and asked them who had won and they said, 'Walter of Birbeck', he realized that our Lady had fought that day in his place. Beatrix, the portress of a convent, ran away with a lover, leaving her keys on the altar of the Virgin: when she returned years later, she realized that our Lady had taken her place so that no one knew she had gone. An acrobat who became a Cistercian monk turned cartwheels with impunity before her statue. Pierre de Siglar, a troubadour, was refused access to the church by a verger, and played softly to our Lady at the back: three lighted candles from her shrine floated through the air to rest on the strings of his lute. Eppo the thief, who was hung on the gallows, had always prayed to Mary: therefore she did not let him die, but held him up for two days until he was taken down and given time to repent. The stories multiplied, and so great were the collections of them that their contact with Laon, Chartres, or other centres was soon obscured. Another Anselm, the nephew of the great Anselm, took a hand in collecting such stories and made one of the major collections of such Mary miracles, which provided imaginative and devotional nourishment for years ahead. Such stories had begun in theology, focused on relics, and flowered in the world of high romance. Mary was now *Domina Nostra*, Our Lady, the friend of sinners, especially of the young, the available one. What men wanted from her was neither mercy nor justice but favour, special pleading, a patron who would regard them as her special people and make sure the righteous judgement of Christ was ameliorated in their case. The links with theology were in places wearing remarkably thin. Most notable perhaps for this was the story of Theophilus, a tale which came originally from the east and was told and retold in the West; it was used by Fulbert of Chartres in his sermon for the Nativity of Mary.

> There was a certain noble named Theophilus who became impoverished ...
> At last he thought of going to the crossroads and talking with the Devil. The Devil offered help if Theophilus would renounce his baptism, his creator and the Mother of Mercy. This he did and the devil, considering his love for this last, said, 'If you will confirm this oath in an indenture written in your blood then all is complete'. This was done ... Years later, Theophilus repented and wept and prostrated himself before the image of the Blessed Virgin Mary, who pardoned him for what he had done.[17]

Eventually, the indenture was returned to Theophilus and he found it was blank.

The story was elaborated in many ways and used again and again in sermons. It was about the fundamental spiritual theme of salvation, and concerned the ultimate unforgivable sin, the selling of a soul to the devil for worldly goods. Its message was that any sin can be redeemed if there is one spark of love remaining in a soul, to cause sorrow and lead to enough humility to ask for help. The scriptural verse behind it is of Christ 'blotting out the handwriting of ordinances that was against us, that was contrary to us, and took it out of the way, nailing it to the cross' (Col. 2.14). It is remarkable that in this medieval Faust story the sinner is saved, and saved by the intercession of Mary, against the justice of God; by the sixteenth century, in another way of thinking which left man alone before God without 'a great cloud of witnesses', Faustus, in spite of his last-minute repentance, was not saved.

It was what began to seem an over-enthusiastic and materialistic side of devotion to Mary which caused the criticism of the cult by sixteenth-century reformers, Protestant and Catholic alike. The link between theology and piety seemed to many to have been for the moment obscured. But this was not to be the end of love for the Mother of God by any means; and I would like to end with two examples of the continued flowering of devotion to Mary on the other side of the protest called Protestantism. Firstly, in the seventeenth century, Bishop Ken continued the theme of Mary and the incarnation, and Mary as queen of heaven, when he wrote one of the most tender of hymns, making love of Mary inseparable from love of Christ:

> Her Virgin eyes saw God incarnate born
> When she to Bethlem came that happy morn
> How high her rapture then began to swell
> None but incarnate love Himself can tell.
>
> Heaven with transcendent joys her entrance graced
> Next to his throne her Son his mother placed;
> And here below, now she's of heaven possessed,
> All generations are to call her blessed.[18]

The theology of the early church was here used to combine the doctrine of the incarnation with that of Mary's assumption into heaven, lovingly and unobtrusively given an English form without diminishing either correct thought or deep devotion.

Secondly, the true veneration of Mary has always been linked inextricably with a profound doctrinal point which was evident in the authors we have considered, that is, the double kenosis of Christ: the emptying of himself as God in order to become man in Bethlehem, and the final emptying of himself as man on the cross for our redemption. The sense that these two are one event has always been a theme of Christianity, and is the secure centre for a veneration of Mary at once theologically correct and emotionally satisfying. It was this combination of death and conception which John Donne encapsulated in his poem written in 1608 'Upon the Annunciation and Passion falling upon the same day'.

> This church, by lettinge these daies joyne, hath shown
> Death and conception in mankinde is one.[19]

But the theme had been present in England much earlier. In 604 the Greek, Theodore of Tarsus, came from Rome to be the seventh Archbishop of Canterbury; he brought with him John the archchanter of St Peter's 'in order that he might teach the monks of his monastery the mode of chanting throughout the year as it was practised at St Peter's in Rome'.[20] It seems that among the many things he taught the Anglo-Saxons was a collect, 'Gratiam tuam', which he himself had perhaps composed, introducing just this link of incarnation and crucifixion:

> Graciam tuam quaesumus domine mentibus nostris infunde:
> ut qui angelo nunciante christi filii tui incarnationem cognovimus,
> per passionem eius et crucem ad resurrectionis gloriam perducamur.

This admirable collect was dropped later to a post-communion prayer, but in the sixteenth century it was retrieved by a Cambridge scholar and theologian, Archbishop Thomas Cranmer, for the new Book of Common Prayer and translated in his own incomparable English as the collect for the feast of the Annunciation, thus preserving an ancient theological insight within a new dimension of devotion in honour of Mary:

> We beseech thee, O Lord, pour thy grace into our hearts; that, as we have known the incarnation of thy Son Jesus Christ by the message of an angel, so by his cross and passion we may be brought unto the glory of his resurrection; through the same Jesus Christ our Lord. Amen.

In the veneration of Mary in the twenty-first century, it may be that the medieval sense of the relics of Mary is not immediately present; but reason and romance are still alive and can be joined in love of the Mary of the Scriptures. At the annunciation, the visitation, the nativity, the presentation in the temple, the wedding at Cana, at the foot of the cross, her part in the cosmic matter of salvation finds its true focus. Reason must be applied to its limits in understanding this truth, and it is equally essential that the love of the heart should be set free. One might perhaps read the name of Mary into the phrase of Dostoevsky, 'Beauty will save the world', and even more surely when it was amplified by Alexander Solzhenitsyn in his Nobel Prize speech, 'One word of Truth', with insight forged in the full horror of a prison camp:

> Not everything has a name. Some things lead us into a realm beyond words. Art thaws even the frozen, darkened soul, opening it to lofty spiritual experience. Through art we are sometimes sent – indistinctly, briefly – revelations not to be achieved by rational thought.[21]

'Mary is taken up into heaven; the angels rejoice, exalting and blessing the Lord.'

Notes

1 Duns Scotus' views on the immaculate conception were presented in Paris and in Oxford in his commentaries on the *Sentences*; for an easily available summary of his views, see C. Balic, *Theologiae Marianae Elementa* (1933).

2 *The Poems of Gerard Manley Hopkins*, ed. W. H. Gardner and N. H. Mackenzie (Oxford 1970), no. 44, p. 79.

3 *Further Letters of Gerard Manley Hopkins*, ed. C. C. Abbott, OUP 1938; 2nd edn. 1956, p. 306.

4 Rupert of Deutz (d.1135), Commentary on John, *PL* 169, col. 789C; for his commentary on the Song of Songs, see *PL* 168, cols. 837–962.

5 Anselm, *Sancti Anselmi Cantuariensis Archiepiscopi Opera Omnia*, ed. F. S. Schmitt (Nelson 1938–61), vols 1–6: vol. 2, *On the Virgin Birth*, pp. 1–37; vol. 2, *Cur Deus Homo*, pp. 27–135; vol. 3, *Prayers and Meditations*, pp. 3–91.

6 I use here my own translation in *Prayers and Meditations of St Anselm with the Proslogion* (Penguin Classics, Harmondsworth 1973), hereafter called 'Prayers'. For Anselm's work on his prayers to St Mary, see his letter 28 to Gundolf, Schmitt vol. 3, pp. 135–6, translated in *Prayers* p. 106.

7 2nd Prayer to St Mary, *Prayers* p. 113.

8 Prayer to St Paul, *Prayers* p. 155.

9 3rd Prayer to St Mary, *Prayers* pp. 118–20.

10 Prayer to Christ, *Prayers* pp. 95–6.

11 Eadmer, *History of Recent Events*, trans. M. Rule (London 1964), pp. 192–4.

12 For the legend of Elsinus and the complex history of the Feast of the Conception, cf. Edmund Bishop, *Liturgica Historica* (Oxford 1917), pp. 238–60.

13 Anselm and Ralph of Laon: see R. W. Southern, *Scholasticism, Humanism and the Unification of Europe* (Blackwells, forthcoming), vol. 2, chs. 3–5.

14 For the journey of the canons of Laon, see *Patrologia Latina* vol. 156, cols. 961–1020. For a more detailed discussion, see J. S. P. Tatlock, 'The English Journey of the Canons of Laon' in *Speculum* 8 (1933), pp. 454–85, and Benedicta Ward, *Miracles and the Medieval Mind* (Scolar Press, 1982), ch. 8, 'The Miracles of the Virgin', pp. 132–66.

15 *Miracles de Notre Dame de Chartres*, ed. A. Thomas (Bibl. de l'École de Chartres, Paris 1881), vol. 42. (The translations are my own.)
16 Fulbert of Chartres (d.1028), *PL* 141, col. 725B.
17 Johannes Herolt, *The Miracles of the Blessed Virgin Mary*, trans. C. C. S. Bland (Routledge, London 1928), no. 13, Theophilus, pp. 68–9.
18 Thomas Ken, Bishop of Bath and Wells, (1637–1711), *The English Hymnal* (OUP 1906), no. 217, p. 315.
19 John Donne, *Complete Poetry and Selected Prose*, ed. John Hayward (Nonesuch Press, London 1929), 'Upon the Annunciation and Passion falling upon one day, 1608', pp. 290–1.
20 Bede, *Ecclesiastical History of the English People*, ed. B. Colgrave and R. A. B. Mynors (Oxford 1969), bk. 4, cap. 18, p. 389. I owe this insight to Professor Eamonn O'Carragain, in his article, `The Annunciation of the Lord and His Passion', forthcoming.
21 A. Solzhenitsyn, *One Word of Truth* (Bodley Head, Oxford 1975).

(This paper was given at the ESBVM Oxford Congress
in August 2000)

12

Homily
given in Oriel College, Oxford
by
Bishop Edward Knapp-Fisher
18 August 2000

**Luke 1.38. Mary said, Behold the handmaid of the Lord.
Be it unto me according to Thy word.**

It is self-evident that *love* cannot coerce. You cannot force those whom you love to love you. You can only seek their freely given response. Even God who is Love cannot compel us to love and serve him. He has made us free to refuse and reject him. God's loving purpose to redeem mankind could proceed only if Mary freely agreed to be the Mother of his Son. We can say that as she pondered the extraordinary words of the divine messenger the salvation of the world hung in the balance. Never had any mere mortal been confronted by responsibility for a decision with such universal consequences. The future of the world was assured when Mary said *Yes* to God.

> Mary said, Behold the handmaid of the Lord.
> Be it unto me according to Thy word.

The vital part played by Mary in God's great work of redemption is a timely reminder that men and women, although different, are equally and infinitely loved by God, and are alike called to be workers together with him. The sexes have been created and designed not to compete but to complement one another. Both are indispensable. The Word was made flesh as a *Man*; but this would have been impossible without the freely given co-operation of a *woman*. This is a truth which needs to be reaffirmed at a time when any recognition of differences between men and women is by many regarded as being politically incorrect.

Obedience to her unique vocation demanded of Mary not only humility but courage – courage to make a blind date with God. She could not know in advance the sacrificial demands to be made upon her, of which Simeon had given some indication: 'A sword will pierce your own soul also'.

Mary's suffering reached its climax on Calvary; but the cost of her obedience must have been apparent from the time of her Son's conception. Her preconceived dream of a happy, hidden and secure family life had to be abandoned; her condition had to be explained to her husband-to-be. The gossip in Nazareth about her pre-marital pregnancy – still, then, a scandal – can well be imagined. We may get a hint of this in the taunt of her Son's enemies recorded by St John: 'We were not born of fornication'. (John 8.15.)

Confronted by the demands of her vocation, Mary went to visit her cousin. This is entirely understandable. It is always a relief to talk to someone whose experience is similar to one's own. Elizabeth, too, had been called to play a part, a minor one of course compared with Mary's, in God's great work of salvation. Called to conceive a child when well past the usual age for childbearing, Elizabeth, too, must have been the subject of gossip and ridicule. Their time together must have been greatly to the mutual comfort and benefit of the cousins.

Your vocation and mine fade into insignificance compared with that of our Lady. We are but minute fragments in the great mosaic of God's loving design for the salvation of the world. Yet each one of us has been created and equipped by God to make some particular and tiny contribution to God's ongoing work in Christ.

You and I are greatly blessed in having been enabled to know his or her vocation, to respond to it, and to find fulfilment and joy in so doing. But, alas, we are a small minority in our secularized society. It is tragic that in an age dominated by computers most people have to settle for mechanical jobs. No longer the masters of machines, they are their servants, condemned to do jobs from which they can derive neither pleasure nor satisfaction. They have no opportunity to discover, develop and use their distinctively human potentialities. They are square pegs forced into round holes. Only those who, like Mary, are faithful practising members of Christ's Church have the chance of finding and embracing their vocations; and mankind at large, as well as the lives of countless individuals, is grievously impoverished.

For us, as for Mary, God's call is often unexpected and unwanted, particularly when it upsets our own cherished dreams and preconceived plans for our lives. To us, too, God's call may come, as it did to Elizabeth, late in life; but whenever and however it comes, our response will make upon us sacrificial demands in small matters and in great. Our obedience has to be constantly reaffirmed and deepened by acts of self-sacrifice, mortification and self-discipline. This is one reason why the Church makes little impact on outsiders in our predominantly selfish and self-indulgent society. To most of our contemporaries faith in a *crucified* Lord makes neither sense nor appeal. We, too, have to be constantly on guard against infection by the prevailing spirit of our times. We do well to recall Bernard of Clairvaux's warning, that it is never possible to be 'comfortable members of a thorn-crowned Head'.

We who struggle to persevere in our vocation, however, have good grounds for encouragement. We know the truth of St Paul's assurance that 'God is faithful, and will not let you be tempted beyond your strength, but with the temptation will also provide the way of escape'. (1 Cor. 10.13.)

Furthermore, we know that the promises made by a secularized world are spurious. The prospects, prizes and pleasures of the world are ephemeral. It is self-evident that in them we can find no enduring satisfaction. It is only beyond *the changes and chances of this fleeting world* that we, dear children of our heavenly Father, can find the fullness and ultimate fulfilment of Eternal Life. *In His Will is our peace.* Heaven is our destination and our destiny.

Supreme above all the saints, unique in her character and in her vocation, Mary was immediately at death received into heaven as its Queen, for which, in the week [of Assumptiontide], we particularly give thanks. There she is seated at the right hand of her risen and ascended Son, sharing with him in his glory and redeeming work.

With him, with her, and with all the saints and the faithful throughout the ages, we worship and adore our heavenly Father as

> With angels and archangels, and with all the
> company of heaven, we praise and glorify His
> holy Name, evermore praising Him, and saying,
> Holy, Holy, Holy, Lord God of hosts,
> Heaven and earth are full of Thy glory:
> Glory be to Thee, O Lord most high.
>
> Amen.

Mary
and
councils

13

The treatment of the Holy Spirit and the Virgin Mary in the documents of Vatican II – analysis and reflection

Cecily Boulding OP

The Western church is sometimes accused of having ignored or forgotten the Holy Spirit. The medieval Western church and the post-Reformation Catholic Church is further sometimes accused of putting the Blessed Virgin Mary in the place of the Holy Spirit. An eminent Dominican ecumenist, Yves Congar, went so far as to say that 'Catholics had a tendency to replace the Holy Spirit with the Magisterium'.[1] How much truth is found in these accusations depends largely on the criteria used to assess the situation: personal spirituality, popular piety or even public liturgy may well have supported them in the past, and perhaps still often fail to reflect the official doctrine of the Catholic Church. I am not in a position to pursue research that could produce serious evidence in any of these fields; I can only survey the stated doctrines as they appear in the latest major corpus of official teaching, the documents of Vatican II. The concluding exhortation to one of these documents, the Dogmatic Constitution on the Church, *Lumen Gentium*, certainly gives some colour to such complaints.

> Let them [theologians and preachers] carefully refrain from whatever might, by word or deed, lead ... any others whatsoever into error about the true doctrine of the Church ... Let the faithful remember that true devotion consists neither in sterile or transitory affection, nor in a certain vain credulity, but proceeds from true faith ... (*LG* 67).

A quasi-official analytical index of the documents lists thirty-three themes,[2] or groups of multiple references to the nature and activity of the Holy Spirit. At least 80 of these occur in *Lumen Gentium*, and more than 180 are scattered through eight other documents. Consideration of the Blessed Virgin Mary is mainly concentrated in the final chapter of *Lumen Gentium*, and supported by occasional references in five other documents.

The Holy Spirit

The key to Vatican II's teaching on the Holy Spirit seems to be the – sadly often misused – comparison by St Augustine of the role of the Holy Spirit in the Church with that of the soul in the human body:

> Whoever has the Holy Spirit is in the Church; whoever is outside this Church does not have the Holy Spirit ... see how the human spirit, which makes me a man, holds together all the members; I command my members to move, direct my eyes to see, my ears to hear ... my feet to walk. What our spirit, our soul, is to our members, so is the Holy Spirit to the members of Christ, who are the Church.[3]

When the first draft of *Lumen Gentium* was discussed in 1962, the Council acknowledged a call, especially from liturgists and sacramentalists both inside and outside, for a more explicit and extensive pneumatology.[4] Consequently the core of its teaching on the Holy Spirit is to be found in *Lumen Gentium* and *Ad Gentes*, the Decree on the Church's Missionary Activity, but this teaching does not appear as a detailed analytical treatise, since the ecclesiology itself does not have that character. Rather it is a description of the life actually lived in and by the Church, expressed at Vatican II by the active process of the Church's reviewing and renewing itself. The pneumatology is therefore to be gathered from constant, spontaneous allusions in the texts, rather than detailed analysis of what is said on some particular occasion. One might almost echo the assertion of Johann Adam Möhler: 'The visible Church is necessary as the visible embodiment of the Spirit, who could not otherwise have any visible embodiment'.[5]

Vatican II's pneumatological ecclesiology springs from an explicitly Trinitarian approach, evident in *Lumen Gentium* articles 2, 3 and 4, where art. 4, consisting of a catena of Pauline references to the Spirit of God and the Spirit of Christ, concludes with the quotation from St Cyprian: 'The universal Church is seen to be "a people brought into unity from the unity of the Father, the Son and the Holy Spirit".'[6] Consequently an earlier, largely structural and somewhat legalistic ecclesiology gives place to a more christocentric vision of the Church, which recognizes in the Church the presence and action of the same Spirit who overshadowed Mary at the annunciation (*LG* 52, *AG* 4), who descended on Christ as he prayed, anointed him as Messiah and sent him forth (*LG* 5, *AG* 4), and who was poured out on the Apostles at Pentecost (*LG* 21, *Dei Verbum* 19–29, *AG* 4). It is the Spirit of Christ who made his own flesh living and life-giving and communicated by him (*Presbyterorum Ordinis* 5), who animates his Church.

The Lord Jesus 'whom the Father consecrated and sent into the world', makes his whole Mystical Body sharer in the anointing of the Spirit wherewith he has been anointed. (*PO* 2).

By communicating his Spirit Christ mystically constitutes as his body those brothers of his who are called together from every nation. (*LG* 7).

The Spirit does not merely dwell in the Church as in a temple; rather, he creates, or co-institutes it:

Christ lifted up from the earth, has drawn all men to himself. Rising from the dead he sent his life-giving Spirit upon his disciples and through him set up his Body which is the Church as the universal sacrament of salvation ... The promised and hoped-for restoration, therefore, has already begun in Christ. It is carried forward in the sending of the Holy Spirit and through Him continues in the Church (*LG* 48).

Firstborn of many brethren, by the gift of his Spirit, he [has] established a new brotherly communion ... of his own body, the Church (*Gaudium et Spes* 32).

Further, the Spirit sustains, enlivens and renews the Church (*LG* 4). The concept of his being the soul of the Church, already alluded to, was taken up in *Lumen Gentium* in a much more nuanced manner than was apparent in nineteenth- and twentieth-century ecclesiology:[7]

That we might be unceasingly renewed in him, he has shared with us his Spirit who, being one and the same in head and members, gives life to, unifies and moves the whole body. Consequently, his work could be compared by the Fathers to the function that the soul fulfils in the human body. (*LG* 7.)

An ecumenist from the Reformed tradition, Harding Meyer, stated succinctly that the '*opus proprium* of the Spirit is that which leads from the act of salvation in Jesus Christ to the appropriation of the act, from the *factum* to the *usus facti*'.[8] The use which the Church makes of the Holy Spirit, if we can put it like that, is extensively alluded to throughout most of the documents of Vatican II. It is apparent that he directs, fosters and energizes a whole range of functions and activities, some of which can be loosely grouped or categorized by way of example. An obvious starting-point is the role of the Spirit in teaching and enlightening. The documents point out that he is active before the visible establishment of the Church, and indeed manifests God's plan: 'The mystery not made known to other generations, but now revealed to his holy apostles and prophets in the Holy Spirit' (Eph. 3.4–6); (*DV* 17, *LG* 2, 44, 59).

He teaches and enlightens the Apostles in the first generation (*LG* 4, 21, 53; *DV* 20); he inspires their teaching (*DV* 7, 18) and accredits the tradition they transmit as truly the Word of God (*DV* 9), and so also inspires their writings (*DV* 11). He makes their successors, bishops and priests, pastors and teachers in the Church (*LG* 20, *Christus Dominus* 2, *Apostolicam Actuositatem* 23, *PO* 12). He enlightens the whole People of God so that it may penetrate and develop that tradition more fully (*DV* 8, *LG* 12), for 'to exercise faith human beings must have the interior help of the Holy Spirit' (*DV* 5; cf. also *LG* 43, 53; *DV* 7, 8, 11, 12, 21, 23; *AG* 2 and *Unitatis Redintegratio* 24). The contemporary relevance of such activity of the Holy Spirit is emphasized in the Constitution on the Church in the Modern World, *Gaudium et Spes*:

> With the help of the Holy Spirit, it is the task of the whole People of God, particularly of its pastors and theologians, to listen to and distinguish the many voices of our times and to interpret them in the light of the divine Word, in order that the revealed truth may be more deeply penetrated, better understood, and more suitably presented. (*GS* 44).

As well as enlightening, it is the Holy Spirit who stimulates a response in the members of the Church, a response alluded to in general, unspecified ways on more than thirty occasions, and very explicitly in, for instance, the Decree on the Church's Missionary Activity, *Ad Gentes*.

> The Holy Spirit calls men to Christ by the seed of the Word ... and arouses the submission of faith in their hearts ... so that, with the Holy Spirit himself opening their hearts, they can respond freely (*AG* 13, 15).

The Blessed Virgin Mary is offered as the model for this response, in the Decree on the Ministry and Life of Priests: the Blessed Virgin Mary made her total dedication under the guidance of the Holy Spirit (*PO* 18). This Spirit-inspired response is again alluded to in *LG* 25 and *DV* 5. A similarly inspired response of Hope and Charity is remarked on in *AA* 3, together with docility and obedience in *LG* 7 and *AG* 15.

The Spirit further inspires a consciousness of ecclesial responsibility in the laity (*AA* 6), as well as a variety of apostolic activities (*LG* 17, *UR* 2), missionary vocations and activity (*AG* 4, 23, 29) and the ecumenical movement (*UR* 1, 3, 24).

The Spirit adorns the Church with various gifts, both hierarchical and charismatic (*LG* 4), and so builds up its organic structure (*LG* 20, 22, *CD* 2). Thus by the Holy Spirit, 'priests are consecrated, signed with a special character and set apart' (*Optatam Totius* 2, *PO* 2 and 15); spouses too are consecrated for the vocation of marriage (*GS* 48). The lifelong practice of the evangelical counsels is prompted and sustained by the Holy Spirit, who inspires the composition and approval of rules governing this way of life (*LG* 39 and 45).

It is by the Holy Spirit that all these various structures, gifts and ministries are harmonized, throughout the ages and across the world (*Orientalium Ecclesiarum* 2; *LG* 4, 13, 49; *AG* 4).

Among these gifts of the Holy Spirit, the sacraments constitute the unique and specifying characteristic of the Church, the source and means of its power to sanctify, precisely because the Spirit is active in every sacramental celebration (cf. especially *Ad Gentes, Lumen Gentium* and *Presbyterorum Ordinis*), for 'the Father has sent Christ that the human race might be built up into one temple of the Holy Spirit' (*AG* 7).

This close association of the Holy Spirit with ecclesiology might lead to the temptation to think that the Church possesses the Holy Spirit, rather than being possessed by the Holy Spirit – a temptation not to be ignored, especially in view of the remark of Adam Möhler quoted earlier. The documents of Vatican II do indeed emphasize that it is one and the same Spirit who is present in both the Head and the members of the mystical body of Christ (*LG* 7, *GS* 45), and that he came on the Apostles 'in a definitive way' at Pentecost to make the Church manifest (*AG* 4); but they also remind us that 'He breathes where he wills' (*AA* 3, *PO* 13), that he often precedes the activity of the apostolate (*AG* 4) and that he is active outside the Church, since he opens the hearts of non-Christians and moves catechumens (*AG* 13, *LG* 4). Bishops are twice reminded that they are to 'prove' but not 'extinguish' the Spirit (*AA* 3, *LG* 12).

It is apparent that the Holy Spirit is the active principle of the entire existence, life and functioning of the Church, so much so that, as the ground of all this, he is so often taken for granted as to remain unnoticed in practice. The presence and role of the Spirit is recognized, believed and confessed, but seldom consciously 'seen', for the obvious reason that the non-incarnate third Person of the Trinity offers less scope for the imagination or to concrete devotional practices. Contrast with the flesh-and-blood woman who is Mother of God is obvious.

The Blessed Virgin Mary

Vatican II treated Mary also in an ecclesiological context. The story is well known of how, during the very radical re-shaping of the second draft of *Lumen Gentium*, the German-speaking bishops, led by Cardinal Frings, called for the inclusion there of a chapter on our Lady, rather than the composition of a separate document about her; how a group led by Cardinal Santos of Manila argued that, as Mother of the Redeemer, she was in some sense 'above the Church', only to be opposed by Cardinal König's assertion that 'she belongs to the community of the redeemed', and so her inclusion in the ecclesiology text would provide the right perspective for mariology. At that stage this proposal was approved by only a very small majority, but when the final, fifth version of the text was voted on, the dissenting minority had shrunk to a mere five votes out of the total of 2,300.

This itself was wryly seen by some as strong evidence of the presence of the Holy Spirit at the Council.[9] The decision is succinctly explained in the text of *Lumen Gentium* itself:

> This synod, while expounding the doctrine on the Church ... intends to set forth painstakingly both the role of the Blessed Virgin in the mystery of the Incarnate Word and the Mystical Body, and the duties of the redeemed towards the Mother of God, who is mother of Christ and mother of men ... It does not, however, intend to give a complete doctrine on Mary ... (*LG* 54).

The passage concludes with a neat epigram combining both the positions advanced in the argument: Mary, 'who occupies a place in the Church which is the highest after Christ and also closest to us'.[10]

Consequently most of what the Council had to say about the Blessed Virgin was concentrated in chapter 8 of *Lumen Gentium*, and while multitudinous references to her occur in other documents, many of these are devotional, illustrative or merely decorative, rather than strictly doctrinal. An analytical index lists treatment of her life, her privileges, her virtues, her relation to the Redeemer and to the Church, as also the devotion shown to her in the Catholic Church and among other Christians. There is a further long list of titles and descriptions which simply serve to illustrate how the doctrinal material is operative in liturgical cult and popular devotion.

Chapter 8 starts with a firmly credal statement: For us and for our salvation the Redeemer was incarnate by the Holy Spirit from the Virgin Mary, born of a woman that we might receive filial adoption. The mystery of salvation is revealed and continued in the Church, in which the faithful revere in the first place the memory of the ever-virgin Mother of God (*LG* 52). These truths of her virginal motherhood of God are reiterated widely in other documents – *Nostra Aetate* 3, *Sacrosanctum Concilium* 103, *DV* 25, *UR* 15 and 30, *OE* 30.

This credal summary is expanded in the terminology that has developed during the history of the Church: a rather brief allusion here, to Mary's own redemption 'in a more exalted fashion, by reason of the merits of her Son and her indissoluble link with him' (an echo of the definition of the Immaculate Conception) is repeated and expanded somewhat in the Constitution on the Liturgy, *Sacrosanctum Concilium*: 'In her the Church admires and exalts the most excellent fruit of redemption' (*SC* 103); and the point is further developed later in *Lumen Gentium*

59, when it is pointed out that she was assumed into heaven that she 'might be more fully conformed to her Son' – a passing reminder that 'the changing of our lowly body to become like his glorious body' (Phil. 3.21) will constitute the completion of salvation for all of us. (*LG* 53.)

Some implications of these beliefs are drawn out: the grace of Mary's motherhood of God means that she surpasses all creatures on earth or in heaven, but as a human being 'of the race of Adam' she is united with all who are to be saved. So she is 'clearly Mother of the members of Christ ... since she co-operates by charity in the birth of the faithful in the Church, who are members of Christ the head'.[11] She is a unique and pre-eminent member of the Church, and its type and model in faith and charity. (*LG* 54.) She is the image and beginning of the perfected Church of the world to come, and at the same time a sign of hope and comfort for the pilgrim People of God on earth. (*LG* 68.)

There follows a slightly more detailed survey of Mary's function in the plan of salvation. References are culled from the Old and New Testaments to the gradually emerging figure of the Mother of the Redeemer, a process justified by allusion to the concept of 'salvation history', and the acknowledged practice of reading earlier scriptural texts in the light of later ones. Four specific images are cited: the woman foreshadowed in the Genesis 3 condemnation of the serpent; the virgin who will bring forth Emmanuel prophesied by Isaiah; the *Anawim*, those poor and lowly folk who confidently wait for the Lord; and the symbolic daughter of Sion in whom the new economy is established in reality when God's Son takes flesh from her. (*LG* 55.)

The significance, willed by God, of Mary's free consent is asserted in contrast with Eve, whose free choice brought death whereas Mary's brings life, and this is used as the basis for description of some of her privileges and virtues. Since Mary brought into the world the life that renews all things, she is enriched with the gifts appropriate to such a role. Full of grace, her free and wholehearted consent was unimpeded by any sin – doctrines here supported by quotation from half a dozen patristic works, from which is deduced the perception that, being by the grace of Almighty God totally devoted to the work of her Son, with and under him, she served the mystery of redemption not merely passively but by her free co-operation. (*LG* 56.)

This theme is illustrated by allusion to the few recorded Gospel incidents concerning Mary. The visitation, Bethlehem, the magi and the shepherds, the presentation and loss of Christ in the temple, summarize her life during Christ's hidden years. (*LG* 57). Common belief in the effectiveness of her intercession is associated with Cana; her own pilgrimage and advance in faith is related to Christ's response about his true relatives being those who hear the word of God and keep it, and her loving consent to his redemptive sacrifice is presumed from her presence at the foot of the cross, where she is given as Mother to the Beloved Disciple, and by implication to all the rest of Christ's disciples. (*LG* 58.) It is perhaps worth noting that, beyond the actual scriptural allusions, this section of the text is supported exclusively by references to Pius XII's 1943 encyclical on 'The Mystical Body', in contrast with manifold patristic references elsewhere, but it does undoubtedly summarize beliefs which are enshrined in common and widespread forms of devotion, themselves an expression of tradition.

It is seen as highly significant that Mary was apparently among the Apostles devoting themselves to prayer before Pentecost, when God definitively manifested and established the Church with the outpouring of the Holy Spirit (cf. also *LG* 21, *DV* 19–20, *AG* 4). (*LG* 59.)

This assertion of Mary's active co-operation in the plan of redemption provoked criticism even during the Council, and is consequently here followed by a careful statement of Christ's unique mediatorship. There is no intrinsic necessity about Mary's salutary influence, which is entirely the result of God's free disposition – as is the entire plan of the incarnation; Mary's influence depends entirely on Christ's merits and sovereign mediation. The point is further explained by reference to the analogy of the mediating role and effect of human priesthood in the Church, both lay and ordained, as a share in Christ's unique priesthood. The same theme is developed somewhat in the Decree on the Life and Ministry of Priests already mentioned (*PO* 18). Mary is cited as an example of docility to God's grace precisely because, guided by the Holy Spirit, she made a total dedication of herself to the mystery of human redemption, and so became mother of the eternal High Priest, a fact which is the basis of her title 'Queen of Apostles' and ground for priestly devotion to her. (*LG* 60–1.)

Consideration of how she co-operated with God's plan during her earthly life leads on to the teaching that she is mother of the human race in the order of grace, epitomized in the statement that her maternal role, initiated at the annunciation, continues uninterrupted until the eternal fulfilment of all the elect. The unstated ground for this is, of course, that the incarnation – and so all its implications – is the unique mode by which salvation is extended to all human beings.

Specific points made here are that her role does not cease with her assumption into heaven, that the cause of her activity is her 'charity' in the fullest sense of that word, and the means of her influence is her intercession of which the Church makes use by invocation. In this context there is some, limited and incomplete, discussion of the various titles applied to her, particularly those of Advocate, Helper, Benefactress and Mediatrix, with a repeated caveat about the unique mediatorship of

Christ. Mary's essentially subordinate role is proffered as a means of more intimate adherence to the Redeemer and Mediator. (*LG* 62.)

Mary's union with her Son unites her to the Church, of which she is a 'type' in faith and charity. She is also an exemplar of the Church in her virginal motherhood, since the Church should similarly regenerate and nourish believers by unadulterated faith. The fact that Mary's Son was to be the firstborn among many brothers (Rom. 8.29) provides ground for re-emphasizing her co-operation in the generation and formation of the faithful, for the maternal Church brings forth by preaching and baptism children who are conceived by the Holy Spirit and born of God to eternal life. (*LG* 63–4.)

In Mary the Church has already reached that perfection towards which the rest of the faithful still strive; stimulated to imitate her virtues, they are led to meditate more deeply on the incarnation, for her place in the history of salvation makes her a kind of synthesis of the main doctrines of the faith, and so directs the attention of the faithful to the sacrifice of her Son and the love of the Father. (*LG* 65.) *Sacrosanctum Concilium* emphasizes that this is the purpose of her liturgical cult. (*SC* 103.) The history of this cult is here summarized, starting with the Council of Ephesus' definition of *theotokos*, and its essential difference from the cult of adoration offered to the Trinity and the Incarnate Word is emphasized. Forms of piety which have been officially approved, on grounds of sound and orthodox doctrine and suitability for the natural human characteristics of different times and places, are commended in order that, while the Mother is honoured, the Son may be rightly known, loved, glorified and obeyed. (*LG* 66.)

Theologians and preachers are strongly urged to refrain equally from exaggeration or niggardliness in treating of the special dignity of the Mother of God. Study of Scripture, patristics and the Church's liturgy will lead to the correct illustration of Mary's role and privileges, which always refer to Christ, the source of all truth, holiness and piety. As we have already noted, they are urged to refrain from any word or deed which could mislead others about the teaching of the Catholic Church, and all should remember that true devotion proceeds from true faith, not merely vain credulity or transitory affection. (*LG* 67.)

The Council's Decree on Ecumenism, *Unitatis Redintegratio*, rejoices in the conspicuous honour paid to the Blessed Virgin by the Orthodox churches, and suggests that this could be a point of ecumenical contact (*UR* 15), while the Decree on the Eastern Catholic Churches, *Orientalium Ecclesiarum*, recommends that her intercession should be sought for the healing of the East–West schism (*OE* 30). *Lumen Gentium* extends this with reference to the fact that the Mother of God is honoured by all Christians, and suggests that she should be invoked in the efforts towards unity among all God's people, to the glory of the Most Holy Trinity. (*LG* 68.)

In the teaching of Vatican II the obvious link between the Holy Spirit and the Blessed Virgin Mary is their ecclesiological context, but the deeper reality that this signifies is surely their relationship as cause and result. This is further apparent from the fact that the treatment of the Holy Spirit is mainly supported by scriptural references, while that of Mary relies much more heavily on patristic works.[12]

In Mary we see the tangible fruit of the Spirit's activity, and so grasp and appreciate it more easily. In the study, liturgy and devotion concerning Mary we see the Church actually contemplating that activity in practice, contemplation which should of course constantly lead back to contemplation of the source of her sanctification – and ours – the action of the Spirit of God. If it does not, if we too often stop at the attractive outward manifestation and do not reach further back to the cause, this is not the fault of the Church's official teaching, though it may sometimes be rightly blamed on her official teachers.

Notes

1 Y. M. Congar, *Je Crois en L'Esprit Saint* (Cerf, Paris 1979), vol. 1, p. 212.

2 Vatican *Editio Typica*, 1966.

3 St Augustine, *Sermo* 268.2.

4 e.g. A. M. Charue, 'Le Saint Esprit dans *Lumen Gentium*' in *Ecclesia a Sancto Spiritu edocta: Homage à Mgr Gerard Philips*.

5 'Karl der Grosse und seine Bischofe: Die Synod von Mainz in Jahre AD 813' in *Theologische Quartalschrift* (1824).

6 St Cyprian, *De Orat. Dom.* 23.

7 Cf. Leo XIII, *Divinum Illud Munus*, 1897, and Pius XII, *Mystici Corporis Christi*, 1943.

8 Harding Meyer, 'A Protestant Attitude' in *Concilium* no. 128.

9 Paul Bernier, '*Lumen Gentium* Fifteen Years After' in *Emmanuel*, October 1979.

10 Cf. Paul VI, *Allocution to the Council*, 4 December 1963 (*AAS* 56, 1964) p. 37.

11 St Augustine, *De Sac. Virg.* 6.

12 St Peter Canisius, Ephesus, Chalcedon, Nicea II, Trent, Constantinople I and II; St Augustine, Germanus of Constantinople; Anastasius of Antioch, Andrew of Crete; St Sophronius, St Irenaeus, St Epiphanius; St Jerome, St Cyril of Jerusalem, St John Chrysostom; St John Damascene, First Council of the Lateran, St Leo the Great; St Ambrose, St Modestus of Jerusalem; ps.Peter Damian, Geoffrey of St Victor, Gerhoch of Reichersburg, St Bede, Isaac of Stella (a total of twenty-seven).

(This paper was given at the ESBVM Leeds Congress in August 1998)

14

Evangelization, Mary and the 'Suenens Amendment' of *Lumen Gentium* 8

Marie Farrell RSM

The decade of evangelization called for by Pope John Paul II fittingly marked the close of the twentieth century. It would seem to be appropriate, therefore, that as members of the Ecumenical Society of the Blessed Virgin Mary, we remember the contribution made by Cardinal Joseph Suenens to the text of chapter 8 of *Lumen Gentium* concerning the role of the Blessed Virgin Mary in the evangelizing activity of the Church.[1] In so doing, explicit consciousness will not be lost concerning the need to carry forward resolutions affecting a handing on of the Good News of Christ across the threshold into this twenty-first century.

Before addressing the theme of Mary and the evangelizing mission of the People of God, I should like to recall a visit to Salisbury Cathedral arranged during the Winchester Congress in 1991. I can still experience my surprise in passing through a narrow archway and being surrounded by an expanse of exceedingly green 'pasture' land – so green, it was explained, because the cathedral was one of those remarkable architectural structures 'floating' on beds of river gravel; certainly amazing for an Australian! An even greater surprise was in store when, at a little distance from the entrance to the historic precincts, just as the pathway began to curve towards the great door of the cathedral, I encountered Elizabeth Frink's *Walking Madonna*. Since 1981 she has, I am sure, happily excited many visitors like myself with her startling modernity in such an ancient setting.

I remember needing to separate myself from the main group for some moments of personal time in order to 'take in' this life-sized bronze of Mary. She is not particularly beautiful – quite unlike many of the other idealized representations met during excursions to various Ladye-shrines in England. In fact she is rather 'angular', initially unattractive even, as she steps out so forthrightly away from the cathedral and into the world of the future. Her shoulders are squared; her arms have a decidedly resolute swing and her head a determined tilt. I return often to the photos taken on that day to recapture a conviction that, for *this* Mary, there is urgent need to be 'out there'... Elizabeth Frink has left comment on her own intent in creating this Mary-figure which she described as: 'Walking with purposeful compassion as a member of the community of the Risen Christ to bring love where love is absent.'[2] I am suggesting that the *Walking Madonna* of Salisbury symbolizes the Church, the eschatological family of Christ bent, in love, upon the task of evangelization, of carrying forward the Good News of salvation into this new millennium.

The following considerations are offered in order to stimulate theological reflection concerning the pastoral implications connected with interpreting Mary as model, exemplar and symbol of the Church in its apostolic outreach. Any naming of precise implications is necessarily tentative, given the virtual silence of the Scriptures about Mary. However, Cardinal Suenens has certainly thrown down a challenge that this be continuous work in progress. In taking up the challenge this Society is not alone. We engage with a number of contemporary liberation theologians and feminist writers who also are working to reconstruct an authentically contemporary Marian theology inclusive of pastoral praxis.

Mary, exemplar of evangelization

It was on 29 October 1964 that a Vatican council reporter announced that Cardinal Joseph Suenens had insisted upon an addition to the text of *Lumen Gentium* 8:65.[3] What were to become the closing sentences of *LG* 65 were read aloud in the council assembly:

> The Church, therefore, in its apostolic work also, rightly looks to her who gave birth to Christ, who was thus conceived by the Holy Spirit and born of a virgin, in order that through the Church he could be born and increase in the hearts of the faithful. In her life the Virgin was a model of that motherly love with which all who join in the church's apostolic mission for the regeneration of humanity should be animated.

Contrary to custom disallowing the names of those responsible for amendments in conciliar documents from being divulged, these sentences just quoted have become known as the 'Suenens Amendment'. Their inclusion in the final text was achieved only after vigorous resistance. As early as 4 December 1963, Suenens had signalled the need for an explicit reference to Mary in the context of the Church's mission. On that day his speech had been greeted with applause as he declared:

> This one thing I underline: at the end of our whole exposition let us raise our eyes to the Blessed Virgin Mary who is the most eminent member, the type and the mother of Christ's Church, indeed the most perfect exemplar accord-

ing to which all the faithful should exercise their apostolic activity for the glory of the Lord.[4]

On 17 September 1964, Suenens reiterated this theme:

> The schema fails ... in an omission of the greatest importance. For nowhere in the text does the bond appear between Mary's spiritual maternity and the *apostolate of evangelization* [emphasis mine] of the world ... So intimate is the bond between Mary's motherhood and today's evangelization ... I ask, therefore, that this bond be clearly indicated, so that Mary not only be an example to be admired, but also that the faithful of Christ be invited to associate themselves actively in some way to her spiritual maternity. If this is omitted, I fear that our schema will have none or little of the practical, vital and pastoral influence that we all wish for it.[5]

Objections to the amendment fell into three categories: (i) that the love motivating apostolic activity in the Church should be understood as originating *only* from the mission of Christ as Son proceeding from the Father rather than from Mary's maternal love; (ii) that not all apostolic activity – especially that of males – should be associated with maternal love; (iii) there was a certain controversy about the idea that Christ's conception and birth of the Holy Spirit and Mary was in order 'to be born and grow in the hearts of the faithful'. The Commission working on the 'Suenens Amendment' failed to be convinced by the objections raised. In particular it was noted that texts such as Gal. 4.9 (Paul's giving birth to his people) and Matt. 32.37 (Jesus' image of the hen and her chicks) testified to association of a maternal context and males. As for the Church's motherhood being modelled on Mary's, it was noted that this patristic idea dating from Origen had already been incorporated into Arts. 53 and 63 of *Lumen Gentium* 8.

In adopting the 'Suenens Amendment' the Council emphasized the mission of the Church *ad extra* – a focus to be expanded in *Gaudium et Spes* and taken up also in the decree on the Apostolate of the Laity.[6] Of significant importance was the stress that in its evangelizing mission, the Church does indeed promote Christ's 'birth' in human hearts. Pope Paul VI expressed a similar sentiment when in concluding *Evangelii Nuntiandi* (celebrating the tenth anniversary of the close of Vatican II) he prayed: '*May she [i.e. Mary] be the Star of the evangelization ever renewed which the Church, docile to her Lord's command, must promote and accomplish, especially in these times which are difficult but full of hope!'*[7]

The 'Suenens Amendment' is no mere postscript to *LG* 8:65; it has the dynamic quality of a punchline. Mary is presented as the one who even now enjoys the full fruition of her pilgrimage of faith. Here, for the only time in chapter 8, she is named *Beatissima* rather than *Beata* with the implication that she is pre-eminent among all those others who are Blessed in the Reign of God. The Church can, therefore, turn to Mary as it 'continually progresses in faith, hope and charity, seeking and doing the will of God in all things'. Still on pilgrimage and not yet glorified, the Church can, as indicated by Suenens in his speech of September 1964, be associated proactively with the spiritual maternity of Mary as it engages in an evangelization marked by active love, *caritas*.[8]

Mary, discipleship and evangelization

In retrospect we can recognize how the presentation of Mary in *LG* 8:65 has helped inspire the subsequent paradigm of discipleship in interpreting the Blessed Virgin. Contemporary studies of the theology of Mary have demonstrated another trajectory also 'seeded' – namely, the essential interconnectedness between the theology of Mary and pneumatology. These two trajectories meet and embrace as we consider Mary as the exemplar of evangelization.

For me, Frink's *Walking Madonna* is undoubtedly a Lukan madonna. Luke's understanding of the role of the Holy Spirit in the evangelizing activity of Christ's disciples suits us well in relating Mary's spiritual maternity to the apostolic activity of the Church.

Luke's entire theology is pervaded with pneumatology. In summary, the Lukan rubric of disciple-ministry in the Spirit-filled community inaugurated at Pentecost would need to include the following features:[9] that Christ Risen is present among the communion of disciples in and through the Holy Spirit who enables their witnessing to him in all aspects of mission (Luke 24.49 and Acts 1.8); that just as Jesus' mission was effected in the Holy Spirit, so the same Spirit catalyses and directs the evangelizing mission of the Church (Acts 1.5) as it proclaims the gospel in word and loving service through sacramental and pastoral ministry; that the Spirit empowers the Church by enabling 'boldness' (*parresia*) in the face of adversity and suffering for the sake of the gospel (Acts 4.13, 29, 31; 9.16, 27 etc.); that the Spirit fosters *communio* among all peoples in a dynamic and continuous manner (Acts 10.34); that anointed by the Spirit as Jesus was, every disciple will champion the causes of right and justice without compromise (Acts 2.44 ff) and that the Spirit's presence in the world by virtue of the mystery of the incarnation occasions experiences of joy and peace (Luke 2.10, 14).

In the Lukan scheme, Mary's call to discipleship occurs within the narrative of annunciation (Luke 1.26–8). Here, in faith and under the shadow of *Shekinah*, Mary's single-hearted and generous *fiat* enabled incarnation of the Word. Such a grace could not be contained. Immediately, Luke tells, Mary went *with haste* into the hill country to be with Elizabeth and Zachary. We know the story well and celebrate the mystery with every singing of Mary's Magnificat. As a very first consequence of Mary's 'visitation' Luke reveals:

> ... a mystery of sharing communion and, most important[ly], of publicising and evangelising. It connects intimacy with God and service to others; it binds vocation and mission into one call; it also proclaims the inversion of earthly values and circumstances, the beginning of a new order of reality, the revolution of love and liberation in the name of love.[10]

Under the action of the Spirit the Lukan Mary is essentially one of those disciples who in the eschatological family of Jesus hears the word, receives it in faith, discerns it carefully, wrestles with it prayerfully, resonates to it joyfully and acts upon it wholeheartedly. A particular 'signature mark' of Mary's character in Luke's infancy narrative is her independence and self autonomy – a feature so different from the Matthean presentation where Joseph initiates major decisions and Mary is passively dependent upon him. Here, she sets out for the hill country without consultation with others, and in proclaiming the Magnificat demonstrates her solidarity with the tradition of dauntless women like Hannah, Judith, Miriam and the mother of the Maccabees.[11]

In this context of evangelization it is noteworthy that Luke's last explicit mention of Mary is with Jesus' followers as they await Pentecost (Acts 1.14). The Spirit who constituted the incarnation of the Word in the womb of Mary here constitutes the Church. Mary, then, becomes both image and exemplar of the Church as it hastens into its own hill country to act out its own Magnificat.

Discerning today's hill country

Since every expression of ecclesial evangelization must of necessity be inculturated, it is virtually impossible to set clear boundaries for its effectiveness in different parts of the world. For our purposes here I propose that one helpful way of proceeding is to follow guidelines drawn up for the Church in Africa when evangelization was a major topic during the 1994 Synod of the Resurrection.[12] Five headings were used: Proclamation, Inculturation, Dialogue, Justice and Peace, and the Means of Social Communication. Each of these areas is fraught with 'hills' (usually 'mountains'!) to be razed for the spread of the gospel of Christ by the Spirit-filled 'cloud of witnesses' with Mary in its midst. Some brief comment ...

Proclamation concerns life in Christ; it is about experiencing the love of Christ poured forth in our hearts by the Holy Spirit (Rom. 5.5). If the force of the 'Suenens Amendment' is allowed to penetrate ecclesial consciousness, then proclamation of the entire paschal mystery will involve being aware of the interrelatedness of the various aspects of the Christian mystery including its Marian dimension. Evangelization implies commitment to truth. As I see it, part of today's 'hill country' is the expansion of those fundamentalist sects whose pseudo-evangelism issues us a clear imperative concerning the hermeneutical enterprise of theologians and pastors. Foundational to evangelization is surely our proclamation of the *truth* of the Word as revealed and doing so in such a manner that it be accepted as relevant to people facing the exigencies of a new millennium. With Mary hastening into hill country, we are agents of the Spirit incarnating the Word, drawing out its *sensus plenior* and quickening Christ in the hearts and minds of those hearing this Word.

Inculturation involves so many aspects of the concrete realities of Christian life – anthropological, pastoral, political, juridical, liturgical, theological ... The *magisterium* of the Catholic Church acknowledges the absolute need for re-thinking, re-formulating and re-presenting the faith in a way vital to every culture.[13] However, movement from theory to praxis is always slow – something which is not necessarily bad as long as steady progress is happening. I agree very much with a comment of Claude Geffre:

> The inculturation of christianity is a task that has to be approached gradually and tentatively. It cannot be entrusted exclusively to theologians, moralists, historians or specialists of any kind. It has to take place in the everyday existence of the christian community. In the many different exchanges of family and social life, christians can show that it is possible to reconcile their christian identity with their ethnic, cultural, linguistic and national identity.[14]

Of course, the primary agent of inculturation is the Holy Spirit.

Dialogue as an enterprise of evangelization is extremely complex. While structured, formal dialogue between both Christian and non-Christian confessions is generally well in place, informal dialogue is equally a vehicle for evangelization. The Ecumenical Society of the Blessed Virgin Mary has achieved a great deal in this respect. In recognizing Mary as sign of unity among the churches, the Society has adopted another madonna as symbol. She is the work of Jacob Lipschitz and stands in the cloister of St Mary's Abbey on Iona. The inscription reads: '*I a Jew, faithful to the faith of my fathers, have made this Virgin for goodwill among all people, that the Spirit may reign.*' Astonishingly, this image depicts Mary as blind; blind too are the images of the lamb and the three angels. Only the Holy Spirit whose dove-wings enclose the Virgin can remove the blindness so that entirely fresh new vision may contemplate the mystery of Christ in the world.

Cardinal Suenens comes to mind again here. His frequent focus at ESBVM congresses was on the mystery of the Annunciation and its implications for the dialogue between the Church and the world. While one of his major works, *The Theology of the Apostolate* (1953) is now dated in many respects, his emphasis there on the active role of Mary with the Holy Spirit in spreading the Word remains forever valid.

Working for **justice and peace** is filled with tension and ambiguity even as Christians are committed to 'assisting the birth of ... liberation, of giving witness to it, of ensuring that it is complete.'[15] There is tension surrounding contemporary liberation theologies and praxis methods of evangelization; tension, too, between the biblical idea of eschatological fulfilment when justice and peace will have embraced in love (Ps. 85.10) and divisions experienced on many levels: human–divine, human–human and human–cosmic. Surely the disciple–love of Mary is significant as ecclesial men and women try to witness to divine love in those many pastoral experiences of apparent hopelessness, lovelessness and meaninglessness.

An 'experiment' suggested some years ago by Gerald O'Collins[16] inviting reflection on love (instead of hope) as an hermeneutic for approaching eschatology may have application here in view of the connection between evangelization and realized eschatology. While the author leaves much unsaid in his analysis of the work of the Holy Spirit as Love at work in the world, he prompts the reader to engage in imaginative ways for being involved in the process. One way to proceed might be to explore an ecclesio-marian theme; to relate the faith pilgrimage of Mary to that of the Church as it works towards justice and peace in seeking to counteract racism, sexism, violence, ecological destruction and all those failures experienced in social and ecclesial structures serving to obstruct messianic *shalom*. The eschatological mystery of Mary's assumption is the fulfilment of the dream of righteousness proclaimed in the Magnificat. This mystery signifies that all people have the right to be treated according to their full human dignity and that everyone is destined for 'glory' in an ultimate communion of Love. Likewise, the assumption acknowledges the worth of the entire created universe; it reflects concern for harmony in relationships between the human family (irrespective of race, gender or creed) and cosmic processes. In its evangelizing outreach, the Church draws energy from Mary-in-glory who within the total communion of saints, personifies the Spirit-ualized destiny of humanity. Confident in her intercessory role before God, the Church can rely on Mary's influence in achieving justice and peace in the world.

It is well over twenty years since *Evangelii Nuntiandi* (n. 451) stressed the urgency of using the mass media as a **means of social communication** and an important method of evangelizing. At this point I shall merely raise the question as to how seriously the various churches have taken the potential of media communication in breaking open the Word not only for first-time hearers but especially for people who have found the 'old' Word lacking in spiritual nourishment.

Feminist retrieval of Mary and evangelization

In the face of dehumanizing and unjust societal structures, theological approaches to evangelization are increasingly using methods which allow the voices of victims to be heard and be related to the scandal of the cross. This, of course, is not to encourage passive acceptance of victimhood but so that transformative action on the part of the Church will overturn obstacles to experiences of the compassionate love of God. Feminist theologians who are attempting to recover the 'real Mary', freed from patriarchal accretions which have too often idealized her in an exaggerated manner, are encouraging others to reach out to people who are experiencing marginalization and injustice.[17] Retrieval of an authentic Marian tradition means that the gospel of mutuality, reciprocity and autonomy within relationships is set over against domination, militarism, hostility and global warfare.[18]

Useful categories being brought to a reconstructed theology of Mary are those of 'memory', 'narrative' and 'solidarity'.[19] The Church remembers Mary in its biblical narratives; it experiences solidarity with her in struggling towards the reign of God. Mary is remembered as someone insignificant in her own right, as belonging to a people oppressed by occupying forces of a foreign power, as an 'outsider' in company with Tamar, Ruth, Rahab and Bathsheba (Matt. 1.1–16) but as someone brought to the centre stage of salvation history in the *economia* of God. She is remembered too within the passion of Jesus as closely victimized by the violence of his torture and death; she is remembered as a prophetic figure proclaiming the justice of God and doing so as a woman.

In each of these memories Mary stands alongside the oppressed in one way or another – with the publicly powerless; with those disparaged by society; with those who mourn murdered innocent children; with those who have suffered because of the 'system'. The memory of Jesus is borne by the Church as a 'dangerous' memory; our task is to stimulate salvific action to overcome the debilitating effects of sinfulness and evil. Within the memory of Jesus, the memory of Mary is moving the Church to transformative action in the 'hill country' of history. The catholic dogmas of Mary's freedom from 'original' sin and of her assumption into glory declare a faith that, because of the gracious self-giving of a loving God, Life will ultimately prevail over forces of death and evil. While the essential meaning of Mary leads inevitably into mystery, we acknowledge nevertheless that:

> [h]er intimate place in the christian pattern enables us to imagine a healed, reconciled [and] finally transformed world. While it is God who works human salvation in Christ, and the Spirit who inspires the active response of the church, it is Mary who is the sign of the final transformation of the world.[20]

Praxis-oriented theologies (including feminist theology) support an important cutting edge of contemporary evangelization. *If* a 'marian' evangelization is marked with the presence of love struggling actively in history, *if* it is sufficiently dynamic then 'liberationalist' movements should eventually disappear.

Conclusion

The 'Suenens Amendment' explicitly links the evangelizing mission of the Church and the Blessed Virgin Mary. It insists that these two belong together and that in witnessing to Christ under the power of the Holy Spirit, Mary is existentially involved. We might well ask, 'How exactly?' How can Mary's past involvement in the economy of salvation translate into present tense? How can she be more that an iconic ideal for the Church? In the past there was a catholic custom of 'having recourse' to Mary before engaging in any apostolic–evangelizing activity. I am convinced that the 'Suenens Amendment' implies much more than 'looking to Mary' as someone in whom the divine work of salvation has been fruitfully accomplished; more is intended than merely drawing inspiration from her. 'Looking to Mary' is intimately connected with experiencing her presence in the midst of the 'cloud of witnesses', alongside us as we attempt to communicate the gospel today.

Given today's resurgence of the goddess cult and the danger of misinterpreting motherhood–fertility images with regard to Mary, we might wonder whether Suenens' way of describing ecclesial activity in terms of 'spiritual maternity' is still entirely appropriate. Perhaps the language of 'sister–discipleship' nuances the meaning better for today? But, whatever the mode of formulation, Suenens' intuition about the importance of having an official statement connecting Church, Mary and evangelization is theologically sound.

A concluding word of hope. May the Salisbury Madonna mirror the Church's and our commitment to evangelization as 'walking with purposeful compassion' and as 'community of the Risen Christ' we 'bring love where love is absent'.

Finally, in the light of previous comment about inculturation of the Gospel, let me illustrate this hope as expressed in two Australian images of Mary as *Theotokos*. Both capture well the Church's call to bring Christ to birth at this time of world history.

The first, a life-sized sculpture completed in 1989, portrays Mary as a young pregnant woman moving out from her own 'place' and into the space of the wider world. The sculptor, John Elliott, has made use of two timbers – laminated beech for flesh, and pine for clothing. Mary's open, expansive hands invite contemplation of the divine largesse surrounding the mystery of incarnation. Elliott intended that Mary's right hand should express a gesture of offering while her left hand should suggest acceptance. Her large, strong right foot appears to move; its motion comes to balanced rest at the left hip.[21] An instant association recalls the prophetic words: *How beautiful upon the mountains are the feet of those who bring good tidings, who publish peace ... and salvation ...* (Isa. 52.7)

The second image is titled *Mary of Warmun*.[22] Here too is a pregnant Mary sculptured in 1983 by George Mung Mung, an aboriginal elder from the Turkey Creek community in the Kimberley region of Western Australia. Mung's work reflects both his aboriginality and his catholic faith in the Incarnation. He travelled deep into the Bungle Bungle Ranges to cut the wood for his masterpiece. Mary is presented as a young unmarried girl; traditional design markings indicate her virginity. Within the womb-shield beneath her heart, Mary carries the Christ-child who is already a man dancing with ecstatic joy. When a very old plaster image of Mary was broken because their dogs knocked over the table on which it stood, George Mung Mung promised his community to make 'a Mary who would never break'; and indeed he has ...

Notes

1 See *Australasian Record* (July 1995) for an earlier version of this paper.
2 Caption on Michael Blackman photograph.
3 For context cf. C. W. Neumann, '*Lumen Gentium* 8: Arts. 60–5' in *Marian Studies* 37 (1986), pp. 96–142.
4 For Latin text see *Patrum orationes, Acta* (iv), 226.
5 *Acta III* (i), 505.
6 *Apostolicam Actuositatem* 4, final paragraph.
7 *Evangelii Nuntiandi* (*EN*) 82.

8 Emphasis on the 'maternity' of Mary in no way detracts from contemporary theological consciousness concerning the 'maternity' of Jesus.

9 See David Bosch, 'The Lukan Missionary Paradigm' in *Transforming Mission* (Orbis Books, New York 1991), pp. 113–22.

10 See Johann G. Roten, 'Memory and Mission' in *Marian Studies* 42 (1991), p. 99.

11 See Elizabeth Johnson, 'Reconstructing a Theology of Mary' in *Mary, Woman of Nazareth* (Paulist Press, New York 1990), for further reflection on this motif.

12 See *National Catholic Media*, 9 and 11 May 1994.

13 *EN* 20.

14 *The Risk of Interpretation* (Paulist Press, New York 1987), p. 237.

15 *EN* 30.

16 'In the End Love' in *Faith and the Future*, ed. J. Galvin (Paulist Press, New York 1984), pp. 25–42.

17 e.g. Anne Carr, Anne Loades, Elizabeth Johnson, Donal Flanagan, Edward Schillebeeckx etc.

18 See Anne Carr, 'Mary in the Mystery of the Church' in C. F. Jegen ed. *Mary according to Women* (Leaven Press, Kansas City 1985), p. 29.

19 Elizabeth Johnson, 'Reconstructing a Theology of Mary', op. cit. pp 69–87.

20 Anne Carr, *Transforming Grace: Christian Tradition and Women's Experience* (Harper & Rowe, San Francisco 1988), p. 193.

21 *The Australian* (October 1991), interview with John Elliott by George Zetlin.

22 Illustrated in *The Catechism of the Catholic Church* (Geoffrey Chapman, London 1994), opposite p. 268.

(This paper was given at the ESBVM Oxford Congress in August 2000)

15

Mary in the ecumenical councils of the Church

Norman Tanner SJ

I am honoured to be invited to give this lecture, especially on this day (15 August) when Mary's assumption into heaven is celebrated by many Christians. At least the title of the talk, 'Mary in the Ecumenical Councils of the Church,' seems to fit well into the tradition of the Society. The ecumenical councils of the Church form a central strand of tradition for all Christians while the importance of Mary requires no emphasis from me – her importance both for the Christian Church as a whole and for this Society more particularly.

By the ecumenical councils I mean, in the first place, the seven councils held before the beginning of the sad schism between East and West in the eleventh century. That is to say, Nicaea I in 325, Constantinople I in 381, Ephesus in 431, Chalcedon in 451, Constantinople II and III in 553 and 680–1, and Nicaea II in 787. These seven councils are recognized as ecumenical councils – that is, councils of the whole Church, as distinct from diocesan or provincial or other local councils – by both the Orthodox and Roman Catholic Churches, generally by the Anglican Church and, when pressed, by many other Christian churches. The disputed eighth council, Constantinople IV in 869–70, need not detain us since it issued no decree touching on Mary. This lecture might, therefore, end with the seventh council, Nicaea II in 787. Yet the Church's clock cannot be stopped even when a major schism occurs. In order to trace the story down to the present, to include the full sweep of Christian history, albeit from a more limited angle, or, to put the matter another way, in order to include all the councils that have usually been regarded as ecumenical councils by one major church, the Roman Catholic Church, at least so regarded from the Counter-Reformation until recent times, I shall include the ten general councils of the Western Church in the Middle Ages, Lateran I in 1123 to Lateran V in 1512–17, and the three general councils of the Roman Catholic Church since the Reformation, Trent in 1545–63, Vatican I in 1869–70 and Vatican II in 1962–5.[1]

A word of caution is pertinent here: do not expect more from the councils than they can provide. That is to say, most of the councils were called principally to meet particular doctrinal controversies and a full treatment of Mary obviously cannot be expected from each of them. Though sometimes omissions are as significant as statements. Teaching about Mary usually comes either incidentally or when she was the subject of controversy: even in the latter case the council normally treats only of the issues in dispute, not mariology as a whole. We may also note the generally reserved or conservative nature of the councils' teaching: they say what they feel needs to be said but do not go further, into uncharted waters. Here the principle of unanimity is important. Church councils are unlike the English Parliament where a majority of one is sufficient to pass an Act. At least in the ecumenical councils unanimous consent, or virtual unanimity, has been required so that formulae have had to be found that were acceptable to all or almost all the members of the council and as a result divisive or adventurous statements have been avoided as far as possible. Within these limitations, however, the councils in question provide a precious insight into the development of understanding about Mary in the Christian tradition.

To begin with the first council of Nicaea in 325, the most striking point, at least for us today, is the omission of Mary from the creed. At the point where she might have been mentioned, the creed reads simply, 'for us humans and for our salvation he came down and became incarnate, became human ...'[2] How significant was this omission? It is an impossible question to answer precisely because no minutes or other background *acta* of the council survive – it is not clear whether they once existed and have been lost or whether in fact they were never made – and none of the subsequent accounts of the council by participants at it and by other writers mention the omission, so far as I am aware, which in itself is an indication that there is nothing noteworthy about it. When one looks at other creeds of the time, most of those from the West, including the old Roman creed, mention Mary; among the eastern creeds, some do and others do not, so since the creed of Nicaea seems based on an existing eastern creed, we may conclude, I think, that there is nothing remarkable about Mary's omission.[3] Besides the creed, the council issued twenty canons and it is not surprising, in this case in view of the disciplinary rather than the theological nature of the canons, that Mary is not mentioned in them either.

It is only in the fuller version of the creed of Nicaea, promulgated by the next ecumenical council, Constantinople I in 381, that Mary is mentioned. Here the relevant sentence runs, 'for us humans and for our salvation he came down from the heavens and became incarnate from the Holy Spirit and the virgin Mary, became human ...'[4] The reason for the inclusion of Mary is unclear. No minutes or other background *acta* of the council survive nor any account of the creed's composition by any of those who were present at the council. Indeed, the creed appears to have remained virtually unknown for seventy years until it surfaced at the council of Chalcedon in 451. An impasse was reached at Chalcedon when the creed of Nicaea seemed to many inadequate to the new situation and yet there was opposition to making alterations to it especially since the intervening council of Ephesus of 431 had forbidden any such changes. It was at this point that the archdeacon of Constantinople drew attention to the creed promulgated by the council of 381, which was based on the creed of 325 and therefore could be interpreted as in conformity with Ephesus's prohibition and yet was an improvement on that creed. The council eventually followed the archdeacon's recommendation.[5]

We can only surmise the reasons for Mary's inclusion. Chalcedon said that the one creed, formed by the two creeds of 325 and 381, 'sets out the Lord's becoming human to those who faithfully accept it' and the creed of 381 was the 'seal' of that of 325.[6] The inclusion of Mary may be seen as part of this seal and of the better setting forth of the Lord's becoming human, also perhaps a 'catching up' with other creeds of the time which did include Mary. The addition of the Holy Spirit, alongside Mary, in the work of the incarnation is more easily explained in the context of the Pneumatomachian controversy, which reached its peak shortly before the council of Constantinople in 381. The Pneumatomachi, or 'enemies of the Spirit', were accused of not according full divinity to the Holy Spirit and the much fuller treatment accorded to the Holy Spirit in the creed of 381 was a way of refuting their views.

All Christians, therefore, especially members of this Ecumenical Society, can be grateful to the archdeacon of Constantinople for his intervention which led to the acceptance of the creed of 381 and its inclusion of Mary. This creed – normally referred to simply as the Nicene creed though sometimes more precisely as the Nicene-Constantinopolitan creed – has remained to this day virtually unchanged as the main creed of the main Christian churches: with the one exception of the unfortunate addition by the Western church of the *Filioque* clause. It is a symbol of unity among Christians and, more particularly in the context of this talk, of a common and enduring devotion to Mary.

At the council of Ephesus in 431 Mary's title of Θεοτόκος, Mother of God or God-bearer, was the central issue. This is not the place to enter in detail into this controversial council especially since the paper by Professor Frances Young [*see pp. 340–54*] deals with the chief protagonist of the title, Cyril of Alexandria. The controversy was principally christological, the relationship between the divinity and the humanity in Christ, yet the implications for Christians' understanding of and devotion to Mary were profound. The title already had a long tradition in the church of Alexandria, certainly extending back to the early fourth century and perhaps earlier to Origen,[7] so that Nestorius's criticism of it seemed an attack upon an ancient tradition and devotion. The acceptance of the title by the leader of the Antiochenes, John of Antioch, in his 'Formula of Union' in 433,[8] two years after the inconclusive end of the council, led to its general acceptance by Christians, apart from the Nestorian church, and it has formed a cornerstone of devotion to Mary ever after. We may note, too, the declaration of Mary's virginity. In both John of Antioch's Formula of Union and Cyril of Alexandria's letter to John, accepting his Formula, Mary is referred to as the 'virgin' Θεοτόκος.[9]

While christological controversies continued during the next three ecumenical councils – Chalcedon, Constantinople II and III – teaching about Mary did not develop further in them. Mary's title of Mother of God had already stretched theological consensus and maybe this discouraged further developments. Chalcedon is important, however, because it established the canon or list of ecumenical councils: Constantinople I in 381, on account of its creed, was in effect raised to the level of an ecumenical council and the controversial council of Ephesus was confirmed as ecumenical.[10] Thereby the teaching of these two councils about Mary became part of the common inheritance of Christianity. Both Constantinople II and III, moreover, confirmed this earlier teaching as well as that of Chalcedon. We may note, too, the introduction of perpetuity into Mary's virginity at Constantinople II, 'the ever virgin Mary, mother of God' (*de sancta Dei genitrice et semper virgine Maria*: the council's decree survives only in a Latin translation).[11] Constantinople III, however, omits the 'ever'.[12]

The second council of Nicaea in 787, the last council generally recognized as ecumenical by both East and West, saved the artistic heritage of Christianity from the assaults of the iconoclasts. Images of Mary received particular attention in its decree:

> We decree that, like the figure of the honoured and life-giving cross, the revered and holy images, whether painted or made of mosaic or of other suitable material, are to be exposed in the holy churches of God, on sacred instruments and vestments, on walls and panels, in houses and by public ways. These are the images of our Lord, God and saviour, Jesus Christ, and of our Lady without blemish, the holy God-bearer, and of the revered angels and of any of the saintly holy men. The more frequently they are seen in representational art, the more are those who see them drawn to remember and long for those who serve as models, and to pay these images the tribute of salutation and respectful veneration.[13]

The decree went on to distinguish the 'tribute of salutation and respectful veneration' (Greek, ἀσπασμὸν καὶ τιμητικὴν προσκύνησιν) that should be paid to these images, including therefore those of Mary, from the 'full adoration' (Greek, ἀληθινὴν λατρείαν) that should be paid only to the divine nature, and concludes:

> People are drawn to honour these images with the offering of incense and lights, as was piously established by ancient custom. Indeed, the honour paid to an image traverses it, reaching the model; and whoever venerates the image venerates the person represented in that image.[14]

Of Nicaea II's decree, two other points regarding Mary may be noted. First, in the passage just quoted she is referred to as 'our Lady without blemish' (Greek, τῆς ἀχράντου δεσποίνης ἡμῶν), perhaps an anticipation of the doctrine of Mary's immaculate conception. Secondly, the decree in another place returns to the perpetual nature of Mary's virginity, she is called the 'ever virgin Mary' (τῆς ... ἀειπαρθένου Μαρίας).[15] Finally, it is perhaps fitting to remember that the decisive figure at this council, so important for the preservation of icons and other artistic aspects of devotion to Mary, was another woman, the empress Irene. As empress and regent of her young son Constantine, she effectively summoned the council, outwitted the iconoclast party at it, presided over the council and directed it in the course it eventually took, then promulgated and enforced its decrees.

When we come to the medieval councils, we are of course in a very different situation. As mentioned earlier, they are not recognized as ecumenical councils by either the Orthodox Church or the churches of the Reformation. Indeed, even within the Western church, they seem to have been regarded, at the time, as general councils of the Western church rather than as ecumenical councils. The common belief in the West was that an ecumenical council was impossible without the participation of the Eastern church: the hope was that the Schism between East and West would soon be ended and then another ecumenical council would be possible; beliefs and hopes that we now know were not to be realized.[16] The status of the medieval and later Roman Catholic councils is of great significance from an ecumenical point of view inasmuch as so many issues in dispute between the Roman Catholic Church on the one hand and the Orthodox and eastern churches and the churches of the Reformation on the other hand hang on statements made by these councils. Are they to be considered as having the same binding authority on Roman Catholics as the first seven councils? – a vital question that is reopening even within the Roman Catholic Church. For this paper, however, the issue need not concern us with regard to the medieval councils since, with one partial exception, they did not issue decrees about Mary.[17]

This absence of teaching about Mary in the medieval councils may seem surprising especially since the medieval church was later criticized, at the time of the Reformation, for encouraging too much devotion to the saints, Mary included: yet we find no such encouragement, or indeed criticism thereof, in these major councils of the Western church. To some extent this may be explained in that these councils mainly concerned themselves with church order rather than with doctrine, reversing the priorities of the councils of the early church, so that teaching about Mary is less to be expected. Devotion to Mary, moreover, seems to have flourished without the need of intervention from the ecclesiastical authorities, perhaps a good sign that this devotion was based on and well in tune with popular religion. Another point, it seems to me, is that Ephesus's declaration of Mary as the mother of God, as well as Nicaea II's defence of images, had provided a sufficiently spacious framework, both doctrinal and iconographical, for much further development to take place without the need of more official definitions. Θεοτόκος was such a strong definition that few wanted to go beyond it, as mentioned earlier. Other doctrines about Mary, such as the immaculate conception or the assumption, could remain open questions that theologians and others might debate legitimately – at least until towards the end of the Middle Ages.

The one partial and perhaps surprising exception to the silence comes from the council of Basel's definition of the immaculate conception of Mary in 1439. I say 'partial' exception because the legitimacy of the council at that time was and still is debated. That is to say, there were then two rival councils, both claiming legitimacy: first, the said council at Basel in Switzerland, which had been meeting since 1431, had constantly been at odds with the pope of the day, Eugenius IV, and as a result the majority of its members had refused to accept Eugenius's transfer of the council in 1437 to Florence, where the pope hoped to be more in control; secondly, the council at Florence comprising those who had accepted the pope's transfer. The remaining council at Basel is often regarded as an anti-council because of its opposition to the pope and it is not usually counted in the Roman Catholic Church's list of ecumenical or general councils, but since it produced the only new teaching about Mary it deserves mention here.

The doctrine of the immaculate conception, the special privilege granted by God to Mary, of being free from original sin and its effects from the moment of her conception, had come to the forefront of theological debate chiefly through its propagation by the Scottish Franciscan friar Duns Scotus in his teaching at Oxford and Paris universities in the late thirteenth and early fourteenth centuries. In the following century the debate had followed largely along the loyalties of the two orders of friars – Franciscans generally following Scotus in support of the doctrine, Dominicans largely opposing it after the example of their great theologian Thomas Aquinas – and it was theologians of the two orders who dominated the debate on the doctrine which began in the council in March 1436. Then the council was still in communion with Pope Eugenius but by the time the council reached its decision in favour of the doctrine, three and a half years later, the rupture with the pope was long a fact. The council's definition read as follows:

> We define and declare that the doctrine according to which the glorious virgin Mary, mother of God, in virtue of a singular grace of the divine will, anticipative and operative, has never been actually subject to original sin, and has always been immune from all original and actual fault, holy and immac- ulate, should be approved, held and embraced as pious and consonant with the worship of the Church, the Catholic faith, right reason and sacred Scripture; and that henceforth nobody is permitted to preach or teach the contrary.[18]

At the same time the council established Mary's Immaculate Conception as a liturgical feast to be observed by the whole Church on 8 December. Despite the uncertain status of the council, the decree proved the turning point in the fortunes of the doctrine and the papacy soon came round to supporting it, beginning with Pope Sixtus IV's constitution *Cum praeexcelsa* of 1477 and culminating with Pius IX's solemn definition in 1854.[19]

Turning now to the council of Trent (1545–63), within half a century of the beginning of the Reformation and responding to widespread crit- icisms about the practice and theology of devotion to the saints in the medieval Church, this council issued, at its final session on 3–4 December 1563, a decree entitled, 'On invocation, veneration and relics of the saints and on sacred images'. Mary is mentioned in person once but in general she appears included alongside the other saints rather than exalted separately. Noticeable, moreover, is the decree's apparent attention to the Reformers' criticisms, contrasting with the rather simple anti-Protestant image of the council that has often been given. Thus, while the decree said that 'it is good and beneficial to invoke the saints and to have recourse to their prayers and helpful assistance', this sentence leads to a Christ-centred conclusion, namely that the purpose of the prayers is 'to obtain blessings from God through his Son our Lord Jesus Christ, who is our sole redeemer and saviour'. And, in a somewhat similar vein, while the decree invoked the second council of Nicaea's defence of saints' images, it rejected any idea that 'some divinity or power is believed to lie in these images ... or anything is to be expected from them, or that confidence should be placed in images as was done by the pagans of old ... but rather the honour shown to images is referred to the original which they represent'.[20]

In its earlier decree on original sin, however, Trent had given individual treatment to Mary, singling her out as exempt from original sin and thereby confirming the doctrine of the immaculate conception. To quote the decree, it said that in its treatment of original sin it did not intend to 'include ... the blessed and immaculate virgin Mary, mother of God, but rather observance should be given to the constitutions of pope Sixtus IV' – obviously a reference to the constitution *Cum praeexcelsa* (1477) in support of the immaculate conception, mentioned above.[21] And, in a similar vein, in its decree on justification: 'If anyone says that a person can avoid all sins, even venial sins, throughout his or her life – apart from a special privilege from God such as the Church holds in the case of the blessed Virgin – let him be anathema.'[22]

After the council of Trent, the Roman Catholic Church waited over three centuries before its next general council, Vatican I in 1869–70. Vatican I's chief concern was papal infallibility and it provided directly no further teaching about Mary. Indirectly, however, the council was important because Pope Pius IX's earlier solemn declaration of the doctrine of Mary's immaculate conception, in 1854, seemed to fit clearly into the conditions for infallibility set by Vatican I. Indeed, in the opinion of what might be termed the minimalist party regarding papal infallibility, it was the only doctrine that clearly fitted within these conditions for infallibility, to be joined a century later in 1950 when Pope Pius XII declared Mary's assumption into heaven, a solemn definition that clearly invoked the conditions set by the first Vatican council. Vatican I, therefore, is important because it placed doctrines about Mary – in particular the immaculate conception and the assumption – at the centre of the debate about infallibility. That neither papal infallibility nor these Marian doctrines were accepted widely outside the Roman Catholic church tended to go hand in hand, while conversely many Roman Catholics tended to link loyalty to the papacy with devotion to these and other doctrines of Mary. In this way Mary unwittingly became a source of tension and even disunity among Christians.

Mary became quite a focus of attention at our next and last council to be considered, the second Vatican council in 1962–5. In the case of this council, too, I am spared giving a full treatment since another paper at the Congress discusses the topic in proper detail: that of Sister Marie Farrell entitled 'Evangelization, Mary and the "Suenens Amendment" of *Lumen Gentium* 8'. [*see pp. 145–55*] So here it may suffice for me to remind you of the main outlines. The decade or so before the beginning of the council had been a time of heightened interest in Mary in the Roman Catholic Church. There had been the declaration in 1950 by Pope Pius XII of Mary's assumption into heaven, as mentioned, and there was pressure for further titles and doctrines about Mary, notably Mary as the mother of the Church and Mary as mediatrix of all graces. At the devotional level, too, this interest was manifested in, for example, the continuing popularity of various Marian shrines, notably Lourdes in France and Fatima in Portugal, as well as a continuing expansion in the number and size of institutions and activities under the patronage of Mary.

Initially the proposal at the council was that there should be a separate decree on Mary and indeed such a decree was drafted by the preparatory commission of the council. However, the separate nature of this decree, as well as its contents, became a source of division between the conservative minority and the progressive majority at the council. (I am oversimplifying with the labels 'conservatives' and 'progressives', I realize, but I cannot think of any more accurate terms: certainly there were the two basic groupings at the council. But for the sake of convenience, I shall henceforth call the conservative party the As and the progressives the Bs.) Most of the As wanted this separate decree on Mary: many of them wanted it to include Mary's title of mother of the Church, and some also that of mediatrix of all graces. Most though not all the leaders of the Bs, on the other hand, argued that Mary should be seen as a model and archetype of the Church, not separate from it, and therefore the treatment of Mary would be much better as part of the decree on the Church rather than in a separate decree, especially since the decree on the Church (usually referred to by its opening words *Lumen Gentium*), was meant to be the most important document of the whole council. Most Bs, moreover, were against the declaration of any further titles for Mary as being of doubtful theological validity, or at least open to misunderstanding, and as detrimental to ecumenical relations with other Christian churches – an aspect of the council that was becoming increasingly important.

Sometimes the division has been portrayed as one between Marian maximalists, the As, and minimalists, the Bs. But this is misleading, rather the difference of opinion concerned the nature of Mary's role: a debate about quality not quantity, if you like. To cut a long story short, the Bs gained the support of the majority. Mary was not accorded a separate decree: rather the eighth and last chapter of the decree on the Church was dedicated to her, and the debated titles of mother of the Church and mediatrix of all graces were not mentioned in the chapter: though significantly Pope Paul VI referred to Mary as Mother of the Church in his concluding address to the council at the end of the session in which the decree was approved; and there is a more general reference to Mary as mediatrix as follows:

> The blessed Virgin is invoked in the church under the titles of advocate, helper, benefactress and mediatrix. This, however, must be understood in such a way that it takes away nothing from the dignity and power of Christ the one mediator, and adds nothing on to this.[23]

On the other hand, it is a full chapter, the longest of the eight chapters into which the decree is divided, and constitutes the longest and most comprehensive treatment of Mary in any of the councils we have been looking at. There is, too, a genuine attempt to include some of the theological and devotional riches of the eastern churches regarding Mary as well as the proper cautions of the churches of the Reformation. The chapter is entitled, 'The blessed virgin Mary, mother of God, in the mystery of Christ and the Church,' and the headings of the five sections into which the chapter is divided give some further idea of the contents: 1. Introduction. 2. The role of the blessed Virgin in the economy of salvation. 3. The blessed Virgin and the Church. 4. The cult of the blessed Virgin in the Church. 5. Mary, the sign of sure hope and comfort for the pilgrim people of God.[24] [For a proper unfolding of the chapter's treasures, see pp. 145–55].

So here this paper draws to a close. We have traversed a long period of time, from the fourth to the twentieth centuries and councils are, of course, only a limited aspect of the Church's history and teaching. In a sense they are better seen as special moments in the Church's history rather than as forming an institution with a continuous history. Even in the first millennium AD, before the schism between East and West, much of the interest in Mary, both theological and devotional, was not reflected in the ecumenical councils. After the schism we have been looking at the tradition of the Western church and then of the Roman Catholic Church, so that we have been missing the contributions of other Christian churches. Still, we have accompanied one group of sailors throughout the voyage, so to speak, and it may be consoling to think that the fullest and most ecumenically sensitive treatment of Mary in all the councils we have been considering came in the Roman Catholic Church's most recent general council, Vatican II, a council of our own time.

Notes

1 References to the conciliar decrees below are taken from N. Tanner (ed.), *Decrees of the Ecumenical Councils*, 2 vols. with continuous pagination (London, Sheed & Ward; Washington USA, Georgetown University Press 1990), = *Decrees*.

'Synod' (Greek, σύνοδος) and 'council' (Latin, concilium) are synonymous terms, though recently a distinction has been introduced in Roman Catholic canon law (formalized in the 1983 revised Code of Canon Law, canons 342–8), between 'ecumenical councils' (such as Vatican II), which have executive and legislative powers, and 'synods of bishops', which may be consulted by the pope and have only an advisory role. In this paper 'council' will be used throughout since it is the more usual word in English.

For the list of councils recognized as ecumenical by the Roman Catholic Church and for earlier and recent discussion of this list within the church, see N. Tanner, *Councils of the Church: A Short History* (Crossroad USA, forthcoming).

2 *Decrees*, p. 5.
3 J. N. D. Kelly, *Early Christian Creeds* (3rd edn., London 1972), chapters 4–7.
4 *Decrees*, p. 24.
5 R. P. C. Hanson, *The Search for the Christian Doctrine of God: The Arian Controversy 318–81* (Edinburgh 1988), pp. 812–13; J. N. D. Kelly, *Early Christian Creeds* (3rd edn., London 1972), pp. 296–301.
6 *Decrees*, pp. 83–4
7 M. Starowieyski, 'Le titre θεοτόκος avant le concile d'Ephèse', in E. A. Livingstone (ed.), *Studia Patristica*, 19 (Louvain 1989), pp. 136–42; *Dictionnaire de Théologie Catholique* (Paris 1903–50), tome 9, part 2, cols. 2351–4.
8 *Decrees*, pp. 69–70.
9 *Decrees*, pp. 69–74.
10 *Decrees*, pp. 83–5.
11 *Decrees*, p. 113.
12 *Decrees*, p. 127.
13 *Decrees*, pp. 135–6.
14 *Decrees*, p. 136.
15 *Decrees*, p. 134.
16 See Tanner, *Councils of the Church*, op. cit. (forthcoming).
17 For occasional references to Mary in the decrees of these medieval councils, see *Decrees*, pp. 230, 360, 573–4, 579, 588 and 590 (as indicated under Index of Subjects, 'Mary', ibid. pp. 1303–4).
18 'Nos ... doctrinam illam disserentem gloriosam virginem Dei genitricem Mariam, praeveniente et operante divini numinis gratia singulari, nunquam actualiter subjacuisse originali peccato, sed immunem semper fuisse ab omni originali et actuali culpa, sanctamque et immaculatam, tanquam piam et consonam cultui ecclesiastico, fidei catholicae, recta rationi et sacrae Scripturae, ab omnibus catholicis approbandam fore, tenendam et amplectandam, diffinimus et declaramus, nullique de cetero licitum esse in contrarium praedicare seu docere.' G. Mansi and others (eds.), *Sacrorum conciliorum nova et amplissima collectio* (Florence etc., 1759–1927), vol. 29, cols. 182–3.
19 J. Galot, 'L'Immaculée Conception', in H. du Manoir (ed.), *Maria* (Paris 1949–64), vol. 7, pp. 71–9; *Dictionnaire de Théologie Catholique* (Paris 1903–50), tome 7, part 1, cols. 1108–15.

20 *Decrees*, pp. 774–5.
21 Decree on original sin (17 June 1546, session 5), chapter 6: *Decrees*, p. 667.
22 Canons concerning justification (13 January 1547, session 6), canon 23: *Decrees*, p. 680.
23 No. 62 of the decree: *Decrees*, p. 895.
24 *Decrees*, pp. 891–8, as well as numerous other versions, for an English translation of the chapter. For the history of the discussions about Mary at the council, see especially: H. Vorgrimler (ed.), *Commentary on the Documents of Vatican II* (London and New York, 1967–79), vol. 1, pp. 285–96; G. Alberigo (ed.), *History of Vatican II* (Leuven and Maryknoll, 1965–), vol. 2, pp. 480–1, vols. 3 and 4 (see under 'Mary' in Index of Subjects) forthcoming in English and already published in Italian (*Storia del concilio Vaticano II*).

*(This paper was given at the ESBVM Oxford Congress
in August 2000)*

Mary
and
unity

16

Prospects for convergence
Ut Unum Sint and *Called to be One*

David Carter

In this paper, I want to develop the thesis that the recent papal ecumenical encyclical *Ut Unum Sint* and the current ecumenical ecclesiological process of Churches Together in England, *Called To Be One*, reveal and illuminate important aspects of the current ecumenical pilgrimage.[1] I shall further argue that they offer us much hope for the future. Both the encyclical and the process are deeply indebted to important trends in recent ecumenical thinking that have, until recently, remained largely the preserve of academic ecumenists and theologians. However, the great merit of the encyclical and the process is that they have powerfully stimulated the vital reception process of such new ecclesiological insights in this country. Thanks to the Pope, and to Churches Together in England, people have been stimulated to respond creatively to such issues. A wider range of people than hitherto have been involved in this process.

I begin with a brief recapitulation of the nature and provenance of the encyclical and the process. The encyclical stems both from the heritage of Vatican II and the Pope's personal and profound ecumenical commitment, which has continued to deepen throughout his pontificate.[2] Much of the encyclical is taken up with a restatement and reaffirmation of the ecumenical principles of Vatican II. However, in certain important respects the Pope explores beyond it into new realms, particularly in respect of his own ministry. The 'Called To Be One Process' has its origins in the 80s and, indeed, owes something to the Pope's visit to Britain in 1982. This visit coincided with an ecumenical disappointment, the failure of the 'Covenanting' scheme which would have established relations of full communion between the Anglican, Methodist, URC and Moravian churches. The Pope, however, played a key role in re-establishing ecumenical morale. He spoke of England with its rich variety of Christian traditions as 'privileged terrain' ecumenically. His encouragement was a factor both in the intensified commitment of the English Roman Catholic hierarchy to ecumenism and in the decision of the Church leaders to restructure the existing organs for ecumenical activity. This led to the 'Not Strangers But Pilgrims Process' which involved the first really thorough grassroots ecumenical study, based on the commissioned book *What on Earth is the Church for?* It then led to the creation, in 1990, of Churches Together in England as a new body for ecumenical co-operation, including, for the first time, full participation by Roman Catholics and some of the 'black-led' churches.[3]

In 1993, the leaders of CTE decided that the time was ripe for a new ecumenical initiative. Bearing in mind the disappointments arising out of 'top-down' schemes of unity, developed by expert commissions mandated by hierarchies and very imperfectly 'received' by many of the ordinary clergy and faithful, they decided that they must first ascertain the current understanding of the key ecumenical issues not only amongst the church leaders but also amongst the faithful in general. They also decided that it was vital to follow up the ecclesiological reflection begun in the 1986 study with further reflection on key ecclesiological issues. They therefore asked partner churches to submit considered answers to a variety of questions relating to the Church and unity. The responses were then studied by a working party and became the basis of the *Called To Be One* book. This summarized the views of the churches and threw out a series of challenges for them to consider.[4] These questions were also sent to all the intermediate county bodies for ecumenical co-operation. Both the churches and the county bodies were asked to consult as widely as possible amongst their constituencies before replying. It was particularly hoped that the county bodies could provide interesting insights arising out of the current, albeit somewhat varied, experiences of unity as lived in the 700-odd local ecumenical partnerships. From the responses received, a monitoring group prepared a briefing document for the Forum of 1997, which responded with a whole series of suggestions for the way ahead.

This has been a remarkably wide consultative process. Nevertheless, one must not prematurely exaggerate its importance. Many of the responses to the questions addressed to the churches and the county bodies show that only partial consideration has been given by some elements in their constituencies to the questions. The Methodist response recorded that replies had been received from only twelve of its twenty-six English districts. Many of the county bodies recorded the fact that their responses were based on evidence from limited numbers of local bodies in association. Many of the responses also comment that, in general, ecumenism is the enthusiasm of a minority rather than of the generality of regular churchgoers.

Nevertheless, there has been widespread debate. In the process, many Christians at the grassroots level have gained a new appreciation of the points of view of their ecumenical partners and of the issues that need, maybe over a very long period, to be addressed. Much of the important new ecumenical thinking of the last fifteen or so years, particularly in the field of ecclesiology, has begun to percolate down and to be received.

The importance of both *Ut Unum Sint* and *Called To Be One* also lies in the clarity with which they approach key ecumenical questions and the style with which they tackle them. Looked at superficially, they, especially *Called To Be One*, may appear to raise more questions than they answer. Both put their finger on continuingly neuralgic issues. Both identify five key questions on which much more work remains to be done. The Pope identifies these as the relationship between Scripture and Tradition, the nature of the Eucharist, ordination as a sacrament, the *magisterium* of the Church and the role and place of Mary, the Mother of God. The *Called To Be One* book contains five appendices on eucharistic communion, Christian initiation, ministry, authority and decision making, and mission. There is clear overlap in three sets of pairs from each document.[5]

Behind, however, the frank admission of these areas of continuing difficulty, lies a common rapprochement in vital areas of ecclesiology and ecumenical style. Both documents presuppose and reinforce the ecclesiology of the Pilgrim Church, so strongly stressed at Vatican II and in the 'Not Strangers But Pilgrims Process'. Both rest on the understanding that the Church is in constant movement towards its promised eschatological fulfilment. Both accept that the future steps, as opposed to the goal of the pilgrimage – the latter lying secure in the promise of Christ – cannot be predicted exactly. What is important is the common acceptance by the churches of the call to make that pilgrimage together. The Pope reaffirms his own previous teaching and that of his predecessors and Vatican II on this point, while the 'red book' recalls the commitment made by the twenty partner churches of CTE when they set it up in 1990.

The second vital common ecclesiological principle is that of understanding the Church as being, in its innermost essence, *koinonia*, that is participation, through incorporation into Christ and the grace of the Holy Spirit, in the mission of the Holy Trinity, and, thus, participation in a life, originating in the eternal circle of Trinitarian love, that flows into every member of the Universal Church. This ecclesiology has been accepted in all the major Christian traditions. It received expression in the 'Canberra Statement' of the last Assembly of the World Council of Churches.[6] It was the central subject for discussion at the last Conference on Faith and Order at Santiago in 1993.[7] It underpinned both the work of

ARCIC II and the fourth quinquennium statement of the Catholic–Methodist dialogue, *Towards a Statement on the Church*.[8] It has received brilliant exposition in the works of such eminent individual ecumenical theologians as the Catholic Tillard and the Orthodox John Zizioulas.[9] It resonates with the depths of patristic and Wesleyan experience and doxology.[10] It has allowed us to refocus old questions. Granted that the Church is essentially communion, what *structures* are needed to express and safeguard this communion? How is this inner *koinonia* best embodied in life and mission? How can the Church best be discerned as sign and sacrament, pointing towards the future kingdom?[11]

Called To Be One threw out several challenges to different churches on these questions. It challenges those churches which have hitherto emphasized the 'invisible' character of the Church to consider how, in fact, *koinonia* is expressed in the life, structure and relationships between Christians. It also challenges those churches that emphasize the visible character and necessity of particular structures as to how they evaluate the churchly significance of bodies which, while lacking those structures, can nevertheless show that they have, over a significantly long period, maintained a consistent Christian witness.[12] All churches are called upon to examine the bonds that hold them together, and to strengthen those bonds where they feel they can do so and without inhibiting legitimate diversity.

Called To Be One also emphasized the remarkable consensus across the ecclesiological spectrum of its members that the word 'church' has two basic meanings, 'local' and 'universal'. It records two different meanings given to the term 'local' church. In the 'independent' tradition, as embraced by Baptists, Congregationalists and some other Free Churches, it means the gathered congregation, assembled to hear the word, and responsible for its life and mission to Christ alone, the invisible head of the Church. For Roman Catholics and Orthodox, the local church is the diocese, gathered around its bishop as the one who keeps it in communion with the rest of the Church. Both concepts, however, emphasize the catholicity of the local church, that it is 'fully' church and not just derivatively so, and that its proper autonomy and responsibility before God and its sister churches must be fostered. Both concepts also emphasize that each local church must relate to all other local churches. Where the differences come is over the bonds that establish this *koinonia*. For those in the 'independent' system, they are strictly voluntary. For the Orthodox, they involve the holding of councils when it is necessary for the bishops, as heads of local churches, to articulate the common faith. For Roman Catholics, the Petrine ministry is seen as an indispensable instrument in enhancing and safeguarding *koinonia*.[13]

Debate, tension and disagreement on such issues continue and are likely to do so for a long time. At least, however, we have identified important points of reference within which they can be meaningfully discussed. Within this context all the churches are asked to examine their bonds of *koinonia*, explain them to each other and listen to the witness of others concerning how, through differing bonds, *koinonia* may be expressed. Increasingly, a theology of *koinonia* is understood as involving concepts of mutual deference and accountability, of interdependence, mutual listening and collaboration; churches are encouraged to look at their structures in this light. The Roman Catholic Church, for example, is challenged on real participation of the laity in decision making. Churches, particularly in the Free Church tradition, which have been suspicious of placing too much authority in the hands of particular individuals and which have practised primarily collegial patterns of leadership are asked to look at the benefits of ministry that is focused on individuals, particularly in the cases of episcopal and Petrine ministries. The more strictly 'independent' churches are encouraged to consider the value of bonds of communion at various levels; interestingly, this question is already being debated vigorously amongst British Baptists.[14]

The challenges that are put are not simply within the context of the theology of *koinonia*, important as that is. They are also put in terms of a context of corporate repentance, rediscovery of the common Apostolic Tradition, dialogue and sharing of riches. Let us look at each in turn.

The Pope places particularly strong emphasis on the importance of repentance. It is clear that by this he means not just repentance for actual 'wrongs' done e.g. in persecution or discrimination. He also means the need to check for reactive distortions that may have occurred in formulations of the truth in separated traditions. Such reactive formulations may have excluded important elements of truth present in the positions against which they were reacting, the result being one-sided presentations of the truth. Equally, the Pope means an acceptance that separated churches may well, despite their errors on some matters, have unveiled elements of the truth that have, as he puts it, 'embellished' the whole tradition of the Church, and thereby, merit reception in the other churches.[15]

In the very moving third section of *Ut Unum Sint*, the Pope confesses, above all, his own weakness, and that of Peter as the first holder – in the Catholic understanding – of his office. He combines an emphasis on Catholic insistence that the Petrine office is of divine institution for the benefit of the whole Church, with the acceptance that the past manner of its exercise may not always have been helpful in revealing and commending its value to other Christians, and that it is therefore, now his responsibility 'to find a way of exercising the primacy ... [that] is, nonetheless, open to a new situation'.[16]

Along with this emphasis on repentance goes the emphasis that the Church is always engaged in a rereading of the Apostolic Tradition. This may involve it in removing distortions or receiving complementary insights which create a better balance of total understanding. It may also involve developing new insights that are genuinely in accord with the Tradition. The Pope understands this re-receiving of the Apostolic Tradition in a holistic way that involves the widest possible reappraisal of all aspects of the life of a church. All communities 'need to examine themselves before the Father to ask whether they have been faithful to His plan for the Church'(*UUS* 83).[17]

Called To Be One complements these emphases. The concluding chapter calls for a process of 're-traditioning' which involves not just elements of repentance and readjustment similar to those advocated by the Pope, but also includes new developments which show the inherent creativity and dynamic of the Tradition. All churches are called to examine anew their own traditions, remembering that they must be constantly reread against the witness of Scripture and the Apostolic Tradition. They must look for new insights and enrichment from the traditions of others. Finally, they must be honest in admitting the diffi-culties that they still encounter with some of the traditions of others. Only thus can there be true dialogue.[18]

The Pope is particularly profoundly affirmative of the importance of dialogue. He is sensitive to the fact that dialogue involves the deepest dimensions of human and corporate existence. It is not just about exchanging ideas but also about exchanging gifts, a point that is partic-ularly strongly re-echoed in *Called To Be One*. He calls it 'an outright necessity, one of the Church's priorities', and links it to a capacity for mutual repentance and conversion, as, in dialogue, Christian partners find each other in Christ, and, in humility, confess their failings to each other and before him. Lastly, he asserts that it 'makes surprising discov-eries possible' and 'the discovery of the unfathomable riches of truth'.[19] These last two points testify to the Pope's openness to his Christian sisters and brothers of other traditions in the course of the common pilgrimage. This in itself is an extremely eloquent testimony to the high degree of *koinonia* already existing between the churches. Perhaps it is most movingly underlined in the Pope's call to the leaders and theolo-gians of the other churches to help him in the process of discerning how most acceptably and effectively his ministry might be exercised in future. The Pope wishes no effort to be spared in taking account of what he calls the 'legitimate concerns of other Christians'. He shows his immense regard for those sister churches with which Rome is not yet in communion. He talks of churches 'helping one another to recover the Tradition', of the importance of 'esteeming the truly Christian endowments' of others.[20]

In the light of these affirmations, it is interesting to note not merely the parallel teaching of the red book *Called To Be One*, but also the responses from some of the intermediate bodies. The Dorset response talks of the increasingly apparent desire of people to 'learn more of each others' traditions'. Lincolnshire talks of the way in which ecumenism 'calls us into maturity, not a fixed static position'. Liverpool says very prophetically, 'What we value most in particular traditions is both a possible gift to others and already desired and cherished by others in their own way'. These moving affirmations parallel the insights of the Pope, and are, I believe, testimony to the way in which the Holy Spirit is moving and inspiring the *sensus fidelium* in England today. The 1997 Forum of CTE called upon churches to 'integrate denominational heritage with the discovery of our common Christian heritage. How can we all receive the treasures safeguarded during our divisions?'[21]

The originally-projected title of this paper also held out the promise that I might consider the Pope's other encyclical, *Orientale Lumen*, as well. I do not propose to do so in detail, since it would rather alarmingly extend the length of this paper. I do, however, agree with my friend, Emmanuel Sullivan, that *Orientale Lumen* is a necessary complement to *Ut Unum Sint*. I also argue, in the present context, that it underlines the Pope's commitment to a richly diversified church, underlining both the teaching of Vatican II and his own earlier teaching that the Church is enriched by the plurality of its ancient traditions. In *Orientale Lumen* he recalls western Catholics to a proper appreciation of the riches of Eastern Christianity. He urges East and West to learn from each other.[22]

In this context it is interesting to notice the call that has consistently underlain the English ecumenical process over the last ten years. At the preliminary conference at Nottingham in the 'Not Strangers But Pilgrims Process' in 1987, it was stated 'Unity comes alive as we learn to live in one anothers' traditions'.[23] There has been an increasing understanding of the importance of affirming, maintaining and deriving mutual benefit from the diversity of traditions in the English churches. One or two of the responses to *Called To Be One* specifically mentioned the concern of both local bodies and some national churches that the witness of numerically smaller bodies should not be lost in any ecumenical rapprochement.

Especially interesting was the affirmation in most of the local responses of 'reconciled diversity' rather than organic unity as the way ahead for English ecumenism in the medium term future. In part, this seems to reflect a fear that organic unity might be monolithically repressive. Perhaps more frequently, it reflects a belief, born of caution after the failures of the Anglican–Methodist and Covenanting schemes of the 60s and 70s, that organic unity is unattainable in the foreseeable future. The exact meaning to be attached to the phrase seems to be rather variable. The Methodist response to *Called To Be One*, noting that many Methodists seemed to endorse the phrase, observed that it could apparently be taken to mean at least three different things. At the most minimal level, it seemed to indicate merely a slight intensification of the sort of close co-operation already existing in many areas. At a higher level, it could be construed as the maintenance of separate denominational structures but with a commitment to much wider consultation and sharing. At the highest level, it could imply common life within one body, but with the existence of considerable variety of style and practice, such as is already found within some single denominations. A very perceptive response from Cornwall argued that if 'reconciled diversity' really were seriously implemented it would have to result in structures for co-operation and mutual counsel that would, in themselves, constitute a form of organic unity.

It is clear that if English ecumenism is to go down this road, a lot of serious theological work will need to be done on such questions as the extent and nature of legitimate diversity. To aid us, there is already the example of the Roman Catholic Church which embraces millions of Eastern-rite Christians as well as those of the numerically predominant Latin rite. There is the theology of *typoi* of church life developed by Cardinal Willebrands and the Lutheran understanding of unity in reconciled diversity.[24]

Where, however, most immediately, do we go from here? I suggest that we explore ever more deeply the ecclesiology of *koinonia*, aided by the insights in *Ut Unum Sint* and the 'Called To Be One Process'. The ecclesiology of *koinonia* calls us to a radical integration of the partial insights, sometimes distorted because of their separation in reaction against other systems, which are contained in what have previously tended to be seen as competing alternative ecclesiologies. In this context we must start from a profound ecclesiological reflection on the relationship of the Father and the Son as it is found in St John's Gospel.

In that Gospel Jesus simultaneously presents himself as totally obedient to the Father and yet as empowered by him and given complete equality. Thus, he says that 'he can do nothing of himself but only what he sees the Father doing.' (John 5.19.) His meat and drink are to do 'the will of him who sent me'. On the other hand, the Father 'has given all things into my hands' that 'all may honour the Son as they honour the Father' (John 5.23). Lest it be thought that this is merely a revelation of inner trinitarian dynamics with no relevance to ecclesiology, let us note the ways in which Jesus speaks so similarly of his relationship to the disciples. He calls them his friends, because he has 'revealed to them everything that I received from my Father' (John 15.16). St John compares the relationship of Jesus to the 'Beloved Disciple', the Johannine 'perfect Christian' with that of the Father and the Son. The same word is used of the 'only Son, who is in the *bosom* of the Father' (John 1.18), and the Beloved Disciple who 'leant against the breast of Jesus' (John 13.23). Clearly there is involved in the relationship of the members of the Church to each other and to Christ, as well as in the relationship of Christ to the Father, a mind-bending generosity of self-giving, on both sides, that defies all other human analogies. It is this that is the key to the elimination of unacceptable distortions in current ecclesiology. For a start, it renders untenable the extremes of independency and papal monarchicalism as they have sometimes been professed and practised. Mutual deference, mutual accountability and mutual respect should be part of the structure of all Christian relationships. They should particularly characterize the relationships of those who are called and set apart for ordained ministry with the rest of the people of God. Such ministries have been known since biblical times and their value and necessity attested in the lives of the vast majority of Christian communities. They are indispensable in terms of maintaining *koinonia* and pastoral work. However, they exist only in the context of the Church to enable the wider ministry and witness of the people of God. They have a duty both of guidance of the people of God and of listening to their witness. They lead, but do not monopolize the corporate discernment of the people of God, as they 'grow more and more in knowledge and complete understanding' (Phil. 1.9, quoted in *The Word of Life*). Their ministry exists 'for the equipping of the saints' (Eph. 4.12).

At all levels, the Church should be characterized by what Jean Tillard calls 'synodality' and 'synergy', and the great Wesleyan theologian, James Rigg, called 'the circulation of love'.[25] The relationship of leaders and led is symbiotic and based on mutual respect and recognition. Tillard emphasizes that, in the early Church, local churches chose as their bishops those in whom they could recognize the authentic faith of the Church and who could, therefore, be trusted to guard it. The bishop had the duty of listening to the witness of his people, speaking their concerns to the wider church and protecting the individuality of the *local* traditions of that church as part of the varied heritage of the whole. The bishop was supposed to be in constant dialogue with his people and clergy, speaking the witness of other churches to them and their witness to other churches. The role of the bishop of Rome was to enhance this circulation of *koinonia* by keeping all the local churches in touch with each other and watching over the common growth in faith.[26]

In the light of this theology of *koinonia* the churches need to reappraise the four key ecclesiologies that have dominated Christian history and look for ways of integrating their valid insights into a greater whole. These are the 'independent', 'connexional', 'episcopal' and 'Petrine ministry' ecclesiologies. Already, of course, much material is to hand in the documents of Vatican II and the work of the bilateral dialogues.[27] More awaits investigation in the writings of the great classical ecclesiologists, such as Möhler and Congar in the Roman Catholic tradition, Ramsey in the Anglican, Rigg and Gregory in the Wesleyan and Forsyth in the Reformed/Independent traditions.[28] More important than the appraisal of such rich material will be the *manner* in which it is done. This should be one of humble self-offering by churches of their insights, of critical self-appraisal by these churches of the empirical weaknesses of their systems, and, above all, humble willingness to listen to and receive from the witness and even the correction of others. In this the Pope has already set an example by his willingness to listen to the witness of other churches' leaders concerning the mode and exercise of his ministry. This humility and openness have made a deep impression on me personally. Believing, as I do in accordance with the Wesleyan theological tradition, that the great truths of salvation receive confirmation in the experience of believers, I consider that we are seeing the value of the Petrine ministry as a universal ministry of *koinonia* for all the churches receiving its 'true and experimental' (to use a phrase of Wesley's) proof.

Already, also, there has been much movement within the churches, as they have taken on board the ecclesiological insights of others. The Anglican, Methodist and United Reformed Churches in this country now all have broadly similar synodical systems, albeit that the URC, following in the 'independent' tradition of its former congregationalist component still allows rather greater autonomy to local congregations, and that the Church of England, following in the episcopal tradition, ascribes wider powers of leadership and doctrinal decision making than is the case with senior leaders in the other two traditions. In some other cases, there is widespread ecclesiological debate, if as yet little actual change. The Roman Catholic Church has yet to work through the practical implications of episcopal collegiality and the recent theology of the local church. The Baptists are still debating what ecclesial reality they can ascribe to intermediate bodies within the Baptist Union. Hitherto, they have denied ecclesial reality to these bodies, seeing them purely as *ad hoc* provisional means of consultation and co-operation. The fact that they are discussing these issues is a sign of real movement.

I believe that we shall increasingly discern the necessary complementarity of the four main ecclesiological emphases. Two, the episcopal and papal, emphasize the importance of personally focused ministries; two, the connexional and independent, emphasize corporate authority and decision making. Both, however, accept the importance of the other emphasis. Catholic theology since Vatican II has emphasized collegiality, particularly, but not exclusively in the context of the relationship of the episcopate to the Petrine ministry. Anglicanism has always believed a lay voice in church affairs to be important.[29] The early Wesleyans emphasized the focusing ministry of superintendents in an almost episcopal way, though never to the detriment of their collegiality with other ministers and the laity.[30] Early independency had its own high doctrine of the ministry and a very real concern for *koinonia* between the varying local churches.[31] We need a theology that reconciles the 'catholic' and 'independent' concepts of local church. I think Methodism here with its sense of the church as an interdependent fellowship at every level, may be able to help. It is important to acknowledge the very real presence of Christ, ruling and guiding in each local congregation gathered around word and sacrament, and to integrate that insight with the understanding of the importance of a minister of *koinonia* expressing and safeguarding the continuity of the Church in a defined area. It is easier in my opinion to reconcile the insights of the other three systems of church government, at least in theory; there will always be practical problems. American Methodism is interesting in this regard. It is an episcopal church in which episcopal ministry is integrated and understood within a connexional framework. It has also stressed, at certain times, that the logic of connexional interdependency points ultimately to a world connexion.[32] This, one can see, would benefit from a world primate, and as ARCIC I said, there is only one obvious contender for this post.[33]

I should end with two sober words of warning. The first is to reiterate that much hard theological thinking and *ecumenical repentance*, on all sides, has to occur first. There are still far too many self-justificatory expositions of denominational traditions coming from leaders and theologians in all traditions. Were they to listen both to the Pope and to *Called To Be One* they might know better. The second warning concerns the reception process. The *Called To Be One* book made the point that there is still far too little ecumenical theological training, particularly, but not exclusively, of clergy. This point was echoed in several intermediate body responses and, notably, in the Baptist one, which called for more ecumenical ministerial formation. Reception, however, is not purely an educational process. It is an essential act of *koinonia* in which the people of God, anointed as they are with that instinct for truth which, according to St John, they have from the Holy Spirit, take to their hearts and practise those new experimental truths which they discern as leading them on to 'full perfection' in their pilgrimage.[34] It is, as Fr Gilles Routhier, ecumenical officer of the Catholic Archdiocese of Quebec, says, an inherently ecclesial process, integral to churchly life.[35] We are called, in the final result, not so much to reconciliation of current viewpoints as to common advance towards a fuller 'imaging of the kingdom of God' (to quote George Tavard) as we 'hand in hand go on to our high calling's glorious hope'. (Wesley, of course!)[36] In this, we have been given some powerful leads in *Ut Unum Sint* and *Called To Be One*. They were followed up by the call of the 1997 Forum of CTE (which sums up so much of what the Pope and *Called To Be One* have said) 'to greater engagement in prayer and worship together. To deepen our communion with one another, we need to listen to one another's concerns and values.'[37]

Notes

1 The basic texts referred to are *Ut Unum Sint* by Pope John Paul II, 1995, CTS edition (hereinafter cited as *UUS*), and *Called To Be One* (hereinafter cited as *CTBO*), edited by Martin Reardon (Churches Together in England Publications, 1996).

2 Much ecumenical wisdom is also to be found in the papal encyclicals, *Tertio Millennio Adveniente* (At the approach of the third millennium) (Rome 1994), and *Novo Millennio Ineunte* (At the beginning of the third millennium) (Rome 2001). See also the striking homily for the Week of Prayer for Christian Unity, 2001, in *Osservatore Romano*, 26 January 2001. For a summary of overall papal ecumenical teaching, see my chapter in the CTS book, *The Wisdom of John Paul II* (CTS, London 2001).

3 *CTBO*, pp. 1–5 gives background to the Process and the wider ecumenical context.

4 *CTBO*, especially ch. 7, pp. 53–9, though other challenges are also thrown out in other chapters.

5 *UUS* 79, *CTBO* appendices, pp. 60ff.

6 'The Unity of the Church as *koinonia*: Gift and Calling', quoted in M. Kinnamon and B. Cope (eds), *The Ecumenical Movement: an Anthology of Key Texts and Voices*, (1997), pp. 127–8.

7 Report, *On the Way to Fuller Koinonia*, T. Best and G. Gassmann (eds), WCC, 1994.

8 *The Church as Koinonia*, report of ARCIC II, 1991. *Towards a Statement on the Church*, World Methodist Council, 1986.

9 e.g. J. M. Tillard, *Church of Churches* (ET), (Collegeville 1993), and *L'Église Locale* (Paris 1995). J. Zizioulas, *Being as Communion* (London 1985).

10 For the patristic sense, see especially the works just cited by Tillard. For the Wesleyan tradition, see H. Bett, *The Spirit of Methodism* (London 1937), especially ch. 5; also the hymns on the church in the present official hymn book of British Methodism, *Hymns and Psalms* (London 1983), nos 752–63.

11 *CTBO*, p. 53, invites all churches to renew their understanding of what it means to be the Church at every level, and the bonds that hold churches together.
12 *CTBO*, p. 20.
13 *CTBO*, pp. 12–14.
14 *CTBO*, p. 55 for appropriate challenges.
15 *UUS* 85.
16 *UUS* 88ff, especially 95.
17 *UUS* 83.
18 *CTBO*, p. 54.
19 *UUS* 28–39.
20 *UUS* 78, 47.
21 For this and other resolutions of the CTE Forum of 1997, see the CTE house journal, *Pilgrim Post*, September 1997.
22 *Orientale Lumen* 45. He quotes Rom. 1.12, in which Paul talks of the encouragement that he hopes he and the Roman Christians will gain from each other's faith. James Rigg, the Wesleyan ecclesiologist, also cites this text in the context of *koinonia*.
23 Statement issued by the Nottingham Conference, 1987, para 2.
24 For Cardinal Willebrands' sermon at Cambridge, in which he developed the notion of *typoi*, see *The Tablet*, 24 January 1970, pp. 75–6. For 'unity in reconciled diversity', see H. Meyer, *That All May Be One* (Grand Rapids 1999), pp. 121–7.
25 Tillard, *L'Église Locale*, op. cit. pp. 362, 554 et al. J. H. Rigg, 'Presidential sermon', published in *Wesleyan Methodist Magazine*, 1878, p. 798.
26 Tillard, op. cit. p. 314ff.
27 See especially the two dialogues already referred to; also the decree *Lumen Gentium* of Vatican II.
    For non-Methodist readers, I give a brief explanation of 'connexionalism'. It is based on the belief that all local churches are interdependent. None can, therefore, take decisions of any nature without considering the effect on the others. Ministers are not 'invited' to churches as in the 'independent' system, but 'stationed' by the national 'Conference' in accordance with its judgement as to the overall needs of the church as a whole. Churches are grouped together in 'circuits' under the authority of a 'superintendent' minister, who, however, always consults with his ministerial colleagues and lay representatives. The principle of subsidiarity is respected, but there is great emphasis on the importance of links of fellowship and co-operation at every level in the Church. The national conferences exercise corporate episcopē over their churches. The classical Wesleyans saw this as a ministry both of *koinonia* and vigilance, in language similar to that used by the Pope in *UUS* 94. The classical statement is A. Barrett, *Ministry and Polity of the Christian Church* (London 1854). For connexionalism in general, see the seminal essays by B. Beck in *Epworth Review*, May/September 1991, and my article, 'A Methodist Contribution to Ecclesiology', in *One in Christ*, 1994, pp. 161–75.
28 For Congar see especially *Divided Christendom* (ET) (1939); *The Mystery of the Church* (ET) (1960); *Tradition and Traditions* (ET) (1966); *Diversity and*

Communion (ET) (1984). For Ramsey, his *Gospel and the Catholic Church* (1936); for Gregory, his *Holy Catholic Church* (1873); for Rigg, his *Principles of Church Organisation* (1887); for Forsyth, *The Church and the Sacraments*.

29 S. Platten, *Augustine's Legacy* (London 1997), p. 40 and discussion in ch. 3 pp. 41–56.

30 B. Gregory, *Handbook of Scriptural Church Principles* (London 1888), p. 87–9. Rigg, op. cit. pp. 171–2, 236.

31 Forsyth, op. cit. especially p. 130ff. on authority of the ministry. A. Sell, *Saints Visible, Orderly and Catholic: The Congregational Idea of the Church* (World Alliance of Reformed Churches, 1986) for an excellent modern overview of this tradition.

32 G. Moede, *The Office of Bishop in Methodism* (Zurich 1964).

33 ARCIC, *Final Report. Authority in the Church I* (CTS/SPCK, 1981), para 23.

34 1 John 2.20. See also *The Word of Life*, report of sixth quinquennium of the international Roman Catholic–Methodist dialogue (1996), Section 1, Part 3. 'The Fruitfulness of Faith', paras 37–9.

35 Gilles Routhier, *La Réception d'un concile* (Paris 1993), pp. 61–3.

36 G. Tavard, *The Church, Community of Salvation* (Collegeville 1992), pp. 244–58, where a whole series of fascinating *theologoumena* on church, kingdom and eschatology are adduced. For the Wesley quotation, *Hymns and Psalms*, op. cit. no. 753.

37 *Pilgrim Post*, op. cit.

(This paper was given at the ESBVM Woldingham Conference in June 1997)

17

Ecumenism and mariology today

Michael Hurley SJ

I. Introduction

The first – and in fact the last – time I spoke on this subject 'Ecumenism and Mariology Today' was almost forty years ago now. The date was 14 November 1962: the occasion was the Winter session that year of the Milltown Park Public Lectures in Dublin.[1] In these past forty years much water has flowed under the bridges of the Thames and the Tiber, under bridges the whole world over. In an introductory part of this paper I therefore ask myself two questions: firstly 'Where is ecumenism now?' and secondly 'Where is mariology now?' In Part II, I attempt a survey of the place of Mary in Interchurch Dialogue in the 90s, the last decade of the century and of the millennium. Finally, in Part III, I make some tentative suggestions for the future: of the Dialogue of Love and the Dialogue of Truth about Mary.

I.1. Ecumenism now

In November 1962 the Second Vatican Council, that watershed in church and in world history, had only just opened. Indeed, 14 November was the very day Cardinal Ottaviani presented to the Council the schema *De Revelatione*, the discussion of which was to be so crucial for the Council's whole future.[2] At that date the Catholic Church had not yet officially committed itself to the ecumenical movement. It would not do so for another two years, until the promulgation of the Decree on Ecumenism on 21 November 1964. In 1962 I myself was a mere ecumenical novice having just two years previously found my way into the field, altogether by accident.[3] After Vatican II, however, ecumenism, as we all know, did come to flourish in the whole Catholic Church. This is not the place to rehearse its achievements, but simply to recall some of the highlights. The Ecumenical Society of the Blessed Virgin Mary was founded in 1967. The Catholic Church, having until Vatican II been negative to the World Council of Churches, became a member of its Faith and Order

Commission in 1968. The Irish School of Ecumenics was established in Dublin in 1970. On New Year's Eve 1971 the Anglican–Roman Catholic Agreed Statement on the Eucharist appeared, indicating 'consensus at the level of faith' 'on essential points of eucharistic doctrine'. The first Irish Inter-Church meeting was held in 1973. The year 1975 saw the publication of the Vatican's document on *Ecumenical Collaboration at the Regional, National and Local Levels*. In 1976 Basil Hume OSB became Archbishop of Westminster and preached at Vespers in Westminster Abbey on the evening of his installation. In 1978 John Paul II became Pope and the following year visited Constantinople and announced his millennium dream project: that the year 2000 'may find us standing side by side in full communion'. The *Final Report* of ARCIC appeared in 1981. Then in 1982 came *BEM*, the Agreed Statement on *Baptism, Eucharist and Ministry* issued by Faith and Order, and in addition Pope John Paul's visit to Great Britain and his splendidly ecumenical, unforgettable visit to Canterbury.

By the mid 80s, however, doubts and complaints were already beginning to be expressed and heard. In April 1985, honesty compelled me to write that 'The twentieth anniversary of Vatican II's Decree on Ecumenism finds all the churches in the middle of an ecumenical recession'[4] but I was able to quote in support the *British Weekly* as well as Yves Congar. Church-going was of course on the decline. The Church was no longer the focus and centre of religion and spirituality which it had been previously, and it was only logical therefore that church divisions should no longer be the major cause of concern which they had been. There was the related fact that, as the *British Weekly* put it, 'all major traditions are today experiencing a resurgence of denominational self-consciousness, even self-preoccupation, and this phenomenon is bound to militate against any sacrificial ecumenism'. And a theory about 'reconciled diversity' scarcely helped by seeming to suggest that peaceful co-existence was the aim rather than organic unity.

This negative trend in interchurch relations unfortunately continued into the 90s. Pope John Paul bravely attempted to reverse it. He had hoped that we could 'celebrate the Great Jubilee, if not completely united, at least much closer to overcoming the divisions of the second millennium'. Some progress has of course been made this past decade. The outstanding example is 'The Joint Declaration on the Doctrine of Justification' solemnly signed by official representatives of the Catholic and Lutheran Churches in Augsburg on Reformation Sunday, 1999.[5] But East–West relations, which for Catholics have traditionally been our first ecumenical priority, were perhaps never worse. The fall of communism, of the Berlin Wall, only aggravated the ancient antipathy. The Orthodox now feel more deeply alienated than ever before, both from their fellow members of the World Council of Churches and from the Catholic Church. The Orthodox–Catholic International Joint Commission which suspended its theological work in 1990 did just last month resume its meetings, but issued what a Zenit News Agency report of 20 July called a 'somewhat pessimistic' concluding statement. And the Ecumenical Patriarch when receiving an honorary doctorate from Georgetown University in Washington in 1997 had not hesitated to declare that

> This deeply rooted conviction of our divergence has led us to a thousand years of separate and autonomous courses. We confirm, not with unexpected astonishment but neither with indifference, that indeed the divergence between us continually increases, and the end point to which our courses are taking us, foreseeably, are indeed different.[6]

This East–West estrangement may not seem particularly relevant here. If therefore we ask whether the ecumenical movement is also showing signs of fatigue in these islands, whether interchurch relations in the West are improving or disimproving, we can hardly ignore the evidence of the 1998 document of our Catholic Bishops entitled *One Bread, One Body*.[7] Much disappointment was expressed on the appearance of this document. Karl Rahner once wrote a short article entitled 'Theology of Risk' in which he spoke about 'the tutiorism of risk' and stated:

> To give an example: in ecumenical matters the question should not be put: What do we have to concede to the separated brethren? But rather: How do we exhaust all imaginable possibilities, all that our Catholic Christian conscience permits, in a courageous and unhampered fashion? Today we just cannot afford to do less, in order to bring Christian unity nearer.[8]

The General Norms established for eucharistic sharing by the Catholic bishops of these islands in *One Bread, One Body* are far from exemplifying such a theology of risk. They are ungenerous, unimaginative, unadventuresome. They provide a sad example of the loss of nerve which characterizes this present ecumenical winter. The abhorrence of casualness which is not only commendable but required in this matter of eucharistic sharing should not have led our hierarchies – as it has not led the hierarchies of other countries – to the extremes of caution shown in *One Bread, One Body*. The question arises: perhaps the anti-Protestantism of our Catholicism is no less real, if more subdued than the anti-Romanism of Orthodoxy? Do we Catholics trust Protestants – including Anglicans – any more than the Orthodox trust us?

I.2. Mariology now

I come then to my second question: 'Where is mariology now, especially in relation to ecumenism?' Vatican II put its Marian teaching not in a separate document but in a chapter of its Constitution 'On the Church'. This decision was made by a majority of just seventeen votes, 'the narrowest majority and the lowest favourable vote in the entire history of the Council'.[9] One year later, however, after a tense debate during which, according to Fr Michael O'Carroll, 'the swaying opinion from one day to the next ... had an element of subdued drama'[10] the text of what became chapter 8 of the Constitution on the Church received almost unanimous approval.[11] Entitled 'The Blessed Virgin Mary, Mother of God, in the Mystery of Christ and of the Church', it acknowledges Mary 'as a pre-eminent and wholly unique member of the Church as well as its model in faith and love and its most outstanding exemplar.' (53). The text attempts to combine a christological and an ecclesiological approach (Mary as type of the Church) and to show these to be complementary rather than mutually exclusive but it still 'bears the marks of the alternating influence of ... its chief drafters, G. Philips and C. Balic'.[12] Despite, however, 'the still persisting tensions which it still embodies', the chapter has been generally welcomed as having succeeded in overcoming the post-tridentine, isolationist trend in mariology and as 'the beginning of a real integration of mariology and ecclesiology'.[13]

But since Vatican II – though by no means simply because of Vatican II – Marian devotions in the Roman Catholic Church are very much on the decline. Pilgrimages to centres such as Lourdes and Fatima and Czestochowa and Medjugorje as well as to Walsingham and Knock do seem not only to have retained but to have increased their popularity. On the other hand the rosary, whether in private or in public, is no longer the devotional staple it once was; and the Jesuit Sodalities of Our Lady have become Christian Life Communities. Happily, however, the Vatican has resisted the campaign by the Fatima priest, Fr Nicholas Gruner, and his supporters to obtain 'the public and definitive collegiate consecration of Russia to the Immaculate Heart of Mary'. This would certainly not improve but seriously aggravate East–West relations. Happily also the Vatican has resisted the campaign which got four million people, including some five hundred bishops and forty-two cardinals, to petition the Pope to have the Marian titles of Mediator, Co-Redemptor and Advocate solemnly and infallibly defined. Such a definition would be an added obstacle in interchurch relations between the churches of the West and between those of the East and the West. One of this Society's most notable supporters, Canon Roger Greenacre, was a member of the special international commission appointed by the Vatican to consider the matter and whose advice was negative. The Ecumenical Society of the Blessed Virgin Mary can therefore take some of the credit for averting this danger of a new marian dogma.[14]

But where now in theological education programmes is the study of Marian doctrine and devotion, the subject Mariology? In the 50s when I studied theology in Louvain and in the 60s when I taught it in Dublin, mariology was a subject in its own right, and obligatory. This was normal then for Roman Catholic faculties and seminaries. It was an expression of the pre-Vatican II isolationist trend in mariology. After the Council, and in order, it would seem, to follow its methodological example, the situation changed. Mariology was largely abandoned as a separate subject. It was taught, but only as an elective. It was of course envisaged that the most significant parts of mariology would be covered in the teaching of ecclesiology and of christology.

In 1988 however the Congregation for Catholic Education issued a document entitled 'The Virgin Mary in Intellectual and Spiritual Formation', which expressed concern that students acquire 'an authentic Marian piety', 'a sound Marian spirituality' . This document concluded that

> it would be unthinkable that the teaching of Mariology be obscured today; it is necessary therefore that it be given its just place in Seminaries and Theological Faculties ... that every Centre of theological study – according to its proper physiognomy – plan that in its *Ratio studiorum* the teaching of Mariology be included.[15]

This, it had stated in the previous paragraphs, should be 'systematic', 'organic', 'complete' and 'suited to the various types of institution and to the level of the students'. The question therefore arises: has the situation changed again as a result of this document? According to the columns of *The Tablet* a Marian Study Centre exists at Ushaw College which in association with the University of Wales at Lampeter offers an MA in Theology (Marian Studies) but unfortunately focuses exclusively on Western Christianity.[16] From soundings made in preparation for this paper in some centres of theology, Mariology, I gather, is now a separate, obligatory subject in some places, for instance, at the Gregorian in Rome and at Allen Hall in London but not so for the most part, it would seem elsewhere. It is certainly not so at Milltown or Oscott. In these centres it is indeed taught, but only as an elective. Students not choosing this elective will, it is envisaged, cover the most significant parts of mariology in their study of ecclesiology and of christology which are of course obligatory subjects for all. Other considerations, however, are now at play besides the methodological insights of Vatican II, as the Dean of Studies at Oscott College kindly explained to me.

> First, [Fr Philip Egan wrote] more and more new elements have been loaded into the programme over the last 20 years (eg Human Development) and over the last 3 years we have been trying to 'downsize'. And secondly, we recognize that learning the habits of prayer and study are more important than imparting information, and so we have acknowledged we cannot cover everything.[17]

But although Marian devotions and the teaching of mariology may have declined since Vatican II, mariological scholarship has continued to flourish, as Fr Eamon Carroll's regular feature 'A Survey of Recent Mariology' in the American journal *Marian Studies* makes abundantly clear. Learned societies continue to meet: the Mariological Society of America, for instance, and the Société française d'études mariales. Scientific journals continue to appear: *Marian Studies*, for instance, in the USA, *Marianum* in Rome, *Études Mariales* in Paris, *Mariologische Studien* in Germany and *Estudios Marianos* in Spain. Individual specialists continue to write and to publish: Eamon R. Carroll OCarm himself for instance. At four-yearly intervals since 1950 international mariological and Marian congresses have been held, organized by the Pontifical International Marian Academy.[18] On the occasion of the millennium Jubilee such an International Congress will be held in Rome from 15 to 24 September 2000, with opening and closing Masses in the Basilica of St Mary Major. And beginning in 1967 these international congresses have included an 'ecumenical round-table' with invited experts from the other major Churches.[19]

II. Mary in interchurch dialogue in the 1990s

II. 1. Mary is for Everyone

What then of the ecumenical dimension? For an overview of the place of Mary in formal interchurch dialogue in the last decade of the twentieth century, three sources which are readily available will be helpful. There is first of all the volume of essays *Mary is for Everyone* subtitled 'Mary and Ecumenism' edited by the Hon. General Secretary of the Ecumenical Society of the Blessed Virgin Mary, Fr William McLoughlin, and Mrs Jill Pinnock.[20] Like the burning and shining lamp which John the Baptist was (John 5.35) the Ecumenical Society of the Blessed Virgin Mary, with its American offshoot founded in 1976, bears faithful witness to the ecumenical dimension of mariology. I do regret that when Martin

Gillett, the Society's founder, visited the Irish School of Ecumenics in Dublin in the mid-70s I unfortunately had to disappoint his hopes that we would help to establish a local branch.[21] If ecumenical work in general is increasingly a lonely furrow, this must be all the more true of you with your very particular, special interest. You will please accept my presence today and this paper as a belated token of my appreciation and gratitude.

Of the twenty-four contributors to *Mary is for Everyone* thirteen are non-Roman Catholic: five Anglican, four Methodist, two Presbyterian, one Lutheran and one Orthodox. This spread illustrates the 'sea-change', as David Butler calls it in his contribution, which has taken place in thinking about Mary within the Protestant tradition in Britain in the last thirty years and which he rightly attributes to the work of the Society. But the book is wide-ranging not only in its authorship but also in its interests, and the diversity of topics discussed shows that there is an authentic Marian dimension to religion, to theology and spirituality. Only one contribution, however, takes up for discussion an official inter-church document: that issued in 1995 by the British Methodist–Roman Catholic Committee entitled *Mary, Mother of the Lord: sign of grace, faith and holiness*. And in the longest section of the book on 'Mary and the unity of the churches' only three of the nine essays treat of a mariological theme. The reason of course is the fact that Mary has not hitherto featured prominently in official interchurch dialogue. While highlighting the undoubted increase of interest in Mary among Protestants, and the acceptance of a relevant Marian dimension in theology as a whole, this collection shows that mariology is still very much a minority interest among what may be called professional ecumenists, and it raises the critical question whether and to what extent Mary *is* for Everyone, whether and to what extent a consensus on Marian doctrine and devotion is a requirement for Christian unity.

II. 2. Mariological Society of America: 1997 meeting

As my second source for an overview of the place of Mary in interchurch dialogue in the nineties I take the Proceedings of the forty-eighth annual meeting of the Mariological Society of America held at San Antonio in Texas in May 1997.[22] In his 1995 Encyclical *That All May Be One* Pope John Paul had listed five areas 'in need of fuller study before a true consensus of faith can be achieved'. One of these was 'the Virgin Mary, as Mother of God and Icon of the Church, the spiritual Mother who intercedes for Christ's disciples and for all humanity' (79). As a result this topic was made the focus of the 1997 San Antonio meeting and the first paper read was by Mgr John Radano, an American priest of the diocese of New Jersey who works in the Pontifical Council for Promoting Christian Unity at the Vatican. Entitled 'Towards the Great Jubilee 2000: Mary and the Search for Christian Unity'[23] this study very strangely makes no mention of the work of the Lutheran–Catholic Dialogue in the USA or of the work of the Groupe des Dombes in France, even though Mgr Radano is identified as head of the Western section of the Unity Council at the Vatican.

The main part of Mgr Radano's paper is entitled 'Some Ecumenical Developments in Regard to Mary as We Prepare for the Year 2000'. It falls into three sections, the first of which deals with 'Mary in the International Multilateral Dialogue: Faith and Order', the World Council of Churches body which, it will be remembered, now includes not only Orthodox but also Roman Catholic members. Here reference is made to two studies. One of these, subtitled 'The Unity of the Church and the Renewal of Human Community', has a final chapter on 'Discipleship and Community' which offers 'Mary, the mother of the Lord' as 'an important example for all who seek to understand the full dimension of life in Christian community'. The second study is 'Confessing the One Faith'. This in its commentary on the article of the Creed 'by the Holy Spirit and from the Virgin Mary' also offers Mary as an exemplary disciple. 'But Mary is also [as well as *Theotokos*] the disciple who hears the word of God, responds to it and keeps it. In her obedience to God and her utter dependence on the Holy Spirit, Mary is the example *par excellence* of our discipleship' (122).

Radano notes that in these Faith and Order papers 'there is no mention of Mary's intercession'[24] and passes on to his second section on 'Sister Churches: Mary in Renewed Eastern Orthodox–Roman Catholic Relations'. Here with the help of liberal quotations from addresses by popes and patriarchs he has no difficulty in showing how by contrast belief in Mary's intercession features very clearly as a common bond and a common tradition between Rome and Constantinople, despite what Patriarch Dimitrios at Vespers in St Mary Major's in 1987 did not hesitate to describe as 'certain unilateral actions of a dogmatic nature ... in times of reciprocal estrangement'.

Radono's third section is entitled 'Mary and the Recent Christological Agreements', but very strangely he makes no mention here of what seem to me to be two very important features of these Christological statements. He passes over in silence the statement approved in 1988 by Pope John Paul and Pope Shenouda III which very strikingly omits the two-natures terminology of Chalcedon. He does discuss the statement signed in 1994 by Pope John Paul and His Holiness Mar Dinkha IV, Patriarch of the Assyrian Church of the East, [*see below, p. 336*] but fails to draw attention to the still more striking fact that this statement does not insist on applying the term *Theotokos* to our Lady. The methodological implications of these omissions will be referred to later in this paper.

At the 1997 Annual Meeting of the Mariological Society of America Mgr Radano was followed by three Protestants. The first is a Presbyterian who is an active supporter of the Ecumenical Society of the Blessed Virgin Mary and read one of the papers at the Bristol Congress in September 1996. Dr Ross Mackenzie refers *en passant* to 'the notoriously anti-Catholic, and therefore anti-Marian vindictiveness that mars much Protestant history'.[25] His is a very positive contribution to the topic of 'Mary Intercessor on our behalf' but he acknowleges it to be very much a personal, untypically Presbyterian contribution and indeed at Bristol subtitled his paper 'a personal, ecumenical journey'.

The second Protestant is a Baptist, Dr Larry Bethune. 'Generally speaking', he said, 'Mary plays little role in Baptist theology and almost no role in Baptist spirituality'. 'Frankly,' he admits 'some of this lack of attention is probably sexist, especially in the American South', where until recently women have been treated 'as secondary spiritual beings in the church'. But though quite negative he does not hesitate to write: 'I envy the way the role of Mary in Catholic theology and spirituality leads people to experience the feminine attributes of God and recognize God's ministry through women'.[26]

The third Protestant speaker at San Antonio was a Lutheran. He is positive not only about Mary as Mother of God and as 'first and model disciple' but also as 'the spiritual Mother who intercedes for Christ's disciples and for all humanity'. He recognizes of course that his is 'not the conventional Lutheran position', but makes no reference to the USA Catholic–Lutheran Dialogue on the topic. This, however, was the subject taken for his paper by the Roman Catholic mariologist, Fr Frederick M. Jelly OP.

The Catholic–Lutheran Dialogue in the USA began in 1965 taking at first such topics as the Nicene Creed, Baptism and the Eucharist, before proceeding in 1978 to that of Justification and then, only then, addressing our present topic under the title 'The One Mediator, the Saints and Mary'. This eighth round of conversations lasted from 1983 to 1990, longer than any previous round, and the report appeared in 1992.[27] This includes background papers and a Common Statement (paras. 1–219; pp. 21–115) which examines the 'divergences' and asks if they need be 'Church-Dividing'. The divergences are chiefly three: the *invocation* as distinct from the *veneration* of Mary, and the two Marian dogmas. In substance the report states, firstly, that our divergence with regard to the invocation of Mary to which Lutherans are negative because of the Augsburg Confession need not be church-dividing, because Trent did not declare it to be obligatory but only 'good and beneficial', or, in the words of Vatican II, 'supremely fitting'[28] (paras. 93–8); and secondly, that our divergences with regard to the Marian dogmas do remain an obstacle to full fellowship but do not 'of themselves exclude all eucharistic sharing' (para. 100).

In his San Antonio paper Fr Jelly noted that this is the first of the official dialogues among our churches to address directly the topic of Mary and the Saints in relationship to the unique mediatorship of our one redeemer, Jesus Christ, and that he himself had served 'both as a consultant and as an active participant'. He dwelt on the substance of chapter 7 of *Lumen Gentium* which deals with the communion of saints. He emphasized the nineteen 'church-uniting convergences' given in the Common Statement which provide the context for the three divergences and in conclusion he stated: 'And we do continue our dialogue with the Lutherans, confident that there are many signs of hope for reunion with them as well as with other Protestants, Eastern Orthodox and Anglican brothers and sisters in Christ . . .'[29] But is reunion our ecumenical goal here and now?

II.3. Jared Wicks's recent survey

The third source to which I would refer in this central section on The Place of Mary Now in Formal Interchurch Dialogue is an article with that very title almost, by the American theologian, Jared Wicks SJ, which appeared earlier this year in *Gregorianum*, one of the periodicals published by the Gregorian University, Rome, where Fr Wicks teaches.[30] This article is particularly helpful because it gives special attention to the work of the French Groupe des Dombes. Being, however, the Luther scholar which he is Fr Wicks very naturally also includes the work of the Catholic–Lutheran Dialogue in the USA. Indeed he can devote himself exclusively to these two because Mary has so far featured in few other interchurch dialogues, national or international.[31]

The Groupe des Dombes is an unofficial French group of some forty Reformed (i.e. Presbyterian) and Catholic theologians well known already for their ecumenical work.[32] Their most recent publication is entitled *Marie dans le Dessein de Dieu et la Communion des Saints* (Mary in the Plan of God and the Communion of Saints). It appeared in two slim volumes, the first in 1997, the second in 1998 and both together in 1999.[33] An Italian translation has already appeared but so far no English translation.

These two ecumenical documents cover more or less the same ground but Fr Wicks very usefully compares and contrasts their different approaches and emphases. They agree that the invocation of Mary is not obligatory; Protestants may restrict themselves to respectful veneration and imitation (284–6). But the French go beyond the Americans insofar as they can acknowledge the two Marian dogmas as no longer church-dividing as well as no obstacle to eucharistic sharing. Indeed the Protestant members of the Groupe can envisage not just eucharistic sharing but a return to full communion without adherence to the two Marian dogmas (326).[34] Again Fr Wicks highlights the distinctive way the French document approaches the Marian texts of Scripture against the background of the articles of the Creed, and also the distinctive emphasis it places on conversion or renewal, which is the subject of its final chapter entitled 'Pour la Conversion des Églises'. The French document, he notes, encourages Protestants (329–33) to give Mary back a proper place in the mystery of salvation and the communion of saints, to reintroduce, for instance, into their celebration of Advent, Christmas, the Passion and Pentecost the Marian dimension suggested by the Scriptures themselves. By contrast the American document, he finds, has 'no critical word directed by the Lutheran members to their own churches' and 'it is hard', he takes the liberty of adding, 'to avoid the impression that these members were also basically contented with the present-day form of Lutheran catechesis and piety regarding the saints and Mary (p. 54). In making this comment Fr Wicks seems to ignore one of the major differences between the two documents: the American is official, the French is unofficial and therefore more open and relaxed. In any case those in the Calvinist/ Presbyterian/ Reformed tradition do not usually feel themselves as bound by their own confessional statements as Lutherans do.

III. The future

III.1. Ecumenical goals now?

Is 'reunion', as Fr Jelly was perhaps suggesting, our ecumenical goal here and now? In the 60s it certainly was, at least for the non-Roman Catholic churches. In September of that great year 1964, the year the Decree on Ecumenism was promulgated, the first British Conference of Faith and Order meeting in Nottingham invited the member churches of the British Council of Churches 'to covenant together to work and pray for the inauguration of union by a date agreed among them. We dare to hope that this date should not be later than Easter Day 1980'. Forty-one of the 350 delegates did vote against the second sentence of that resolution because of its specific date, but only five of them voted against the first sentence.

On the Roman Catholic side, however, ecumenical euphoria was more subdued and our expectations more modest. Ecumenism did begin to flourish, as we all fondly remember. We were hoping, however, not so much that the churches would be united by the 80s but that they would be 'ecumenized' by then. Even this more realistic hope has, however, also been disappointed. The 90s brought statistics showing a growing if not mounting indifference to church membership[35] and by an inexorable logic a growing if not mounting indifference to ecumenism. 'In Europe', Cardinal König wrote in 1995, 'the People of God at the local level in parishes and dioceses has become somewhat sceptical ... The commitment at the base remains feeble.'[36] In consequence despite new flurries of activity, in Scotland for instance, and in India,[37] prospects of Church union have also receded. And as far as the Roman Catholic Church is concerned, the [then] Secretary of the Pontifical Council for the Promotion of Christian Unity, Bishop Walter Kasper, speaking in Vienna in March 2000, did not hesitate to state that it would take patient and protracted dialogue 'for a century or more' to solve the issue of papal primacy.[38] Church union therefore, between Rome and Constantinople at least, is therefore not an immediate prospect, and therefore not here and now a reasonable, practical ecumenical goal.

III.2. Dialogue of Truth or Dialogue of Love?

After all these years of ecumenical effort the question arises whether we have not given too much attention, too much time and energy to Faith and Order issues, to the problem of truth, and too little to the problem of charity and mutual forgiveness? The theory we have followed was that, whereas doctrinal unity would have to wait and be worked hard for, here and now the exercise of mutual charity could and must begin. John Wesley enunciated the theory in his famous *Letter to a Roman Catholic:* 'if we cannot as yet *think alike* in all things, at least we may *love alike*'.[39] Pope Paul VI endorsed the theory when greeting Patriarch Athenagoras on 6 January 1964.

> Divergences of a doctrinal, liturgical and disciplinary nature will have to be examined, at the proper time and place, in a spirit of fidelity to truth and of understanding in charity. What can and must now begin to develop is that fraternal charity which is ingenious in discovering new ways of showing itself; which, taking its lessons from the past, is ready to pardon, more ready to believe good than evil.[40]

Pope Paul spoke again in similar terms when greeting Archbishop Ramsey in March 1966. 'In the field of doctrine and ecclesiastical law, we are still respectively distinct and distant ... From now on charity can and must be exercised between us, and show its mysterious and prodigious strength'.[41]

This priority of unity in charity over unity in truth – the former being easier, the latter more difficult to achieve – has now become an ecumenical commonplace but has time not shown that, on the contrary, agreement in truth has in a sense been much easier to reach than agreement in charity? Bilateral Commissions at national and international level have made great progress in producing agreed statements. Already indeed in 1978 Karl Rahner could write that 'today there are no theological opinions that with certainty can be pointed to as absolutely binding on Catholics and Protestants of such a nature as to require or to legitimate the separation of Churches'.[42]

But the common truth which has emerged in the dialogues has not made us free, because of course it has not been truth done, lived in love (cf. Eph. 4.15) – except for the privileged few. What evidence is there that in general we Christians have fallen back in love with each other, that we have really abandoned the culture of contempt (to use the phrase from Jewish–Christian dialogue) which makes us suspect and doubt each other's faith? We are groups, we can hardly deny, who in the past have hurt and offended each other and who in places still discriminate against each other; groups, however, who have so far never really forgiven each other, who carry doubts and suspicions about each other, who often unknown to themselves carry bitter memories. These doubts and suspicions and bitter memories may remain hidden for the most part. But they surely make their presence felt in our general ecumenical apathy and they surface only too clearly in resistance to Agreed Statements or in the ungenerous provisions of a document such as *One Bread, One Body* or indeed in some places in sectarian violence. In any case we are groups who, even where there is peaceful co-existence, too often ignore each other's presence as neighbours, as fellow-Christians, as partners in mission. Our sins of omission in the present if not our sins of commission in the past rise up to condemn us. Our prime need, as Pope John Paul emphasized in Jubilee year, is for mutual forgiveness, for unity in love to facilitate unity in truth. And in this context I should like to endorse what Fr Yarnold wrote a few years ago:

> The focus of importance is shifting from centralised discussions to local activity. A multitude of small actions can combine to establish a climate of mutual trust and affection which might eventually justify the Churches in putting a favourable interpretation on one another's teachings and practices, and create the readiness to do all possible to satisfy the demands of one another's consciences. The responsibility for pursuing this process of reunion by stealth falls above all not on Rome and Canterbury [and Geneva] but on dioceses, parishes and neighbourhoods.[43]

III. 3. Mariology and the dialogue of love

Because relations between East and West are at present at such a low ebb and because the Marian doctrine and devotion of the East has never been seriously questioned, a renewed dialogue of love between East and West must follow the general lines of what Pope John Paul proposed in his 1995 Apostolic Letter *Orientale Lumen* where, among other things, he emphasized the importance of meeting and experiencing each other's ways of worship. After my 1980 visit to Mount Athos where St Benedict is held in honour I stressed what I saw as the role of Western-rite Latin monks in helping to redress the present situation in which there is very little love lost between the Christian East and the Christian West. 'Twinning', as it has been practised between Anglican and Roman Catholic monasteries, would hardly be possible as yet, but I would like to see more visits by Western monks, by those at least who are sympathetic and who will not be discouraged if they are not welcomed to join the monks in church or perhaps even in the refectory.[44]

But above all a renewed dialogue of love between East and West must of course find concrete expression in the implementation of the Balamand Statement of 1993 agreed as a means of overcoming the alienation caused by the influx of the Western churches into Russia and Eastern Europe without reference to the relevant Orthodox authorities. This Statement recommends a 'will to pardon', mutual respect, the condemnation of violence, the avoidance of 'everything that can foment divison, contempt, and hatred between the Churches', the rejection of proselytism, and the sharing of church buildings. But the implementation of Balamand has only barely begun.

A dialogue of love designed to ease the mariological difficulties between the churches of the West must surely begin by recognizing that Protestants in general (as distinct from the relative few who have been members of bilateral commissions or ecumenically involved in other ways) are not convinced that Catholics accept that Jesus Christ is, in the words of 1 Tim. 2.5, our sole mediator. Rather they are convinced that we Catholics (of whatever denomination) do not accept that 'our entire hope of justification and salvation rests on Christ Jesus ... we do not place our ultimate trust in anything other than God's promise and saving work in Christ'.[45] And, on the face of it, are they not right? Do we not say the 'Hail Holy Queen' and pray to Mary as 'our life, our sweetness and our hope'? And as the Jews say in the gospels: 'What further testimony do we need?' (cf. Luke 22.71).

According to Vatican II in its Constitution on the Church we Roman Catholics must 'carefully refrain from whatever might by word or deed lead the separated brethren or any others whatsoever into error about the true doctrine of the Church' about Mary (67). In this context some of you may remember the story in Cardinal Bea's Preface to volume 7 of Fr du Manoir's 'Études sur la Sainte Vierge'. The parish priest in a largely Protestant village wanted to dedicate its new Catholic Church to our Lady because, he submitted, we should not dissimulate our views but give witness to them. His parish committee on the other hand wanted to dedicate the church to Christ the Redeemer or Christ the King. Cardinal Bea when asked for his advice sided with the latter but added that the principal or one of the principal side altars in the church be dedicated to our Lady.[46] For the same reasons in my lecture forty years ago I suggested statues of the Madonna and Child in preference to statues of the Madonna by herself.[47]

Is it not true that much of Roman Catholic life since the Reformation has been deliberately non-Protestant if indeed not anti-Protestant. We (and they too, of course, at least as much) have wanted to emphasize our distinctness and differences. A curious instance of this tendency – it has recently emerged – is to be found in the Greek style of Dublin's Pro-Cathedral, the foundation stone of which was laid in 1815. According to the professor of the History of Art at University College, Dublin, the fluted Doric columns inside and outside the cathedral may be due to a wish to distinguish it from the Royal Chapel at Dublin Castle, seat of the politico-religious establishment, which had been recently built in the 'diametrically opposed' Gothic Revival style.[48] And if, though a guest, I may take the liberty of mentioning it, one possible example here in England of the non-Protestant background to Roman Catholic Marian devotion may be the fairly common practice (unique to this country) of reciting the Hail Mary in the concluding part of the General Intercessions or Bidding Prayers at Mass. The National Centre for Liturgy in Ireland considers this practice inappropriate. It has been generally held that the English bishops were granted an indult from Rome in the matter, but the English authorities whom I consulted would no longer maintain this. Indeed I am informed by them that Archbishop Bugnini as Secretary of the Vatican Congregation for Divine Worship recommended that the practice be brought to an end 'over the coming years with appropriate catechesis'.[49]

A dialogue of love in Western Christianity to ease mariological difficulties must include Protestants as well as Catholics. They too have emphasized differences and therefore for them too the dialogue of love must be a process of renewal or of conversion, as the Group des Dombes put it, or of reform as the *ecclesia semper reformanda* adage expresses it. Reference was made earlier to the suggestions in this regard made by the Groupe des Dombes and to Fr Wicks's remark that the American Lutherans had 'no critical word' for their own churches.[50] When writing on this topic some forty years ago I suggested that 'isolation from its own sources and indeed infidelity to its own origins is one of the major obstacles hindering on the side of Protestantism mutual understanding between Christians on the subject of Marian doctrine and devotion'.[51] I was emphasizing then, what everyone now knows, that the Protestant reformers themselves saw no incompatibility in holding to the unique mediatorship of Christ and retaining a high doctrine about Mary, and indeed a warm devotion to her, especially to her Magnificat. Protestants in our day might surely begin to feel more tolerant of Roman Catholic doctrine and devotion if they were more conversant with that of their founders, even though the personal views of these founders carry none of the authority which the Book of Concord or the Thirty-Nine Articles do.

III.4. Mariology and the dialogue of truth

When in Rome in 1987 Patriarch Dimitrios made the following statement:

> ... Of all the entire Christian world our two sister Churches have maintained throughout the centuries unextinguished the flame of devotion to the most venerated person of the all holy Mother of God ... Truly the all holy Mother of God dominates in the consciousness of the faithful of both our Churches like a common bond and common tradition ... The person of the all holy Mother of God occupies a central and principal position in the faith of our Churches.[52]

Against the background of statements such as this it is very much to be regretted that in the age of controversy and confrontation Roman Catholic theologians expressed doubts about Orthodox belief in the doctrine of the immaculate conception. The dogmatic character of this doctrine is of course a problem but relatively minor. What matters is the doctrine itself. The Orthodox for their part in the context of East–West controversy have of course been negatively critical of the doctrine but only of the doctrine in its Western, Augustinian clothing.[53] In a recent article Bishop Kallistos of Diokleia quoting Fr George Florovsky was referring to the 'Babylonian captivity' of the East to 'Western scholastic categories'[54] and, he might have added, not only to scholastic categories but to Western theological and canonical categories in general. In the Second Vatican Council, in paragraphs 14–18 of the Decree on Ecumenism, the Roman Catholic Church solemnly committed itself to releasing the East from this captivity so that, in the words of the present Pope, the Church may once again be able to 'breathe with both its lungs'.[55] Roman Catholic doubts about Eastern belief in what we misleadingly call the immaculate conception[56] are perhaps the prime example of this Babylonian captivity. In the words of Florovsky, our Roman Catholic 'unfortunate terminology only obscures the indisputable truth of the Catholic belief'[57] which the East expresses by calling Mary the *panagia*, the all-holy.[58]

Mention was made earlier of the fact that the present Pope signed a Common Declaration with the Catholicos–Patriarch of the Assyrian Church of the East without using the term *theotokos* which, since the Council of Ephesus, that church has rejected on the grounds that it seems to prejudice the full humanity of Mary's son. This ecumenical methodology in its willingness not to insist on previous formulations is an application, but a surprising, a daring application of the principle famously enunciated by Pope John at the opening of Vatican II: 'the substance of the ancient doctrine of the deposit of faith is one thing, and the way in which it is presented is another'. This a very liberating principle in the whole dialogue of truth about Mary, and about the controversial Marian dogmas. Some Protestants, especially those in the Calvinist tradition who have had difficulties with the term *theotokos*, will be happy to hear about these recent developments in Roman Catholic dialogue with the Assyrian Church of the East – a Church whose members have often been thought of as the Protestants of the East. In the past Catholics have had little sympathy for these Protestant difficulties over the title '*theotokos*'. Forty years ago I stated that;

> We seem to have forgotten that it requires theological courage and daring to apply this title to Our Lady and that the very document of the Council of Ephesus which sanctions the application admits this, using as it does the words: *houtos tetharsekasi theotokon eipein ten hagian parthenon*. 'So [the holy Fathers] have made bold to call the holy Virgin Mother of God'. We seem to have forgotten too that to justify the title is to become involved in all the intricacies of trinitarian and christological doctrine, and that to express accurately the truth contained in the title demands many extremely and exquisitely, not to say excruciatingly, subtle distinctions.[59]

I have, however, to admit a reluctance to accept 'god-bearer' as an acceptable translation of *theotokos*. The more common translations of the Constitution on the Church of Vatican II (Flannery, Flanagan, Vorgrimler, Tanner[60]) use the traditional term. Fr Jelly however prefers 'God-bearer' and his own translation of the title of chapter 8 reads: 'The Blessed Virgin Mary, God-bearer, in the Mystery of Christ and of the Church'.[61] Although we still speak of 'women of child-bearing age' and of 'childbirth', 'bearing' is in general parlance simply another word for 'carrying'. Lampe translates 'God-bearing, who is mother of God'.[62] I very much doubt if we will ease Protestants' difficulties by substituting 'God-bearing' for 'Mother of God'.

III.5. The last article of the creed

What most of all perhaps preparation of this paper has revealed to me in a new way is the undeveloped state of the theology of the Four Last Things, of eschatology in all our churches. We would, I suggest, do a real service to theology and not just to mariology if in our dialogue of the truth we concentrated on the last article of the creed. The need for such a service is evident in the relative weakness in this regard of, for instance, the Faith and Order Study on *Confessing the One Faith*[63] and of the American Catholic–Lutheran conversations on *The One Mediator, the Saints, and Mary*. I still remember the shock I felt when I first read the chapter on 'The Cult of the Blessed Virgin' in John Gregg's *The Primitive Faith and Roman Catholic Developments*.[64]

> We owe her [Mary] reverence and gratitude. But that is in return for what she was, not for what she is—for what she once did, not for what she does. What she did she did once; and, once done, her unique position is no longer of importance. She steps down once again into the ranks of humanity. Her work is done; it belongs to history, to memory, to the past.
>
> The Blessed Virgin did the work she was called to do, and when it was done, there was (so far as has been revealed to us through the holy scripture) nothing more that she, and she alone, could do.

The author was later to become Archbishop of Dublin and Church of Ireland Primate in Armagh and as such prominent in Anglican circles – he attended four Lambeth Conferences.[65] But it was the eschatology of the sermon just quoted rather than its mariology that shocked me most. As it happened, just ninety years after Dr Gregg preached that controversial sermon, I had the privilege of standing in the same pulpit in St Fin Barre's Cathedral, Cork, to deliver the address at a memorial service for Bishop Henry McAdoo, of happy memory. On that occasion I took the liberty at the end of expressing the following not very Protestant sentiments:

> Baptized into the death and resurrection of Jesus, marked with the sign of faith, Henry McAdoo has now gone to the Father and his joy no one can ever take from him. And it is for our good that he has gone: to make intercession for us and for our fumbling ecumenical efforts, and to prepare a place for us so that where he is we may also be: in our Father's house where – as here – there are many rooms.[66]

It is for me incredible that any of us suffers a basic change of personality with death: Henry McAdoo has not lost his ecumenical interest nor the Blessed Virgin her maternal love for her Son and for all of us, his friends and followers. With Karl Rahner I would hold that

The Assumption of the Blessed Virgin, body and soul, into heaven says nothing else about Mary but what we also profess about ourselves in an article of faith in the Apostles' Creed: the resurrection of the body and eternal life.[67]

III.6. Taking Mary into their system?

'To take episcopacy into their system' was the phrase famously used by Archbishop Geoffrey Fisher in his landmark 1946 Cambridge sermon which led to official unity conversations between the Church of England, the English Methodists and the Scottish Presbyterians.[68] This paper concludes by asking: 'Do Catholics make a similar call to Protestants in view of Church union?' 'Is Marian doctrine and devotion an essential of the Church somewhat as episcopacy is?'

Before addressing this question however we do well perhaps to remind ourselves, if only very briefly, that the aim of the ecumenical movement is not so much to promote Christian unity and establish Church union as to reduce and end the scandal of Christian disunity. It is surely scandalous, especially in these days of mounting unbelief, if we Christians belittle each other's belief and beliefs, if there is anything that savours of anti-Catholicism, anti-Protestantism or anti-Romanism in our Churches and our Christian lives. Unfortunately there is still, it would seem, some post-Tridentine anti-Protestantism in our Roman Catholic Marian piety, and some anti-Romanism also in Protestant doctrine and piety. Is it not still our main means of differentiating ourselves? Our first responsibility is surely to recognize this fact and take the beam out of our own eye. We are unlikely to recognize it, however, if we continue to live in isolation and have little or no experience of each other's ways.

But do Protestants have to take Mary into their system? 'Mary *is* for everyone'. There is a Marian dimension to the Scriptures, to the early Councils, to the Creeds – and indeed to the spiritual lives of the sixteenth-century Reformers. Protestants have tended to play down this dimension. A due recognition and appreciation of this dimension, within the parameters of course of a Protestantism which venerates without invoking the saints, is indeed to be desired. But otherwise is a Marian spirituality any more obligatory for Protestants than it is for Catholics, Roman or any other? A Christian life in which devotions to Mary – for instance saying the rosary – are prominent is not necessary for church union. In any case the most in the way of Christian unity that can realistically be expected in the foreseeable future, as far as Roman Catholics are concerned, is a less restricted pulpit and table fellowship. For this, however, to happen adherence to the two Marian dogmas is certainly not necessary. When for Roman Catholics church union does eventually become a practical proposition, developments in Christian anthropology and Christian eschatology, as well as in ecumenical theology generally, will surely have shown the two Marian dogmas to be much less controversial than they may now appear, to be no longer 'church-dividing'. Paragraph 79 of *Ut Unum Sint* does not mention them. This omission is at least of some significance. And when church union does become a practical proposition, times will have changed so much that the question posed by Anglicans in the 1981 'Authority in the Church II' statement of the Anglican–Roman Catholic International Commission (para. 30) as to whether 'in any future union . . . they would be required to subscribe to such dogmatic statements' as the Marian dogmas will not be problematic any longer.[69] In any case, what here and now at this stage seems most important from an ecumenical and Marian point of view is not what the churches of the West may have to take into their system at some future date, but what they ought here and now to throw out, to jettison. Mary is still more of a stumbling block than a bond of union. We have all contributed to this by making her a main focus of our mutual antipathy, by unduly emphasizing Marian doctrine and devotion as a way of differentiating our respective traditions and of justifying their separate existence.[70] What Michael Ramsey wrote of 'the Papal controversy' may I think be applied to Marian doctrine and devotion. 'Ultimate reunion', he wrote, 'is hastened not by the pursuit of "the papal controversy" but by the quiet growth of the organic life of every part of Christendom.'[71] In that spirit we can surely say that the ultimate reunion of our churches is hastened not by the pursuit of controversy over Marian doctrine and devotion but, as the Groupe des Dombes was suggesting, by the quiet growth of the Marian dimension which is inherent in the Christian religion and which has been fostered so zealously since 1967 by the Ecumenical Society of the Blessed Virgin Mary, the hosts of this International Congress.

Notes

1   The text was published the following year in *The Furrow* 14/4, 6 (1963), pp. 212–24, 349–60.
2   Xavier Rynne, *Letters from Vatican City* (New York 1963), p. 170; Ralph M. Wiltgen, *The Rhine Flows into the Tiber* (New York City 1967), passim. The Constitution, under the title *Dei Verbum*, was finally passed only on 18 November 1965.
3   No one else being ready and willing to give a Milltown Park Public Lecture on the topic, I made it up myself, and the public interest was such that I was never allowed to look back. Cf. Michael Hurley SJ, *Christian Unity: An Ecumenical Second Spring?* (Dublin 1998), p. 265.
4   'Ecumenism: time for the breakthrough', in *The Month* (April 1985), pp. 126–8.

5 Michael Hurley SJ, 'The Joint Declaration on the Doctrine of Justification: Another Ecumenical Milestone?' in *Milltown Studies* 45 (Summer 2000), pp. 44–57.

6 Quoting from a Georgetown University press release.

7 Cf. Michael Hurley SJ, *'One Bread, One Body' Studies* (Summer 1999), pp. 225–30; Ruth Reardon, *'One Bread, One Body:* an Interchurch Family Commentary', in *One in Christ* 35/2 (1999), pp. 109–30.

8 *The Furrow* (May 1968), p. 267.

9 Michael O'Carroll CSSp, *Theotokos. A Theological Encyclopedia of the Blessed Virgin Mary* (Wilmington 1982), p. 353.

10 ibid. p. 355.

11 Frederick M. Jelly OP, 'The Theological Context of and Introduction to Chapter 8 of *Lumen Gentium*' in *Marian Studies* 37 (1986), pp. 43–73.

12 Stefano De Fiores SMM, 'Mary in Postconciliar Theology' in *Vatican II: Assessment and Perspectives*, ed. René Latourelle (Paulist Press, New York 1988), vol. 1, p. 471.

13 By, for instance, Donal Flanagan in Kevin MacNamara, ed., *Vatican II: The Constitution on the Church* (Chapman), pp. 317, 323.

14 Cf. Michael Hurley SJ, *'Mary is for Everyone: Essays on Mary and Ecumenism'*, in *The Month* (May 1998), pp. 202–3.

15 Paragraphs 27, 30. I am very grateful to Fr Chris O'Donnell OCarm, who teaches Mariology at the Milltown Institute, for bringing this document to my attention. I quote from the English version published in 1989 by the Congregation for Catholic Education.

16 *The Tablet*, 22–29 April 2000, p. 584. 'Theological, historical, social scientific approaches to the cult of the Virgin Mary in Western Christianity'.

17 In a letter of 7 April 2000. In his reply the Secretary of the Theology Faculty at Maynooth, Fr Hugh Connolly, wrote that 'there did seem to be some agreement among colleagues that Mariology is at something of a low ebb at present and that there may be a case for a rediscovery of this area as a counterbalance to some of the more esoteric marian devotions which are gaining currency at this time'.

18 Eamon R. Carroll OCarm, 'Mary in Ecumenical Perspective', in *Ecumenical Trends* 26/5 (May 1997), pp. 8–72.

19 ibid.

20 Gracewing, Leominster 1997.

21 Fr Carroll, in the article cited in the preceding notes 18–19, quotes a bishop who worked closely with Martin Gillett to the effect that 'Martin had the remarkable charism of not being able to take "no" for an answer, and indeed, in the face of his charity and commitment few people could deny his requests on behalf of the Ecumenical Society'. I regret having been one of the few.

22 Published in *Marian Studies* 48 (1997), pp. 6–137.

23 ibid. pp. 16–50.

24 ibid. p. 28.

25 ibid. p. 54.

26 ibid. p. 113.

27 H. G. Anderson, J. F. Stafford, J. A. Burgess eds. *The One Mediator, the Saints, and Mary* (Augsburg Fortress, Minneapolis 1992). Cf. John Reumann, 'A Perspective on the Lutheran–Roman Catholic Dialogue in the United States, 1965–1993', in *One in Christ* 34/4 (1998), pp. 277–88.

28 *Lumen Gentium* 50.

29 *Marian Studies* loc. cit. p. 136.

30 'The Virgin Mary in Recent Ecumenical Dialogues', in *Gregorianum* 81/1 (2000), pp. 25–57.

31 Reference was made above, p.191, to a British Methodist–Roman Catholic study on Mary. The *Final Report* of ARCIC I had a significant paragraph on Mary in 'Authority in the Church II' (para. 30), and in 1977 the Old Catholics and Orthodox had already produced an Agreed Statement on Mary; cf. H. Meyer and L. Vischer, *Growth in Agreement* (Paulist Press, New York, WCC, Geneva 1984), pp. 299–401. The *Catholic Herald* (26 May 2000, p. 3) reported that ARCIC was considering a new study on the place of the Blessed Virgin Mary in the life and doctrines of the Church.

32 In 1991 they produced a report on Church Renewal, an English translation of which was published by the World Council of Churches in 1993 under the title *For the Conversion of the Churches*. Here they are described as 'an independent group of Catholics and Protestants in France'. In the beginning an Orthodox observer was present, Paul Evdokimov, but he was not replaced. Cf. Maurice Jourjon, 'Marie dans le Dessein de Dieu et la Communion des Saints', in *Études Mariales* (MediasPaul 1998), p. 219.

33 All published in Paris by Bayard Editions/Centurion. Quotations here are from the two-volume edition in which happily the numbering of the paragraphs and chapters (though not of the pages) runs on – is continuous. References here are given to paragraphs rather than pages.

34 In an earlier paragraph (298) the whole group and not just its Protestant members appear to hold this view.

35 'Church-going figures are still plunging', in *The Tablet*, 22–29 April 2000, p. 584.

36 *The Tablet*, 21 October 1995, pp. 1340, 1341.

37 Thomas F. Best and others, 'Survey of Church Union Negotiations 1996–1999', in *The Ecumenical Review*, 52/1 (January 2000), pp. 3–45.

38 *The Tablet*, 8 April 2000, p. 495.

39 Ed. Michael Hurley SJ, (Geoffrey Chapman, London 1968), p. 56.

40 Quoted ibid. p. 15.

41 ibid.

42 *Journal of Ecumenical Studies* 1978, p. 225.

43 '*Apostolicae Curae*: Past and Future Processes', in *The Month*, November 1966, p. 434.

44 This was my experience on Mount Athos in 1980: cf Michael Hurley SJ, *Christian Unity: An Ecumenical Second Spring?* pp. 40–5, 292–307. In June 2000, however, when I was a guest for a week at the Stavropegic Monastery of St John the Baptist at Tolleshunt Knights in Essex, I was made welcome at all their common meals and at all their services, including the Divine Liturgy, but not at the Holy Table itself. The offer of eucharistic hospitality made to

the Orthodox by Vatican II and by *One Bread, One Body* is sadly, however understandably, not so far reciprocated.

45 *The One Mediator, the Saints, and Mary* (above note 27), 103.

46 H. du Manoir SJ, *Maria* (Paris 1964), p. xii. The volume dealt with 'the harmony of Marian doctrine and devotion with the ecumenical spirit'.

47 Michael Hurley SJ, 'Ecumenism and Mariology I: The Contribution of Catholics', in *The Furrow*, 14/4 (April 1963), pp. 222–3.

48 Michael McCarthy, 'Dublin's Greek Pro-Cathedral', in *History of the Catholic Diocese of Dublin*, eds. James Kelly and Daire Keogh, (Four Courts Press, Dublin 2000), p. 246. The author is Professor of History of Art at UCD.

49 Sean Swayne, *Gather Around the Lord* (Columba Press, Dublin 1987), p. 86; correspondence with Rev. Patrick Jones of the National Centre for Liturgy at Maynooth (4 May 2000), with Mgr Anthony Boylan, formerly Secretary of the National Liturgy Commission (NCL) of the Bishops' Conference of England and Wales (BCEW) and now Episcopal Vicar for Worship in the Diocese of Leeds (7 July 2000); telephone conversations with Mgr Anthony Rogers (24 July) and with Mr Martin Foster (1 August), the former being Secretary, the latter Assistant Secretary of what was formerly the NCL and is now the Department of Christian Life and Worship of the BCEW at Westminster. The letter from Bugnini, I gather, is not at present in place. According to Mr Foster, it was occasioned by the suggestion in a second edition in the early 70s of an official booklet on the Bidding Prayer that other Marian prayers might be included as well as the Hail Mary. His reaction was to disapprove of this further suggestion and to ask that the recitation of the Hail Mary be itself discontinued.

50 Above II.3.

51 Michael Hurley SJ, 'Ecumenism and Mariology II: The Contribution of Protestants' in *The Furrow* 14/6 (June 1963), pp. 350–2.

52 Quoted by Mgr Radano loc. cit. (above II. 2: notes 22–3), pp. 36–7.

53 Cf. Paul McPartlan, 'Mary and Catholic–Orthodox Dialogue', in *One in Christ* 34/1 (1998), pp. 3–17.

54 'The Witness of the Orthodox Church' in *The Ecumenical Review* 52/1 (January 2000), p. 52.

55 *Ut Unum Sint*, 54.

56 It is a misnomer insofar as what is said to be immaculate is not the act of conception by Joachim and Anne, but the child conceived by them. Cf. Michael Hurley SJ, 'The Immaculate Conception', in *Doctrine and Life* 46/10 (December 1996), pp. 601–3.

57 Quoted by McPartlan, art. cit. p.11.

58 Which against the background of Isaiah 6 I call 'theological brinkmanship with a vengeance *à outrance*', art. cit. p. 600. The term 'hyperagia' is also used, for example in the services at the Monastery of St John the Baptist in Essex.

59 Michael Hurley SJ, 'Ecumenism and Mariology I: The Contribution of Catholics', in *The Furrow* 14/4 (April 1963), pp. 213–14.

60 Austin Flannery OP, *Vatican II on the Church*, (Scepter Books, Dublin 1966), p. 307; Donal Flanagan, *Vatican II: The Constitution on the Church*, ed. Kevin

MacNamara (Chapman, London 1968), p. 317; Otto Semmeroth, *Commentary on the Documents of Vatican II*, ed. Herbert Vorgrimler (Burns Oates/Herder & Herder, 1967), vol. 1, p. 285; *Decrees of the Ecumenical Councils*, ed. Norman P. Tanner SJ, (Sheed & Ward/Georgetown University Press 1990), vol. 2, p. 891.

61   Frederick M. Jelly OP, 'The Theological Context of and Introduction to Chapter 8 of *Lumen Gentium'*, in *Marian Studies* 37 (1986), p. 239.

62   G. W. H. Lampe, *A Patristic Greek Lexicon* (Clarendon Press, Oxford 1961), p. 639. Liddell and Scott give 'mother of God'. According to Henry Bettenson, 'God-bearer' is 'not so startling as the English "Mother of God", the Greek stressing the Deity of the Son rather than the privilege of the mother' (*Documents of the Christian Church*, OUP 1943, p. 65).

63   Faith and Order Paper no. 153 (World Council of Churches, Geneva 1991).

64   Dublin, Association for Promoting Christian Knowledge, 1957, pp. 48–61. The book contains the text of six sermons delivered in 1909. As late as 1962–3 they were still indicated for reading and study at secondary school level by all Irish Protestant boys and girls.

65   George Seaver, *John Allen Fitzgerald Gregg* (The Faith Press, London: Allen Figgis, Dublin 1963).

66   Michael Hurley SJ, '*In Memoriam:* Henry Robert McAdoo', in *Doctrine and Life* 49/6 (July–August 1999), p. 354.

67   Karl Rahner, *Foundations of Christian Faith* (London 1978), p. 388.

68   S. L. Greenslade, 'The Church of England and the Free Churches from 1660', in *Anglican Initiatives in Christian Unity* (SPCK, London 1967), p. 122.

69   *The Final Report* (London 1982), p. 96.

70   'One consequence of our separation has been a tendency for Anglicans and Roman Catholics alike to exaggerate the importance of the Marian dogmas in themselves at the expense of other truths more closely related to the foundations of the Christian faith.' ibid.

71   Arthur Michael Ramsey, *The Gospel and the Catholic Church* (Longmans, Green & Co, London, 2nd edn. 1956), p. 228.

(This paper was given at the ESBVM Oxford Congress
in August 2000)

18

Interchurch relations:
Forty years in the desert?

Michael Hurley SJ

Maynooth is not Oxford and a Regional is not an International Conference but rightly or wrongly I feel that I have been invited back. This is very encouraging, especially perhaps as at Oriel last year I provoked my good friend and perfect gentleman, Ted Yarnold, to disagree with me in public. There is very good reason therefore why, to begin with, I should ask the organizers of this Conference of the Ecumenical Society of the Blessed Virgin Mary to accept my very sincere thanks for their kind and generous invitation to give this paper – which I have subtitled: 'Forty Years in the Desert?'

It was at Ascensiontide that I began to put pen to paper and the ascension, we know from St Luke, took place forty days after the resurrection. This may well be the immediate reason why just recently I have come to see that ecumenism is now in its forties, and to realize that this fact may be of some considerable significance.

Ecumenism of course is already in its nineties; it began in 1910 in Edinburgh at a meeting of the International Missionary Council. It is Roman Catholic involvement in ecumenism which is in its forties, but the birth of Roman Catholic ecumenism in the 1960s meant a rebirth for Anglican, Orthodox and Protestant ecumenism. The 1960s were a climacteric in the ecumenical movement in general. The winds of change were blowing strongly not only in the secular world but also in the religious world.

In any case it remains that for Roman Catholics at least and certainly for myself personally ecumenism is now in its forties and that the significance of this fact merits some consideration. Vatican II took place from 1962 to 1965. The Council's Decree on Ecumenism was promulgated on 21 November 1964 and was welcomed on all sides as 'revolutionary', 'epoch-making'; 'a remarkable achievement, far surpassing what even the "ecumenical romantics" would have anticipated'.[1] It was on Whit Sunday 1960 that Pope John XXIII had announced the establishment of what was initially called the Secretariat for Promoting Christian Unity. Thanks to this body and its Moderator, Cardinal Bea, all the other churches became involved in the Vatican Council and to quite a considerable extent both in the preparations for it and in the actual proceedings. Later that same year, on 3 December, Archbishop Fisher of Canterbury, an Evangelical who had no great sympathy for Rome,[2] called on the Pope at the Vatican and his first words were: 'Your Holiness, we are making history'.[3] It was in fact the first visit of an Archbishop of Canterbury to the Pope since that of Archbishop Arundel in 1397.[4] One immediate result was the appointment of a representative of the Archbishops of Canterbury and York to take up residence in Rome and the eventual establishment of the Anglican Centre in Rome.

Then no sooner had Vatican II ended in December 1965 than Pope Paul VI was off to Jerusalem where he and Archbishop Athenagoras, Patriarch of Constantinople met and in what they called an 'act of justice and forgiveness' solemnly consigned to oblivion the excommunications of 1054. In March of the following year, 1966, Archbishop Michael Ramsey, Archbishop of Canterbury, was visiting Rome and receiving as a gift from the Pope his very own Episcopal ring: a gesture richly if ambiguously symbolic in significance.[5] Soon afterwards the Anglican–Roman Catholic Joint Preparatory Commission was established. This was quickly followed by bilateral Commissions with the other churches, especially the Lutheran and Methodist – I myself was involved in the Methodist–Roman Catholic International Commission. And as early as 1968 the first fruits of this work began to appear. That year the Roman Catholic Church became a full member of the Faith and Order Commission of the World Council of Churches and that year the Anglican–Roman Catholic Joint Preparatory Commission produced its 'Malta Report' which urged a strategy of Unity by Stages. Already however the first signs of difficulties to come made their ominous appearance. The Congregation for the Doctrine of the Faith would not agree to the publication of the Malta Report.[6]

For me the question now arises: has it any significance that it is forty years ago that all this happened? Sometimes both in biblical and secular usage the figure 'forty' may indicate little more than a round number: the length of David's reign of forty years (2 Sam. 5.4), the depth of 'the forty-foot' at high tide here in Dunlaoire, the number of Ali Baba's Forty Thieves. At other times however the meaning of 'forty' in the Bible is quite definitely much more than merely mathematical. It is hardly a coincidence that the Flood lasted forty days, that Israel wandered in the desert for forty years, that Jesus too spent forty days in the desert and forty hours in the tomb and remained on earth forty days after his resurrection, and that our Lent lasts for forty days.

For the Christian therefore the figure 'forty' suggests a mysterious, fateful period. But if salvation history, as we have just seen, consists of such periods of forty, the central, fundamental one is Israel's wandering in the desert which the Book of Deuteronomy (8.2) describes so beautifully: 'And you shall remember all the way which the Lord your God has led you these forty years in the wilderness, that he might humble you, testing you to know what was in your hearts, whether you would keep his commandments, or not.'

The Synoptic account of Jesus's forty days in the desert – especially that of Matthew and Luke culminating in the triple temptation – is generally accepted as a deliberate reference to Israel's desert experience. The desert is a place of danger, hardship and death, the haunt of demons and wild animals, a place to wrestle with evil, eventually to be saved, of course,[7] but primarily to be tempted and tested and, as the New Testament reminds us more than once (eg Acts 7.41, 1 Cor. 10.5; Heb. 3.8), to fail and be unfaithful, to drink the chalice of doubt and mistake, of failure and unfaithfulness.

Looking back now on the period since the 1960s it makes sense to me to see it as a desert experience for the ecumenical movement and it reassures me, it gives me hope to realize that we are now in the last decade of this forty-year period. These forty years have for ecumenists in particular been a period of ups and downs, of mistakes and failures, of disappointments, of trials and tribulations. It has been a period of probation, of formation. But the movement has grown in maturity.

These forty years of ecumenical endeavour have seen a heavy emphasis placed on doctrinal unity and on joint research and study as the privileged means of achieving this unity. The results have been quite remarkable. Agreed statements on the eucharist have been produced not only by the Anglican–Roman Catholic International Commission but by other bilateral commissions as well and indeed by the Faith and Order Commission of the World Council of Churches. The Pope has signed Common Christological Declarations with Patriarchs of churches which rejected not only the Council of Chalcedon but also the Council of Ephesus. Rome no longer insists on a two-nature terminology nor on the term '*theotokos*'. As Pope John XXIII put it at the opening of Vatican II: 'the substance of the ancient doctrine of the deposit of faith is one thing, and the way in which it is presented is another'. And more recently a Joint Declaration on the Doctrine of Justification, the article on which the Lutherans see the Church stand or fall, has been agreed by them and by the Roman Catholic Church.[8] Unfortunately Marian doctrine and devotion does not so far feature in this success story, despite all the good work of the Ecumenical Society of the Blessed Virgin Mary.[9]

But this remarkably successful dialogue of truth has for all practical purposes remained a dead letter. Addressing Patriarch Athenagoras in 1964, Pope Paul VI had stated:

> Divergences of a doctrinal, liturgical and disciplinary nature will have to be examined, at the proper time and place, in a spirit of fidelity to truth and of understanding in charity. What can and must now begin to develop is that fraternal charity which is ingenious in discovering new ways of showing itself; which, taking its lessons from the past, is ready to pardon, more ready to believe good than evil.

In general, however, it is the doctrinal divergences between the churches which since the 1960s have received attention and indeed showed themselves amazingly amenable to solution. No comparable dialogue of charity, of joint action, has developed either in parallel to the dialogue of truth or in consequence of its conclusions. The boldness which has characterized the churches' thinking has been conspicuously absent from their ways of acting. The 'co-operation among all Christians' to which Vatican II's Decree on Ecumenism had exhorted Roman Catholics in its longest and most eloquent paragraph has not for the most part become the norm but only the exception. Neither has the ecumenical tithing which I took the liberty of suggesting some twenty years ago, in 1983.[10]

We do not in fact relate to each other or treat each other as sisters, and to that extent the controversial Vatican documents of 2000 simply exposed the hollowness of our ecumenism. It is our deeds rather than our words which express our real feelings and opinions about each other, our deeds in the matter for instance of integrated education and joint schooling, and in the matter of eucharistic sharing. From our deeds rather than words what emerges is sadly that we Christians have not yet fallen back in love with each other, that we have not yet abandoned the culture of contempt which makes us suspect and doubt each other's faith. As the incoming President of the Methodist Church in Ireland (the Revd Harold Good) was saying last week, all the churches have been plagued by 'irrelevant and wasteful denominationalism, our unhealthy preoccupation with self-preservation'.[11]

But as we enter the last decade of our forty years of wandering in the ecumenical desert, I discern one sign of a new maturity in interchurch relations: there is a change of vocabulary, of terminology, a changed theological emphasis. Whereas in earlier years we spoke in terms of unity and renewal, now we prefer to think and talk in the related but distinct terms of reconciliation, of repentance and forgiveness. Reconciliation is a term which these recent years has become very popular in secular as well as religious discourse. And so it comes as a surprise to find that there are very few – only five or six, it would appear – references to 'reconciliation' in the whole corpus of Vatican II.[12] The change of vocabulary, the new emphasis on reconciliation instead of unity is, I suggest, highly significant: it implies a distinction with a real difference. What is merely implicit in the language of unity and renewal becomes explicit in the language of reconciliation, of forgiveness and repentance. Here in this latter there is formal recognition of the following highly relevant facts: that it is groups of people, not sets of doctrinal or theological propositions; communities of belief, rather than systems of belief, which primarily need to be brought into agreement; that the disunity to be overcome among Christians is a disunity of estrangement and alienation; that down the years we have hurt and offended each other and discriminated against each other and that, if this does not still continue, the memory of it does; that we have so far never really forgiven each other; that we harbour bitter memories, doubts and suspicions about each other; that if these lie hidden for the most part, they surface only too clearly in resistance to Agreed Statements, in various forms of sectarianism, not excluding violence, in general ecumenical apathy, in the ungenerous provisions of *One Bread One Body*, and of course in the clumsy insensitivities of the Vatican Declaration *Dominus Jesus* and its Note on 'Sister Churches'.

But where there has been hurt and offence, renewal in a relationship must take the form of forgiveness and repentance, and unity must take the form of reconciliation. The unity which is reconciliation, whether it be the reconciliation of two individuals or two groups or two societies, either secular or religious, makes demands on both victims and offenders. Faults however are rarely if ever all on one side. Each of us, therefore, is very likely both victim and offender, so that it is mutual forgiveness and mutual repentance which are in order. In any case if there is to be reconciliation it is necessary that the victims forgive: that they abandon thoughts of revenge or retribution; that they persevere in love for the offenders but paradoxically without in any way condoning the offence. And certainly if there is to be reconciliation it is also necessary that the offenders repent, i.e. that they confess, apologize, say sorry and give concrete expression to these words of sorrow by making amends, by undoing the wrong committed, making compensation, restoring justice.

But all this is very complex and still quite controversial. There are some who reject the concept of reconciliation because it seems to them to soft-pedal, to downplay if not ignore the claims of justice–repentance or who accept it with a one-sided emphasis on justice–repentance, soft-pedalling the claims of forgiveness.[13] These differences surfaced in 2000. In his 1994 Apostolic Letter on 'Preparation for the Jubilee of the Year 2000' Pope John Paul emphasized that the Church 'cannot cross the threshold of the new millennium without encouraging her children to purify themselves, through repentance, of past errors and instances of infidelity, inconsistency, and slowness to act.' (33)

After six years of research into the Church's record of past errors, the Pope on Sunday 12 March celebrated a Jubilee Day of Pardon. Each of seven leading figures of the Roman Curia confessed in turn 'sins committed in the service of the truth', 'sins which have harmed the unity of the Body of Christ', 'sins against the people of Israel', 'sins committed in actions against love, peace, the rights of peoples and respect for cultures and religions', 'sins agains the dignity of women and the unity of the human race' and 'sins in relation to the fundamental rights of the human person'. In each case the Pope asked for forgiveness. At the beginning he had mentioned 'the wrongs done by others to us', to the Christians who had 'suffered injustices, arrogance and persecution for their faith', urging a renewed offer of forgiveness in order 'to purify the memory of those sad events from every sentiment of rancour or revenge'.

This Day of Pardon was a deeply moving occasion but, as mentioned, the prospect had given rise to a good deal of misgiving among some theologians and historians. To address these misgivings the Pope had asked the International Theological Commission to study the issue. Their report, in the drafting of which the Revd Professor Tom Norris of Maynooth had taken part, was published earlier in the month. Entitled *Memory and Reconciliation: The Church and the Faults of the Past,* this document discusses the problems arising, and by way of answer emphasizes the 'solidarity that exists among them [the children of the Church] through time and space because of their incorporation into Christ and the work of the Holy Spirit' (3.4.)[14] In other words, the principles of logic and theology which enable us to pride ourselves on our past and its glories – these same principles enable and require us to be ashamed about, to ask forgiveness for, to do penance for what is inglorious and sinful in that same past, for the evils which our ancestors perpetrated; and also, of course, to offer forgiveness for the evils suffered by those ancestors, to offer it to those who are and who recognize themselves as the heirs and successors of the perpetrators.

In Ireland in a 1996 letter our Catholic Bishops had stated: 'We must all respond generously to the Pope's call to the whole church for a collective examination of conscience regarding the mistakes and sins of this Millennium, especially sins against Christian unity'. And the following year a report of the Department of Theological Questions of the Irish InterChurch meeting (an association of all the churches, Catholic and Protestant) recommended, among other things, that the churches come together in a common confession of guilt, and a common desire for reconciliation, in Ireland North and South. In that spirit the Anglican and Catholic Bishops of Ferns, Bishop Brendan Comiskey and Bishop John Neill issued a Joint Pastoral Letter for Pilgrimage Sunday, 21 May

2000. In this Letter they recalled how 'relationships between us as Churches ... have undergone a sea-change' and added:

> Grateful as we are for that flowering of ecumenical fellowship, good will and cooperation, we cannot but feel called to ask God's and each other's forgiveness for the many divisive, wounding and unchristian attitudes, policies and practices that found their way into both our churches during the centuries since the Reformation. We each express true repentance on behalf of our own church for these hurtful and damaging words and deeds and we pray that the reconciliation all of us in both Churches seek may be brought nearer by our request for forgiveness and our expression of true conversion of heart in relation to these ecumenical faults and failings.

The Catholic Archbishop of Dublin and other individual Catholic bishops did during the Jubilee year emphasize forgiveness and reconciliation, but mainly with particular reference to recent scandals rather than in the comprehensive way adopted by the Pope. The Jubilee Day of Pardon which the Pope celebrated in Rome on 12 March 2000 went unobserved here. And as a body the Irish Catholic Bishops seem to have no plans to follow the Pope's example in this matter. Many Catholics of course disapprove of this papal initiative. When in 1997 Bishop Walsh of Killaloe asked forgiveness from Protestants for the 'pain and hurt' caused by the *Ne Temere* decree and mixed marriages in the past, his gesture was dismissed in articles in the *Irish Catholic* and in an editorial in the *Catholic Herald* (17 May 1997) as 'cultural cringe' and 'misleading digression'.[15] With reference, however, to our neglect of the Day of Pardon the editor of the *Irish Catholic*, David Quinn, wrote as follows in his *Sunday Times* column:

> Let down by the usual failure of imagination, nothing was forthcoming from the Irish hierarchy, apart from Dublin's Archbishop Desmond Connell ... The Irish Bishops collectively could have done something dramatic last Sunday [12 March] for all the wrongs committed in the name of the Irish church. It might even have convinced some people and won back lost ground. Instead they did nothing. Another opportunity lost.[16]

While the change of terminology and of theology from unity to reconciliation is a sign of maturity, resistance to it is also a sign that we are still wandering in the desert. In particular this resistance highlights the fact that we have paid too little attention to the dialogue of charity, that this has suffered by contrast with the dialogue of truth. This resistance therefore invites and challenges us to begin at last to follow the advice of Paul VI in 1964 when addressing Patriach Athenagoras: 'What can and must now begin to develop is that fraternal charity which is ingenious in discovering new ways of showing itself, which, taking its lessons from the past, is ready to pardon, more ready to believe good than evil.'

The same advice is given by Pope John Paul II when in his Apostolic Letter 'At the Beginning of the New Millennium' he urges us 'to launch out into the deep' (Luke 5.4). This must mean abandoning our fears, of joint schools, for instance, and of eucharistic sharing, and taking seriously the call to co-operation according to conscience in paragraph 12 of the Decree on Ecumenism. In the words of the Decree: 'Through such co-operation, all believers in Christ are able to learn easily how they can understand each other better and esteem each other more, and how the road to the unity of Christians may be made smooth.' Such co-operation, doing everything together as far as conscience permits, has been the ecumenical ideal since the Faith and Order Conference in Lund in 1952. The Churches in Europe in their recent *Charta Oecumenica* have formally committed themselves to such co-operation: 'We commit ourselves ... to seek encounters with one another, to be there for one another, and to work together in every way possible'. And, as Bishop Poyntz conveys in his paper which follows (pp. 219–231), the promotion of such co-operation seems to be the main concern of the new Anglican–Roman Catholic International Commission.

In any case despite this resistance an ecumenical journey in the desert, a desert experience of forty years for the ecumenical movement, is not a cause for doom and gloom. At the end must lie the promised land. So I look forward to the next decade and it begins, I note, very promisingly and very providentially in its very first year, in 2010 with the centenary of Edinburgh 1910, and continues in 2014 equally promisingly and providentially with the Golden Jubilee of the promulgation of Vatican II's Decree on Ecumenism, in 1964. These past forty years of ecumenism have indeed been a time of trial, of temptation, a time of too much inept leadership and too many botched initiatives; they still are. But against the background of biblical salvation history it is, in the words of Moses in Deut. 8.2, the Lord our God who is leading us during these forty years in the ecumenical wilderness. It has been a learning experience; we have grown in ecumenical maturity. We believe that as a people we will get to the promised land of Christian unity. And we know that we shall get there not by the methods used by Joshua, not by conquest, and not by a dialogue of truth alone, but by a dialogue of truth and a dialogue of charity in proper combination. We do not yet know what the promised land of Christian unity will really be like. At times, like Moses and like Martin Luther King, we've been to the mountain top; we've looked over and seen the promised land, a land overflowing with milk and honey; with the milk and honey of human kindness, of Christian charity, of mutual forgiveness and repentance, of reconciliation, with shared pulpits and shared eucharists. So we travel 'buoyed up by hope' (Rom. 12.12) with the hope that does not disappoint (Rom. 5.5) but still accepting that, while we wander in the desert, to hope is to hope against hope (cf. Rom. 4.18).

Notes

1 *Ecumenical Review*, April 1965, pp. 93–112.
2 Owen Chadwick, 'The Church of England and the Church of Rome, from the beginning of the nineteenth century to the present day', in *Anglican Initiatives in Christian Unity* (London 1967), p. 101.
3 ibid. p. 103.
4 B. and M. Pawley, *Rome and Canterbury Through Four Centuries* (London 1974), p. 334.
5 According to Owen Chadwick, in his *Michael Ramsey: A Life* (Oxford 1990), p. 322: 'No Pope could have said anything louder about that vexing sore over the validity of Anglican Orders. It spoke more loudly than any bull or encyclical.' He goes on (ibid.) to quote Ramsey himself stating at a press conference that 'What it does betoken is the official recognition of the Church of England as an official Church with its rightful ministers. That from Rome means a great deal.'
6 William Purdy, *The Search for Unity* (London 1996), pp. 112–14, 121–3. Copies of the Report were distributed to the Bishops of the Lambeth Conference during the summer and eventually on 31 November the text was published in *The Tablet*.
7 This note of hope, the assurance of salvation, is missing in the phrase 'the roaring forties'. This nautical phrase refers in general to 'stormy ocean tracts' and in particular to 'the exceptionally rough part of the Ocean between 40 and 50 degrees South latitude'. To speak of the ecumenical movement being in the roaring forties would, I think, merely suggest that it was having a stormy time, a stormy passage, without holding out the hope of a safe passage and safe arrival.
8 Michael Hurley SJ, 'The Joint Declaration on the Doctrine of Justification: Another Ecumenical Milestone?' in *Milltown Studies* 45 (2000), pp. 44–57.
9 Michael Hurley SJ, 'Ecumenism and Mariology Today' in *One in Christ* 36/4 (Winter 2000), pp. 295–316.
10 Michael Hurley, 'Ecumenical Tithing' in *Christian Unity: An Ecumenical Second Spring?* (Dublin 1998), pp. 78–88.
11 *Irish Times*, 9 June 2001, p. 5.
12 I have noted elsewhere that there is no entry for 'reconciliation' in the quite detailed index of the Dehoniane Latin–Italian edition of the documents of Vatican II. Cf. Michael Hurley, 'Reconciliation and Forgiveness', in *Christian Unity* (op. cit.) pp. 55–6.
13 Cf. Michael Hurley, 'Reconciliation and Forgiveness', in *Christian Unity* (op. cit.) pp. 54–77.
14 Extracts are available in *One in Christ* 36 (2000), pp. 185–93.
15 Two articles in the issue of 15 May 1997. A reply by Martin Browne to these

sharply critical articles was printed in the issue of 19 June: cf. art. cit. (above note 8), pp. 67, 358.

16 *Sunday Times*, 19 March 2000, p. 19.

(This paper was given at the ESBVM Maynooth Conference
in June 2001)

19

Anglican–Roman Catholic
ecumenical dialogue

Samuel Poyntz

I share four snapshots depicting changes in Anglican–Roman Catholic relations at the international level over the past four decades. It all began in 1960 with the final pastoral visit of Archbishop Geoffrey Fisher's episcopate to Jerusalem, Istanbul and Rome (note the order), from the birthplace of Christianity, on to the head of the Orthodox world at Constantinople, Istanbul, and finally to the head of the Roman Catholic Church. In 1966 Archbishop Michael Ramsey and Pope Paul VI said together that they intended 'To inaugurate between the Roman Catholic Church and the Anglican Communion a serious dialogue which, founded on the Gospels and the ancient common traditions, may lead to that unity in truth for which Christ prayed.'

While in Rome, Dr Ramsey visited the English College: on leaving, he received rapturous applause from the students, and threw into the air his Canterbury cap, which got lost in the scrum, and perhaps today is a cherished possession in some presbytery. Such was the euphoria of the times, and so began Phase I. In 1982 when Pope John Paul II visited Great Britain he knelt in prayer with Archbishop Runcie in Canterbury Cathedral. Subsequently together they initiated a new stage in the dialogue (Phase II). Finally, at the beginning of the recent Holy Year 2000, Archbishop George Carey and a representative of His All Holiness the Ecumenical Patriarch of the Orthodox Church were invited by Pope John Paul II to the opening of the Door in the Basilica of St Paul. When it came to the moment of opening, it was discovered that the door was not too well oiled. All three had to combine to get it opened, although the programme had it planned for the Pope to do this himself. So the Holy Year inauguration required a suitable degree of ecumenical co-operation, and that is a parable of where we are today.

I hope in this paper

1. To outline briefly the ARCIC dialogue to date.
2. To say something of the Anglican–Roman Catholic Episcopal Consultation at Mississauga, Toronto, 2000.

3. To offer some comments on *One Bread, One Body* and *Dominus Jesus* and the Note.
4. To outline some conclusions and hopes.

ARCIC began with the establishment of a Preparatory Commission which was mandated to draw up an agenda for serious dialogue. The Preparatory Commission Report stated

> We record with great thankfulness our common faith in God our Father, in our Lord Jesus Christ, and in the Holy Spirit; our common baptism in the one Church of God; our sharing of the holy Scriptures, of the Apostles' and Nicene Creed, the Chalcedonian Definition, and the teaching of the Fathers; our common Christian inheritance for many centuries with its living traditions of liturgy, theology, spirituality, Church order and mission. [It is good to remember that common faith which we share. It is good to remember that from the very beginning we] acknowledge that both Communions are at one in the faith that the church is founded upon the revelation of God the Father, made known to us in the Person and work of Jesus Christ, who is present through the Holy Spirit in the Scriptures and his Church and is the only Mediator between God and Man, the ultimate Authority for all our doctrine.

The importance and the depth of the common faith shared by the Anglican Communion and the Roman Catholic Church should be carefully noted. Based on this, ARCIC discussions began with a dozen or so theologians under the joint chairmanship of Bishop Henry McAdoo, Bishop of Ossory and subsequently Archbishop of Dublin, and Bishop Alan Clark of the Roman Catholic hierarchy of England and Wales.

ARCIC methodology

There are those who may insist on testing ARCIC reports against the formularies of the sixteenth century, especially the Thirty-Nine Articles; not surprisingly those who take up this position will find ARCIC documents and statements wanting, and the same could be said of a Roman Catholic harking back. Such an approach either involves a misunderstanding or a rejection of the ARCIC methodology encouraged by successive twentieth-century archbishops of Canterbury and popes. The ARCIC Agreed Statements tried to emulate the spirit of Phil. 3.19: 'Forgetting what lies behind and straining forward to what lies ahead'. The attempt is to discover the other's faith as it is today, and to appeal to history only for enlightenment, not as a way of perpetuating past controversy (*Final Report* preface), and above all to avoid emotive language.

The word *koinonia* is the key to understanding the various ARCIC reports. It can be translated as 'communion', 'participation'. *Koinonia* is the union with God in Jesus Christ through the Holy Spirit. In the New Testament the term is used in various contexts, but it signifies a relationship between persons which results in their participation in the same reality. Jesus Christ, the Son of God, sends upon us his Holy Spirit, making us members of the Body of Christ, so that we are able to call God 'Abba, Father'. Because we share in the same Holy Spirit we become members of the same Body of Christ, adopted children of the same Heavenly Father, and consequently are bound together in a totally new relationship.

Koinonia runs like a refrain through the various statements. The Eucharist is a sign of *koinonia*. Episcopē or oversight serves the *koinonia*, and primacy or authority is a visible link and focus of *koinonia*, so it is wonderful to recall that this word also sums up our relationship with God the Father in the Holy Spirit through Jesus Christ. That relationship with each other, *koinonia*, communion, is the Church, and it is because we are 'in communion' with each other that we are able to dialogue, to speak about the Church and to grow in things that are fundamental to its unity.

Recently I have been reading John Zizioulas' book *Being as Communion*. Following the Cappadocian Fathers, he states that God is an event of communion of the three Persons of the Trinity permeating our theology of creation, the divine image in humankind, redemption and the work of the Holy Spirit. Now if we are incorporated into God through baptism, how is it possible for our communion with God and one another to be impaired or imperfect? Is it just possible that the 'Institutional' Church/Churches are getting in the way?

ARCIC's first Agreed Statement was on the Eucharist/Holy Communion/Mass, published in 1971. I highlight two aspects of the agreement claimed in the document. Firstly, there was agreement that the Eucharist is truly the sacrifice of Christ. It is true of course that Christ's death on the cross was the one perfect and sufficient sacrifice for the sins of the whole world – never to be repeated or added to. But Christ gave the Church a means through which that sacrificial–atoning work on the cross is proclaimed and made effective in the life of the Church. The Eucharistic celebration is not just a calling to mind of a past event but the Church's effectual proclamation of what God has done in Christ. To quote from the Agreed Statement:

> In the eucharistic prayer the church continues to make a perpetual memorial of Christ's death, and his members, united with God and one another, give thanks for all his mercies, entreat the benefits of his passion on behalf of the whole church, participate in these benefits and enter into the movement of his self-offering.

The Agreed Statement proclaims the Eucharist to be a living memorial of the sacrifice of Jesus Christ.

Secondly, there was agreement on the Real Presence of Jesus in the Eucharist. As the Report puts it: Before the eucharistic prayer, to the question: 'What is that?' the believer answers: 'It is bread'. After the eucharistic prayer, to the same question the believer answers: 'It is truly the body of Christ, the Bread of Life'. The reality of Christ's presence in the Eucharist is a fundamental of the agreement. In evaluating the Agreed Statement, both authorities at the highest level agreed that no further work need be done on the Eucharist at this stage, yet we have not agreement on Eucharistic hospitality and perhaps we will not have until it is recognized that our Anglican Eucharistic rite is based on that of the early Greek-speaking Church and not on that of the Latin Church. Perhaps some day Anglicans and Roman Catholics will come to realize that their understanding of the Eucharist rests on two divergent but ancient Christian traditions. If that is recognized there should be no hindrance to intercommunion between us.

The second Agreed Statement of ARCIC was issued in 1973 on Ministry and Ordination. Again the members of ARCIC claim to have reached substantial agreement. It was concerned with the nature and origin of the ordained ministry, and asserted firmly our agreement about different gifts of the Spirit of those ordained to the priesthood and episcopate, and about the common Christian priesthood. Again this was a very important contribution to reconciliation, because there has been much misunderstanding and disagreement about the nature and validity of ordination, particularly over the past hundred years or so. However, it is necessary to say that this substantial agreement was concerned with the origin and nature of the ordained ministry, and not with the question of who can be ordained. It did not, for instance, address the issue of the ordination of women, which is a grave obstacle for the Roman Catholic Church. Although it left aside this vexed question, the agreement showed the recognition of Anglican Orders in a new context.

There followed in 1976 a preliminary statement on Authority in the Church. Underlying the themes of Phase I, Eucharist, Ministry, and Authority (of which more anon) and the Responses which followed, there is a common Ecclesiology. The work on these themes culminated in the Final Report of 1981.

Phase II brought a fresh emphasis on Communion and has given us a number of important reports. To the question: How are the Church and salvation related? and Does the Reformation issue of justification separate Anglicans and Roman Catholics? the Commission gave its response in a report entitled *Salvation and the Church*, in 1986. It was stated that the doctrine of justification and the role of the Church in salvation need no longer separate the two communions, and it went on to claim that the doctrine of salvation and the Church 'is not an area where any remaining differences of theological interpretation or ecclesiological emphasis either within, or between, our Communions can justify our continuing separation'.

(It is of interest that the Lutheran Churches also reached a new agreement with the Roman Catholic Church on the doctrine of justification in 1999.)

In 1993 another report called *Life in Christ – Morals, Communion and the Church* was issued, in which Anglicans and Roman Catholics set the scene for their agreements and disagreements about moral teaching. In both papers, *The Church as Communion*, and *Life in Christ*, the Commission believed it had reached further common ground and was able to point to more of the real, even if not full, communion that exists between us. *Life in Christ* includes the acceptance of the same basic moral values. In the realm of moral teaching there have been many misconceptions and misperceptions of each other and this is thoroughly explored. There has been a real convergence in our understanding because we possess a shared vision of Christian discipleship and a common approach to the moral life, and this has been wholly positive.

There are, of course, a number of moral issues on which we disagree. There is the question of the remarriage of a divorced person during the lifetime of a former partner, and it must be admitted by Anglicans that we disagree among ourselves. There are the permissible methods of family planning and controlling conception. There is the whole difficult debate about abortion and homosexual relations. All these issues are not unimportant as we consider the effectiveness of our dialogue and our desire for a common witness, not only in faith but in moral teaching.

There in outline is the work of ARCIC to date – the Eucharist, Ministry, Salvation, the Church, morals – all areas where we have expressed very real agreement. Not all of these statements have been officially recognized by the authorities in our churches, but they have been in different degrees evaluated between our two communions.

I turn now to the question of authority on which there have been a number of statements issued, in 1976, another in 1981, and in 1998 *The Gift of Authority* (Authority III). What has ARCIC said about authority? It is agreed that

1. The Spirit of the Risen Lord maintains the people of God in obedience to the Father's will. By this action of the Holy Spirit the authority of [Jesus Christ] is active in the Church.

2.   Because of their baptism and their participation in [what is called] the *sensus fidelium*, [the faith of the people], the laity play an integral part in decision making in the Church.
3.   The work of Bishops and the role of the laity are elements in the whole oversight of the Church, i.e. the complementarity of primacy and conciliarity.
4.   There is a need for a universal primacy exercised by the Bishop of Rome as a sign and safeguard of unity within a reunited Church.
5.   This universal primate should exercise his ministry in collegial association with other Bishops.
6.   An understanding of universal primacy and conciliarity complements and does not supplant the exercise of episcopē or leadership – the oversight of local churches.

These were the recommendations of the authors of the reports. However, already there have been requests for further work to be done, because it is believed that a real consensus or agreement has not been achieved. I have to say that for many in the Church of Ireland, and in worldwide Anglicanism, 'Authority III' represents 'a bridge too far'. I have never met a report which evoked so much criticism, and this is a painful experience for many committed ecumenists. The Church of Ireland has already made an initial response to this report which can be found in the *Book of Reports* issued for this year's General Synod, pp. 160–6. Among the criticisms offered I mention but three: firstly, the highly significant role for the global ministry of a universal primate. We believe that a universal primacy in a reunited Church (a) should be constitutional in form; (b) should not have any unique magisterial powers; (c) should be non-jurisdictional and (d) should not necessarily be associated with Rome. The universal primate in such a Church, we believe, should perform a primarily pastoral role as distinct from a magisterial/jurisdictional one. Secondly, following the suggestion for a more centralized and effective authority within the Anglican Communion, it was pointed out that Lambeth 1998 and the Anglican Consultative Council in 1999 revealed that Anglicanism had not been won over to the concept of a more centralized authority. Ways in which mutual accountability can be developed are generally welcomed by Anglicans, but – while recognizing the role of the Archbishop of Canterbury as *primus inter pares*, the Lambeth Conference, the Primates' meeting and the Anglican Consultative Council – further development beyond a moral and consultative form of authority is not seen as helpful. Thirdly, considering infallibility, and the claim for statements in faith and morals to be absolutely free from error, the response pointed to *indefectibility* as more generally the Anglican approach – meaning that the Church, despite its fallibility, is maintained in the truth. 'Authority III' tries to conflate infallibility and indefectibility by arguing that 'infallible teaching is at the service of indefectibility'. However, an infallible *magisterium*, we believe, is not necessary for the Church to be maintained in truth, and where the idea of infallibility has been practised the result has not been helpful. Indefectibility works not through an infallible *magisterium* but through the unfathomable provi- dence of God. 'Indefectibility' has a vital and dynamic eschatological dimension that the much more static, cut-and-dried 'infallibility' lacks.

At Toronto there was no great wish to enter into detailed discussion on this report, because the churches are now committed to an in-depth study of it with final responses not due until 2005. The document is an invitation to join in the debate, and the authors hope it will be discussed where possible in conjunction with Roman Catholics locally and at provincial level. While it says many uncomfortable things to Anglicans – perhaps even unacceptable – it will also pose difficulties for Roman Catholics; e.g. what will they make of the concept '*sensus fidelium*'? We do well to listen to the advice of Professor Henry Chadwick, one of the Anglican architects of ARCIC Phase I with Archbishop McAdoo, when he says, 'this docu- ment does not deserve an instant response'. (*The Tablet*).

Looking back over Phase I – Eucharist, Ministry, and the early state- ment on Authority – these were approved by the Holy See in 1991 after collaboration between the Congregation for the Doctrine of the Faith (CDF) and the Pontifical Council for Promoting Christian Unity. From the Anglican side the responses have come from various provinces of the Communion. Because the structures and resources of the Provinces are not all the same, the responses have come in various forms. We can learn some ecclesial lessons from this diversity of methods of response. In addition to the official response there have been a number of other authoritative reflections from competent bodies in both churches. For the Roman Catholics, there have been responses from Episcopal Conferences and in some cases Ecumenical Commissions. Some of these have been published.

In the Anglican Communion, some provinces referred the Final Report (Phase I) to their Dioceses before giving a response. There followed a series of supporting resolutions passed by the Lambeth Conference 1988. It should be realized that a Lambeth Conference does not possess any canonical or juridical authority, although it is a world- wide gathering of chief pastors. It has a moral authority (which some would describe as theological). However, most people take the Lambeth Resolutions as the official response of Anglicans. These Resolutions were largely reflections of the provinces, while the Vatican response often appeared to take a different line from those published by

Episcopal Conferences. Questions arise; for example, Roman Catholics may ask Anglicans, Who speaks for the Anglican Communion? Can Anglicans do more than reflect the majority opinion in a number of autonomous provinces? Where is the integrity of authoritative teaching in the Anglican Communion? Is dispersed authority adequate?

Anglicans can ask Roman Catholics, for example, To what extent are the views of Episcopal Conferences taken into account before Rome declares some statement to be the position of the Roman Catholic Church? For instance, some French Roman Catholic Episcopal Conferences, as in Oceania, were far more enthusiastic about a number of the Agreed Statements than the official Vatican line. What in the Roman Catholic Church is the relationship between the Bishop of Rome and the Curia on the one hand and between Rome and the particular churches on the other? These questions were highlighted recently, with two German cardinals clashing about centralization of the Church. Cardinal Walter Kasper, now President of the Pontifical Council for Promoting Christian Unity, has maintained that Cardinal Joseph Ratzinger, Prefect of the Congregation for the Doctrine of the Faith, has approached the issue of the relationship between bishops and the Vatican from 'a purely abstract and theological point of view'. Kasper maintains that the local church is neither a province nor a department of the universal Church. The local bishop is not a delegate of the Pope but one sent by Jesus Christ. He maintains that this is the teaching of Vatican II. Such an understanding should have led to the decentralization of the Church's government, but the opposite has happened since Vatican II. Cardinal Ratzinger will not accept this understanding.

The Toronto Experience

It seemed good at the beginning of the millennium year 2000 to attempt to review Anglican–Roman Catholic relations officially, to discern what had been accomplished so far, and whither we are going. Bishops attended the meeting at the invitation of the Archbishop of Canterbury and Cardinal Edward Cassidy, who was then President for the Pontifical Council for Promoting Christian Unity. They met at Mississauga near Toronto from 14 to 20 May. In addition to Cardinal Cassidy and the Archbishop of Canterbury, who chaired the meeting, there was an attendance which included twelve archbishops (two have recently become cardinals) and eighteen bishops, from New Zealand, Australia, Brazil, Canada, England, India, Ireland, Nigeria, Papua New Guinea, South Africa, USA and the West Indies. In addition there was considerable secretarial backup, including two women theologians.

The result of a four-point questionnaire sent out to a number of countries in the early stages of preparation for the Consultation showed that we should concentrate on 'Communion in Life Together', under four headings:

1. The nature and current state of relationships between the Bishops of the two Communions.
2. Strengths and weaknesses of the relationship between Anglicans and Roman Catholics.
3. Significant examples of ongoing joint witness and work.
4. Current issues and challenges which should be addressed together.

Our deliberations produced what is now known as the 'Toronto Action Plan'.

Toronto Action Plan

Joint Unity Commission

(Mainly bishops; reporting to PCPCU and Inter-Anglican Standing Commission on Ecumenical Relations)

- To set priorities
- To oversee Joint Declaration
- To promote ARCIC statements
- To promote coherence of other bilateral dialogues
- To examine the range of possible ways to deal generously and pastorally with inter-church marriages involving Anglicans and Roman Catholics
- To commission resources on ARCIC
- To set up more national ARCs (Anglican–RC Committees)
- To invite one or two ARCs to study implications of common baptism for roles of men and women in the Church
- To promote local co-operation
- To promote collegiality (including joint bishops' meetings at province level within two years; search for ways of ensuring formal consultation before decisions on faith and morals).

Follow-up by pairs of bishops
Reporting sharing results

Anglican–RC International Commission (ARCIC)
Invited to consider producing

- a coherent summary of the work so far
- study of the place of Mary

Also urged to consider producing

- Volume of agreed statements

Annual Informal Talks
(PCPCU, ACO, Lambeth, Anglican Centre, ARCIC co-chairmen)

- November meeting to consider relations of Joint Unity Commission with ARCIC

Pontifical Council for Promoting Christian Unity
(PCPCU), and Anglican Communion Office (ACO)

- To explore publication of papers and other documents from Toronto in book form.

Recent Publications

I offer some comments on recent publications which do not arise out of Anglican–Roman Catholic relations but certainly have affected them.

The document, *One Bread, One Body* was published by the Roman Catholic bishops of England, Wales, Ireland and Scotland. The constantly-reiterated desire to achieve Christian unity and the high-lighting of aspects in eucharistic teaching shared by Roman Catholics and Anglicans is welcome. We are impressed with the beautiful way in which the Mass/Eucharist is described in Part I; however, it is to be regretted that there was no ecumenical consultation prior to the publica-tion of this document as required by the 1993 Vatican Directory for the application of norms. We greatly regret references to churches such as the Church of Ireland being referred to as 'A Christian Community', and the narrow approach to interpreting various rules when we have heard of a more liberal interpretation elsewhere. We have noted the openly critical approach of many Roman Catholic theologians, lecturers, priests and laity to this document: I quote but two. Professor Enda McDonagh said, 'In a situation where political settlement within Northern Ireland and between Ireland and Britain was, and still is, so delicately poised, and where the churches have been part of the problem, a more generous, practical directive, or a patient and silent waiting upon the working of the Holy Spirit among God's people, would have been gospel-like.'

Another theologian, Father Donal Dorr, a priest of St Patrick's Missionary Society in Kiltegan has called for 'a more lenient and flexible interpretation of intercommunion rules'. He maintains, 'Catholics could be present at a Reformed Communion Service without needing to make any judgement as to whether the Eucharist was "valid" in their Church's terms, so why then should a question arise if they received?' He goes on to point out that Reformed Church members receiving in a Roman Catholic Church did not 'necessarily erode or dishonour the meaning of our Catholic Eucharist', provided Catholics do not allow it to dilute their beliefs. He also interestingly comments that any rule laid down by official leaders which is not in line with the conscientious convictions of members of their churches does not bind the members in conscience, and whenever this is done it not only damages the credibility of the Church but also does great damage to the consciences of church members.

The second document is *Dominus Jesus*. This document was published by the Congregation for the Doctrine of the Faith in 2000, and has been replied to by the Church of Ireland (see *Book of Reports to the General Synod 2001*). There is much in *Dominus Jesus* to which we can say Amen, as, for example, what is said about our Lord and his uniqueness. We believe that it was unfortunate to bring together Inter-Faith Relations (i.e. other religions) with ecumenical relations between churches where members are baptized into Christ. This undervalues the real measure of communion that exists between baptized Christians. Time constraints permit me to only refer to two aspects: firstly, the tone of *Dominus Jesus* and the Note is a chilling, stark and insensitive harking back to infallible teaching about the Single Church of Christ subsisting in the Roman Catholic Church: even Roman Catholics have noticed this. To quote from *The Tablet* of 9 September 2000: 'What a pity that it sounds notes of triumphalism that the sympathetic style and way of acting of Pope John XXIII, newly beatified, seemed to have dispelled for good.' Cardinal Martini of Milan suggested that the tone 'risks being rather strong'. Cardinal König, formerly of Vienna, wished that the document 'could have been expressed more politely and could have reflected a greater eagerness for dialogue'.

Then there is the Note on Sister Churches – a terminology which has been used in times past to refer to Orthodox Churches, but also on occasions with regard to Anglicans, and indeed other churches as well. The Note seems to have changed the interpretation of this phrase in such a manner as to change the way in which it has been understood in ecumenical theology. Just as recently shown by the Northern Ireland election results, the central ground appears to be slipping towards extremism, so these two documents, *One Bread, One Body* and *Dominus Jesus*, seem to give inadequate recognition to the agreed *central ground* established in Anglican–Roman Catholic dialogue, leaving ARCIC open to sneering attacks from unecumenical fundamentalists in both traditions.

Conclusion

Firstly, I stress the profound agreements which have been reached in the various statements. One of the difficulties is that these various agreements have been evaluated to a greater or lesser degree but have not, as yet, been totally received by either Anglicans or Roman Catholics.

Secondly, there are the continuing 'Neuralgic Issues:'

- Curial and papal power
- Infallibility
- Marian dogmas
- *Jus Divinum*
- Pain of inter-church families over Eucharistic hospitality
- Marriage discipline which means that in some instances marriage in the Anglican Church is not recognized
- Different attitudes and policies in relation to remarriage of divorced persons
- Diversity in the interpretation of moral behaviour
- Ordination of women, especially to the episcopate
- Lack of recognition of Anglican Orders
- Both Churches are in the process of change. The Roman Catholic Church is struggling to understand what it is to be local, while Anglicans are struggling to understand what it is to be a world-wide communion.

Thirdly, the Agreements in faith that ARCIC has enunciated must not be allowed to wither, nor the official Agreed Statement from Toronto which sets out the stage of communion that has been reached between Anglicans and Roman Catholics. I quote in full Section 9.

The marks of this new stage of communion in mission are: Our trinitarian faith grounded in the Scriptures and set forth in the Catholic Creeds; the centrality of Christ, his death and resurrection, and commitment to his mission in the Church; faith in the final destiny of human life; common traditions in liturgy and spirituality; the monastic life; preferential commitment to the poor and marginalized; convergence on eucharist, ministry, authority, salvation, moral principles, and the Church as Communion, as expressed in the agreed statements of ARCIC; episcopacy, particularly the role of the Bishop as symbol and promoter of unity; and the respective roles of clergy and laity.

We must not be too disheartened by the difficulties and obstacles which lie ahead. When I look back to the position of Roman Catholics and my own Church of Ireland over fifty years of priesthood, I can only thank God how much our relationships have changed for the better. And they have changed because the heart of ecumenism is spiritual ecumenism. This involves conversion to Christ, newness of attitudes towards each other and unstinted love. Experience of ecumenical dialogue has not only led to seeing theological agreements but also to more common prayer and the common life that we live together, studying and thinking together and, of course, the close friendships that have been made and have endured. One of the main purposes of Anglican–Roman Catholic Conversations has been to achieve convergence, agreement in faith, but also to encourage a more common life together. This is what members of this Conference have been living during the past week.

At the Toronto Conference we had a devotional address from Bishop (now Cardinal) Walter Kasper, now President of the PCPCU. I leave you with some words he said;

> God will always surprise us. He cannot be understood through our human systems or correspond to our positive or negative predictions of the future … In our ecumenical efforts we should keep in mind that one day we will rub our eyes and be surprised by the new things God has achieved in His Church. It is true that in the course of history we have done much against love and unity but God – this is our hope – will make all things new again.

(This paper was given at the ESBVM Maynooth Conference in June 2001)

20

Co-redemptrix

Edward Yarnold SJ

In all the recent discussion whether Mary's role in the process of redemption should be defined as that of Co-redemptrix,[1] one fundamental fact is accepted on all sides, namely that there is 'one mediator between God and men, the man Christ Jesus' (1 Tim. 2.5). The same message is found in the Fourth Gospel: 'I am the way and the truth and the life; no one comes to the Father but by me' (John 14.6). In this paper we shall first examine some of the ways in which Mary's part in the process of redemption under Christ is expressed in Scripture and the Church's tradition; secondly, we shall set out the different ways in which her influence is exercised; thirdly, we shall consider the sense in which this activity can accurately be described as 'co-redemption'; fourthly, we shall recall the reasons why the Church defines a dogma, and ask whether these reasons are present in this case; fifthly, we shall take account of the probable ecumenical consequences of such a definition.

Mary's role in salvation-history: Scripture

A number of passages feature repeatedly in the debate, chief among them being the following:

Gen. 3.15: 'I shall put enmity between you and the woman, and between your seed and her seed; he shall bruise your head, and you shall bruise his heel.' According to R. J. Clifford and R. E. Murphy, 'Christian tradition has sometimes referred it [the word "he"] to Christ, but the literal reference is to the human descendants of Eve, who will regard snakes as enemies'.[2] There is a third interpretation based on the Latin of the Vulgate: 'ipsa conteret caput tuum', which makes Mary the one who crushes the serpent; this reading forms the basis of the frequent representations of Mary trampling on a snake. However, even without this unsound third interpretation the passage has a Marian reference: though it is Eve's offspring and not Eve herself who crushes the

(For abbreviations in this paper see p. 244, note 1.)

serpent's head, the 'enmity' is still between the serpent and the woman. Later interpretations of Mary as the Second Eve imply that she continues to be involved as the Woman in her Son's warfare against the devil.

Gal. 4.4: 'When the fullness of time had come, God sent forth his Son, born of woman.' Mary is integrally involved in God's plan for the redemption of the world, providing the Saviour with his biological link with the human race.

Luke 1.38: 'Let it be to me according to your word.' Mary is invited to consent to God's plan (though we are not told she understood it all). Her consent takes place *before* Jesus is conceived (2.21); it is therefore the occasion, even if not the condition, of the Incarnation.[3]

Luke 2.35: 'A sword will pierce through your own heart too.' These words have traditionally been taken as a prophecy that Mary will suffer together with her Son. Thus Pope John Paul II explains that Simeon's words reveal that 'she will have to live her obedience of faith in suffering, at the side of the suffering Saviour'.[4] This however seems not to be the whole, or even the primary, meaning of the text. The context of Simeon's prophecy is the ambivalent sign which Jesus constitutes: for fall or rising, to be disputed (*antilegomenon*), to reveal thoughts. Thus if the clause concerning the piercing sword refers to Mary's *suffering*, it must be taken as a parenthesis inserted into the three phrases concerning the sign of Jesus and *changing the subject*. There is, however, another sense in which the saying about the sword can be taken, which is preferable, as it does not interrupt the sequence of thought concerning the ambivalent sign. In this interpretation the sword seems to be what R. J. Karris describes as a 'sword of discrimination';[5] the same sense is found in the passage in Hebrews concerning the word of God, which is 'sharper than any two-edged sword, piercing to the division of soul and spirit, of joints and marrow, and discerning the thoughts and intentions of the heart' (Heb. 4.12). The point of Simeon's words would thus be that Mary, like everyone else, will find her Son a challenge which can be either accepted or rejected – a test which she passed, being the woman who heard the word of God and kept it.[6] Pope John Paul, beside his other interpretation of the passage, hints at the view I am expounding, linking it with Mary's *faith*: 'this announcement on the one hand confirms her faith in the accomplishment of the divine promises of salvation' (*RM* 16).

The wedding at Cana (John 2.1–11), where Mary makes of her Son a request which he grants, is often taken as an illustration of her wider role in the Church. Thus Pope John Paul ascribes a 'symbolic value' to Mary's concern over an unimportant human need: it brings those needs 'within the radius of Christ's messianic mission and salvific power. Thus there is mediation: Mary places herself between her Son and mankind in the reality of their wants, needs and sufferings. *She puts herself "in the middle"*, that is to say *she acts as a mediatrix ... in her position as mother'* (*RM* 21). Some commentators detect a deeper symbolism in the passage: the title 'Woman' by which Jesus addresses his mother is not to be taken as a mark of cold formality or even disapproval, but as an echo of the 'Woman' of Genesis 3 who is at enmity with the serpent; Jesus' words thus would imply that Mary is the Second Eve.

Jesus' words from the cross – 'Woman, behold your Son ... Behold your mother' (John 19.26–7) – can also be interpreted as a reference to the Second Eve. Pope John Paul sees them as an indication of 'the unique *place* which she occupies *in the whole economy of salvation'* as Mother of the Church (*RM* 24).

Mary appears again in a similar light in a third Johannine passage, namely the vision of the woman clothed with the sun, standing on the moon and crowned with twelve stars (Apoc. 12.1–17). The symbolic woman is the mother of the Messiah, who will 'rule the nations with a rod of iron' (Apoc. 12.5, quoting the messianic Ps. 2.9)[7], and therefore the mother of the historic Jesus, namely Mary. At the same time she is the personification of 'the heavenly Israel, the spouse of God',[8] the rest of whose offspring is at war with the dragon (Apoc. 12.17).

To sum up, several of these passages can bear more than one interpretation. If they are taken in the sense I have proposed, they show us a composite picture of Mary as the Woman, the Second Eve, who in the fullness of time bore the Son who crushed the serpent's head, who was invited to consent to God's plan for redemption before it took place, who represents to her Son the needs of others, whose intercession leads to her Son's first miracle, who is appointed Mother of the Church at the foot of the cross, who is the personification of the people God has chosen as his own, but who, like her Son, was tempted as we are, and emerged from the temptation still stronger.

Mary's role in salvation-history: tradition

The two earliest exponents of Mary's role as the Second Eve were Justin (d. *c.* 165) and Irenaeus (d. *c.* 200). Irenaeus incorporated this insight into his systematic understanding of Jesus as the 'recapitulation' of the history of Israel, who relived it as it ought to have been lived and so set it right.[9] Thus, since Jesus is the second Adam, his mother is the second Eve. The first Eve, when betrothed but still a virgin, brought death to the entire race by her disobedience; the second, also a betrothed virgin, through her obedience brought salvation (*Adv. Haer* 3.22.4); the virgin Mary rescued the human race from the slavery to death into which the virgin Eve had brought it (*Adv. Haer.* 5.19.1). The poet-deacon Ephrem (d. 373) developed the same theme: just as death entered the world through the 'womb' of Eve's ear when she listened to the serpent's temptation, so new life entered through the ear of Mary (*Hymn on the Church*, 49.7); Eve was humanity's blind left eye, Mary its sighted right eye (*Hymn on the Church*, 37.5); Mary gave us the living bread instead of the bread of sorrow brought by Eve (*De Azymis*, 6.7); Mary is the 'praised sheaf' from which the Eucharist comes (*Hymn on the Crucifixion*, 3.9). In a work of disputed authenticity which has come to us in Greek, not Syriac, 'Ephrem' addresses Mary as the 'dispenser' (*chorēgia*) of all good things, the 'mediator (*mesitēs*) of the world after the mediator'.[10]

The abbey of Canterbury made major contributions to the developing understanding of Mary's co-redemptive role. In a series of prayers to our Lady, St Anselm is, as far as I know, the first to indicate the freedom of God's decision to associate Mary in the work of salvation: 'the one who could make all things from nothing chose not to remake them after their violation without the Virgin Mary'. Because she gave birth to the Father of created things, Mary became the mother of their re-creation (*PL* 158.956). Through giving birth to the Reconciler, she became the mother of our justification (956–7). 'Both salvation and damnation depend on the will of the good Brother and the merciful Mother' (957). While Anselm had referred in passing to Mary's 'merits' (958), his disciple and biographer Eadmer in his work entitled *On the Excellence of the Virgin Mary* makes this point more explicit: Mary is the ruler of creation (*domina rerum*), who re-established everything to its original dignity by the grace which she merited.[11] In these theologians of Canterbury we find two key axioms: first, Mary's mediation of salvation is due to God's free decree, but is linked with her merits; secondly, Mary's mercy is contrasted with her Son's justice.

From the time of St Bernard (d. 1153), Western writers allow greater play to their imagination in descanting upon Mary's prerogatives. Bernard himself in a sermon for the Nativity of the Blessed Virgin Mary compares her to an aqueduct. She is not the source of the living water, but passes on to us what she has first received herself. Although we have Christ as our Advocate, since sinners might be afraid of having recourse to him directly, we are given Mary as an advocate with our Advocate. God could have given us grace directly, but it was his will that we should receive everything through Mary. She has thus corrected the mischief done by the first woman, so that mankind can now say: 'The woman you gave me has fed me with blessed fruit' (*PL* 183.437–43). So too Bernard's sermon on the twelve stars for the Sunday after the feast of the Assumption remarks how fitting it is that both sexes should be involved in our redemption as both were involved in our fall: in the redemption as in the creation of the human race, it is not good for man to be alone. Moreover, as Christ combines justice with compassion, 'we need a mediator in order to reach Christ our Mediator ... There is no severity in her' (*PL* 183.429).

The Franciscan St Bonaventure (d. 1274) developed the Second Eve theory in a new way: Eve had sold us to sin, but Mary brought us back by accepting God's will at the foot of the cross and consenting to the sacrifice of her Son.[12] After Bonaventure many writers were to elaborate this idea of sinners being redeemed by Mary's sacrifice.

From the middle of the twelfth century writers begin to find a new expression for Mary's distribution of grace, which Bernard had compared to an aqueduct. Beginning with Hermann of Tournai, writers now speak of Mary as the Mediatrix, the 'neck' which links Christ's Mystical Body with its head (Graef 1.234). In the fifteenth century the mystical theologian and Chancellor of Paris University John Gerson used the same metaphor, adding that she is the 'Mother of the Eucharist', the 'key-bearer of the wine-cellars of the King of Peace'; though not ordained like the apostles at the Last Supper, she was present there and was 'anointed into the royal priesthood, not indeed to consecrate, but to offer this pure Victim ... on the altar of her heart'.[13] In the same century another Franciscan, St Bernardine of Siena (d. 1444) shows rhetoric running riot in his praises of Mary: 'One Hebrew woman invaded the house of the eternal King; one girl, I do not know by what caresses, pledges or violence, seduced, deceived, and, if I may say so, wounded and enraptured the divine heart and ensnared the Wisdom of God'. 'Even if she had not been the Mother of God, she would nevertheless have been the mistress of the world'.[14] Through her assent at the incarnation, she merited more than all other human beings and angels put together: she merited the dominion of the world, the fullness of grace, and all knowledge.

St Louis-Marie Grignion de Montfort (d. 1716) carried the idea of Mary's mediation to the limits.[15] To go directly to God without passing through Mary's mediation is to fail in humility – a statement in which Hilda Graef detected the influence of the court of Louis XIV. Because Christ always obeys his mother, 'the greatness of the power which she exercises even over God himself is incomprehensible'. If we offer our good works to Jesus through Mary, he will turn a blind eye to the imperfections of our gifts. The Holy Spirit produces Christ in his members through Mary: when the Spirit finds Mary in a soul, he flies there.[16] This theology is echoed in two later developments. The first is G. M. Hopkins's poetic conjecture that Mary continues to exercise 'high motherhood', giving birth to Jesus in the hearts of Christians.[17] The second is the 'Morning Offering' recommended by the 'Apostleship of Prayer', which begins: 'O Jesus, through the most pure heart of Mary, I offer you all the prayers, works, sufferings and joys of this day ...'

The idea of Mary's mediation is to be found also in the East. Theophanes of Nicaea (d. *c.* 1381) compared Mary to the Holy of Holies into which the High Priest has entered, and from which God speaks to his people. Just as no one can come to the Father except through the Son, so no one can approach the Son except through Mary.[18] Following Dionysius' conception of a heavenly hierarchy, Theophanes teaches that all grace flows undivided from God to Christ and from him to Mary, who distributes it, in the first instance to the seraphim. In the sixth-century Akathist hymn, which still forms an important part of the Greek Orthodox liturgy, Mary's mediation is expressed in a variety of images, the purpose of which is

> precisely to indicate the Virgin's relationship to Christ. The Marian titles in which the Hymn abounds – such as ladder, bridge, vine, star, earth, table, key – have all of them a christological reference: if she is the star, Christ is the sun; if she is the earth, Christ is the harvest; if she is the table, Christ is the feast; if she is the key, Christ is the door. When the Orthodox say to the Mother of God, 'Save us', as we sometimes do, it is clearly understood that in the strict sense Christ alone is our Saviour. It is because of the Son that we honour the Mother.[19]

(Similar titles appear in the Western Litany of Loreto.)

Mary's different roles

Stripping away the exaggerations of some of these writers, we can sum up the important truth they are all seeking to clarify, i.e. Mary's part, under her Son, in the process of salvation. There can be no disputing her unique role in Christ's life: she and she alone was the Mother of God the Son made man, not only providing the biological source of his humanity, but bearing the immense responsibility of bringing up the Saviour, caring for his physical needs, and providing the love, security and wisdom which contributed to his human growth and therefore to his saving work. In the life of the Church she exercises a mother's role in her intercession for her Son's followers. This role, however, unlike her divine motherhood, seems to be different from that of other saints not in kind but in degree: the doctrine of the communion of saints implies that we all support one another by our prayers. It is important in our rejection of exaggerations, not to under-emphasize the vital importance of these functions of Mary in salvation-history, or to allow a critical spirit to eclipse the devotion and love we should have towards her. All generations should indeed call her blessed.

Nevertheless some other explanations of Mary's mediation must be questioned, for example that Mary made satisfaction for sin by sharing her Son's sufferings at the foot of the cross and offering them to God; or that she is the gentle mediator between us and a stern Christ; or that she decides how God's favours will be distributed.

The term Co-redemptrix

We must now face the question whether Mary's role in the process of salvation, which we have tried to clarify above, is accurately described by the term 'Co-redemptrix'. First, however, we would do well to consider the gradual adoption of the title.

Perhaps the first use of the term is to be found in a fourteenth-century hymn from Salzburg:

> Ut compassa Redemptori,
> Captivato transgressori
> Tu Co-redemptrix fieres.[20]

> So that, suffering with the Redeemer,
> For the captive sinner
> Co-redemptrix you might be.

Since the time of Leo XIII several popes have taught that Mary co-operated in her Son's redemption of the world, although the term 'co-redeemer' itself occurs relatively rarely, and in homilies rather than encyclicals. Thus Leo explained that Mary was not only the 'servant' or 'steward' (*administra*) of redemption during the life of her Son, but continues for all time to be the steward of grace, which the Church derives from her.[21] Benedict XV analysed Mary's role in the process of redemption more deeply, explaining that she 'immolated' her Son by renouncing the rights that she held as his mother: she 'gave up her maternal rights to her Son[22] for the salvation of mankind and immolated her Son to appease the justice of God in so far as it pertained to her, so that it can truly be said that with Christ she redeemed the human race'. The boldness of this statement is softened by the saving clause 'in so far as it pertained to her',[23] which leaves undetermined the level of Mary's co-operation. Pius X expressed Mary's share in the redemption in technical terms connected with merit: because of her personal holiness and because Christ chose to associate her in his saving work she merited *de congruo* what her Son merited *de condigno*.[24] An illustration may clarify the meaning of these terms. Condign merit is a matter of strict equivalence, as when one pays the just price for a work of art; congruous merit, on the other hand, is based on what is appropriate rather than just, as when a little child's mother describes her daughter's gift of a childish daub as 'beautiful' not because of its intrinsic merits but with regard to the good intentions with which it was painted. Only the One Mediator can earn salvation condignly; but it was appropriate that God should enable Mary to participate in this work. Pius XI in his encyclical *Miserentissimus Redemptor* (1928) used several different titles to express Mary's part in the process of redemption: she is 'Repairer', 'Advocate', 'minister and mediator of grace', 'fosterer of heavenly gifts'.[25] However, he did not refer to Mary as Co-redemptrix in this or any other encyclical, although he used the title in a broadcast prayer addressed to Mary who 'as Co-redemptrix stood by your most sweet Son'.[26] The Dogmatic Constitution on the Church of Vatican II explained that Mary's mother-hood of the Church does not diminish her Son's unique mediation, because it depends on God's good pleasure, flows from the superabundance of Christ's merits, and draws all its power from his mediation; nevertheless Co-redemptrix is not among the titles Advocate, Auxiliatrix, Adjutrix, Minister of grace and Mediatrix which the document lists as legitimate expressions of Mary's maternal relationship to the Church.[27] Pope John Paul II in his 1984 encyclical on the redemptive value of suffering entitled *Salvifici Doloris* emphasized the significance of Mary's suffering 'for the Church' at the foot of the cross; her sufferings were 'a contribution to the redemption of all' and were 'supernaturally fruitful for the redemption of the world'. Thus Paul's words apply to Mary: 'I complete in my flesh what is lacking in Christ's afflictions for the sake of his body, which is the Church' (Col. 1.24).[28] Three years later the Marian encyclical *Redemptoris Mater* developed the theme: at the foot of the cross Mary is 'perfectly united' with the 'shocking mystery' of Christ's 'self-emptying'. 'Through faith the Mother shares in the death of her Son, in his redeeming death'.[29] Although these encyclicals made no use of the term 'Co-redemptrix' to describe this share in Christ's redeeming death, Pope John Paul, like Pius XI, used the term in the more devotional circumstances of an address.[30]

The meaning of 'Co-'

While there are several passages in the Pauline writings which use the Greek prefix *sun-* (in Latin and English *co-* or *con-*) to denote human participation in the redemptive process, that participation is of limited scope. Most common is the use of such expressions in reference to the Christian's participation in Christ's death and resurrection: our old humanity is 'con-crucified' with Christ so that we shall 'co-live' with him;[31] we become 'co-heirs' with Christ if we 'co-suffer' and are 'co-glorified' with him;[32] having 'co-died' with Christ, we shall 'co-live' and 'co-reign' with him;[33] God in his love and rich mercy has 'co-vivified' us with Christ, 'co-raised' us with him and 'co-set' us in heaven.[34] We are to be 'con-formed' to the image of Christ.[35] We are 'co-workers of God'

– a phrase which could mean either that we collaborate *with* God or that we work together *for* God.[36] The prefix *sun/con* never occurs however in a word denoting co-redemption, and with good reason: Mary is one with us in being redeemed, though in a unique way, for while we are rescued from a sinful state, through the merits of her not yet incarnate Son[37] Mary was redeemed in anticipation and preserved from sin from the first moment of her conception.

Why a definition?[38]

So, despite certain exaggerations, there is sound and important truth behind Mary's title of Co-redemptrix, though the title itself needs hedging against misinterpretation. But whether the title could or should be defined as a revealed article of faith is a different question. It seems to me it should not. The legitimate desire to honour our Lady is not a sufficient reason for a dogmatic definition; if the Church decided to make the title official out of devotion to her, there would be other more appropriate ways of doing so. The Church could formally proclaim the title without a dogmatic definition, as Paul VI did with the title 'Mother of the Church' during Vatican II; it could institute a new liturgical feast with appropriate liturgical texts, as the Church instituted the feast of Our Lady of Lourdes without making any dogmatic pronouncement about the apparitions there; the Pope could write an encyclical on the subject. There are many ways in which the Church can exercise its *magisterium* short of a dogmatic definition.

Two important principles are relevant here: the principle of 'minimism' and the principle of subsidiarity. The first of these principles was invoked by John Henry Newman in connection with the doctrine of papal infallibility in 1870: dogmas should not be defined unnecessarily. 'When has the definition of doctrine de fide been a luxury of devotion,' he wrote to Bishop Ullathorne, 'and not a stern painful necessity?'[39] '... so difficult a virtue is faith ... that she [the Church] has ever shown the utmost care to contract, as far as possible, the range of truths and the sense of the propositions, of which she demands this absolute reception.' A 'true Catholic', who has a 'generous loyalty towards ecclesiastical authority', 'has a claim ... to be met and to be handled with a wise and gentle *minimism*'.[40]

The principle of subsidiarity, which was devised originally by Catholic political theorists and subsequently applied to discussions of the constitution of the European Union, states that higher authorities should leave lower authorities to fulfil their own responsibilities, intervening only when intervention is necessary; for example, responsibility for the education of children belongs in the first instance to parents, so that the city or state should intervene only to do what the parents cannot do for themselves. Pope Pius XII applied the same principle to the government of the Church, without filling in the details.[41] Already Vatican I had explained that the purpose of papal primacy was to 'assert', 'strengthen' and 'defend' the power of bishops in their dioceses, and not to 'impede' it.[42]

Thus papal intervention at the highest level should be no more than is necessary to preserve the unity of the Church and to maintain it in the truth. Throughout history the most usual need of this kind has been to clarify the Church's faith in the face of heresy – a need which cannot however be plausibly alleged as a reason for the definition of the title Co-redemptrix. Granted, we are faced here with a problem: the same argument seems to apply to the dogmas of the immaculate conception and the assumption, the definition of which was not required in order to combat any particular heresy. The need for these two dogmas can perhaps be explained in two other ways. First it was desirable to set clear limits to what is to be believed of Mary in an age of Marian excesses, typified by the tag: *de Maria nunquam satis* (with regard to Mary it is impossible to exaggerate). The second explanation might be that the dogmas in question were definable for their *symbolic* value: they illustrate in the case of Mary more general truths concerning God's saving action for the whole of mankind, according to the principle of Vatican II that Mary is a type or model of the Church. Thus the immaculate conception illustrates the truths that God's favour is not to be earned, for everything is grace, and that, just as God prepared Mary by grace for the vocation he had in store for her, so too he equips every Christian for his or her vocation in life. The assumption shows that salvation and glory apply to the body as well as to the soul: the body is not to be exploited or made an end in itself, but has its part in the salvation and glorification of a human being.

This would be in effect an application of another insight of Vatican II, namely the hierarchy of truths: 'in catholic doctrine there exists an order or "hierarchy" of truths, since they vary in their connection with the foundation of the christian faith.'[43] The Decree on Ecumenism does not explain the meaning of this statement, which was inserted into the text of the document in the final stages of its redaction; but it seems to imply that while all dogmas must refer to the 'foundation of the christian faith' – i.e. the fundamental doctrines of the creeds, namely the Trinity, the incarnation, salvation, the Church and its sacraments – some dogmas have this reference only indirectly. These, which one might call 'second-order' doctrines, can become dogmas only in so far as they are expressions of the foundational doctrines. Doctrines about Mary are a case in point, expressing as they do the consequences of the incarnation (e.g. the divine motherhood, the Virgin birth) and the pre-eminent accomplishment in *her* of her Son's saving work, which in *us* still remains to be completed.

Ecumenical Implications

One could perhaps make a similar case for the definition of Mary as Co-redemptrix: in teaching that she is the supreme instance of human co-oper-ation in her Son's redeeming work, the Church would be affirming the corresponding, though lesser, vocation of all Christians. There are, however, other reasons, based on the Church's commitment to ecumenism, which seem decisive against the definition of the Co-redemptrix. In his encyclical of 1995 on Christian Unity *Ut Unum Sint*, Pope John Paul II invoked the principle of Acts 15.28: 'one must not impose any burden which is not strictly necessary' (*UUS* 78); the reference is to the Council of Jerusalem, which decided that gentile converts should not be obliged to observe Jewish ritual law. In the same vein Pope Paul VI had earlier more than once stated that charity required churches where possible to avoid language which would seem incomprehensible and scandalous to non-Catholics. Thus in 1965 at the end of Vatican II Pope Paul VI explained to leaders of other churches that the Council had made a 'unanimous effort to avoid any expression lacking in consideration for you'.[44] Again in 1967 he spoke to the Orthodox Patriarch of Constantinople concerning the 'charity' of the Church Fathers which had led them to 'refrain from using certain terms which, accurate though they were, could have given rise to scandal in one part of the Christian people' (*TAIE* 69).

Consequently when other ways of expressing the truth about Mary are available, the Catholic Church must not choose expressions which non-Catholics would find hard to reconcile with the belief in one Mediator who by his death and resurrection achieved redemption once for all. There is another reason why non-Catholics would find such a definition burdensome: it would seem to trivialize the pope's *magisterium* by exercising it for devotional reasons rather than out of neces-sity. In fact, such fears should be superfluous, since already in 1870 the first Vatican Council in its decree defining papal infallibility had empha-sized the strict limits within which the pope's extraordinary *magisterium* can be exercised: 'For the holy Spirit was promised to the successors of Peter not so that they might, by his revelation, make known some new doctrine, but that, by his assistance, they might religiously guard and faithfully expound the revelation or deposit of faith transmitted by the apostles.'[45] Nevertheless the first Anglican–Roman Catholic International Commission, despite reaching a remarkable degree of accord concerning the universal primacy of the Bishop of Rome, felt it necessary to acknowledge that 'special difficulties are created by the recent Marian dogmas [of the immaculate conception and the assumption], because Anglicans doubt the appropriateness, or even the possibility, of defining them as essential to the faith of believers'.[46]

The Catholic Church has acknowledged the relevance of the ecumenical factor to the exercise of papal *magisterium*. In his 1995 encyclical on Church unity entitled *Ut Unum Sint*, Pope John recognized his 'particular responsibility ... in heeding the request made of me to find a way of exercising the primacy which, while in no way renouncing what is essential to its mission, is none the less open to a new situation' – i.e. the situation of the 'ecumenical aspirations of the majority of the Christian Communities'.[47] In 1987 the Pope had invited bishops and theologians of the Orthodox Church to join their Catholic counterparts to 'seek – together, of course – the forms in which this ministry may accomplish a service of love recognized by all concerned';[48] now in 1995 he extended the same invitation to the pastors and theologians of all Christian communities. To exercise the infallible *magisterium* unnecessarily and without consulting other churches would make it look as if this invitation by Pope John Paul was not intended seriously.

The commitment of their respective churches to the search for 'that unity in truth, for which Christ prayed' made by Pope Paul and Archbishop Michael Ramsey in their Common Declaration of 1966 implied the 'determination ... to strive in common to find solutions to the great problems' facing Christians today. Thirty years later in a new Common Declaration Pope John Paul II and Archbishop George Carey spoke of the need to avoid *new* problems: 'We pray that the spirit of dialogue will prevail which will contribute to reconciliation and prevent new difficulties arising.'[49] This prayer would be futile unless there were also the determination not to create new problems – except in grave necessity and only after every effort had been made to obtain the agreement of the other side. Thus Pope Paul VI was justified in 1975 in criticizing the Anglican Communion for its decision to ordain women, on the grounds that it introduced 'an element of grave difficulty' into the dialogue between the two churches.[50] Pope John Paul II reaffirmed his predecessor's judgment; while acknowledging the 'thoughtfulness' which had led Archbishop Robert Runcie to inform him of the decision of the 1988 Lambeth Conference to leave the matter of ordination of women to the discretion of individual provinces, the Pope spoke of 'new obstacles' to the reconciliation of the churches, and suggested that the Anglican decision 'preempts' the study of the subject implied by the mandate given to ARCIC II six years earlier.[51] Now if Rome were to define the dogma of Mary Co-redemptrix, the boot would be on the other foot: it would be the Roman Catholic Church which was unilaterally erecting a new obstacle to reunion.

Thus, although Mary's proposed title of Co-redemptrix, when properly explained, expresses important truths, to define it would be a violation of the Catholic Church's ecumenical undertakings. It is a pity that fears and hopes concerning the possibility of a new definition may overshadow important truths concerning Mary which can be more effectively expressed in other terms.

Notes

1 I have found three studies especially helpful: H. Graef, *Mary: a History of Doctrine and Devotion* (2 vols., London and New York 1963–5); H. du Manoir (ed.), *Maria* (8 vols., Paris 1949); M. I. Miravalle, *Mary: Co-redemptrix, Mediatrix, Advocate* (Santa Barbara, Cal. 1993).
   I have employed the following abbreviations:
   AAS   *Acta Apostolicae Sedis*
   ASS   *Acta Sanctae Sedis*
   DS   Denzinger-Schönmetzer, *Enchiridion Symbolorum, Definitionum et Declarationum*
   LG   Vatican II, Dogmatic Constitution on the Church *Lumen Gentium*
   LXX   The Greek Septuagint translation of the Old Testament
   NJBC   *The New Jerome Biblical Commentary*, ed. R. E. Brown, J. A. Fitzmyer and R. E. Murphy, Englewood Cliffs, NJ, and London 1990–1991
   PL   *Patrologia Latina*
   RM   Pope John Paul II, Encyclical *Redemptoris Mater* on the Blessed Virgin Mary in the life of the Church
   TAIE   E. J. Yarnold, *They Are in Earnest: Christian unity in the statements of Paul VI, John Paul I, John Paul II*, Slough 1982
   UUS   Pope John Paul II, Encyclical *Ut Unum Sint.*
2 *NJBC* 2:5.
3 This is the interpretation of *LG* 56.
4 *RM* 16.
5 *NJBC* 43:34.
6 Cf Luke 11.28; 8.21.
7 According to the LXX, where the King will 'be shepherd' for the nations (*poimaneis*), rather than the Hebrew, according to which the King will 'break' them.
8 A. Y. Collins in *NJBC* 63:43.
9 Irenaeus gives his own interpretation to the verb 'recapitulate' (or 'sum up' or 'unite') as used in Eph. 1.10.
10 *Prayer to the Mother of God*, Assemani iii.528; quoted in du Manoir, *Maria*, vol. 1, p. 481.
11 *per illam quam meruit gratiam*: *PL* 159.578.
12 *On the gifts of the Holy Spirit*, 6.15 (Quaracchi edn 5.486).
13 Quoted in Graef 1.313–14.
14 Quoted in Graef 1.316–17.
15 Pope John Paul II commends St Louis-Marie's 'Marian spirituality' (*RM* 48),

without endorsing his theology in detail.

16 *True Devotion to the Blessed Virgin Mary*, quoted in Graef 2.59; see also pp. 57–8.

17 'The Blessed Virgin Compared to the Air we Breathe', in *The Poems of Gerard Manley Hopkins*, 4th edn, ed. W. H. Gardner and N. H. Mackenzie (Oxford 1970), p. 95, line 47.

18 *Sermon on the Most Holy Mother of God*, quoted in Graef 1.335.

19 Bishop Kallistos T. Ware, in *The Akathistos Hymn to the Most Holy Mother of God*, Ecumenical Society of the Blessed Virgin Mary, (Wallington, Surrey 1986).

20 Latin text in Miravalle, p. 14.

21 Encyclical *Adiutricem populi* on the Rosary, 1895 (*ASS* 28 (1895), p. 130).

22 *materna in Filium iura* (Apostolic Letter *Inter sodalicia* on devotions for a happy death, *AAS* 10 (1918), p. 182).

23 *quantum ad se pertinebat*.

24 Encyclical *Ad diem illum* (1904) (*ASS* 36 (1903–4), p. 453). On the distinction between condign and congruous merit see Aquinas, *Summa Theologia* 1a 2ae.114.3.

25 *Reparatrix, advocata, ministra ac mediatrix, auspex* (*AAS* 20 (1928), p. 178).

26 *L'Osservatore Romano* 29–30 April 1935, quoted in Miravalle, p. 17.

27 *LG* 60–2.

28 *n*.25.

29 *n*.18.

30 Address in Guayaquil, January 1985 (*L'Osservatore Romano*, 11 March 1985, quoted in Miravalle, p. 23).

31 *sunestaurōthē, sunzēsomen* (Rom. 6.6,8).

32 *sunklēronomoi, sunpaschomen, sundoxasthōmen* (Rom. 8.17).

33 *sunapethanomen, sunzēsomen, sunbasileusomen* (2 Tim. 2.11–12).

34 *sunezōopoiēsen, sunēgeiren, sunekathisen* (Eph. 2.5–6).

35 *summorphous* (Rom. 8.29).

36 *sunergoi* (1 Cor. 3.9).

37 'in view of the merits of Jesus Christ, the Saviour of the human race' (Pius IX, Bull *Ineffabilis Deus* defining the dogma of the Immaculate Conception (DS 2803)).

38 Four articles on the question by Bishop Kallistos Ware, René Laurentin, Roger Greenacre and Elaine Storkey appeared in *The Tablet* between 17 January and 7 February 1998. They have been assembled and reprinted by the Ecumenical Society of the Blessed Virgin Mary (11 Belmont Road, Wallington, Surrey SM6 8TE) together with a fifth article by Fr Michael O'Carroll, thus presenting comments from members of the Anglican, Orthodox and Roman Catholic churches.

39 *Letters and Diaries*, 25.18–19.

40 'Letter to the Duke of Norfolk' in *Difficulties of Anglicans*, London 1910, pp. 320, 339.

41 *AAS* 38 (1946), p. 145.

42 'asseratur ... roboretur ... vindicetur ... officiat' (DS 3061).

43 Vatican II, Decree on Ecumenism *Unitatis Redintegratio* 11 (in N. Tanner, ed., *Decrees of the Ecumenical Councils*, London and Washington 1990, 2.915).

44 Extracts from Pope Paul's address can be found in my *They Are in Earnest: Christian Unity in the statements of Paul VI, John Paul I, John Paul II (TAIE)* (Slough 1982), p. 52.
45 Tanner 2.816; DS 3070.
46 ARCIC I, Authority I, 24 (d).
47 *UUS* 95.
48 Homily in the presence of the Ecumenical Patriarch, 6 December 1987, quoted in *UUS* 95.
49 The text of the Common Declaration can be found in *A New Spirit: The Archbishop of Canterbury's visit to Rome 1996*, Anglican Communion Publications, London 1997.
50 *AAS* 68 (1976), p. 599.
51 *Pontifical Council for Promoting Christian Unity Information Service*, 70 (1989). p. 60.

(This paper was given at the ESBVM Leeds Congress in August 1998)

21

Homily
given at the Little Oratory, Brompton,
at the thirtieth anniversary celebrations
of the Ecumenical Society of
the Blessed Virgin Mary
by
Alberic Stacpoole OSB
12 July 1997

Cast back your minds from the Second Millennium to AD 200: it was then that Tertullian wrote: 'Plures efficimus quoties metimur in vobis, semen est sanguis Christianorum' (*Apol.* 50.13). That means, in our universal language, 'As often as we are mown down by you, the more shall we grow in numbers – for, you see, the blood of the martyrs is the seed of the Church'. Tertullian went on to edit the *Passio Sanctae Perpetuae et Felicitas*.

Ours is a proud church in Britain, a church which has suffered grave martyrdom for a prolonged period; indeed both aspects of the *Ecclesia Anglicana* have fiercely undergone and inflicted martyrdom. For the Catholics who never flinched, there were the years from 1535 till 1681 of blood martyrdom – by the axe and the sword, or by being hanged, drawn and quartered. To mark the terminal dates: first a Cardinal of the Church was beheaded, and then an Archbishop of Armagh (Primate of Ireland in post-Cromwell days) was hanged. What followed was the 'white martyrdom' of ostracism, boycotting, denial of State rights or any social participation, until the penal laws were withdrawn in 1778–93 and catholic emancipation was proferred by the victor of Waterloo in 1829. The English hierarchy was restored in 1850, from which blossomed a Second Spring of life.

Enough it is to speak of John Foxe's *Book of Martyrs* (1563), covering the period of the reign of Mary Tudor, otherwise called 'Bloody Mary'. There is a whole record of bloodletting by Catholicism, which does need rehearsing. Thus, when we all came on scene in the twentieth century, in our realm we were not yet in common dialogue one with another, despite Cardinal Mercier of Malines, and Viscount Halifax of York. The Lambeth Conference of 1920 made its *Appeal to all Christian People* 'to move towards worldwide Christian unity'. Pius XI took eight years to respond for worldwide Catholics, with his encyclical on *Fostering True Religious Unity*. He (and Pius XII after him) claimed that Catholicism and the Church Christ founded are necessarily co-terminal and wholly inclusive. Cardinal Bourne, from Westminster Cathedral, declaimed thus: 'The Catholic Church must ever be, as she has been from the beginning, an *exclusive* Church, both in her teaching and in her worship.' It needed a world war to soften this view, in which Catholics, Protestants and Jews in their hordes died together, clinging to the last vestiges of humanity. Then the Phoenix of resuscitation became the ancient Roman Church Phoenix of resurrection; and humanity found itself holding out hands for survival and common prayer – the prayer Christ gave his dozen martyr-Apostles.

In the *Ecclesia Anglicana*, the search for mutual understanding issued in talks, official and grass-root. Two Anglicans names stood out, Canon Leonard Prestige and Dr Alec Vidler; and from among the English Roman Catholics it was the monks (like Bede Griffiths) and Jesuits (like Bernard Leeming) who were spiritually or intellectually most flexible and fertile. Then hierarchies began to lead: then Archbishops of Canterbury made visits to Popes in Rome. William Temple began it in 1944, but was taken by God; Geoffrey Fisher reached Rome, but was told that his part was no more than 'Dr Fisher of Lambeth'; Michael Ramsey went as the one hundredth Archbishop of Canterbury, coming away with a pontiff's gold ring. Ever since then, no Pope has refused to receive a Cantuar, and one Cantuar received a Pope, both kneeling before the place of martyrdom of Becket (one of the Church's first prelates ever to be canonized).

But in England and Wales, all was not so sweet. As the Anglican–Roman Catholic International Commission (ARCIC I) gathered weight and impetus – what we call kinetic energy – issuing in Common Declarations beforehand and Common Agreements afterwards, even such nodal figures as Cardinal Heenan of Westminster felt compelled to write to this monk:

> My dear Father … a statement of substantial agreement (such as that of Canterbury) is too like the communiqué issued by diplomats and statesmen after their meetings. These conversations always turn out to have been frank and full – usually agreement is said to have been reached on all points under discussion. Theological dialogues with the same team make these excellent men fast friends, and it would break their hearts to admit any discord in their views. This is the real danger. I am all for conversations – there will be no reunion without them – but against Joint Statements of the kind we have had.

When Heenan was taken by God a year later (7 November 1975) the monk who was Vicar Capitular of Westminster wrote of him: 'He tended to see theology not only as the handmaiden of the priesthood, but as almost valueless apologetic and indeed positively menacing except to the extent that it directly subserved an apologetic purpose'.

To some, ecumenical growth must have appeared rather as a jousting field, armed knights flaunting fierce banners under the cry, 'In hoc signo, vinces'. But there were gentler souls who spoke to God in a different tone, hearing God encourage brotherhood. Was it not Giuseppi Roncalli who met the Jews at the outset of Vatican II with those gentle words: 'I am your brother, Joseph'. What issued from that approach? The great document, *Nostrae Aetate*. The Vatican Council generated a revolution between churches, most of them being directly represented in the St Peter's Aula for the formative debates. When the Observers left Rome, Paul VI said much to them, among it all this:

> If we want to summarize the fruits ... of the Council, we can state first the fact of a deepening awareness of the existence of the problem of reunion in the unity of the Church itself: a problem which concerns us all and calls us all. We can add another fruit, yet more precious: the hope that the problem – not today, certainly, but tomorrow – may be solved; slowly, gradually, loyally, generously. That is great; and it is a sign that still other fruits have ripened: we have learned to know one another better – as Christian communities which live, pray and act in the name of Christ – with Christian treasures of great value.

And so Observer brethren left Rome in real sorrow, but in responsible, committed hope.

It was in this climate that our Ecumenical Society came into being. From such sentiments emerged a sharing – of pulpits, of scriptural translation, of theological study courses, of prayer and liturgy, even of church buildings. Thus the Ecclesia Anglicana chose to commemorate, with the Belgian hierarchy under Cardinal Suenens, the bow-wave Malines Conversations of 1921–6, terminated only by the death of Cardinal Mercier, who gave his ring to Halifax. Across the water, the once Anglican deacon turned Catholic layman, Martin Gillett, ventured to propose an enterprise near his Marian heart (for he had come to collect Marian shrines, books and events as his ecumenical years unfolded). 'Why', he asked thin air in the presence of such as Suenens, 'why should Our Lady not lead our reunion? Why should she be a stone of stumbling, not a stone in the bridge of unity?' In his mind, in October 1966, there came to life our Ecumenical Society of the Blessed Virgin Mary (ESBVM), a society that was to be founded with this unlikely charter – 'to promote ecumenical devotion, and the study at various levels of the place of the Blessed Virgin in the Church, under Christ ... in the cause of Christian unity'. Léon-Joseph Suenens was enthusiastic; the evangelical

Bishop Allison of Winchester was acquiescent; Bishop Gordon Wheeler, (once an Anglican, and warm to his past) was supportive; Cardinal Heenan was approached and did not dissent. Soon a formal foundation was made at the Methodist Central Hall, Westminster – for all things were done with grandeur from inception. In the presence of the most positive Apostolic Delegate, Igino Cardinale, four Co-Chairmen were installed, Catholic, Anglo-Catholic, Orthodox and Methodist: let us name just one, Graham Leonard, later Bishop of London and finally a Roman Catholic priest with a KCVO. Gillett then vowed the rest of his life to the ESBVM, a vow he kept till he died, on St George's Day 1980.

Martin Gillett proved industrious beyond his health, earning a Knighthood of St Gregory, as a successor in his shoes was similarly to do. He founded a national organization, with local branches, all composed of several denominations (what we call 'the four-legged stool': Orthodox, Catholic, Anglican and Free Churches). Membership was drawn widely from folk encompassing many levels of the religious life, prelatal or pious, scholarly or simple. They all caught the fever of shared traditions (despatching the word 'denomination'). They caught the tide incoming in so many holy activities, which seemed splendidly led by seniors enthusing as equals. Were one to select a name vital to the Society's success, it would be the Italian–American Delegate from Paul VI, Archbishop Cardinale. Heenan said of him: 'All his friends seem to be in the Church of England and Free Churches'. He was quick to proffer a public paper entitled 'Pope Pius XII and the Blessed Virgin Mary', which we were quick to publish in the first ESBVM collection, *Mary's place in Christian dialogue*. It gave an impression that the papacy was behind the Society's work; and indeed soon enough papal blessings came to send off our Congresses. Meanwhile branches burgeoned over England, with their own shared and pooled study papers.

'Far back, through creeks and inlets making
Comes silent, flooding in, the main'.

At this point there is a danger of subsiding into organizational reportage. Yet some account of our widening activities needs to be given, to illustrate our high intention. Prelacy embraced the ESBVM, and the Society was not slow to employ the advantage offered. International Congresses became the main work, the high profile of the Society, and it was found *convenable* to gather in a Father for each of these. Our two most assiduous fathers have been Cardinal Léon-Joseph Suenens, often preaching on his leading spirituality – the place of the Holy Spirit at the heart of all theology or spirituality, even mariology (and indeed *a fortiori* there). The other was Cardinal Jan Willebrands, who led the Secretariat for Promoting Christian Unity, sometimes from his place as leader of the Dutch Church in all its turmoil. Willebrands' present successor, Cardinal Edward Cassidy, has also fathered our works; and now we have the presence of Cardinal Cahal Daly of Armagh. Our Patrons have included Cardinal Basil Hume and Archbishop Robert Runcie; and our working Moderators have included bishops and leading churchmen like Dr John Newton of the Methodists, and with him Dr Gordon Wakefield.

So quickly did ESBVM take off, that it held its first Congress at Coloma College, Kent in April 1971, where the speakers included Dean Alan Richardson KBE of York, Dr Eric Mascall of King's College, London, the Dominican Fr F. M. Jelly of Washington and Mgr Philip Delhaye, Dean of the Louvain Theology Faculty. But enough of names. Two Congresses were held at Newman College, Birmingham – to which Paul VI and Cardinal Villet sent messages. Leading mariologists throughout the world (one more name, Abbé René Laurentin, has to be uttered), came with study papers. Participants began to come from all over western Europe, North America and Australasia. The Congresses travelled to Oxford, Westminster, Dublin, and places where our branches were strongest – notably Chichester and Liverpool. A chapter, with its own life there, was inaugurated in the United States by Martin Gillett, hoping 'to form further chapters in the major cities of the United States', based on Washington.

The work of ESBVM became categorized as study, prayer and social-izing – what we coined as 'say – pray – play' or 'learning – liturgy –living'. Besides publishing ESBVM Congress proceedings and papers in journals, then books on each event, there developed a steady flow of published pamphlets, drawn from branch lectures and weekend events. The best of these have been gathered into further books, displaying deep thought within all of the four traditions: Catholic, Anglican, Orthodox and Free Church (especially Methodist); and indeed non-Christian tradi-tions were granted their say (especially Islam, where Mary is much honoured). Besides those who sought to further Marian ecumenical crusades, many of our members became so for the joy of their own Marian spirituality, remembering Mary's words at Cana, 'Do whatever Jesus tells you' (knowing that it echoed Genesis 41, where the Pharaoh of the famine ordered all Egypt 'to go to Joseph and do as he tells you'). What is most remarkable abut ESBVM is its range, and its quite unfore-seen success – high, low and immediate, *ut in omnibus glorificetur Deus in Maria Dei genitrice Deipara.*

Mary
and
gender

22

Our Lady and women in the new century

Josephine Robinson

'We want religion to be a severe inner discipline without any consolations whatsoever. The colder and clearer the better ... Religious activity has now to be undertaken just for its own sake as an autonomous and practical response to the coolly-perceived truth of the human condition. This is true religion: all else is superstition.' So wrote Don Cupitt in 1984. However we interpret these words, the image they conjure up is worlds away from the second most familiar image in Western art – that of Mary and the Christ child. The warmth of that portrayed embrace has cheered the hearts and uplifted the spirits for perhaps a thousand years of Christian picturing. It is, indeed 'true religion' – God incarnate as a child in the sheltering arms of his human mother.

In the last century the French philosopher, Simone de Beauvoir, wrote in her book *The Second Sex*, 'One is not born, but one becomes a woman'. I think that by this runic statement, she intended to convey the idea that the differences between the sexes were largely social constructs. It is not clear whether she thought that all human beings began as male, and certain of them were then classified as female, perhaps on grounds of fragility, or whether she meant that human beings were born neither male nor female, and that they developed as bully or as victim and became male and female under that dispensation. Either way I find this view a little passé. I am speaking rather flippantly but these are my two themes: Our Lady, and women at the start of the new century. Many influences dominant in contemporary society deform the existential personhood of women. The Blessed Virgin Mary is, I believe, the first of all models for the daughters of Eve.

Origins of Feminism

It cannot be denied that the political and social 'cause' of feminism is having a signal effect on human society, especially, so far, in the affluent world, but its votaries are spreading this cult world-wide. I would argue that this is not an unmixed blessing. On the surface, of course, equality for women is a matter of justice. Votes for women, women's lib., the women's movement, all had the power to improve women's status in society. It must indeed be terrible to live in a culture which does not allow one as a woman to have a measure of education, to choose a husband, or own property or even to be able to influence by the ballot box the society in which one lives. There are many societies where women are denied these rights There are many societies where many men do not have much in the way of rights, either. All manner of limitations have been and still are placed on men and women alike.

The modern feminist movement seems to have started in strength in America in the nineteenth century. Women played an important role in the building up of the United States, enduring the hardships of hazardous terrain and weather and the hostility of the indigenous peoples. Many of their early campaigns were admirable, concerned with sobriety and the rescue of women from prostitution. Strong women, with a firm, Biblical Christian faith, did much good.

In nineteenth-century Europe, Marx, and in particular Engels, had developed another view of women. Engels in his *Origins and History of the Family* asserts that the earliest societies were matriarchal, but that as wealth increased each man came to want his own exclusive woman, as a personal possession. However, one of the best-known of feminist theologians, the American Rosemary Radford Ruether, sees this as 'historically inaccurate and ideologically distorted'. Marx, for his part, saw women as well as men as economic units, useful producers of future workers, but wasted on home-making and care for the family. In every Marxist-inspired revolution, women were expected to do everything that men did. A clear and interesting example of this is chronicled in the book *Wild Swans* in the context of China. In Soviet Russia, many blocks of flats were constructed without kitchens and communal feeding was provided by the authorities. A home without a kitchen is an empty shell. The preparation of meals, the warmth, the security, the laughter, the stories, the love were discounted and diminished. Women were denied the realm that was particularly their own. Other societies, too, deny women the proper freedoms that belong to human beings.

There is a religious element in the concept of the family. Totalitarian states cannot, almost by definition, admit the validity of religious faith, because it takes the totality out of totalitarianism. The lure of Marxism for some women, even today, is that it seeks to overturn the established structures of society. Even in the relatively free Western world, an after-taste of Marxism downgrades marriage and family.

Freud is another founding father of feminism. His emphasis on sex as the basic human drive has been enthusiastically adopted by many feminist women in the affluent world. They tend to see sexual desire and pleasure as self-justifying and without any context. We also find also a 'romantic' vein among certain feminists, who pursue a pantheistic form of belief. They aim to exclude men from their lives entirely, and often turn their affections to embracing trees and plants, sometimes worshipping the earth as goddess.

Some time ago, I met a priest who is rector of a seminary in the Philippines. He said that he gets religious sisters coming to him and saying that they feel oppressed at the sight of a number of priests in the sanctuary concelebrating the Mass. I am afraid I replied, rather tartly, 'You can't imagine our Lady saying that!' The Rector laughed. But thinking it over, it occurs to me that it was perhaps the early experiences of these sisters, before they came to the convent, that made them anxious at the sight of a group of men As Pope John Paul II wrote in *Mulieris Dignitatem*, the male's tendency to dominate is a result of the Fall. So it must be said that males cannot shrug off feminism as nothing to do with them.

Many women in the Western world develop a fixed belief that women should do whatever men do, good, bad or indifferent. One could say that the liberation they seek is the liberation from womanhood. They share the 'liberal' beliefs of the majority of civilized Western society which depends on a kind of personal *laissez faire*. Rosemary Ruether describes this, rather acidly, as 'the preferred view of the bourgeois'. They hope that education and opportunity in the workplace will produce a society of equals, while keeping private property in place.

The Judaeo-Christian tradition

We Christians, as heirs to the Judaeo-Christian tradition, can go back to the beginning of Genesis and the unequivocal and inclusive statement that God made man in his image and likeness; 'male and female He created them'. This statement makes plain the equality of males and females in the sight of God, and one has to say, as a Christian, that equality before God is what matters. This Biblical statement is very different from the Greek view of women in classical times. Plato says in the *Timaeus* that the souls of males who had failed in controlling their feelings were incarnated in women: women are therefore failed males and rated as halfway between males and brute beasts.

Women in Judaism, though not affirmed as Christianity was to affirm them, nevertheless played a great part in Jewish history, with many notable women making their mark for good or ill. Furthermore, some important Jewish religious rituals take place in the home – the Sabbath meal, preceded by the ritual cleansing of the house, the candles of Hanukkah and so on – and the value placed on the bearing of children endorses the position of women. Even the well-known prayer of the Jewish male thanking God that he was not born a woman, is countered by the lesser-known prayer of women thanking God for their woman-hood.

There is a charming picture of the Good Wife in the Book of Wisdom. More Martha, perhaps, than Mary, she is busy about many things. She runs her household with the skill of a company director. She under-stands woman management; she rises early to get the best bargains in the market, but has already set her maids their tasks for the day. She is continually busy, but, I suspect, not wholly driven. She does two things at once, one intellectual and one practical. This is one of God's gifts to women! She thinks best with knitting needles, (or rather spindle) in hand. She has her cottage industry, selling the girdles she makes to the merchants. It may well be that when she sees her husband, well-dressed, thanks to her, setting off for the gates to discuss weighty matters with his cronies, she thanks God for the quiet about the house and the chance of a chat with her friends. Yet she loves her husband, who trusts her absolutely, brings up her children to bless her, and is kind to the poor. Despite her husband's 'patriarchy', can we doubt that she was the centre of the home?

Patriarchy, which is fatherhood writ large, and androcentrism, which is the male as monopolizing leadership and dominating culture, are the twin bugbears of feminism, but have really to be considered in a more ample context than is often the case. A patriarch, properly so named, leads, guides and guards his people. Democracy muddles through without patriarchal national figures, and the twentieth century, more than most centuries, threw up dictators, who were a grotesque and evil parody of patriarchy. One has only to think of Hitler, of Stalin, of Mao Tse-Tung. As a woman of the Roman Catholic tradition, I see a real patriarch of our present age in Pope John Paul II. He protects the weak, defending them against utilitarian values, be they pre-born, sick, elderly, disabled, or denied the proper autonomy of the human being in any sphere. It is significant that John Paul II is vocal in his love of Mary and carries her initial on his coat of arms. He is her *preux chevalier*.

Women and families

As for the cultural domination of society by the male, that is surely coun-tered by the fact that women, usually mothers, dominate the lives of small children and present values which influence them for the rest of their lives, and which are necessary for the survival of individual members of the human race. Children cannot thrive without being nursed, fed and loved, and mother and child have a symbiotic relationship which develops continuously during the nine months of life in the womb. This fact tells us why the act of bringing up children is initially, at any rate, the usual job of the mother – with, one hopes, the help of the father or others. There is a truth in the old saying that 'The hand that rocks the cradle rules the world'. When the mother shapes the new person, can we still seriously say, with confidence, that males dominate the culture?

The God-given strengths of women are often discounted by feminists. They value achievements in the public sphere; and feminist writers tend to be interested only in the high-flyers of this world and view everyone who is not rich and famous as a failure or a victim. In every century the vast majority, of men and women alike, have lived in obscurity, working hard in difficult circumstances, worried and to a greater or lesser degree, oppressed. Women have had, at least, something amounting to their own tiny realm, with the satisfaction of producing a nourishing meal, or watching a baby grow, or sewing a garment to keep someone warm in winter. These small triumphs should not be underestimated.

We know now, with ever deeper pain, that children who lose either parent, but especially the mother, suffer a deprivation the results of which are often seen in anger, and disruptive behaviour of various kinds, which may last for years or even a lifetime. A child who loses either parent through illness and death suffers, but the child whose mother or, to a lesser extent, father leaves him or her, by choice, is likely to feel not merely unloved, but unloveable.

Oddly enough, one of the consequences of feminism, along with other modes of thought, is a revival of a kind of nominalism – the heresy of the Middle Ages, which saw every substance as irreducibly individual. For many Western women, brought up in the wider, more diffuse feminism that permeates the educational system in this country, females can, even must, do all that males do, in order to assert their individuality. One of the saddest photographs I have seen was in one of the newspapers which showed a young American woman soldier in full combat gear, cradling her three-month-old baby, before she went off to the Gulf war. Why? Pray God she got back safely.

This individualism has been most dangerous in the sphere of sexuality. Science has played its part, by making it possible for the link between sexual acts and procreation to be broken. People now speak about recreational sex, as if it were a sort of party game, and the child as sometimes an inconvenience to be destroyed in the womb, sometimes a feather in the cap of the successful woman. The child is often not considered as the fruit of the love between husband and wife. And because fornication and adultery carry fewer risks when pregnancy can be avoided, the inbuilt monitor that weights women's psyche towards fidelity and chastity is overruled. This is, however, to some extent theoretical , because there is ample evidence of contraceptive failure.

This is the picture of untrammelled individual choice which has been constantly presented to young women of the last generation or two. There is another deleterious development. In the past educators stressed the importance of purity and of marriage. Now, adolescents are presented with 'value-free' so-called 'sex education'. So-called sex education providers, many of whom have some official standing, have not promoted continence outside marriage, have not upheld marriage and certainly imply that as long as the adolescent feels 'ready for sex', he or she should go ahead – only making sure that no child results. We have seen continual increases in the number of teenage pregnancies, most ending in abortion, and huge increases in sexually-transmitted diseases. Indeed, any form of sexual activity is often presented as a valid 'life-style choice'. It requires heroic virtue for young people to combat tyrannies like these.

Sexual activity has different consequences for men and women. The male can move away from a sexual encounter – although he should not do so – without any practical consequences to himself this side of judgement. Even if no pregnancy results, a woman is constituted to receive, to embrace, her emotions sharpened to the meeting. A young girl's need to be loved is, I believe, more immediate than that of the young male. He needs guidance to curb his predatory instincts.

This approach to sexuality has had further results in the disastrous breakdown of marriage and the appalling consequences for children. As we have seen, the child's security depends on continuity, and family fragmentation must destroy that. It also denies the child the chance to learn the ways of both sexes. It also often brings with it the hazards of stepfamilies and it is not by chance that stepmothers, stepsisters, stepfathers, are so often the catalysts for disaster in fairy stories. I was recently reading a cookery book about the glories of the potato. From the introduction, it transpired that the two authors, a man and a woman, were living together unmarried, and each had a daughter from a previous union. The woman writing told a little story of how her daughter, fourteen years of age or so, had rung her at her office one day and said, 'Mum, there's no food in the house.' 'Yes, there is,' the mother said, 'There are pizzas in the freezer and bread and cheese and fish fingers' and so on. 'But,' the girl said fiercely, 'there are no potatoes!' Potatoes are often described as comfort food. Was that girl saying 'no potatoes', when she really wanted to say 'no comfort'?

It is commonplace in our time to denigrate the Christian churches and, I have to say, the Catholic Church, in particular, for harping negatively upon sex. Sexual sins are not the only sins. But it is because the

Church knows how sexual sin can have consequences far beyond even the intention of the sinner that she stresses her teaching. It is because sex is so important, and so often trivialized. Feminism, while seeking to uphold women in their status as human beings, has in the event, urged them to disregard their particular qualities of gracefulness and gentleness which are largely inborn , a necessary preparation for motherhood, which is the common lot of the majority of women.

Our Lady and the Church

The Blessed Virgin Mary, a true woman, is held by the Church in high honour, as the greatest human being, apart from God-made-man, who ever lived. One would expect, therefore, that all women would hold her in the highest esteem. By contrast, some women rather regard her as the wrong sort: an unassertive woman. They confuse receptivity with passivity, which is odd when you think that even receiving a confidence requires as much energy and discernment as making the confidence. Many of them despise her virginity, many downgrade her motherhood. One contemporary writer has Mary saying that her pregnancy 'was not exactly planned'. I think she was trying to present our Lady in modern-day language and with contemporary concerns. But it jars. Imagine Mary 'planning' when she would open herself to God's gift of new life! Another writer suggests that Mary's conception was the result of rape, an instance of God's transforming power to bring good out of evil. I would guess that she mentions this to avoid the 'embarrassment' of the doctrine of our Lady's virginal conception, though if Jesus had had a human father, he would only have been the son of God in the same way as any other human being is the son of God. It also avoids the threat of a patriarchal family – that Church-endorsed detention camp so feared in some quarters!.

The changes Christianity brought to women

It is surely a paradox that a religion that gives pre-eminence among all creation to a woman should be seen by many today as the enemy of women. Yet the love and reverence felt for our Lady is a development of the Jewish tradition of women's equality with men before God. I mentioned Plato's view in the *Timaeus*. When we look at the position of women in the Roman empire, we see that they were, with few exceptions, outside the rule of law. They were part of the property of the male, whether father or husband. Jurists studying Roman documents have noted what was called 'the forced disappearance of little girls'. Few families had more than one girl in them. The Roman father had the right to look over his new-born offspring and 'disappear' weak or deformed boys, but he was apparently not obliged to keep girl children at all. The French writer and archivist, Régine Pernoud, notes that girls were often not given a personal name, but were called by a femininization of the family name, a clear indication of disregard.

Yet, by the beginning of the third century of Christianity, in the early 200s, we learn of young girls, within the Roman empire, who defied their fathers, not to assert their right to a good time, or a masculine life style, but because they wished to devote themselves to God. They would not marry the pagan husbands their fathers selected for them, not because of some sexual anorexia or peculiarity, but because they would have had to renounce Christ. They gave up their lives and became virgin martyrs. Pope John Paul II maintains that love of the Virgin Mary played a part in this. Certainly, it appears as if Christianity brought a huge rush of spiritual energy to women. When the Romans had weakened and the empire was fragmented and defeated, it was Christian women, in many cases, wives of savage, marauding kings, who brought their husbands and thus kingdoms, to Christianity. How many prayers and what human guile must have gone into those conversions!

Love of our Lady grew and flourished in the Middle Ages in devotion and in art. The grace, in both senses, of Mary illuminated those centuries amid the darkness of wars and many kinds of deprivation.

After the Reformation, Mary was, as we know, neglected by the reformers. No doubt the exuberant love of Mary seemed, to those austere Christians, to verge on idolatry. I think idolatry, on the one hand, and adoration, the praise that we give to God alone, directed to Mary, was rare. It was the very humanness of Mary that drew people to her. Christ is indeed the sole mediator between God and man. Her part was to mediate the coming of God the Son into the world through her own body. I would argue that some of the warmth of the faith was lost without the embrace of the virgin mother, while the social status of women was not notably improved. It was, after all, Martin Luther who said that a woman was like a nail, fixed to the wall of a house, which is not a very comforting image.

Mother of God and Mother of us

Eve shared the failure of Adam, the man. Mary, prepared, as the Church came to understand, by God himself for her unique encounter with the divine – the God-man, a child in her womb – responded to the state of sinlessness in which she herself remained from her conception, by a richness of loving. According to the *Protoevangelium Jacobi*, an apocryphal gospel, her parents Joachim and Anna presented her in the

Temple, as a thankoffering to God. There is a most beautiful painting by Titian hanging in the Accademia in Venice which shows the scene: the great staircase at the head of which stands the high priest, tall and imposing, and at the bottom stand a number of people, Mary's parents among them, in wonder and a certain anxiety. And half-way up the stairs runs an enchanting little girl, her hair hanging down, one hand holding up her blue dress and the other outstretched in unselfconscious confidence towards the high priest. She knows that the two of them are in it together, in worship, in love and reverence for God.

The Association of Catholic Women, with whom I work, is much moved by the idea that Mary, the Maid of Israel, was taught the Psalms by her mother and her father too, perhaps, – those prayers to God the Father, which she may well herself, with Joseph, have taught her divine Son. There are many statues dating from the Middle Ages, which show Mary as a little girl with a book in her hands, and St Anne with her. We have taken this as providing us with a guide to the way in which Christians should seek to pass on the faith to the next generation. Within the tradition of the communion of saints, we ask the mother and father of the blessed Virgin Mary, as well as Mary herself, to intercede for all who try to do this. We hope that these prayers will be answered in such a way as to produce a seed-bed for vocations to the priesthood and religious life, as well as steadfast lay people. We have formed the League of St Anne and St Joachim to this end.

At the annunciation, we see the same directness of response that is caught in Titian's picture; no false modesty, no self-serving; only the graciousness that comes from purity in God's grace and the perfect human response to it. If our Lady's virginal conception of Jesus was miraculous, we may suppose that his growth in the womb followed the pattern of all humanity. His divine heart, for us the potent symbol of his love, would have started beating about twenty-one days from the annunciation. No wonder that one of the titles that we give to Mary is 'Ark of the Covenant', the precursor of the Church. John Saward has pointed out that she carried in her the greatest treasure, not merely of Israel, but of the whole world, from Nazareth, through Jerusalem, to Elizabeth's home. As she went towards her cousin's house, 'in the hill country of Judah', the living Covenant between God and man, that was to redeem the world, was growing in her womb. In our time, which kills babies in the womb, we women, and men too, need to be reminded of the sacred, God-given life of the zygote, the embryo, the foetus, the baby.

Mary is no feeble, ordinary girl. The unimaginable wonder of her position is fearlessly accepted by her. The poet Gerard Manley Hopkins speaks of her as 'Wild air, world-mothering air' She 'proclaims the greatness of the Lord ... who has done great things' for her.

Every woman who gives birth mediates through her own body a person in the image and likeness of God with an immortal destiny. Every woman, whatever her life, whether married, dedicated to God as a religious, or pursuing her life in the world, has the gift of spiritual motherhood through empathy with others. We have no need to feel uneasy before Mary, our mother. Her tenderness and her fearlessness, her rich loving as virgin and mother manifest the glorious possibilities of womanhood.

The joy Mary must have felt when Simeon described her Baby as 'a light for revelation to the Gentiles and for glory to thy people Israel' was countered by the foretelling of the sword that was to pierce her heart. She pondered on all these things. The anthropologist Philip Lersch wrote that men look directly at an object, whereas women tend to cast their eyes over the whole scene, so that they observe the background and the shadows. Do we, contemporary women, ponder enough?

Again, when she found her Son in the Temple, asking questions of the teachers, she sought to discover the reason for his apparently thoughtless behaviour. She did not understand why he had done what he had done. That, again is a lesson for us before our own children, or others. We have to have the humility to accept that we do not always understand. Sometimes we have to accept, unknowing.

Our Lady did not hang on to her Son. We know, of course, that she was at the wedding at Cana and prompted Jesus to perform the miracle, so rich in symbols of the Last Supper, that inaugurated his public ministry. Hans Urs von Balthasar links the occasion when Jesus, having been told that his mother and family were asking for him, made plain that all who believed in him were kin and even mother to him, with the Godforsakenness that Jesus felt on the cross. Mary was to share even in this. Rejection was the experience both of Jesus and his mother. Our Blessed Lady is our guide here as well.

Jesus, from the cross, gave his mother into the care of his Beloved Disciple. And he gave her to us, in the person of St John, as our mother. She is called 'Our Lady' in many languages and this 'our' is familial.

The future

In this new century, Christians will have to fight the ethos of the age. Many women, and men, do reject the culture of deformation and death. Many women recognize in themselves the lineaments of womanhood, which are part of God's plan. Christian women, within the restored tradition of seeking to imitate Mary, of loving her as both virgin and mother, must spearhead the culture of life and grace. She tells us to do whatever Jesus tells us.

When I was researching my book *The Inner Goddess, Feminist Theology in the Light of Catholic Teaching*, I became aware of the contradiction of feminism. It often generates an envious desire for, not merely equality, but identity with the male: a society with only masculine values would be a poorer place. But, by focusing all their energies on themselves, feminist women become their own objects of worship, inner goddesses, impotent and sad. As to Mary, no one ever worshipped herself less than she did!

Von Balthasar once daringly used the existence of Mozart as proof of the existence of God. Mozart exists, therefore God must exist. May I , on this occasion and in this context, say that the beauty of Mary leads us to deepen our faith in God? *Theotokos*, Mother of God, pray for us.

(This paper was given at the ESBVM Oxford Congress
in August 2000)

23

The ordination of women, gender symbolism and the Blessed Virgin Mary

Edward Yarnold SJ

We are all well aware what decisions each of the churches has taken concerning the ordination of women to the priesthood. In this paper I have no intention of calling any of those decisions in question. This is an ecumenical society; it should be our method to avoid accentuating differences, and instead to accept one another as we are, and try to maximize and deepen the 'real but imperfect communion' which already unites us in Christ. What the Holy Spirit may do with us subsequently is not for us to guess.

My purpose is rather to consider one factor which is invoked by both sides of the debate, namely the symbolic power of gender and its relevance to ordination. Other scriptural, historical and theological considerations lie outside my self-assigned brief. Whatever the outcome of our reflections today, we will not have resolved all the differences between the churches and between their members.

Let us examine an example of this appeal to gender-symbolism, namely the Declaration *Inter Insigniores (II)* promulgated by the Congregation of the Doctrine of the Faith (CDF) in 1976, while Cardinal Seper was still its Prefect. Its full title is *Declaration on the Question of the Admission of Women to the Ministerial Priesthood*.[1]

The Declaration does not begin with the symbolic force of gender. It first sets out three other factors under distinct headings: 1) 'The Church's constant tradition'; 2) 'The attitude of Christ'; 3) 'The practice of the Apostles'. A fourth section then maintains 'the permanent value of the attitude of Jesus and the Apostles', concluding that 'the practice of the Church ... has a normative character' (n. 4);

> In the final analysis it is the Church, through the voice of her Magisterium, that ... decides what can change and what must remain immutable.

It is only then that the Declaration proceeds to propose further considerations. It is made crystal clear that the aim is not to bring forward a 'demonstrative argument'; the aim is to 'clarify[ing]' the teaching, not to prove it, to 'illustrate' the norm by showing its 'profound fittingness'. The appeal is to the 'analogy of faith' (n. 5): that is to say, considerations drawn from one area of theology, such as Christian anthropology, are expected to cast light on other areas, such as the theology of priesthood, because Christian truth is a harmonious whole.

The Congregation's fundamental notion is that the bishop or the priest, in the exercise of his ministry, especially at the Eucharist, 'does not act in his own name, *in persona propria*'. He acts through the *power* conferred on him by Christ, and also in the *person* of Christ, 'taking the role of Christ, to the point of being his very image, when he pronounces the words of consecration' (n. 5) The Declaration confirms this view by quoting several passages from Vatican II. It also appeals to the teaching of St Thomas. For Aquinas, just as the celebration of the Mass is the 'representative image' of Christ's cross, so too the priest 'enacts the image of Christ, in whose person and by whose power he pronounces the words of consecration'.[2] It is a fundamental principle of sacramental theology that sacraments are not only causes, but also signs, of grace; as such, they not only signify the grace they effect, but effect it precisely as signs, effecting it through signifying it. Moreover, such signs are not arbitrary symbols, like an asterisk used in a time-table to denote a change of trains. In the words of St Thomas, 'sacramental signs represent what they signify by natural resemblance.'[3] This resemblance, the CDF concludes, would not exist if the priest were not male, for 'Christ himself was and remains a man' (n. 5).

The CDF acknowledges that Christ is the firstborn of *all* humanity, female as well as male; nevertheless it was in the male sex that the Word became flesh. This fact is not accidental to God's plan; it is 'in harmony with the entirety of God's plan as God himself has revealed it, and of which the mystery of the Covenant is the nucleus' (n. 5). To develop the CDF's argument, there are some facts about our Lord's humanity which are not essential to his saving work, such as his social class or the colour of his eyes; but other features are essential, above all the fact that he was male. Consequently, if the priest is to bear the natural resemblance to Christ of which the Declaration has been speaking, he need not be a dark-eyed member of a country artisan's family, but he *will* need to be male. (But what of his Jewishness, which was also essential to God's plan?)

The Prophets explained the Covenant between God and his Chosen People in nuptial imagery, in which he is the Bridegroom, and his people are his 'ardently loved spouse'; the CDF refer to Hosea 1 — 3 and Jeremiah 2. The New Testament develops the same imagery to describe the New Covenant, only now the Bridegroom is Jesus Christ, and the Bride the Church. St Paul expresses these ideas in 2 Cor. 11.2 and Eph.

5.22–3; in the Johannine writings they occur in John 3.29 and Rev. 19.7,9. In the Synoptic Gospels too, our Lord speaks of himself as the Bridegroom (Mark 2.19). 'And therefore', the Declaration infers,

> unless one is to disregard the importance of this symbolism for the economy of Revelation, it must be admitted that, in actions which demand the character of ordination and in which Christ himself, the author of the Covenant, the Bridegroom and Head of the Church, is represented, exercising his ministry of salvation – which is in the highest degree the case of the Eucharist – his role (this is the original sense of the word *persona*) must be taken by a man. This does not stem from any personal superiority of the latter in the order of values, but only from a difference of fact on the level of functions and service (n. 5).

Of course it has long been acknowledged that the priest acts also *in persona Ecclesiae*, representing the whole Church made up of women as well as men. It consequently can be argued with good reason that a woman priest could be an appropriate symbol of the Bride. The Congregation's response to this counterargument is to indicate that the priest represents the Church, the Body of Christ 'precisely because he first represents Christ himself, who is the Head and Shepherd of the Church' (n. 5).[4]

When Pope John Paul II reaffirmed the teaching of *Inter Insigniores* in his 1994 statement *Ordinatio Sacerdotalis*, his brief summary of the reasons for the Church's decision made no mention of gender symbolism.[5] Nevertheless, the symbolic function of gender played an important, though not a decisive, part in the Declaration of 1977, and has continued to feature largely in discussions of the subject. It seems worth while therefore to explore this symbolism further. This is the aim of my paper.

It is implied in the argument above that this symbolism is living and effective; the resemblance between Christ and the priest must be 'natural' and not merely theoretical. I ask you accordingly to reflect without prejudice on your own experience, to see to what extent this is indeed so. In simplest terms, when we take part in the Eucharist, what difference does the gender of the priest make to the way in which he or she represents Christ the Bridegroom and the Head of the Church to our minds and our hearts? I am inviting you therefore to an exercise of imaginative introspection. It may help if I offer certain observations.

1. The importance of gender symbolism

I would like to reflect a little more deeply on the importance of the symbolism of gender symbolism in many areas of life, not only in the liturgy. But let us first consider briefly some of the problems.

First, there is today a general recognition of the danger of stereotypes based on gender. So keen are we sometimes to avoid these stereotypes that in one North American University in which I have taught, certain procedures are proposed to faculty members. One procedure consists of a form of reverse discrimination: if you wish to write about an active, adventurous child, make it a girl: 'Jane climbed boldly to the top of the tree'; if about a sensitive child, make it a boy: 'Tom cradled the kitten carefully in his hands'. Moreover some women are stronger, or taller, or more aggressive, or deeper-voiced than some men. Again, there are almost always present in men in a diminished degree some of the qualities which we regard as typically feminine, such as compassionate insight; and in women some of the qualities which we regard as typically male, such as competitive energy.

Secondly, gender symbolism does not sit comfortably with the egalitarian ethos of modern Western society. Even in his day St Thomas Aquinas judged it necessary to indicate that his appeal to the 'subjection' of women was independent of whatever status they held in society. After arguing that a woman could not be a priest because she could not represent Christ the Head, he continued that this remained true even if temporal power might be open to her (*temporaliter dominari*).[6] Unfortunately, in this passage at least, Aquinas does not explain the considerations – whether of anatomy or biology or psychology – which lead him to this conclusion.

How can such attacks on gender-symbolism be answered? I suggest the basic answer may be that the fact that a symbol depends on a stereotype does not rob it of validity. A symbol depends on what is *perceived*. A Rolls Royce is a symbol of opulence, even though there exist Rolls Royces with broken springs and slashed upholstery. Even in modern society a woman is a symbol of something which a man is not, and *vice versa*. Of course, if it became the norm for women to be hard-nosed, thrusting, childless executives, and for men to be ineffectual wimps, then the symbolism would cease to work; but, please God, we have not reached that state yet.

Or am I conceding too much here? Should not one rather say that gender-symbolism is based on permanent differences between the sexes which are too deep to depend upon the changing conditions of a particular society? The sexes are related in such a way that, except in the most freakish circumstances, the man is necessarily the initiator of sexual activity, and the woman the recipient, and the main carrier of the consequences. To put it bluntly, women cannot commit rape, and men cannot have babies. I am not of course suggesting that the reason why the male priest can represent Christ at the altar is that he is a potential rapist; my

270 Mary for Earth and Heaven

point is that the violent sexual initiative of the deviant is the corruption of the initiative which is present in healthy form in normal sexual activity. I know no reason to believe that these different sexual roles are restricted to the physiological level, and have no echoes in psychology. Gender differences are inescapable, and provide a basis for gender symbolism.

It would be useful to take into account whatever empirical studies psychologists have made concerning the differences in the behaviour of boys and girls at play. I have not had time, and have no competence, to do this. Nevertheless, the evidence of one's eyes suggests that in the playground of a primary school you will find the boys playing different types of games from the girls; and if you were to listen, I believe you would find them talking of different things.

Anecdotal evidence suggests that men and women undergraduates work in characteristically different patterns: the men often show more self-confidence than the women, even though their ability and knowledge may not warrant it; while the women often manifest greater concern with producing the kind of work which they judge is required of them. Moreover, while the achievements of women in some intellectual and cultural fields often equal or surpass those of men, there are some surprising areas in which men seem to outperform them. In the English language, women novelists have a record at least as good as that of men; it is surprising therefore that it is not easy to name two world-class women dramatists. What could be the reason why there have been so few great women painters or composers? Why are there so few first-class women chess-players, so that the Polgar sisters seemed to burst from a clear sky? Since it is hard to find adequate sociological explanations for these admittedly loosely-observed facts, one is left with the conclusion that there are characteristic differences between the male psyche and the female which help to provide an objective basis for the different symbolic power of each of the genders.

Again, speaking unscientifically – which is, to repeat, the level at which symbols operate – although the external, homemaking roles of the father and the mother may no longer be as easily distinguishable as they used to be, there is something lacking to the child cared for by a single parent or by two partners of the same gender; at least they lack a role-model for forming a responsible relationship with the opposite sex.

2. Pope John Paul II on gender symbolism

I have so far tried to justify the belief that the symbolic significance of male and female remains different even in contemporary Western society. I shall now turn to Pope John Paul II's more philosophical exposition of the same point which he proposed in his Encyclical *Mulieris Dignitatem* (*MD*) 'On the Dignity and Vocation of Women', written for the Marian Year of 1988.[7]

The Pope takes as his starting-point a statement in the documents of Vatican II to the effect that human beings find themselves only in the gift of self.[8] This principle *'gives an essential indication of what it means to be human'*. In the Genesis account of creation the image and likeness of God is linked with the relationship between men and women: 'in his own image God created them, male and female he created them' (Gen. 1.27). This relationship finds its fullest expression in the mutual self-giving of marriage, which 'opens to the gift of a new life' (*MD* 18). (It is not our purpose to consider the Pope's other way of self-giving, which is 'Virginity for the sake of the Kingdom' (*MD* 20).)

Within this relationship, Pope John Paul believes that the different 'parts' of man and woman can be identified. The woman's part is 'motherhood', which

> implies from the beginning a special openness to the new person ... In this openness, in conceiving and giving birth to a child, the woman 'discovers herself through a sincere gift of self'.

This contact with the new life which the mother carries in her womb gives rise to an attitude to all human life which 'profoundly marks the woman's personality'. (We can see here some of the reasons why the Pope is so implacably opposed to abortion and contraception.) 'It is commonly thought that *women* are more capable than men of paying attention *to another person'*. Because the man remains outside the process of pregnancy and birth, 'he has to *learn* his own *fatherhood from the mother'* (*MD* 18).

3. Gender symbolism in scripture

Let us now consider some of the many ways in which the Bible applies gender-imagery to the relationship between Yahweh and his People in the Old Covenant, and between Christ and his Church in the New. We have already given a little thought to the use of nuptial imagery by the prophets and St Paul in the course of our examination of *Inter Insigniores*. To this we can add the use of symbols derived from fatherhood and motherhood. Yahweh is the Father of his people: 'Is he not thy Father who has bought thee? Has he not made thee and established thee?' (Deut. 32.6). More surprisingly, in the prophetic writings Yahweh becomes also the mother: 'Can a woman forget her sucking child, that she should have no compassion on the son of her womb? Even these may forget, yet I will not forget you' (Isa. 49.15). 'As one whom his mother comforts, so I will comfort you' (Isa. 66.13). Our Lord also applied a maternal image to himself: 'O Jerusalem, Jerusalem, killing the prophets and stoning those who are sent to you! How often would I have gathered your children together as a hen gathers her brood under her wings, and you would not' (Matt. 23.37). Later Paul also compared himself to a mother 'in travail' giving birth to his spiritual children (Gal. 4.19).

The same maternal imagery is applied to the Church, especially under the form of the new Jerusalem. Under the old covenant Isaiah had invited the people to 'Rejoice with Jerusalem ... that you may suck and be satisfied with her consoling breasts' (Isa. 66.10). Paul directs his readers' attention from the 'present Jerusalem' to the 'Jerusalem above', who is 'our mother' (Gal. 4.26). (Revelation on the other hand envisages the new Jerusalem as the Bride coming down from heaven for her wedding with the Lamb (Rev 21.2,9). Early in the second century the *Shepherd* of Hermas recounts a vision of the Church in the form of an old woman. Since then it has become almost a cliché to speak about 'holy Mother Church'.

4. Gender symbolism and the Blessed Virgin Mary

Images, when applied to divine mysteries, cannot always be used consistently. Thus, while the Church is called our Mother, we also address Mary as our Mother and as the Mother of the Church. This last title can be traced back to John 19.26–7, where Mary is entrusted with maternal responsibility for the whole Church, in the person of the Beloved Disciple. Although there is no passage in the New Testament which speaks of Mary explicitly as the Mother of the Church, the title is close enough to Scripture for Pope Paul VI to have made its promulgation a matter of first importance during the Second Vatican Council.

The title 'Mother of the Church' needs to be understood in two ways. First, Mary is the mother *within* the Church, while herself being a member of it. While each member has his or her special endowment given by the Holy Spirit to equip them for their personal service of the whole Church – some are apostles, some teachers etc, for the building up of Christ's Body (Eph. 4.11–12) – Mary's special charism is to be the member of the Church who serves as Mother. One may recall the analogy of the 'father (or mother) of the House of Commons', the senior Member of Parliament, who is a father- or mother-figure among fellow members.

Mary is not only the one *within the Church* who has the responsibilities of a mother; she is also Mother of the Church in the sense that her *rela-*

tionship to the Church is that of a mother to her offspring. This follows immediately from her relationship to her Son: she is the Mother of the one whose body is the Church. This is not just the commemoration of a relationship which has ceased, now that her mothering of Jesus has been completed. It is an enduring relationship with practical consequences; Mary, who took the Beloved Disciple as her son at the foot of the cross, continues to support the Church with her prayers. Gerard Manley Hopkins expressed Mary's continuing motherly action in the well-known passage from his poem 'The Blessed Virgin Mary compared with the air we breathe'.

> Of her flesh he took flesh:
> He does take fresh and fresh,
> Though much the mystery how,
> Not flesh but spirit now
> And makes, O marvellous!
> New Nazareths in us,
> Where she shall yet conceive
> Him, morning, noon and eve;
> New Bethlems, and he born
> There, evening, noon and morn . . .

Mary's role as the Mother of the Church is not separate from her role as type or model of the Church, which received such clear emphasis at Vatican II. In the contemplative faith and obedience, which the Third Gospel picks out as her characteristics (Luke 1.45; 2.19; 2.51; 8.21; 11.28), she provides an example of what it is to be her Son's disciple. She demonstrates uniquely in her own person the working of God's grace in us all. This is especially true of the two most recently defined Marian dogmas. Mary's fullness of grace and preservation from original sin through her immaculate conception, and her reception, body and soul, into heaven at the assumption, are divine actions *already* accomplished in her, pointing to a similar destiny to which we are all *called* in eternity.

Hans Urs von Balthasar developed the understanding of Mary's maternal relationship to the Church in a new way, which Pope John Paul II has taken into his own thought, paying him the very rare honour of citing him by name in a footnote to an encyclical (*MD* 27 and note 55); for by custom it is only the deceased who are quoted as authorities. For von Balthasar, there are two fundamental symbols of the Church, namely Mary and Peter. The Church is Marian in its 'active receptivity', after the model of the one who heard the word of God and kept it. This Marian, and therefore feminine, dimension corresponds to the priesthood of all the baptized, who through the sacrament become a 'royal priesthood' (1 Pet. 2.5,9). But within this general priesthood the Church is also endowed with the hierarchical or ministerial priesthood of the ordained, which von Balthasar called Petrine, and which is character-ized by the masculine quality of service.[9] (But why is service mascu-line?)

The Marian dimension is 'antecedent' to the Petrine, which can be understood only in relationship to it. For the universal priesthood involves a call to holiness, to worship God with the gift of one's whole life. The Petrine dimension is secondary to the Marian, because the ordained priesthood exists for the sake of the universal: the authority of the ordained 'has no other purpose except to form the Church in line with the ideal of sanctity already programmed and prefigured in Mary'. It is at this point that the Pope quotes von Balthasar: Mary is 'Queen of the Apostles without any apostolic powers: she has other and greater powers'(*MD* 27, note 55). (We can see here one solution to the objection that to bar women from ordination is to confine them to an inferior status. On the contrary, women have other and greater powers.)

5. In the person of Christ

Let us now give further thought to the idea of the priest acting in the person of Christ at the Eucharist. This is not a phrase that goes back to the time of the early Church, still less the New Testament. The CDF is not fully justified in seeking confirmation in the Letters of St Cyprian; for the latter did not exactly say that the priest acts in the person of Christ, but that he 'truly acts in the place of Christ' (*vice Christi vere fungi-tur*), a phrase which does not carry the same symbolism as acting in Christ's person.[10] Moreover, Cyprian's concern is to show that the priest must not say Mass with water instead of wine, because he must follow the example and the command of the Christ in whose place he acts. There is no evidence yet for the idea that the priest is acting in Christ's person in speaking Christ's words of institution: 'This is my body ...' The CDF can, however, claim the authority of St Thomas Aquinas, according to whom 'the priest also enacts the image of Christ, in whose person and by whose power he pronounces the words of consecra-tion'.[11] The first council to have followed Aquinas in this teaching seems to have been the Council of Florence in the fifteenth century: 'for the priest, speaking in the person of Christ (*in persona Christi*) brings about this sacrament [of the Eucharist]'.[12]

However the expression has never formed part of a dogmatic defini-tion by the Roman Catholic Church, although it has gained common currency, and can claim to represent the Church's mind. For example, the Vatican II Decree on the Liturgy states that the priest presides in the person of Christ and prays in the name of the people (*Sacrosanctum*

Concilium 33) – a principle which reminds us that he also acts *in persona Ecclesiae*, in the person of the Church, as we have already seen in our investigation of *Inter Insigniores*.

We can perhaps go a little more deeply into what action in the person of Christ means. According to the CDF, at the Eucharist the priest acts *in persona Christi* 'to the point of being his very image, when he pronounces the words of consecration' (*II. 5*). The line of thought is that of Aquinas.[13] One might also recall St Ambrose's explanation of the Real Presence to the newly-baptized of Milan towards the end of the fourth century. In the first part of the Eucharist the bishop prays on his own account, but when he recites the Words of Institution, he is speaking the words of Jesus Christ; so that since it is Christ who is saying 'This is my Body', those words have power to bring about what they state, namely the presence of Christ.[14]

The logic of this position requires that the words of consecration be seen as an effective or declaratory formula, intended to bring about what it affirms. Other sacramental examples are easy to find: 'I baptize you in the name ...'; 'I absolve you'. However this is neither the origin nor the function of the words of consecration within the Eucharistic Prayer as a whole, as is shown by the syntactical and logical connection between the words of consecration and the rest of the Prayer. The words of consecration do not form a free-standing unit, but are linked with the rest of the Prayer by a connecting word. For example, in the Roman Canon this takes the form of a relative pronoun: the Father is asked to ratify the gifts of bread and wine and make them acceptable, so that they may become the Body and Blood of Jesus Christ, '*who*, the day before he suffered took bread ...' In the Egyptian liturgy of St Mark the words of consecration are introduced by a causal particle, which implies that the account of the Institution gives the reason for what goes before, namely the invocation of the Holy Spirit on the offerings: may the Holy Spirit make these offerings the body and blood of Christ *because* on the night before he suffered Jesus took bread ...[15] In short, the words of consecration are not a unit in which the priest ceases to speak for the Church and instead speaks in the person of Christ, but are part of the overall prayer of thanksgiving ('Let us give thanks') which the priest speaks on behalf of the Church.

Thus, while it is certainly true that the priest at the Eucharist does represent Christ to the people, this does not seem to be by virtue of speaking the words of Christ like an actor playing a role. Perhaps it is as the one who *presides* at the Eucharistic assembly that the priest's representation of Christ is most evident. This seems to accord with the Vatican II Decree on the Liturgy, which (while discussing the prayers spoken at the Mass) speaks of the priest as the one who, 'in the person of

Christ, presides over the assembly' (*SC* 33). The *General Instruction on the Liturgy of the Hours* uses similar terms in explaining that in the liturgical celebration of the Office the bishop and the priests united to him 'represent the person of Christ' (28).

Other more recent documents confirm this view. Thus the *Catechism of the Catholic Church* makes no reference to words of consecration when it explains that

> Through the ordained ministry, especially that of bishops and priests, the presence of Christ as head of the Church is made visible in the midst of the community of believers (n. 1548).

So too Pope John Paul's Apostolic Exhortation on the Laity *Christifideles Laici* (written a few months after *Mulieris Dignitatem*) speaks of the priest's action in the person of Christ without applying this action to the recitation of the words of consecration: ordained ministers receive from the Holy Spirit

> the authority and sacred power to serve the Church, acting *in persona Christi Capitis* (in the person or Christ the Head) and to gather her in the Holy Spirit through the Gospel and the Sacraments (22).[16]

The mention of the Gospel is a reminder that one of the essential ways in which the priest represents Christ is in proclaiming the Gospel and teaching its meaning and application.

6. Need Christ's representative be male?

After these considerations of the meaning of the priest's action in the person of Christ, let us reflect a little on the contention that to perform this representative function the priest needs to be male. Pope John Paul in *Mulieris Dignitatem* suggested tentatively ('it is legitimate to conclude') that in linking the Eucharist with the Apostles, Jesus 'wished to express the relationship between man and woman, between what is "feminine" and what is "masculine"'. For it is above all the Eucharist which

> expresses *the redemptive act of Christ the Bridegroom towards the Church the Bride.* This is clear and unambiguous when the sacramental ministry of the Eucharist, in which the priest acts *'in persona Christi'*, is performed by a man (*MD* 26).

Now the argument seems to be that what the priest signifies is not the maleness of Christ as such, but Christ's role as the Bridegroom of the Church. But does this act of signifying necessarily require sharing Christ's male gender? Indeed, might not a woman be an appropriate symbol of Christ's redemptive action, especially of his compassion and healing in the sacrament of reconciliation?

7. Priesthood or ministry

One last observation – a cat among the pigeons? – before we try to draw our musings together. Almost invariably throughout these deliberations we have been speaking in terms of priesthood. However, that is not the only possible terminology. It is well known that the New Testament, while freely speaking of a royal priesthood shared by all the baptized, never refers to the ordained minister as a priest; it took several centuries for the term to be regularly applied first to bishops and later to presbyters. What would happen to the argument if we spoke throughout of ministers rather than priests? Could this jog our imagination into considering the possibility of an ordained ministry for women which did not necessarily include the call to preside at the Eucharist? The Canon Law Society of America has recently explored the possibility of establishing or restoring a permanent diaconate for women.[17]

Conclusion

So let me try to draw the threads of this rambling paper together. My aim is not to question the teaching on the ordination of women of any of the churches, but rather to consider the relevance of gender-symbolism to the issue. We noted that in the fullest official Roman Catholic exposition of the arguments, the decisive appeal was to authority and tradition; considerations derived from the symbolic force of gender were seen to provide clarification and confirmation, but not proof. We have given reasons for believing that gender-symbolism retains its validity and its relevance even in modern society; and we have examined Pope John Paul's innovative understanding of that symbolism. We also recalled some of the ways in which the Old and New Testaments use both male and female imagery to express the relationship between Yahweh or Jesus Christ and his people. In this context, following the lead of von Balthasar, we considered Mary as the Mother of the Church and as its model in her feminine quality of receptivity, which is complemented by the masculine, Petrine function performed by the ordained priest. Finally we tried to identify the sense in which the priest acts in the person of Christ.

Throughout I have been asking you to do one thing: by examining your own reactions to try to discover what symbolic difference it makes to you whether the priest is male or female. This requires not only unprejudiced honesty on your part, but considerable intellectual discipline. You have to get down to essentials. Many reactions you may have to disregard: for example, if you see the female priest as the vindication of the rights of downtrodden woman, or the pretentious claimant to powers to which she is not entitled, put such feelings aside; they are not at the heart of the matter.

There was once a woman whose son had died in a Japanese prisoner-of-war camp, and who could not find it in her heart to forgive the Japanese. One morning, while waiting in church for Mass to begin, she was kneeling with her head bowed, struggling with her emotions. When the bell rang, she looked up and saw that the priest was Japanese. At once the block to her forgiveness and peace of mind was removed.

That priest had a symbolic power for the woman in her effort to forgive: not because of his gender or his good looks, but simply by virtue of the fact that he was Japanese. I invite you to make a similar effort of the imagination, and to pare down your attention to the one fact of the action of Christ in the liturgy, especially the Eucharist. What does it symbolize to you if the priest is a man? What does it symbolize to you if the priest is a woman? There are no correct answers.

Notes

1 Published in English as *Women and the Priesthood*, CTS Do 493, London.
2 *Summa Theologiae*, III.83.1 ad 3.
3 *In IV Sent.*, dist. 25, q.2, art. 2.
4 The CDF refers to the Vatican II Decree on the Ministry and Life of Priests (*PO* 2 and 6).
5 Pope John Paul's statement can be read in *Origins*, 24 (1994), pp. 49–52.
6 *In IV Sent.*, dist. 25, q.2, art. 1.
7 Published in English by the CTS Do 584, London.
8 Pastoral Constitution on the Church in the Modern World (*GS* 24). In this and other quotations from the writings of Pope John Paul II the italics occur in the original text.
9 See Paul McPartlan's helpful paper 'The Marian Church: Hans Urs von Balthasar and the ordination of women' in W. McLoughlin and J. Pinnock (eds), *Mary is for Everyone* (Leominster 1997), pp. 41–55.
10 Cyprian, *Epistles* 63.14; *PL* 4.397; *CSEL* 3.713, quoted in *MD* 5.
11 St Thomas, *Summa Theologiae*, III.83.1 ad 3, quoted in *MD* 5.
12 Decree for the Armenians, Denzinger-Schönmetzer 1321.
13 *Summa Theologiae* III.83.1 ad 3, quoted above. D. M. Ferrara maintains that the CDF misunderstands St Thomas's thought: he argues that when Aquinas says the priest acts in the person of Christ, he does not mean that the priest is like Christ, but that he serves Christ 'as the instrument in whom Christ himself acts' (D. M. Ferrara, 'Representation or Self-Effacement? The Axiom *In Persona Christi* in St Thomas and the Magisterium', *Theological Studies* 55 (1994), pp. 195–224; quotation on p. 223). Sara Butler's argument against this

position convinces the present writer: S. Butler, 'Quaestio Disputata: In Persona Christi: A Response to Dennis M. Ferrara', *Theological Studies*, 56 (1995), pp. 51–80.

14 Ambrose, *De sacramentis*, iv.14.

15 See R. C. D. Jasper and J. G. Cuming, *Prayers of the Eucharist: Early and Reformed* (3rd edn, New York 1987), p. 64.

16 The Exhortation is published in English by the CTS, Do 589.

17 'Canonical Implications: Ordaining Women to the Permanent Diaconate', in *Origins* 25 (1995), pp.344–52. The report concludes that '... ordination of women to the permanent diaconate is possible and may even be desirable for the United States in the present cultural circumstances' (p. 351).

(This paper was given at the ESBVM Woldingham Conference
in June 1997)

Mary
and
justice

24

Jewish–Christian relations

Janet Barcroft

'Remember that Jesus was born of a Jewish mother . . .' This is the second of the Ten Points of Seelisberg, and is surely an appropriate phrase to begin this paper on Jewish–Christian relations, at this conference whose theme is Mary's Vision of Justice as shown in the Magnificat in Luke 1. 46–55. Mary's vision of justice was worded by Luke as a parallel to 1 Samuel 2, in which Hannah, offering her son Samuel to the service of the Lord, glorifies the Lord for his justice and compassion towards the oppressed. Here are two Jewish mothers with their vision of justice. In all human relations, in all human dialogue, it is so important to remember God's justice and compassion towards us, so important that we show justice and compassion towards each other. It is so important in Jewish–Christian relations.

A pioneering gathering of Christians, both Protestant and Catholic, together with their Jewish colleagues, met at Seelisberg in Switzerland in 1947, just two years after the end of the Second World War. They were primarily concerned with anti-Semitism – and the Ten Points of Seelisberg represented ten issues which those present believed should be emphasized in order to avoid false or inadequate presentation of Christian doctrine.

The Ten Points of Seelisberg

Published by the International Council of Christians and Jews in 1947

1. Remember that One God speaks to us all through the Old and the New Testaments.
2. Remember that Jesus was born of a Jewish mother of the seed of David and the people of Israel, and that His everlasting love and forgiveness embraces His own people and the whole world.
3. Remember that the first disciples, the apostles and the first martyrs were Jews.

4. Remember that the fundamental commandment of Christianity, to love God and one's neighbour, proclaimed already in the Old Testament and confirmed by Jesus, is binding upon both Christians and Jews in all human relationship, without any exception.
5. Avoid distorting or misrepresenting biblical or post-biblical Judaism with the object of extolling Christianity.
6. Avoid using the word *Jews* in the exclusive sense of the enemies of Jesus, and the words *The Enemies of Jesus* to designate the whole Jewish people.
7. Avoid presenting the Passion in such a way as to bring the odium of the killing of Jesus upon all Jews or upon Jews alone. It was only a section of the Jews in Jerusalem who demanded the death of Jesus, and the Christian message has always been that it was the sins of mankind which were exemplified by those Jews and the sins in which all men share that brought Christ to the Cross.
8. Avoid referring to the scriptural curses, or the cry of a raging mob: *His Blood be Upon Us and Our Children*, without remembering that this cry should not count against the infinitely more weighty words of our Lord: *Father Forgive Them, for They Know not What They Do*.
9. Avoid promoting the superstitious notion that the Jewish people are reprobate, accursed, reserved for a destiny of suffering.
10. Avoid speaking of the Jews as if the first members of the Church had not been Jews.

The Ten Points certainly presented a fundamental corrective to New Testament texts and the presumption that Christianity was the 'New Israel', over against reprobate, deicidal Israel. (Eckardt in Croner (ed) 1985, p. 19: see Bibliography p. 291 below.)

I am sure we must all agree that today these Ten Points or Laws are observed – but that they are still sometimes broken – in Christian teaching and preaching. These Ten Points were to occupy a pivotal position in the whole theological and academic debate over Jewish–Christian relations, in the years that followed 1947.

The Jewish Jesus became the focus of both Christian and Jewish scholars. Mention should certainly be made of the writings of Geza Vermes – Jewish by birth, baptized as a child into the Roman Catholic Church, he later returned to Judaism. He became Reader in Jewish Studies in the University of Oxford. The titles of three of his books illustrate this interest in the Jewish Jesus: *Jesus the Jew; Jesus in the World of Judaism; The Religion of Jesus the Jew*.

Christian scholars turned to a study of Jesus the Jew also. This provided a balance to a christology which sometimes had hidden the man Jesus, and his background. Christian scholars, such as Rosemary Radford Ruether and Paul van Buren, examined the supersessionist theology which had long dominated in the Christian Church: the concept of the Church as the New Israel, the concept of the New Covenant superseding the Old Covenant. This led to an examination of the concept of Covenant, and gradually Christian theology began to think in terms of two covenants, one between God and the Jewish people and one between God and the followers of Jesus Christ – and both covenants equally alive and valid today. Judaism was a religion in its own right. It was sometimes described as the Older Brother, with Christianity the Younger Brother. Some theologians spoke of One Covenant, embracing both Jews and Christians. St Paul's Letter to the Romans, chapters 9–11, was studied afresh by Jewish and Christian scholars. In these chapters Paul, the Jew, called to preach the Gospel to Gentiles, declared that his own people were still loved by God. Christianity was like a branch grafted on to the olive tree of Judaism. Jewish scholars are saying more and more that, if only Paul's teaching had been correctly presented and understood by the Christian Church, terrible Jewish suffering could have been avoided down the centuries which followed. All this shows how much new and exciting thinking there now is in scholarly and theological Jewish and Christian circles.

The Ten Points of Seelisberg and subsequent theological and academic debate were reflected in a great wave of statements issued by many Assemblies of Christian Churches, by the World Council of Churches, and by the Vatican, which began to pour forth in the post-war years. There was agonizing over Christian responsibility for attitudes which had contributed to the Nazi Holocaust of Europe's Jews. There was Christian remorse and penitence that such terrible events should have taken place in so-called Christian Europe. There was the guilt of the perpetrators and the bystanders, and there was the trauma of the survivors. Gradually the survivors, such as Elie Wiesel, began to break silence, and to tell the world what really happened in the concentration camps. The immensity of the suffering in those camps was revealed. Elie Wiesel's first book, *Night*, says it all.

In the post-war years, the attitude that the Christian Church offered the one means of true salvation persisted for some time, though the way in which mission to the Jews was carried out was to be in accordance with the principles of the Ten Points of Seelisberg. Gradually, however, in the light of the theological and academic debate which I have just outlined, a very large question mark emerged in connection with 'Mission to the Jews'. If Jews were still loved by God, and in Covenant with God, had Christians the duty, the right, to try to convert them to Christianity? Should there be a different approach altogether in Jewish–Christian relations? The Jewish attitude towards Christian mission to the Jews is clear-cut (I quote from George Wilkes, a Jewish historian): 'In the minds of many Jews, anti-Semitism and mission are two sides of the same coin.' Looking right back into history, it is not difficult to see why Jews see anti-Semitism and mission as two sides of the same coin. There is a sorry tale of the Church's anti-Jewish legislation, of forced conversions and baptism of Jews, waves of brutal persecution, death, expulsion from the land. All this was Christian mission to the Jews at its worst. (Fry, 1996, pp. 8–9.)

What about Christian mission to Jews at its best? It is true that Christianity has always had a sense of mission to the world, to share the Gospel, the Good News of Jesus Christ – with all mankind. The point at issue, however, is: Should an exception be made with regard to missionary activity among the Jews? There are many Christians who express a sincere love of the Jewish people and a pity for the Jews' plight in times of anti-Semitic persecution. However, the fact that this persecution had its roots in the New Testament and in early Christian teaching is not always fully recognized. Yet there is a Christian belief that the Good News of the Gospel should be offered to the Jewish People. In 1965, a Presbyterian, George Knight, wrote this: 'There is one, and only one thing that we must communicate to Jews, as to all men, and that is Christ. To refrain from doing so ... is a form of religious anti-Semitism which is as basically evil as the philosophy of the Nazis. (Knight, 1965, p. 174.)

Let me put beside that statement another statement: this time by Bishop Hugh Montefiore, a Bishop of the Church of England and himself a Jew who, as a teenager at school in England, experienced a call to be a Christian. It was a personal experience, which he writes about in his recently-published autobiography, *On Being a Christian* (1998). Hugh Montefiore sees mission as an integral part of the Gospel, but particularly where Jewish people are concerned, he believes that evangelism is better accomplished not by naming the name of Christ, but simply by manifesting the love of God through personal life style.

> Why do I say that it is better not to name the name of Christ to my fellow-Jews? Not all my fellow-Christians would agree with this, and not all my Jewish fellow-Christians. But I believe it is better not to name the name of Christ to Jews because down the centuries the word Christ has been a curse to them, causing discrimination against them, forfeiture of possessions, social deprivation, civic disabilities and even torture and death. So the name of Christ has become the very reverse of good news: it is bad news.
>
> (Montefiore, 1998, p. 174.)

I add to that a comment by Rabbi Mordecai Waxman of Temple Israel, writing in 1985:

> Jews see no need to seek to convert Christians, for their own salvation or any one else's. But by the same token, Jews desire that Christians view Judaism as a faith predicated upon the Torah and Covenant, with its own view of Jewish destiny, with its own vision of the Messiah and of the means of salvation.
>
> (Croner, 1985, pp. 30–1.)

Thus the issue of Mission to the Jews is difficult. In fact, I believe it can truly be said that no issue in the history of Jewish–Christian relations has caused as much antagonism as Christian efforts to convert Jews.

I have shown the effect of the Ten Points of Seelisberg on theological and academic debate, and how the Christian Churches have been responding ever increasingly with statements of penitence and a realization that the Holocaust must always be remembered.

Mission has changed into Dialogue – and it is dialogue between Jews and Christians as equal partners on a journey which seeks mutual understanding and reconciliation. Jews and Christians, in this dialogue, both bear witness to their beliefs. There is a growing warmth and frankness in this dialogue. Recently, Rabbi Jonathan Gorsky was in Dublin giving a lecture to the members of the Irish Council of Christians and Jews. It was an in-depth analysis of dialogue: the title of his lecture was 'What can we say to each other? Dialogue and Sensitivity in Jewish–Christian Relations'. He explained that dialogue means talking, talking in the multi-cultural, multi-faith situation of today's world. Speech is not difficult. The key issue is *listening*, and this means affirming the other person in the totality of all that that person is. It is a process of mutual sharing. This approach is gradually transforming Jewish–Christian relations.

Jewish and Christian scholars are talking and listening to each other. They study together. For example, Rabbi Dan Cohn-Sherbok has written a *Dictionary of Judaism and Christianity* (1991). Included in this, he gives a clear, accurate, account of Christian beliefs about Mary, and the various doctrines formulated by the Church. He then gives a clear account of the Jewish viewpoint on Mary and the doctrines about her:

> Perpetual virginity is not seen as a meritorious condition. A wifeless man is said to be a deficient man. The Matriarchs – Sarah, Rebekah, Leah, Rachel, the wives of Abraham, Isaac and Jacob – do have an honoured role in Jewish folk religion. They are invoked in the Sabbath blessing of daughters and in the prayer said after the birth of a child. Jewish feminist liturgies also include these matriarchs whenever the patriarchs are mentioned, but they are never perceived as anything more than virtuous human beings, and worship of anyone other than God is completely rejected in Judaism.

Cohn-Sherbok has just published a book on Messianic Jews, an issue that can be contentious in Jewish–Christian relations.

There is so much interesting, positive, forward-looking work going on today in Jewish–Christian relations: there is indeed a revolution going on in Christian approaches to Judaism.

A response has come from the Jewish side to Christian penitence for the past and changed Christian attitudes towards Jews. It is the document *Dabru Emet* (which means Speak Truth). Its emphasis on justice seems to me most appropriate for your conference here in Maynooth, and I wish the conference every success.

This statement, the result of a scholarly dialogue which began five years ago, was signed by 172 Jewish thinkers and leaders from all four branches of Judaism: Orthodox, Conservative, Reform and Reconstructionist. The statement was co-authored by Dr Michael A. Signer, University of Notre Dame; Dr Tikva Frymer-Kensky, University of Chicago Divinity School; Dr David Novak, University of Toronto; Dr Peter W. Ochs, University of Virginia. The Institute for Christian and Jewish Studies in Baltimore, MD provided the educational setting in which the work of the project was conducted. The phrase '*Dabru Emet*' comes from the verse: 'These are the things you are to do: speak the truth to one another, render true and perfect justice in your gates' (Zech. 8. 16).

The statement appeared on Sunday, 10 September 2000 as full-page paid advertisements in the *New York Times* and *The Sun* of Baltimore.

Dabru Emet: A Jewish Statement on Christians and Christianity. 10 September, 2000.

In recent years, there has been a dramatic and unprecedented shift in Jewish–Christian relations. Throughout the nearly two millennia of Jewish exile, Christians have tended to characterize Judaism as a failed religion, or, at best, a religion that prepared the way for, and is completed in, Christianity. In the decades since the Holocaust, however, Christianity has changed dramatically. An increasing number of official church bodies, both Roman Catholic and Protestant, have made public statements of their remorse about Christian mistreatment of Jews and Judaism. These statements have declared, furthermore, that Christian teaching and preaching can and must be reformed so that they acknowledge God's enduring covenant with the Jewish people and celebrate the contribution of Judaism to the world civilization and to Christian faith itself.

We believe these changes merit a thoughtful Jewish response. Speaking only for ourselves – an interdenominational group of Jewish scholars – we believe it is time for Jews to learn about the efforts of Christians to honour Judaism. We believe it is time for Jews to reflect on what Judaism may now say about Christianity. As a first step, we offer eight brief statements about how Jews and Christians may relate to one another.

1. Jews and Christians worship the same God

Before the rise of Christianity, Jews were the only worshippers of the God of Israel. But Christians also worship the God of Abraham, Isaac, and Jacob; creator of heaven and earth. While Christian worship is not a viable religious choice for Jews, as Jewish theologians we rejoice that, through Christianity, hundreds of millions of people have entered into relationship with the God of Israel.

2. Jews and Christians seek authority from the same Book – The Bible (What Jews call '*Tanakh*' and Christians call the 'Old Testament')

Turning to it for religious orientation, spiritual enrichment, and communal education, we each take away similar lessons: God created and sustains the universe; God established a covenant with the people of Israel; God's revealed word guides Israel to a life of righteousness; and God will ultimately redeem Israel and the whole world. Yet, Jews and Christians interpret the Bible differently on many points. Such differences must always be respected.

3. Christians can respect the claim of the Jewish people upon the land of Israel

The most important event for Jews since the Holocaust has been the re-establishment of a Jewish state in the Promised Land. As members of a biblically-based religion, Christians appreciate that Israel was promised – and given – to Jews as the physical centre of the covenant between them and God. Many Christians support the State of Israel for reasons far more profound than mere politics. As Jews we applaud this support. We also recognize that Jewish tradition mandates justice for all non-Jews who reside in a Jewish state.

4. Jews and Christians accept the moral principles of *Torah*

Central to the moral principles of *Torah* is the inalienable sanctity and dignity of every human being. All of us were created in the image of

God. This shared moral emphasis can be the basis of an improved relationship between our two communities. It can also be the basis of a powerful witness to all humanity for improving the lives of our fellow human beings and for standing against the immoralities and idolatries that harm and degrade us. Such witness is especially needed after the unprecedented horrors of the past century.

5. Nazism was not a Christian phenomenon

Without the long history of Christian anti-Judaism and Christian violence against Jews, Nazi ideology could not have taken hold, nor could it have been carried out. Too many Christians participated in, or were sympathetic to, Nazi atrocities against Jews. Other Christians did not protest sufficiently against these atrocities. But Nazism itself was not an inevitable outcome of Christianity. If the Nazi extermination of the Jews had been fully successful, it would have turned its murderous rage more directly to Christians. We recognize with gratitude those Christians who risked or sacrificed their lives to save Jews during the Nazi regime. With that in mind, we encourage the continuation of recent efforts in Christian theology to repudiate unequivocally contempt of Judaism and the Jewish people. We applaud those Christians who reject this teaching of contempt, and we do not blame them for the sins committed by their ancestors.

6. The humanly irreconcilable difference between Jews and Christians will not be settled until God redeems the entire world as promised in Scripture

Christians know and serve God through Jesus Christ and the Christian tradition. Jews know and serve God through *Torah* and the Jewish tradition. That difference will not be settled by one community insisting that it has interpreted Scripture more accurately that the other; nor by exercising political power over the other. Jews can respect Christians' faithfulness to their revelation just as we expect Christians to respect our faithfulness to our revelation. Neither Jew nor Christian should be pressed into affirming the teaching of the other community.

7. A new relationship between Jews and Christians will not weaken Jewish practice

An improved relationship will not accelerate the cultural and religious assimilation that Jews rightly fear. It will not change traditional Jewish forms of worship, nor increase intermarriage between Jews and non-

Jews, nor persuade more Jews to convert to Christianity, nor create a false blending of Judaism and Christianity. We respect Christianity as a faith that originated within Judaism and that still has significant contacts with it. We do not see it as an extension of Judaism. Only if we cherish our own traditions can we pursue this relationship with integrity.

Jews and Christians must work together for justice and peace

Jews and Christians, each in their own way, recognize the unredeemed state of the world as reflected in the persistence of persecution, poverty, and human degradation and misery. Although justice and peace are finally God's, our joint efforts, together with those of other faith communities, will help bring the kingdom of God for which we hope and long. Separately and together, we must work to bring justice and peace to our world. In this enterprise we are guided by the vision of the prophets of Israel:

> It shall come to pass in the end of days that the mountain of the Lord's house shall be established at the top of the mountains and be exalted above the hills and the nations shall flow unto it . . . and many peoples shall go and say, Come ye and let us go up to the mountain of the Lord, to the house of the God of Jacob and He will teach us His ways and we will walk in His paths. (Isa. 2.2–3)

Bibliography

Buren, Paul van, 'Probing the Jewish–Christian Reality' in *Christian Century* XCVII, 21.

Cohn-Sherbok, Dan, *A Dictionary of Judaism and Christianity* (SPCK, London 1991).

——*Messianic Judaism* (Continuum, London and New York 2000).

Croner, Helga (ed.), *More Stepping-Stones to Jewish–Christian Relations* (Paulist Press, New York 1985).

Fry, Helen P. (ed.), *Christian–Jewish Dialogue* (EUP, Exeter 1996).

Knight, George, *Beyond Dialogue: Jews and Christians, Preparation for Dialogue* (Westminster, Philadelphia 1965).

Montefiore, Hugh, *On Being a Jewish Christian* (Hodder & Stoughton, London 1998).

Ruether, Rosemary Radford, *Faith and Fratricide* (Seabury Press, New York 1974).

Vermes, Geza, *Jesus the Jew* (2nd edn) (SCM, London 1983).

——*Jesus and the World of Judaism* (SCM, London 1983).

——*The Religion of Jesus the Jew* (SCM, London 1983).

——*Providential Accidents: An Autobiography* (SCM, London 1998).

Wiesel, Elie, *Night* (Penguin Books, Middlesex 1958, 1981).

Wilkes, George, Module 801, MA Course, Centre for Jewish–Christian Relations, Cambridge 2000.

Dabru Emet: A Jewish Statement on Christians and Christianity, 15 November 2000.

*(This paper was given at the ESBVM Maynooth Conference
in June 2001)*

25

The Bearer of God and the politics of Ireland

Richard Clarke

I have to begin with what is a pleasurable confession – that what began, in the preparation of this paper, as an intellectual exercise became, somewhat to my surprise, a devotional encounter.

But let me give the background.

My own setting is that of Irish Anglicanism, in my particular case probably somewhere in the liberal and catholic overlap, or is it overspill? It is, I think, fair to say that when it comes to the Blessed Virgin Mary, the *normal* Church of Ireland stance (perhaps in common with other Anglican churches) is one of *respect*, albeit a slightly distant and somewhat formal respect, a raising of the hat rather than a falling to one's knees. There are certainly many saints who would engage public and personal affection within the Irish Anglican community more readily – in particular the Irish saints, Patrick, Brigid or Columba, in addition of course to the more prominent of the biblical apostles and evangelists.

On the other hand, there is no shortage of churches dedicated to Saint Mary in the Church of Ireland; the Magnificat is part of the devotional core of our worship, and the Blessed Virgin is seen, and portrayed in sermons on her festivals, as a great exemplar of obedience and of faithfulness. The theological deference is there, but it is, as I have suggested, respect rather than devotion.

I would have to go on to say that within the Anglican tradition (as I have experienced it), there is – albeit very much at a cerebral rather than a devotional level – a very clear understanding that the theology of the Blessed Virgin as *Theotokos*, the bearer of God (even if those terms are not often employed) is crucial, if a proper christology is to be maintained; or, to put it the other way around, a true understanding of the incarnation demands a theology of Mary as *Theotokos*. Again, however, we are speaking of a theological cipher rather than of a real person. Perhaps for that reason alone, the term 'Mother of God' is one which would find virtually no place in much mariological talking or thinking within, I suspect, any of the Reformed churches. It would, however, have to be acknowledged that, whatever the theology, the actual term 'Theotokos' would be seldom employed in the Church of Ireland, and that the Council of Ephesus is not, so far as I know, a normal topic of conversation at clerical dinner parties in the dioceses, nor even, I fear, at clerical study groups. In short, the typical Irish Anglican perspective on our Lady would be one of theological correctness rather than personal spirituality.

There are exceptions and, in turning to *classical* Irish Anglicanism in a technical sense, to whom would we move instinctively but Jeremy Taylor? And, in his *Life of Christ*, Taylor indeed draws a wonderful parallel between St Paul, who obtains the crown of righteousness in a life of frenetic action and activity, and the Holy Virgin who in a quiet and a gentle life obtains the greatest crowns. The uniting of love, humility and obedience, the bringing together of faith and love, of patience and meekness, of hope and reverence, in what Taylor speaks of as 'a life of an ordinary and small oeconomy', make, he reminds us, what are the greatest ascents to God. We are still speaking, however, of the Blessed Virgin primarily in her role as *exemplar,* or as a model of the virtues.

I cannot speak with any assurance on the Orthodox view of the Blessed Virgin Mary but I do know enough to realize, obviously, that *Theotokos* is the principal Orthodox title for our Lady and that her place is seen very much in theological terms, when it comes to the doctrine of the incarnation. However, and I do not say this glibly, my suspicion is that the attitude towards the Blessed Virgin in the Orthodox churches is a great deal less cool and distant, than that which I have tried to describe within my experience of Irish Anglicanism.

And what, then, of the *politics* of Ireland? I do not think that it could seriously be denied that when we speak of religion in Ireland, we are always on the edge of talking politics. And certainly, in the recent history of Irish Christianity – let us say the past century and a half – our Lady unhappily represents something of a fault-line between different religious traditions which, in Ireland, too easily denote socio-political lines of demarcation. In *Mary – A history of devotion in Ireland*, Fr Peter O'Dwyer outlines the history of Roman Catholic devotion to the Blessed Virgin Mary through the centuries. What comes through is the huge increase in public devotion and public devotional ceremonies in honour of our Lady through the nineteenth and twentieth centuries. This period corresponds almost exactly with what is (in the context of Irish history over the centuries) the relatively recent identification of Catholicism with Irishness, and of the Reformed traditions with non-Irishness. Until the mid-nineteenth century it would not have occurred to any observer of the Irish scene to equate nationalism with Roman Catholicism.

Indeed, one could readily produce a catena of celebrated Irish national-
ists – Wolfe Tone, Henry Joy McCracken, Robert Emmet, Thomas Davis
and many more – whose origins were very definitely in the Protestant
culture. However in the mid-nineteenth century, nationalism – and even
Irishness itself – began to be identified with Roman Catholicism. This
development was in part a natural progression, in other aspects a care-
fully-calculated political strategy.

If we now superimpose this identification of Roman Catholicism with
Irishness, on the huge growth in Catholic public devotion – a sincere and
deep devotion – to our Lady, it is not difficult to see how the Blessed
Virgin Mary becomes what is an unfortunate and unintentional fault-
line, not only between religious traditions, but between religious and
political cultures.

Fr O'Dwyer goes on to show how our Lady was identified with the
1916 Rising, in that the Rosary was said – in every sense *religiously* –
every night in all the different rebel garrisons in Dublin during that
Easter week that changed forever the face of Irish life. And, just before
his death, the acknowledged leader of the Rising, Patrick Pearse, wrote
a strange mystical prayer for his mother in which he drew a type of
parallel between *her* son going out to die for Ireland, and our Lady's Son
going out to die for mankind. Leaving aside what is in this instance
almost certainly blasphemy – from the perspective of the intervening
eighty-five years at any rate – the deep devotion to the Blessed Virgin
Mary in those who would die for Ireland was clear and decisive.
Interestingly – and this is a personal observation – when the Pope
visited Ireland in 1979, he gave what was, ecumenically, an immensely
sure-footed performance, delicately avoiding those tiresome shibboleths
that could have spelt disaster for the visit, but with perhaps one exception when he spoke of the Blessed Virgin Mary as Queen of Ireland. I
remember speculating quietly at the time that would not perhaps be the
perception of 'the Queen' on the Shankill Road in Belfast.

But Ireland has changed and is changing rapidly, economically, politically, and spiritually. Certainly the southern part of the island has
become both less insular and more secular, and there is certainly a
connection between the two. The Republic of Ireland looks as easily to
the continent of Europe as to its sister island of Britain, or even inwards
to itself. It has become more materialistic, less hospitable, and spiritually
almost rudderless, at least in contrast to thirty years ago. This applies to
society as a whole, and it has subtly (and sometimes not very subtly)
affected all the Christian traditions.

Northern Ireland, on the other hand, has inevitably been shaped by
thirty years of fear, suspicion and violence. It has in consequence
remained a great deal more introspective than the south, and its reli-

gious life, again in all its manifestations, is also more self-absorbed and more rooted in history and in the perceptions of history. There is also, I think it is fair to say, less apparent public devotion to our Lady among the majority, Roman Catholic, tradition in the south of Ireland than I can remember from my childhood and youth. Lourdes and Knock are not as noticeable in Catholic spirituality as would have been the case even twenty years ago, when Pope John Paul visited Ireland. It is also probably true to say also that, with a greater rapprochement between the churches in the south (and a far greater understanding between the churches in Northern Ireland than is often realized), there is less emphasis on the Blessed Virgin Mary within the Christian dialogue, a dialogue which thankfully is now in Ireland part and parcel of the life of the Church as a whole.

I am not sure that this near-sidelining of the Blessed Virgin is good for any of us. I become increasingly convinced that if we can indeed marry the human, unaffected, and deeply *personal* love for our Lady – so innate to traditional Roman Catholicism – to a cool and careful theological understanding of the Blessed Virgin Mary as *Theotokos*, which latter is, as I have suggested, characteristic of what I would see as the best of Anglican and Reformed thinking (in addition to being, more obviously, the classical Orthodox stance), we could do much for the religious life of Ireland, which is still very much in part the politics of Ireland. When we use *both* strands in order to see in Mary a proper *type* or model of Church, we may yet rescue the Church, in all its forms, from decay and trivialization.

Many of you may well know a Breughel painting, *The Adoration of the Kings*. (It was prominent, I believe, in the National Gallery exhibition of a few months ago, Seeing Salvation.) I saw that painting in an entirely new light some weeks ago, coincidentally (or was it perhaps providentially) as I was putting thoughts together on this paper. If you know the picture, you will know what I mean when I say that it gives an entirely different view of the adoration of the Magi. Herein also lies a personal progress, of which I spoke at the outset, from the intellectual to the spiritual.

In Breughel's painting, the kings appear, not as worshipping and adoring, but as old, cynical and even sinister. In the background of the picture there are soldiers – the same soldiers that we are to picture, we may assume, soon going about the business of butchering the Holy Innocents. In the picture there are also greedy, uncouth and vicious-looking onlookers, one of whom seems to be whispering into Joseph's ear, perhaps offering a good price for the gifts being brought by the Kings. One of the Kings is kneeling before the infant Christ, but he is offering not the gift of gold (which is what we usually see in such paintings), but the gift of myrrh, the ointment of death. But what caught my eye on this occasion was a look of real fear on the face of the infant Christ and his instinctive shrinking in terror into the protection of his mother. What we see in that Breughel painting is not the carefully-measured theology of *Theotokos*, but the frighteningly human picture of a child in need of his mother's protection.

If we are then to move towards this tender fusion of the personal and the intellectual, of the Mother of our Lord Jesus Christ as real *in addition to* being a necessary theological entity, we need to move towards the picture of Mary as *type* – type of a vulnerable Church, type of a vulnerable Christian community, and we need to do this not only with heads but with hearts, nowhere more than in Ireland.

That picture of the vulnerable Christ is the one we most avoid in our attempts at evangelism, at preaching Good News.

We rightly see Christ as Lord of the Church.

We rightly see the Church as being Christ's.

We rightly see the grace of Christ *alone* as that which protects the Church.

What we have now also to see with the heart's eye is the vulnerable Christ who is not only Lord of the Church, but *of whom* the Church is also the Bearer and even, in no profane sense, the Defender. After all, if we are to look at the Blessed Virgin Mary properly, I believe that we have to see also that although Mary, as within the created order, is *in need of redemption*, she is also to be found *within that process of redemption* through her action of free and loving response to the providence of God. As is probably clear already, I come from a Christian tradition which fears greatly any exaltation of the Blessed Virgin Mary which would even tangentially take from the perfect and complete redeeming work of God *in Christ*, but there is an equal sense in which we are all, through God's grace, called to partake and participate in the divine scheme of redemption for humankind. In that process, the Blessed Virgin Mary and the Church of which she is, in human form, *type*, have their place of veneration.

In the Irish context, we can look only with shame and penitence, at a Church – a Bearer of God – which has handed Christ over to the forces of darkness portrayed so vividly by Breughel. Too often, also, the politics of the Church and even the politics surrounding the Blessed Virgin Mary, have been the politics of power: How can we demonstrate that we have control? How can we demonstrate that we are the most influential of the churches? How can we make sure that we are taken seriously by the secular rule of the age?

Mary's Magnificat, which is the cry for spiritual force and the demand for justice over the material dominance and the political corruption of the age has been ignored if not reversed. Magnificat makes social, political and economic demands on the individual Christian disciple – on Mary herself as the first of those within the scheme of Christian redemption, and on the community of the Church as those who follow with her on that road to holiness. They are demands which we have marginalized.

To give a very topical example, Ireland is now one of the electronic communications centres of Europe. The communications revolution effected by electronic means has divided society as never before. Those who have access to electronic communications, and in particular to media communication, have the power to change the world – how the world thinks and what the world does. And yet those who are excluded from this magic circle of electronic communication – whether for economic or for social reasons – are now at the mercy of the mighty. Magnificat cries out for righteousness to prevail against 'the proud in the imagination of their hearts'. And yet the Church, in Ireland as in so much of the developed world, wishes only to be part and parcel of the new technology, without wishing to acknowledge the pitfalls, the temptations and the sheer vacuity of all the slickness and the spin, and 'the imagination'.

Magnificat calls us, with Mary, to ally holiness with a radical trans-formation of society – but from the underside of society, not from the seat of mightiness. And when we can see *Theotokos* in that light, we can indeed transform the politics and the society of our environment. Only a few weeks ago, a good friend – brought up in a traditional Irish Roman Catholic home on the border between Cork and Kerry – told me that it was only in recent years that she had come to love the Blessed Virgin Mary. Mary, through my friend's youth – had been an omnipresent and all-seeing prude who would be certain to be offended and hurt by almost anything one might do or want to do. But to see her now in a new light, my friend said, as a young innocent girl given those cosmic responsibilities by God and being asked to carry, in every sense, those burdens, made her not only an object for a much more profound awe and even sorrow, but also a person with whom there could be a genuine solidarity.

The politics of gender in Ireland have as much need of *re-creation* as the politics of society and it is within that re-creation of gender politics that the politics of the country will be given a new life and hope. We do our Lady no honour when we cast her in a role only of subservience. Obedient to the call of God, certainly; but not a model for an ecclesiastical politics that subjugates the female in favour of the male. We need to find Mary, not simply as embodied in Magnificat but in the courage at the cross, when so many of those males who should have been there had fled. We need to find her also in the confidence that would *interrogate* her Son – after the escapade in the Temple when he was a child, or at the wedding in Cana. There is a strength and toughness of character that should make us re-align our ideas about the place of womanhood in the divine economy. It is only too easy for the Church to say, in effect, to women, 'You may have our Lady as your model, but just leave us with the real power'.

Although it is true that in the modern history of Ireland there have indeed been women who encouraged their menfolk to acts of savagery, and who have themselves participated in acts of viciousness, the balance is on the other side. I believe that many impartial observers of the Northern Irish scene would say without hesitation that it has been the women of Northern Ireland who have, without fanfares or self-promotion, ensured that the present peace process was not smothered at birth but was allowed to grow. We have also, as you know, elected two female Presidents in the Republic of Ireland, both named Mary, and both of whom have brought distinction to their office, albeit in very different ways. Perhaps the revolution of the Magnificat is indeed gathering force, amidst the strange and twisted politics of Ireland. And it may well be some of the mighty of the Church who will be thrown down by its impetus, and who will be able to say that it may not be a work of the Holy Spirit of God, through the witness of the Bearer of God?

But it is not with Magnificat but another poem I wish to conclude – a familiar hymn of Gerard Manley Hopkins to our Lady – 'The Blessed Virgin compared to the Air we Breathe'. It is, by any standards, a very strange poem, but it strikes a rich chord as Hopkins teases out the implications of the naturalness of the relationship between Mary and humanity – not only 'that men are meant to share / Her life as life does air', but that as Christ is born in Mary, so too he is *born in us*, and born repeatedly throughout our earthly pilgrimage.

All of it centred on Mary –

> Merely a woman, yet
> Whose presence, power is
> Great as no goddess's
> Was deemèd, dreamèd; who
> This one work has to do –
> Let all God's glory through,
> God's glory which would go
> Through her and from her flow
> Off, and no way but so.

(This paper was given at the ESBVM Oxford Congress
in August 2000)

26

Mary, model of the Church

Brendan Leahy

The topic 'Mary, Model of the Church' became particularly popular in the decades around the Second Vatican Council.[1] Indeed, that Council's decision to insert its document on Mary into its Constitution on the Church encouraged deeper reflection on the link between Mary and the Church and, more importantly, imitation of Mary as model.

As time moves on, there is a growing recognition within ecumenical circles that as disciples of Jesus Christ we find in Mary, the first disciple who generated and accompanied Jesus, a woman of faith who is, as it were, what we *ought to be* as disciples. And as Christians who are called to journey 'the Way' of Christ, we are those who *can be* like Mary generating him mystically through the 'Word of life' lived out in our lives.[2]

The renowned theologian, Hans Urs von Balthasar, emphasized the need particularly for us today to focus on this model that has been given to us in the pages of the Gospel:

> ... Perhaps it is particularly necessary for our times to look at Mary ... We are for ever concerned with reshaping and improving the Church in accordance with the demands of the time, following the criticisms of opponents and our own models. But do we not thereby lose sight of the one fulfilled standard, indeed the Model? Should we not constantly keep our eyes fixed on Mary in our reforms, not in any way to multiply the Marian feast-days, devotions or indeed definitions, but rather simply to know what Church, what ecclesial Spirit, and what ecclesial behaviour really is?[3]

There are many things that could be said about Mary as model of the Church, but I shall take my lead from the overall theme of this conference: 'Mary's Vision of Justice as shown in the Magnificat: Luke 1.46–55'. Whether intended or not, the theme of justice suggests a link also with the recent joint declaration on the doctrine of justification between the Lutheran World Federation and the Roman Catholic Church.[4] In the light of this, I propose to structure this article as follows:

Firstly, I shall focus on Mary within the perspective of God's great act of justice in the paschal mystery of Jesus Christ's death and resurrection.

Secondly, I shall go on to examine how Mary is a model a) of the Church's origins in the event of justice, b) of the Church's form shaped by this event, and c) of the Church's mission in communicating the Good News of this event.

God's great act of justice in Jesus Christ – a justice that overwhelms

Mary's rapturous opening line of the Magnificat: 'My soul "magnifies" the Lord ... for he has regarded the low estate of his handmaiden ...' (*tapeinosis*, Luke 1.48) is followed by an outline of the extraordinary social effects of the whole event of redemption: 'he has put down the mighty from their thrones, and exalted those of low degree; he has filled the hungry with good things, and the rich he has sent empty away' (Luke 1.52–3). The sheer intensity of sentiment, Scripture reference[5] and vision bring us to realize that what we have in the Magnificat is exultation at the whole overwhelming, unimaginable, scene of justice.

Just as from the top of a mountain you see a whole breathtaking landscape that you cannot capture because it is too vast, likewise it is as if Mary's Magnificat is an expression of wonder at the panoramic overview of God's great act of rendering just, of bringing about justice in Jesus Christ.

Scripture scholars remind us, in fact, that while the actual context of the Magnificat is the visitation, we should also keep in mind that it is an Easter text, projecting on to the story of Jesus Christ's conception and birth the glory and power of the crucified and risen Christ.[6] As depicted in Luke's Gospel we have Mary exercising charity – we remember this gift is poured into our hearts through the event of Jesus' death and resurrection (Rom. 5.5) – by running to visit and help Elizabeth with the good news of God's Advent among us. What Mary proclaims in the Magnificat is, in fact, a prelude to the Easter proclamation. In Jesus Christ's death and resurrection, God has indeed done something great. God now dwells among us and we dwell in God.

Mary is the first to experience the in-breaking of a new creation, a new humanity, a new destiny, and, as Jesus' first disciple, she is the one in whom we see the first-fruits of his redemption. In this regard, it is worth recalling Luther's words:

> Mary begins with herself and sings what he has done for her ... Mary confesses that the foremost work God did for her was that he regarded her, which is indeed the greatest of his works, on which all the rest depend and from which they all derive. For where it comes to pass that God turns his face toward one to regard him or her, there is nothing but grace and salvation, and all gifts and works must follow ...[7]

When we think about the almost breathtaking tone in Mary's Magnificat we begin to see it is due to a turning upside down of a notion and concept of God and his justice. It follows on from what has happened in the annunciation. On the one hand, in the annunciation (Luke 1.26–38), Mary, the creature, has given God his due. And this is a central dimension of justice. She has put God in the first place, the proper place, in her life and is totally transparent to whatsoever it is he wants to give her as gift.

And God has responded in a way that has given her a place, but one she could never have remotely expected – through the incarnation she has been taken into God's own interior dialogue between the Father and the Son in the Holy Spirit. The annunciation is, as von Balthasar never tired of reminding us, the first revelation of the triune face of God.[8] In seeing God give her this place, Mary, the *Theotokos,* discovers the amazing justice exercised by God *vis-à-vis* us.

Exalted in her lowliness, humility, nothingness she finds herself projected into a new communion with 'all generations' of her brothers and sisters in a new 'reconciled world', as St Augustine calls the new creation.[9] The dramatic intervention of God in her life and the turning upside down of all her notions of God is not merely a religious fact, but will involve political, social and economic consequences.[10]

The model justice: Love your 'neighbour' as yourself

Delving deeper into what has happened to Mary we see that God's justice is rooted in his Trinitarian logic. The central definition Christians give of God is that he is Love (1 John 4.8,16). God is triune Love – three Persons who are totally Being-for-one-another in mutual love. This is the central doctrine of the Christian faith.[11] Each of the three Persons contains the Other. Each of the three Persons makes themselves 'nothing' before each other so as to be 'wholly in each Other'.[12]

When it comes to God's relationship with creation, God cannot but work out of the Trinitarian logic that he is in himself. Here we find the remote origins of Jesus' commandment to 'love your neighbour as yourself'. (Matt. 19.16–19). Here too we find the origins of creation and humanity's vocation to justice. God does not command more than he himself is and does. God is the first to live out this commandment to 'Love your neighbour as yourself'. This echo of his own interior life resonates throughout all of God's exterior action and plan for humanity.

Creation is, in a certain sense, God's 'neighbour' created as such by himself. And what we see happening in the incarnation is that God loves this 'neighbour' as himself in that he makes himself nothing before his creation and brings all of creation to share in his own triune life. God loves Mary (and all of humanity on whose behalf she responds in faith with her 'yes' at the annunciation[13]) so immensely that he makes himself small, almost 'nothing' before her. He has made himself small to the point of being contained in her womb. Yes, Mary proclaims her 'lowliness' and 'nothingness' for so she is as creature and so she rightly magnifies God. But God magnifies Mary. In this sense he loves his neighbour as himself.

The first explicit revelation of the Trinity to Mary at the annunciation is not simply an extrinsic proclamation. In Jesus Christ and through the power of the Spirit, the Father introduces Mary into the depths of the Trinitarian life. She becomes 'trinitized'.[14] As *Lumen Gentium* 53 puts it, she is 'Mother of the Son ... daughter of the Father and the temple of the Holy Spirit'.

In accordance with the norm 'Love your neighbour as yourself', Mary is shaped by the Trinitarian event that is being revealed in Jesus Christ. And through Jesus Christ's death and resurrection and the outpouring of the Holy Spirit, the disciple Mary is formed by the Trinity for that 'homecoming' that sees her final destiny – to be inserted into the life of the Triune God.

This is what the doctrine of the assumption tells us. In Mary we see already realized the end of creation. Our future hope is no longer simply an hypothesis but already, in the Risen Christ, realized in Mary. We are set into the life of the Trinity and the whole of creation groans towards this great outcome of history (Rom. 8).

Mary personalizes God's project of justice

Mary personalizes the arrival point of creation and human history that results from the paschal mystery. It is worth noting here that Carl Jung was so impressed by the proclamation of the doctrine of the assumption that he wrote a book in which he exulted at this proclamation of the assumption of the feminine in God alongside the masculine personified in Christ.[15]

But to say all this of Mary is not to exalt her beyond us. The doctrine of the assumption tells us no more than what all of Scripture points to – we have already arrived home although we still journey in time. St Paul puts it 'our lives are hidden with Christ in God' (Col. 3.3). Mary is the radical concretization of what baptism realizes in everyone in the Church of Christ: 'It is no longer I who live but Christ who lives in me (us)' (Gal. 2.20). And in Christ we find ourselves in the bosom of the Father. Our 'living space' is the Trinity. God us loves so immensely that he makes himself nothing before us in order to bring us to share in his triune life.

When we see in Mary, the model of the Church, our destiny, our 'living space' in the triune life of God, we can now come back to the Magnificat and look again at how she links God's glory, the social revolution of love that has entered the world, and her spiritual communion with all of humanity.

The really real is that everything and everyone is in relationship with everything and everyone else. Through grace, God really has brought his 'neighbour' (creation and humanity personified in Mary) on to a par with himself, bringing his 'neighbour' to share in his own life, and thereby making us all neighbours to one another, neighbours who contain one another and neighbours who are responsible for each other. This is the justice that God wants to promote in Jesus Christ. And Mary personifies the new kind of person–communion created in that event of justice.

Mary as model of the Church

In this second section we can now turn to some implications of what we have been saying so far. By way of introductory comment, it can be noted that a focus on a Trinitarian perspective of justice that opens up in consideration of what has happened to Mary (and humanity) in the paschal mystery is a theme that resonates with the renaissance in Trinitarian theology currently going on within all denominations.[16]

A. Mary as model of the Church's origins in the event of justice
Like Mary and echoing her 'low estate' as she 'magnifies' the Lord, the Church is called to recognize her 'low estate' and 'magnify' the Lord. The Church never creates herself. She is born in the original event of justice: the paschal mystery. It is through Jesus Christ that we are brought to share in God's triune life. Christ continues in every generation to be the 'Spouse' of the Church who generates her through the Word (Eph. 5), the sacraments and apostolic ministry (Matt. 28.18–20; John 20. 19–23) as well as charisms (1 Cor. 12.4–7; Eph. 4.7–16; Eph. 2.20).

Accordingly, just as Mary never sought to possess herself but allowed God to love her as himself, the Church is never her own possession, but always a renewed gift of her Spouse, Jesus Christ. Standing before him, the Church, like Mary, is called constantly to welcome the Word with a continuous 'yes', giving herself back to him in an ever new love as the Word lived.

Mary is the model to be imitated by the Church of Christ in contemplating and adoring within the great event of justice that has created her and let herself be shaped by sacrament and charism. With this model before us we discover a number of the fundamental dimensions of our vocation:

1. The Orthodox theologian Alexander Schmemann, in his *For the Life of the World* says that secularism is above all the denial of human being as an adoring being.[17] Lack of adoring affects not only our relationship with God but also with the world. The tendency towards a false autonomy neglects how world itself is a gift from God revealing God. Ultimately this tendency towards a false autonomy is really wanting not to have to say 'thanks' to anyone, denying the giftedness of being, of grace. Paradoxically, it means wanting to be freed from being loved. This is the strange form of not giving God his place in our day.

In terms of justice, therefore, the first and crucial task for the Church today is herself first and foremost to know and believe more and more that she is loved immensely by God. In doing this she will bear witness to the ontological condition of creation – being a gift with a destiny directed towards God. In Mary we see personified the Trinitarian ontology of gift in which 'losing' is not slavery but true freedom. All of creation finds its true being in a true/just relationship with God which is that of adoration exemplified in Mary. As a community the Church is called to bear witness to the joy and freedom of this relationship.

2. With Mary as model, we remember our origins are not activism! It is good to recall here the first and last chapters of *Lumen Gentium*. They point us in the direction of rediscovering the dimension of Mystery and the Marian profile of the Church. Von Balthasar comments that, without keeping before our eyes the first disciple of Christ as a model,

> ... Christianity threatens imperceptibly to become inhuman. The Church becomes functionalistic, soulless, a hectic enterprise without any point of rest, estranged from its true nature by the planners. And because, in this manly-masculine world, all that we have is one ideology replacing another, everything becomes polemical, critical, bitter, humourless, and ultimately boring, and people in their masses run away from such a Church ...[18]

Apart from encouraging a more contemplative attitude, the rediscovery of the Marian profile of the Church is also linked to the recognition, esteeming and appreciation of the pastoral implications of the new charisms being given to and poured out by the Holy Spirit upon the Church in our time. It is significant that many of the new communities and movements emerging from the new charisms are all linked with Mary. Many of them promote new social projects.

3. In directing our gaze towards Mary, model of the Church's origins in God's great act of justice, we find fertile ground for ecumenical life and thought. Focus on Mary's 'nothingness' and recognition that it is God's initiative that raises us to share in his triune life provides us with a

common starting point in our dialogue of life and thought. Martin Luther writes: 'God's love does not find in the world what he loves, but he creates it'. And again: 'God looks upon those who, like Mary, live in the consciousness of their own nothingness, and fills them with his gifts. He smites and rejects those who are full of themselves and consider themselves just.'[19]

The recent Joint Declaration on the Doctrine of Justification tells us: 'By grace alone, in faith in Christ's saving work and not because of any merit on our part, we are accepted by God and receive the Holy Spirit, who renews our hearts while equipping and calling us to good works' (s. 15).[20]

This describes the sheer giftedness of our justification, that 'rendering just' of our lives before and in God. It needs to be thought through, however, not only individually but socially and in terms of the humanity-related Church. Attention to Mary, the woman related to 'all generations' will help us in this. Reflection on the Marian–Ecclesiological dimension of justification may go some way to responding to the conclusion of the Declaration to the effect that Lutherans and Catholics (and by extension all of us) 'will continue their efforts ecumenically in their common witness to interpret the message of justification in language relevant for human beings today, and with reference to individual and social concerns of our times'.

B. Mary, model of the Church's form

Mary is the first disciple in whom we see that the form of life that emerges from Jesus Christ's death and resurrection is one of Trinitarian communion. Her own 'yes' at the annunciation was on behalf of all of humankind. The visitation, Cana and other episodes during Jesus' life present her as a woman of communion – with others and for others. At the foot of the cross she repeats her 'yes' again on our behalf as the mystical body of Christ comes to life. At Pentecost she is found in the Upper Room with the apostles and the early community.

In his recent letter marking the Church's entrance into the third millennium, John Paul II promotes 'a spirituality of communion' precisely because seeing the Church as communion has been the great rediscovery for the Roman Catholic Church since the Second Vatican Council.[21] We go to God not on our own but in communion with and through our neighbour.

The communion that results from the paschal mystery and which Mary is the first to experience is nothing less than a share in God's own triune life of communion between Father, Son and Holy Spirit. Just as Mary was totally formed by the Christ event as a woman immersed in the Trinity, so too the Church finds its form, in the words of *Lumen*

Gentium 4, as a 'people united in the unity of the Father, the Son and the Holy Spirit'. The Church is herself a reality like Mary immersed in the Trinity. This has a number of implications:

1. We discover we ourselves are called to live 'Trinitarian' relationships among one another. We ourselves are to be an icon of that reconciled world, a 'seed of unity'[22] where God's act of justice in Jesus Christ is to be made manifest. John Paul II writes of our calling 'to live the Trinity'.[23] How? Through mutual love among individual Christians and also between church components, between churches and communions. The New Commandment of mutual love is the 'law' of the Church.[24] But to live it requires that we know how 'to be nothing', not just before God but before one another. St Paul in Phil. 2.3–8 tells us we are to have the same sentiments in relationships with one another as Jesus Christ who 'emptied himself'.

Here Mary is a model because she is totally shaped in the 'how' of this life. Her discipleship of Jesus taught her lessons in this spirituality that at times were quite tough. From Simeon's prophecy in the Temple to her apparent rebuffs by Jesus during his public ministry, and culminating in her stance at the cross, Mary knows how to 'lose God for God' as the way to build up ecclesial communion. 'Those who lose their life find it.' (Luke 17.)

To be a gift of oneself is written into the life of communion that itself is a sharing in the life of the Trinity. Jesus Christ loved 'right to the end' and this is what Mary imitated and lived as she 'lost' her Son at the foot of the cross in taking on the new maternity indicated to her by her dying Son.[25] And it is in living this 'emptying', 'losing' not just *vis-à-vis* God but *vis-à-vis* one another that the Church as communion is born.

2. One cannot but think of Mary as model in reading John Paul II when he reminds us of the elements involved in a spirituality of communion. It involves an ability to think of our brothers and sisters in faith within the profound unity of the Mystical Body as 'those who are part of me', sharing their joys and sufferings, sensing their desires, attending to their needs and offering deep and genuine friendship. It implies an ability to see what is positive in others, to welcome it and prize it as a gift from God. It means knowing how to 'make room' for our brothers and sisters, bearing 'each other's burdens' (Gal. 6.2) and resisting the selfish temptations which constantly beset us and provoke competition, careerism, distrust and jealousy.

The Gospel picture of Mary presents her spiritual path as a model involving all of these elements just outlined. It is a spiritual path of communion. The importance for the Church of following such a spiritual path is stressed by Pope John Paul II as he comments: 'Let us have no illusions: unless we follow this spiritual path, external structures of communion will serve very little purpose. They would become mechanisms without a soul, 'masks' of communion rather than its means of expression and growth'.[26]

3. There is another perhaps paradoxical aspect of viewing Mary as model of the Church's form of communion. In doing so we discover a key enabling us to interpret our church history which so often speaks of a lack of communion and encounter with injustice. Mary followed Jesus Christ right through the moments of darkness in his public ministry and the cross. As the first disciple she eloquently reminds us that the way of discipleship in communion, the way of the Church as Bride of Christ cannot be different from that of the Spouse.

Jesus himself told us so: 'If anyone wants to be a follower of mine.. let him take up his cross' (Matt. 16.24). And the Book of Revelation tells us that the elect are those who have passed through the great trial; they follow the Lamb (the Crucified Christ) wherever he goes. Just like Mary's journey, the Church too often experiences moments of crucifixion, moments of crying out in abandonment, moments when there appears to be little or no communion.

Pronouncing 'yes' on behalf of all, Mary's embrace reaches out even to cover all the sins and divisions of humankind. Imitating Jesus' 'into your hands I commend my spirit' that led to the resurrection, Mary 'stood' by the cross as a monument of virtue. The Church was born in this event. So too throughout history the Church will know its moments of persecutions, the sins of her own members, internal divisions, and even periods of de-Christianization. But like Mary she stands by the cross and continues to be generated anew in communion in the Risen Christ. Often it is the moments of greatest suffering that prove the most fruitful.

C. Mary, model of the Church's mission

With Mary as model, the Church discovers her mission of justice. Mary was not one of the twelve apostles, and yet she has been given the title 'Queen of the Apostles'[27] because who more than Mary gave Christ to the world? Her silence, her nothingness, her discipleship was nothing other than letting God speak his Word to and in humanity. Mary let the Word evangelize in the world and usher in the kingdom of justice and peace.

It was the Word of God, Jesus Christ, 'our peace' who 'broke down the dividing walls' (Eph. 2. 14). The Church continues his mission of justice, peace and the breaking down of the walls of division. As a 'co-operator' with Christ (see 1 Cor. 3.9) Mary herself reached union with

God and indeed saw the beginnings of the unity of 'all generations'. She reminds us that the Church's mission of justice centres on unity with God and unity among humankind. A number of points come to mind in this context:

1. As seldom before in history, the Church is very conscious today of this calling. As the very opening paragraph of *Lumen Gentium* puts it: 'The Church is in Christ a sacrament, a sign and instrument of union with God and unity of all humankind'. Our participation in the great event of justice that occurs in the paschal mystery is not limited simply to hearing the Word, reception of sacraments or religious practices. Of its nature it is communicative. We are called to enter into and be builders of unity, builders of the Kingdom of God come among us.

But looking at Mary as a woman immersed in the Trinity and in its logic of mutual love, we see unity is not simply a getting along together. As a people gathered in the Trinity, the Church's mission is to communicate the Trinitarian life of God to the whole of humanity. The Church is to be the leaven in humanity, gradually 'trinitizing' relationships in all expressions of human life – from the family to the workplace, from intercultural encounter to economics and politics. The Church's great mission of justice is to contribute to the building up of 'a new city' (Rev. 21) where mutual love is the norm in all spheres of existence.[28]

2. Focus on Mary helps us also rediscover the centrality of lay vocations within the Church's mission of building up the new united humanity generated in Jesus' death and resurrection. In his Apostolic Exhortation, *Christifideles Laici* John Paul II writes: 'Lay faithful find themselves in the advance life of the life of the Church. Thanks to them the Church is the life principle of society ... they are church ...[29] There is indeed a rediscovery today of the common priesthood and the prophetic role of the laity in various fields such as journalism, urbanization, media, ecological problem, political commitments.[30]

As a lay woman, Mary is a model for all those who seek to live as members of the Church radiating Christ in their daily lives. The creativity of the Marian profile of the Church is vital to the Church's mission.[31]

3. With Mary as model, the Church can always rediscover the plot in her missionary endeavour. Mary could have done thousands of things. But her greatness consisted in focusing on Christ, following Christ, searching him out. In living out the social teaching of Jesus and in pursuing dialogues at every level, the Church is continuing to search Christ out in situations of marginalization and otherness.

Our life can never be closed in upon ourselves (1 Cor. 9.19–23; Rom.

9.3). We go out to those living in situations of distance from God, darkness, disunion. We seek what is different and 'other'. In her mission, the Church is directed towards all of humanity in a love that knows how to make herself all things to all people. Rather than concentrate upon devotions to Mary's sorrows and wounds, the Church is called to imitate her in how she lived through her great wound – that of division, feeling the separation that her Son experiences when he cries out 'My God, my God, why have you forsaken me?' (Mark 15. 34; Matt. 27.46) .

All the separations and distances from God that characterize our time, symbolized in the *Shoah*, are reflections of the Crucified Christ who cried out from the cross. Just as Mary sought only Christ wherever that brought her, so too in the contemporary 'death of God' culture that Nietzsche foresaw, the Church feels called to go out in search of her Spouse who entered that darkness. It is worth noting that it has been particularly women who are sensitive to this search. We can think of Thérèse of Lisieux, Simone Weil, Edith Stein, Mother Teresa, Chiara Lubich.[32]

The Church's mission revolves around various dialogues. These too are directed towards knocking down racism and building up a peaceful and more fraternal society. The Church is conscious in a new way that Christ has 'united himself in some way to every person'.[33] And so she is discovering herself 'outside herself', as it were. She sees all men and women already united to Christ, already united because of his gift of love, of himself, but not yet fully united in their response to the great event of justice that is the paschal mystery. So, gathering 'children wherever they may be', helping them discover the greatness of the Father's love, the Church reaches out to all. Mary is clearly a model in this. Because of the almighty God, Mary's outreach, as proclaimed in the Magnificat, is universal.

Conclusion

In this article I have attempted to open up windows upon how Mary is a model for the Church in terms of the theme of justice suggested by the conference's title. Throughout the centuries many have found in Mary a woman to be imitated in life. By way of conclusion, therefore, I should like to refer to a woman I heard about recently who likewise sought to imitate Mary, with amazing consequences.

Her name is Ginetta Calliari. She was one of the very first girls of the Focolare Movement that started during the Second World War with the rediscovery of the Gospel and its promises. She went to Brazil in 1959 and remained there till her death some weeks ago. When she arrived in Recife forty years ago she was stunned to see the enormous gap between the rich and the poor, the discrimination, the hunger. She could see it on the faces of so many. There was widespread destitution and a lack of compassion on the part of the rich for the poor. She resolved that in the face of all this she and her companions would not remain passive spectators. Something had to change.

But how could there be change? Through what she had seen of the effects of the Word of God put into practice among her companions and those who had come into contact with them, she had come to realize that the best way for change is to bring about a change in people's hearts. A new people was needed from which new structures would come that would then form new cities. She was convinced that only God could resolve society's problems.

And indeed, over time, through the mutual love to which she and her companions bore witness, around her a new community spread, soon reaching several hundred thousand. Soon too, around her spiritual and social situations developed, culminating in two small towns of the Focolare Movement in Brazil. Soon there were people from the shanty towns of Recife and Sao Paulo relating with those of upper classes putting themselves at the service of the poorest. Politicians, church leaders and the media recognized these developments.

One enterprise to which she devoted herself in particular was the so-called 'Economy of Communion' project. Launched by Chiara Lubich, foundress of the Focolare, upon a visit to Brazil in 1991, this project sees businesses living a communion whereby a portion of their profits is given to the poor, a portion to building up structures for the spiritual formation of people and, of course, a portion to the business itself for its continuance. From Brazil this project has spread worldwide.

When Ginetta died some weeks ago it was said of her that, looking at all that was accomplished in her lifetime you could not but think of Mary's Magnificat happening in today's world.[34]

Notes

1 As well as *Lumen Gentium* 63–5, see the works of O. Semmelroth, *Urbild der Kirche: Organischer Aufbau des Mariensgeheimnisses* (Würzburg 1950); H. Rahner, *Maria und die Kirche* (Marianischer Verlag, Innsbruck 1951); H. de Lubac, *Méditation sur L'Église* (Montaigne, Paris 1952); Max Thurian, *Marie: Mère du Seigneur, figure de l'Église* (Les Presses de Taizé, Taizé 1963); Hans Urs von Balthasar, 'Die marianische Pragung der Kirche' in Wolfgang Beinart (ed.), *Maria heute ehren* (Herder, Freiburg 1977), pp. 263–79.

2 See the Groupe des Dombes study, *Marie dans le dessein de Dieu et la communion des saints* (Bayard Éditions & Centurion, Paris 1999); David Carter, 'Mary – Servant of the Word: towards convergence in ecclesiology' in William McLoughlin and Jill Pinnock (eds.), *Mary is for Everyone* (Gracewing,

Leominster 1997), pp. 157–70. See also A. Stacpoole (ed.), *Mary and the Churches* (Columba Press, Dublin 1987), and Jared Wicks, 'The Virgin Mary in Recent Ecumenical Dialogues' in *Gregorianum* 81 (2000), pp. 25–57.

3 'Maria in der kirchlichen Lehre und Frömmigkeit' in Joseph Ratzinger and Hans Urs von Balthasar, *Maria-Kirche in Ursprung* (Herder, Freiburg im Breisgau 1980), pp. 41–79, especially p. 72.

4 For documentation see Pontifical Council for Promoting Christian Unity *Information Service* 98 (1998/III), pp. 81–100.

5 Raymond Brown lists the following: Ps. 35.9; 1 Sam. 2.1–2; Hab. 3.18; 1 Sam. 1.11; Gen. 28.32; Gen. 30.13; Deut. 10.21; Zeph. 3.17; Ps. 111.9; Ps. 103.17; 1 Sam. 2.7–8; Ps. 89.11; Sir. 10.14; Job 12.19; Ezek. 21.31 (26); Ps. 107.9; Isa. 41.8–9; Ps. 98.3; cf. R. Brown, *The Birth of the Messiah* (Image Books, New York 1977), pp. 358–60.

6 A. Valentini, 'Editoriale' in *Theotokos* V (1997), p. 395 e 'Approcci esegeti a Lc 1, 42b–55' in *Theotokos* V (1997), pp. 405–8, 419–20; cf R. Brown et al, *Mary in the New Testament* (New York 1978), pp. 139–40. On the critical–exegetical question of the Magnificat, see A. Valentini, 'Il Problema dell'attribuzione del Magnificat' in *Theotokos* V (1997), pp. 642–74; J. McHugh, *The Mother of Jesus in the New Testament* (Darton Longman & Todd, London 1975), p. 445; R. Brown, *The Birth of the Messiah*, op. cit. pp. 334–5.

7 Quote from Luther's Commentary on Mary's Magnificat in Eric W. Gritsch (ed.), *Martin Luther: Faith in Christ and the Gospel: Selected Spiritual Writings* (New City, New York 1996), pp. 41–2.

8 See for example *Mary for Today* (St Paul Publications, Middlegreen, Slough 1987), p. 35; *Prayer* (Ignatius, San Francisco 1986), pp. 193–5.

9 Sermo 96.7: *PL* 38.588.

10 See De Fiores, *Maria Madre di Gesú* (Edizione Dehoniane, Bologna 1992), pp. 81–2; Joseph Paredes, *Mary and the Kingdom of God* (St Paul Publications, Middlegreen, Slough 1991), pp. 91–4.

11 Catechism of the Catholic Church, para. 234.

12 See Council of Florence (1442): DS 1331.

13 S. *Th.* III, q. 30, a 1, c.

14 See Piero Coda, *Magnifica il Signore Anima Mia* (San Paolo, Milan 2000).

15 Carl Gustav Jung, *Answer to Job* (Princeton University Press, 1972).

16 It is sufficient here to mention the popularity of theologians such as Bulgakov and Zizioulas (Orthodox), Von Balthasar and Rahner (Roman Catholic), Moltmann (Lutheran), Colin Gunton (United Reformed Church).

17 St Vladimir's Seminary Press, Crestwood NY 1998, p. 118.

18 *Elucidations* (Ignatius, San Francisco 1998), pp. 112–13.

19 Eric W. Gritsch (ed.), *Martin Luther* op. cit. pp. 36–47. See also Hubertus Blaumeiser, *Martin Luthers Kreuzes-theologie* (Bonifatius, Paderborn 1995).

20 Pontifical Council for Promoting Christian Unity, *Information Service*, 2000.

21 *Novo Millennio Ineunte* (6 January 2001), 43.

22 *Lumen Gentium* 9.

23 *Novo Millennio Ineunte* 43.

24 *Lumen Gentium* 9.

25 See De la Potterie, *The Hour of Jesus* (St Paul Publications, Middlegreen, Slough 1989), pp. 132ff.

26 *Novo Millennio Ineunte* 43.

27 See 'Apostles' in M. O'Carroll, *Theotokos* (Liturgical Press, Collegeville MN 1982), pp. 44–5.

28 See the Vatican II document on the Church in the Modern World, *Gaudium et Spes* 38.

29 30 December 1988, n. 9.

30 See Hans Urs von Balthasar, 'Riflessioni per un lavoro sui movimenti laicali nella Chiesa' in Inos Biffi et al, *I laici e la missione della Chiesa* (Istra, Milan 1986) pp. 85–106.

31 See B. Leahy, *The Marian Profile* (New City, London and New York 2000), pp. 182ff.

32 See Chiara Lubich, *The Cry* (New City, London and New York 2001).

33 *Gaudium et Spes* 22.

34 See 'Ginetta' in *Living City* 40 (2001/6), pp. 6–10.

*(This paper was given at the ESBVM Maynooth Conference
in June 2001)*

27

Mary's vision of justice as outlined in the Magnificat

Peter McVerry SJ

My soul proclaims the greatness of the Lord,
And my spirit exults in God my Saviour,
Because he has looked upon his lowly handmaid.
Yes, from this day forward all generations will call me blessed,
For the Almighty has done great things for me.
Holy is his name
And his mercy reaches from age to age for those who fear him.

He has shown the power of his arm,
He has routed the proud of heart,
He has pulled down princes from their thrones and exalted the lowly.
The hungry he has filled with good things, the rich sent empty away.
He has come to the help of Israel, his servant, mindful of his mercy
– according to the promise he made to our ancestors –
of his mercy to Abraham and to his descendants for ever. (Luke 1.46–55).

I am not a professional theologian and so I cannot give you a theological reflection on the Magnificat. What I can do is to share with you what, after a long time working with those who are homeless and on the margins, the Magnificat says to me.

Context

Sometimes my faith grows dim. Sometimes I wonder, is there a God at all or are we all just fooling ourselves? Why did God make it so difficult for us to believe in God if it is so important? Could God not do a little parting of the Liffey waters from time to time, just to prove that God exists – though you still wouldn't be able to walk across with the dirt you'd find there! I resonate with the authorities in Israel who, when Jesus came and said that he was from God and had a revelation from God, asked him to give them a sign that he was who he said he was. 'If you are the Son of God, tell this stone to turn into a loaf.' (Luke 4.3). And again, 'If you are the Son of God, throw yourself down from this tower.'

(Luke 4.9). And what does Jesus say? 'No sign shall be given to this generation.' (Mark 8.12). I always thought that that was most unreasonable of him – the least he could do was to give them a little sign. So what was going on?

In fact, Jesus was giving signs all the time but they couldn't read them. One person asked for a sign and got it. That was John the Baptist. John, from his prison cell, sent his messengers to Jesus with the question: 'Are you the one who is to come or have we got to wait for someone else?' (Matthew 11.3). In other words, give us a sign. And what does Jesus say? 'Go back and tell John what you hear and see: the blind see again, and the lame walk, lepers are cleansed and the deaf hear and the dead are raised to life and the Good News is proclaimed to the poor; and happy the man who does not lose faith in me.' (Matthew 11.4–6). In other words, the signs that Jesus was from God were the *signs of compassion*. Jesus was trying to say: 'Miracles prove nothing – every generation has its magicians! But if you knew who God was, if you knew that our God is a God of compassion, then you would recognize that I am from God by the signs of compassion that I do. If you do not recognize that I am from God, then you do not know God.' We look at a child in the pram and we say: 'Oh, he's lovely, he's the image of his father/mother'. So Jesus was trying to say: 'The only way to know whether I have come from God is if you see in me the same likeness that you find in the Father'. Our God is a God of compassion and the only way we can recognize the Son of God is through the Son's compassion. So when my faith grows dim, where do I go to have my faith restored? Moving statues? Forget it. What sort of God would have even the remotest interest in playing games with statues? When my faith grows dim, my faith is restored by the countless acts of compassion of innumerable people who are reaching out to the sick, to the lonely, to the poor and the marginalized, to the dying and the unwanted. There I find the evidence that God exists.

Of course this is not evidence in the scientific sense of the word. I cannot *prove* that God exists, neither to anyone else, nor even to myself. But what I can do is to *confirm, in my own experience, that I am loved, infinitely and unconditionally, by a being I call God.*

I am loved *infinitely*: God wishes me to be happy. There is no happiness that God withholds from me. God desires my infinite happiness. And so I am loved infinitely. It is this love that gives me my value. I am like a Picasso painting: a Picasso painting, valued at £50m: where does its value come from? It comes from *outside* itself. Its value is *given* to it. It is valued at £50m because others give it that value, others love it to that extent. But although its value comes from *outside* itself, its value resides *in* the painting itself. If I put an exact, identical copy of the painting

beside it, the copy has little or no value. The value is *in* the Picasso painting but the value is given to it from *outside* itself.

And so my value comes from outside myself, from the infinite love of
God for me. And so I am of infinite value. I have this unsurpassable
dignity, which has been given to me.

And I am loved *unconditionally*. Nothing can separate me from the
love of God, 'neither principalities nor powers ...' The one thing in this
world that never changes is God's love. And so no one, nothing, not
even my own sinfulness, can take away, or reduce, the value and dignity
that God's love bestows on me. Being loved infinitely and unconditionally gives me an infinite dignity and value that can never be taken from
me.

This conviction, that I am loved infinitely and unconditionally, is the
foundation stone of justice. Because if I can confirm that I am loved infinitely and unconditionally, then so can everyone else. If I have this infinite dignity, then so has everyone else. This conviction is a challenge to
our culture, which seeks to give value to people by what they do, what
they achieve, how they succeed. Our culture seeks to value people by
what comes *out* of them; our faith seeks to value people by the love of
God, which has been put *into* them.

Link between faith and justice

For me the link between faith and justice is this *dignity* of people. We
could sum up the whole Gospel by saying that Jesus came to proclaim
that God is the Father of every human being; and conversely that evey
human being is a child of God and has the dignity of being a child of
God.

But if our faith proclaims in *words* the dignity of every human being,
then our commitment to justice seeks to make that dignity a *reality* for
every human being. Faith without justice is hypocrisy – it is empty
words that mean nothing because we have taken the meaning out of
them. Justice seeks to put that meaning back into the words, to make
reality reflect what we say, and what we say to reflect reality. And so
compassion is the heart and soul of justice, it is the beginning, the
middle and the end of our commitment to justice. Our reaching out to
those whose dignity is being denied or threatened by the way in which
they are treated by society, is the meaning and the content of our struggle for justice.

Motivation for our commitment to justice

Why do I commit myself to this reaching out, which can be difficult, self-sacrificing and problematic? Is it for the sake of the reward, the Kingdom of God, which is promised to those who reach out to the poor? No. Is it for fear of punishment, if I fail to show love? No. The motivation for our commitment to justice is *gratitude*, gratitude for the infinite and unconditional love which God has given to me. The deeper my appreciation of that love, the greater my gratitude and the greater my commitment to justice can be. So the foundation stone for justice is my appreciation of that love of God.

So the first half of the Magnificat speaks to me of Mary's total conviction, born from her own experience, of the love of God for her, freely given, not deserved, and given in all the abundance which God is able to give. Mary is rooted in that deep appreciation of the dignity and value which she has been given by the love of God. She expresses her deep gratitude to God for that love.

In the second half of the Magnificat, Mary recognizes that that same love, which has been poured out on her, moves God to reach out, in a special way, to the poor and the powerless.

Commitment to justice

1. A preferential option for the poor and powerless

An image of God which I often use is this: Imagine a parent with two children: one of the children is doing their homework. They ask the parent to help them with the homework. So the parent goes over to help the child with the homework. While they are doing that, they look out the window and see their other child being beaten up outside. So what do they do? Well, obviously they *leave* the child doing the homework and *go to* the aid of the child being beaten up. Why do they do so? It is not because they love the child being beaten up more than they love the child doing the homework. No, they love both children equally. But they leave one child and go to the aid of the other because of the situation that that child is in. The child is in a situation of danger, of pain, and so has a priority call on the parent's care and concern at that moment of time, which the other child does not require.

As I imagine God looking down at our world, God sees me talking here to you and loves me with an infinite and unconditional love. I cannot ask for more than that. But God is also looking down on some poor mother in Sudan whose children are dying from hunger in her arms, or some homeless child in Dublin or London or Calcutta wondering where they are going to eat and sleep tonight, or some young mother waiting in her flat for her alcoholic husband to come in and wondering if he is going to beat her up again tonight. I would have to say, that if they did not have a priority concern for God, in a way that I do not require at this point in time, then God would not be a parent.

God's preferential option for the poor and the powerless comes, not from loving the poor and powerless more than the rest of us, but because God is compassion. The God who is compassion must, it seems to me, have a special concern and care for those children who are suffering, who are in danger or in pain.

And so in a world of injustice, must we take sides? I believe, Yes – because God is compassion. To be for the poor and the powerless is not to be against anyone, it is to be *for*, to be for the poor and powerless, and to be an invitation to others also to be for the poor and powerless, an invitation which of course they may reject.

When Jesus was asked who would be in the Kingdom of God, he answers: 'How happy are you who are poor; yours is the Kingdom of God'. In school, I was taught that at the Last Judgement, I would have to stand up on the platform and all my sins would be revealed, and all the god things I did would be revealed, and the weighing scales would come out and maybe I would get in, or maybe not. Then, after me, some other poor soul would have to get up, and so on. Well, after the first few hundred thousand it is going to get very boring! So maybe the Last Judgement scene is not about the revelation of McVerry or anyone else to the world; maybe it is God's final revelation of who God is, to the world. Here we have the whole world gathered before God and God finally reveals who God is. And who is our God? Our God is compassion. And how better could God reveal that God is compassion than to usher into the Kingdom all those who were made to suffer here on earth, whose dignity was taken away from them, who were unwanted and rejected. The Kingdom belongs to the poor. So I am left watching the poor being given the Kingdom, and wondering do I get in or not! Well, I get in, if I have made friends with the poor. If through my compassion, I have made friends with the poor, then they will welcome me into the Kingdom which they have been given. However, if I have ignored them, failed to reach out to them, despised them, how can I then expect them to invite me into their Kingdom.

In our reaching out to the poor and our attempts to take some of the suffering from their shoulders, nothing is untouchable, nothing is sacred. Some of the suffering, the poverty and marginalization that is imposed on many in our world, is due to political failure, political policies and decisions. There is a debate in many of the churches about whether the Church should get involved in politics. Many would say it is no business of the Church to meddle in politics, it knows nothing about politics and should stick to what it is supposed to do – bring people to know God and teach them to pray. But the Church proclaims the dignity of all people and where that dignity is undermined, threatened or taken away, then no area of human life is exempt from the Church's criticism and efforts to bring about change, no door is closed to the Church's prophetic call for justice. If political decisions, policies or programmes impose suffering and marginalization on people and take away the dignity that is theirs by right, then such decisions, policies or programmes must be challenged.

Another image I often use is of a fellow lying by a river on a lovely sunny day. He is enjoying the peace and feeling very contented. Suddenly, he sees a body floating down the river. So he jumps in, pulls the body out, gives them the kiss of life and sends them on their way. He settles back to enjoy the rest of the day, feeling very satisfied with himself, when another body comes floating down the river. So he jumps in, pulls them out, gives them the kiss of life and sends them on their way. And a third body and a fourth, the bodies just keep coming. At some point, he has to say to himself, 'I must go up-river and see where all the bodies are coming from'. So up he goes and finds a bridge where an oil tanker has crashed, spilt its oil on the bridge and broken the side of the bridge. Everybody crossing the bridge slips on the oil and falls into the river. So, he cleans up the oil and puts a rope along the side of the bridge and there are no more bodies floating down the river.

In our compassion for the poor and the powerless, we must not only pull the bodies out of the river, but we must go up-river and fix the bridge. It is still important to pull the bodies out of the river – the poor fellow floating down the river doesn't want you to fix the bridge until *after* you have rescued him out of the river. But we cannot be content with just pulling the bodies out of the river. At some point we must also fix the bridge. Fixing the bridge may involve toppling princes – I think of President Marcos in the Philippines or Papa Doc Duvalier in Haiti. There may be smaller princes to be challenged, toes to be trod upon! If some do not want the oil to be cleaned up, because it is too costly, or because it threatens their position or power or status or wealth, they must be challenged – I think of homeless children, homeless adults, people with disabilities, travellers, the list goes on.

The Gospel is not a political gospel – it is a Gospel of compassion. But it may have to tread on political ground if it is to truly reach out to the poor and the powerless.

2. A church that *is* poor and powerless

> He has pulled down princes from their thrones and exalted the lowly,
> The hungry he has filled with good things, the rich sent empty away.

Why would we think that this vision does not also refer to the churches? I believe that a church that proclaims the Gospel must be a church that is poor and powerless. A church, rich and powerful, will be pulled down and sent empty away. A church that is poor and powerless involves a new vision of priesthood. If the criteria for priesthood emphasizes the necessity to complete a third-level qualification in Theology and Philosophy, then, given the educational structure of our world and of our society, candidates for the priesthood will be drawn predominantly from middle-class backgrounds. That shapes the Church's *expectations, aspirations,* its *value system,* its *understanding* of, and *attitude* towards the structures of our world and our societies.

Another image I use is that of a person living in a flat on the top floor of a building. Eight o'clock in the morning comes and they pull back the curtains; the sun shines in. They look out the window into the back garden and see the freshly-cut grass, the beautiful multi-coloured flowers swaying in the gentle breeze, the birds hopping on the lawn looking for worms. They think, What a beautiful day.

However, someone may be living in the basement flat of the same house. Eight o'clock in the morning comes, they pull back the curtains, nothing happens. The sun can't get in. They look out the window into the back garden and all they see is the whitewashed wall of the outside toilet; they cannot see the garden, or the grass or the flowers or the birds.

Here we have two people looking out of the same house, into the same garden, at the same time of the same day, but they have two totally different views; there is the view from the top and the view from the bottom.

If the leadership in our church comes from predominantly middle-class backgrounds, then the church will predominantly have the view from the top. To seek a church that is poor and that *aspires to be poor* is to seek out and welcome candidates for the priesthood from among the poor. Of course, if such candidates come into a church that is middle class, that aspires to a middle-class quality of life, then priesthood becomes an upwardly mobile vocation choice for people who are poor, as with the Roman Catholic Church in parts of Africa today.

A church that is poor is a church that is *free.* Wealth and property and power tie the Church into those aspirations and structures that are dominated by the comfortable and make the Church less free not only to be critical, but even to realize that it *ought* to be critical. A church of wealth and property and power tends to be – as we have seen in Ireland – a church that accepts the *status quo* and is welcomed by and accepted by those whose interests lie in retaining the *status quo*. A church that is wealthy and powerful can *never* be prophetic – and our world today needs a prophetic church, it cries out for a prophetic church. Those who are poor and excluded in our society and in our world, whose dignity the Church proclaims again and again from the altar, have a right to expect the Church to proclaim that dignity in the way it lives.

In Luke's Gospel, the person chosen to be the Mother of God was a nobody from Nazareth, a despised region of Israel; the person who first recognizes Mary's honour is an elderly barren woman, Elizabeth, who would have been despised in society because of her barrenness, which was understood to be a sign of God's displeasure; and the first persons to witness to the birth of Jesus were shepherds, a despised group of people. God chose the poor and the powerless to be witness to, and instruments of, the salvation which Jesus came to bring. The Church, which continues to witness to, and to be the instrument of, God's salvation must too be poor and powerless.

Conclusion

The Magnificat then poses for me a two-fold challenge:

- first, to enter more deeply into my experience and conviction of the infinite and unconditional love of God, given to me, not because I deserve it, or have earned it, but because I am God's creation.
- and secondly, resting on this foundation and driven by gratitude, to reach out in compassion to those whose dignity as children of God is being denied or undermined and to accept the radical, all-embracing consequences of being the compassion of God, even if those consequences bring us, as they brought to Jesus, marginalization, suffering and even perhaps death.

*(This paper was given at the ESBVM Maynooth Conference
in June 2001)*

Mary
and
patristics

28

The Blessed Virgin Mary in Relation to her Son

The Significance of her Title 'Second Heaven' in the Church of the East Tradition

Bawai Soro

I feel particularly privileged, and I am grateful, for having been given the opportunity to address the subject of the Blessed Virgin Mary, the Mother of our Lord Jesus Christ (and, in a profound sense, the Mother of all who name his Name in faith), and her relationship with her Son. I shall speak specifically of the place she holds in the affection and pious veneration of the sons and daughters of the Church of the East, and discuss the implications this has had for the theological tradition of that Church. I will seek to convey a sense of the church's deep appreciation of her role, and its attachment to the memory of her life as a vivid model of righteous obedience and faith in God's will and providence.

I. Mary's christological title 'Second Heaven': Some liturgical and patristic references

The place of honour Mary holds in the Church of the East is one which elicits a sense of affinity and profound veneration among the faithful. This follows from the church's emphasis upon Mary's unique role in the history of our salvation, and its recognition of her relationship both to Christ and to the community of the faithful. According to the Gospel of Luke, she is the *'Handmaid of the Father'*, the *'Mother of the Son'*, and the *'Temple of the Holy Spirit'* (Luke 1.30–5, 38). In the Gospel of John, the Blessed Mother and the beloved disciple are brought together at the foot of the cross, where Jesus defines their new relationship as *'mother and son'*. Accordingly, the Church of the East venerates Mary because she is seen to be forming, with John, the first Christian family – each seeing Christ in the other – thus having a profound relationship to the Christian community (John 19.26–7).[1]

Following the axiom, *Lex Orandi Lex Credendi*, and quoting directly from liturgical and patristic sources that have been received and celebrated in the Church of the East for centuries, we will be able to demonstrate the significance accorded to Mary, and appreciate the unique terminology employed to describe the Blessed Mother. With such language, we will be able to gain some insights into the ways this tradition honours the Holy Virgin, and the implications this may have for its christological understanding.

There are three feasts of our Lady in the Assyrian Church of the East, which are celebrated in January, May and August. The Church of the East never exhausts itself in extolling Mary in terms that could not be applied to any other human being.[2] Among the numerous glorious epithets for Mary, the most significant is the title 'Second Heaven'. This title is one of the most prominent themes in these celebrations:

1.   From the *Second Heaven*, the Ever Virgin
2.   [Christ] shone forth temporally for our salvation
3.   Holy and the fount of divine holy things
4.   She is splendid and fair and the ark of spiritual mysteries
5.   She is renowned in virtue and holy exploits
6.   A treasury of grace and storehouse of heavenly riches
7.   Our Lady, Mary, is more exalted and sublime than [any] name
8.   *Temple of the Holy Spirit* and *Mother of the Son of God*
9–10. She alone, among all the daughters of Eve is the one [whom God] chose to be a *'Temple for the Holy Spirit'* and a *'Mother for the Son of the Highest'*[3]
11.   In her womb she bore fire; in her body she carried the *Shekinah*[4]
12.   Within her soul the Spirit brooded, and [Mary] became, all in all, a *Heaven*
13.   Do not reproach me, O reader, because I have designated [Mary] a *heaven*
14.   And, as I think, [Mary is] more excellent, sublime, and exalted than *heaven*.[5]

This indicates that, in the eyes of the Church of the East, Mary deserves the honour of being called *'Heaven'*, due to her intimate and active participation in the mystery of the Incarnation. Furthermore, she is venerated as such since the eternal Lord of all, the Only-begotten Son of God, whose eternal dwelling-place is in Heaven, did, in the fullness of time (at the incarnation), descend to the world and make the womb of the Virgin his dwelling-place, truly a *'Second Heaven'*. Mary is therefore named Heaven because of God's unique relationship with her, whose womb became the Sanctuary of his Son.

Mary's title *'Second Heaven'* implies that the two Apostolic Marian traditional teachings of the *'virginal conception'* of Jesus and of his mother's *'perpetual virginity'* are consequently taken in their literal sense, both in theological and pastoral usage. The title *'Second Heaven'* helps the believer to avoid a mere symbolic approach to describing God's intervention in human history.[6] Accordingly, for the Church of the East, as for all Christians, Mary becomes a figure of great spiritual significance. For the Christian believer she is a model of the co-operation which should take place between humanity and God. The example of Mary's co-operation establishes a parallel between the coming of the Holy Spirit upon Mary at the annunciation (Luke 1.35) and the invocation of the Holy Spirit at the Eucharist, with the subsequent sanctification of the whole community.[7] She is also an example of holiness and chastity for those who desire to consecrate their lives to virginity and celibacy for the sake of the Kingdom.[8]

In an anonymous Syriac hymn of the Virgin Mary found in a British Library manuscript, the Virgin is depicted as follows:

1. An orphaned girl has become the very *Heaven*
2. And supernal beings stand in awe at the daughter of Man
3. Heaven was too small for Him who descended
4. And resided within her so as to save all creation.[9]

From another Syriac traditional hymn called 'The Angel and Mary', Church of the East Fathers express their understanding of Mary's role in the mystery of incarnation in the following words given through the lips of the Angel:

1. Let your hand be raised up, O maiden
2. Let your heart rejoice, O Virgin
3. O *'Second Heaven'*, let the earth rejoice at you
4. For in your Son it does gain peace.[10]

In another tradition that is attributed to Ephrem the Syrian, Mary is again imaginatively depicted, in accordance with the gospel story of the nativity, as a *'Heaven'* and also as *'Second Heaven'*:

1. Welcome, young girl in whom is the ancient Babe
2. Welcome, the Dove, which bears Christ the Eagle
3. Welcome, most chaste of women who bears her Lord
4. Welcome, *Heaven* in which the world finds rest
5. Welcome, the Lock, wherein is the Key of fire
6. Welcome, High Hill, more exalted than all the heights
7. Welcome, *'Second Heaven,'* who has appeared to us
8. Welcome, O Wondrous One, who has given birth to Emmanuel.[11]

Finally, this hymn on the Virgin expresses definitively the relation between Mary and the Godhead of Christ, her Son:

1. And, among us He was born from one of us
2. This day Mary has become for us
3. The *Heaven* that bears God
4. For in her the exalted Godhead has descended and dwelt.[12]

The title *'Second Heaven'* emphasizes significantly that Mary is not venerated in isolation, but in relation to her Son. This term is designated to stress the divine origin of her Son and reflect the presence of Christ in her womb.

II. Theological parallelism with Theodore and Nestorius

We have seen in the above texts attributed to St Ephrem (fourth century), and the hymns from the *Book of Khodra* (seventh century), examples of this church's distinct Marian title *'Second Heaven'*. The *'ancient Babe'* referred to lovingly as the resident of that heaven on earth is none other than the eternal Son, 'begotten of his Father before all ages'. He is Emmanuel, God with us, whose dwelling-place becomes a celestial haven because of its Inhabitant. The one who is 'with us', the sole subject of the incarnation extolled in these anthems, whose manhood, though complete, is not perceived as an *'other'*, is the eternal *'Word made flesh, who dwelt among us'*, whose glory shone forth from the Virgin. The newly-conceived is more ancient than the everlasting hills of Jacob's blessing. Here is a high christology indeed, and the singers of these anthems down through the ages could not be confused as to the identity of the infant within the *'Second Heaven'*.

Our next task will be to demonstrate a similarity in christological faith between this ancient tradition of the Church of the East and two of its Greek-speaking teachers, namely, Theodore the Interpreter, Bishop of Mopsuestia, (d. 428) and Nestorius the Patriarch of Constantinople (d. 451). The influence of these two 'Westerners' on the native church of Persia was profound – even decisive in the matter of christology – and therefore must be taken into consideration whenever this subject is addressed.

The meaning of the incarnation according to Theodore

The reader of Theodore is always confronted with the task of understanding and assimilating Theodore's thought through concepts and terminology that were relevant to his own cultural and philosophical backgrounds. The most significant factor to take into account in such an effort is that Theodore lived in an atmosphere charged with 'monophysite'[13] teachings and other 'heretical' tendencies that emphasized the divine aspect of Christ's person, while at the same time denying the fullness of his humanity.

The moment of becoming

On the one hand, Theodore's concern was to argue against these teachings and, consequently, he laid great stress on the fact that the humanity of Jesus was a true and perfect humanity, bestowed with all the human faculties and operations, including a rational human soul. On the other hand, and in order to balance this approach, he taught that the second Person of the Trinity, God the Word, or the Only-begotten of God the Father, was to be distinguished from that which was *'begotten of Mary'*, born of the seed of David, yet, at the same time, by virtue of the very close and intimate union existing between the natures, the two distinct and radically different natures which were begotten did not constitute two sons but only one Son.[14]

At the moment of conception the Word of God dwelt in Mary's womb, and the Virgin was the chosen vehicle in and through whom God the Word united himself to a particular human nature, which is taken from her by the power of the Holy Spirit. However, Theodore emphasizes that through this divine act the resultant 'becoming' should not be understood as if God the Word, the Only-begotten Son of the Father, was born of her in the sense that his divinity originated at that time, or that he owed his existence to her. Theodore prefers to distinguish the two natures even during the becoming, but necessarily refers to them both as *one* by virtue of the one *prosopon* of the Son of God and due to the ineffable union between Godhead and manhood. Here is how he taught the faith:

> It is obvious that they do not teach that the Divine nature of the Only Begotten was born of a woman, as if it had its beginning in her, because they did not say that the one who was born of His Father before all the worlds and who is eternally from Him and with Him had His beginning from *Mary*, but they followed the Sacred Books which speak differently of natures while referring [them] to one *prosopon* on account of the close union that took place between them, so that [it] might not be believed that they were separating the perfect union between the one [nature which] was assumed and the one [nature which] assumed.[15]

Elsewhere by stating the following about the bearing and the birth of Christ by the Virgin Mary, Theodore explains what it means to him that God the Word dwelt in the womb of Mary.

> In saying that He was made of a woman He showed that He entered into the world from a woman according to the Law of the children of men, and the

fact that 'He was under the law to redeem them that were under the law that we might receive the adoption of sons',[16] happened so that He might pay our debt to the Lawgiver and procure life for us.[17]

Theodore tells us that when speaking about the distinction of the two natures we must simultaneously and immediately assert the truth of the union. The following texts illustrate his point.

> If this union were destroyed the one [nature], which was assumed, would not be seen more than a mere man like ourselves.[18]

> He thus hid himself at the time in which He was in the world and conducted himself with the children of men in such a way that all those who beheld Him in a human way and did not understand anything more, believed Him to be a mere man.[19]

Indeed, those who historically have not perceived the reality of Christ's united divinity and humanity since the time of the incarnation have judged him according to his outward *schema*, alone. It was as a mere man who claimed divinity that men sought to put him to death (e.g. the Jewish authorities). Conversely, others, acknowledging his divine nature, have sought to deny his real human nature and to withhold from it the glory due to it by virtue of the union (e.g. the Arians).

Elsewhere it seems that in Theodore's mind the one *prosopon* in Christ is the same as the Divine Person. This one *prosopon*, or one subject, we can address now as God and now as man.[20] However, according to modern critics of Theodore's christology,[21] Theodore faced the problem of what in modern theology is called the *'theandric composite'*.[22] In this context, they maintain, Theodore could not attribute and would not ascribe the resultant 'person' of the union to the Word of God. But at the same time other theologians,[23] more sympathetic and understanding to the context and essence of his thought, show the inaccuracy of such criticism by citing passages through which Theodore himself, in advance, excludes such a viewpoint. There are two passages in which we can see how explicitly Theodore states that what is applicable to the human nature is ascribed to the divine, and what is due to the one nature is also due to the other.

> While all these things are clearly and obviously said [by the Apostle Paul][24] of human nature, he referred them successively to Divine nature so that his sentence might be strengthened and be acceptable to hearers. Indeed, since it is above human nature that it should be worshipped by all, it is with justice that all this has been said as of one, so that the belief in a close union between the natures might be strengthened, because he clearly showed that the one [nature] which was assumed did not receive all this great honour except from the Divine nature which assumed [it] and dwelt in [it].[25]

The one who assumed is the Divine nature that does everything for us, and the other is the human nature which was assumed on behalf of all of us by the One who is the cause of everything, and is united to it in an ineffable union which will never be separated ... The Sacred Books also teach us this union, not only when they impart to us the knowledge of each nature but also when they affirm that what is due to the one is also due to the other, so that we should understand the wonderfulness and the sublimity of the union that took place.[26]

Communicatio idiomatum

As a result of the union of the two natures, which took place in the womb of the Virgin, Theodore confesses the necessity of exchanging predicates between the two natures in Christ.[27] The whole need for the *'communicatio idiomatum'* is, in Theodore's words, *'so that the belief in a close union between the natures might be strengthened'*. An example is presented in his exegesis on Phil. 2.8–11 in the commentary on the Creed. Theodore maintains that it is not true to say that the gift of adoration – *'every knee shall bow and every tongue confess'* – will be granted to the divine nature, for this [adoration] already belongs to it; however, adoration will be granted to the 'form of a servant' by virtue of the union. Yet, though this is *'clearly and obviously said of human nature [Paul] referred [it] ... to Divine nature'*.[28] In other words, though the natures are two, what is technically specific to one is referred to the other, and there is but a single *subject* of adoration in Christ.[29]

The final subject in Christ

In this text, Theodore ascribes to the subject, Jesus Christ, the experience of rising from the dead and receiving immortality and immutability, and to the same he ascribes the ability to raise others and to give them perfection as well. It is plain that it is not natural to the divine to undergo, nor to the human to give, resurrection, or change from mortality to immortality or from mutability to immutability. Yet the subject of both receiving and giving is the one *'Christ our Lord'*. The critical question concerning Theodore's christological orthodoxy is who is the *subject* of the title *'Christ our Lord'* who divinely bestows and humanly receives. Is this one and only subject in Jesus Christ the same as the *Word of God*, the Only-begotten Son of the Father? The following two Theodorian texts, commenting on the phrases of the Nicean Creed, *'who for us children of men and for our salvation came down from heaven,'* and *'he shall come again to judge the living and the dead,'* address this legitimate concern.

He [the blessed David][30] called the condescension of God the 'coming down' of God, in the sense that He who was so much above all condescended to deliver them from their tribulations. It is in this sense that God the Word, the only Son of God, is said to have come down for our salvation[31] ... He condescended to come down to such a humility as to take upon Him[self] the form of a servant[32] and be in it so that through it He might grant us the delight of His abundant gift ... [33]

'This same Jesus which is taken up from you into heaven shall so come in like manner as you have seen Him go into heaven.'[34] This was to demonstrate to [the disciples] that it would be the very man who was seen by them, and was with them, and was now being separated from them, who would be coming and be seen by all men. To this man the word *again* is not fitting. Indeed, it is not He [the man] who came but it is the Godhead that came down from heaven, not that it moved from place to place, but by its condescension and its Providence for us which it [fulfilled[35]] in the man who was assumed on our behalf. The word *again* will refer in the next world to the man whom [the Godhead] assumed on our behalf. The man who was assumed on our behalf went now first[36] into heaven and will come again first from heaven, but because they [our blessed Fathers] were referring in their words to the Divine nature they counted His coming twice, first when He came down through that man,[37] and secondly when He will come *again* through the same man who had been assumed, because of the ineffable union that that man had with God.[38]

Jesus' human nature which Theodore calls 'man' is that 'medium' through which God the Word manifests himself in both revelations – the incarnation and the parousia. For Theodore, it is God the Word who came down to this world through the Virgin Mary, and who later suffered and rose through his humanity – through that which Theodore calls 'man' – and most clearly who will come again to judge the world. For Theodore, as for the Fathers in Nicea, the word *'again'* indicates that the Word, appearing in his own manhood, is the subject of the Parousia. The word *'again'* eliminates the possibility for the human nature (that which Theodore calls 'man') to be the subject in Jesus Christ. It is rather the united vehicle of the second appearance, as it was of the first. The Word's 'man' ascended for the first time into heaven, therefore his coming from heaven will be for the first time as well. The logic runs thus, the man whom the Word assumed did not 'come down' from heaven, but the divine nature did. But the man whom the Word assumed will 'come *again*' from heaven because he is the Word's united man. Here (and in its context) we see clearly Theodore's view of the Word as the subject/agent of our redemption, and his assumed human nature in the womb of the *'Second Heaven'* Mary, as his united instrument of manifestation and redemption.

Nestorius

The direct excuse for the '*Nestorian*' controversy was the controversy ignited by Anastasius, one of Nestorius' confidants from Antioch and his presbyter in Constantinople. In November 428 Anastasius preached an infamous oration in which he said, '*Let no one call Mary the mother of God, for Mary was a human being; and that God should be born of a human being is impossible*'.[39] By asserting such a statement, Anastasius was perceived to be imposing the Antiochean christology on the Church of Constantinople, which for the people of that city was an unfamiliar teaching. During his Christmas lectures on the Nativity in December 428, Nestorius did not reprimand his friend nor did he correct him. And so this incident caused a great uproar among the monks and the public alike, in particular to the partisans of the Marian cults, who were then beginning to form in Constantinople and elsewhere. The faith of these people, whose devotion to the Blessed Virgin was emotional (her veneration was highly popular), had prompted them to bestow upon the mother of Jesus the religious epithet *Theotokos*, 'Mother of God'. What Anastasius pronounced about Mary was perceived as a direct denial of the divinity of Christ. So consequently, violence erupted in Constantinople, ultimately bringing the enemies of Nestorius down upon him like wolves. Nestorius was later accused of being the actual source of the offensive teaching and had to be judged and silenced by force.[40] Later events of this controversy became so involved that the conflict which broke out as a result of Anastasius' sermon soon grew to encompass, in addition to Cyril,[41] the Alexandrian clergy, Pope Celestine I and the Roman Synod, the imperial court, and other episcopal supporters of one side or the other.[42] Ultimately, Nestorius and his teaching were condemned by the Council of Ephesus in 431.

However, Nestorius personally preferred to venerate the Virgin Mary with something other than the term '*Theotokos*'. He gives us an account in this regard of a situation in which he was called upon to settle a question as the Patriarch of his church in Constantinople.

> Those on the one hand who called the blessed Mary the mother of God they called Manichaeans, but those who named the blessed Mary the mother of a man Photinians. ... But when they were questioned by me, the former denied not the humanity nor the latter the divinity, but they confessed them both alike, while they were distinct only in name: they of the party of Apollinarius accepted 'Mother of God' and they of the party of Photinus 'Mother of man'. But after I knew that they disputed not in the spirit of heretics, I said that neither the latter nor the former were heretics, [the former] because they knew not Apollinarius and his dogma, while similarly the latter [knew] the dogma neither of Photinus nor of Paul.[43] And I brought them back from this inquiry and from this dispute, saying that: If indistinguishably and without

extrusion or denial of the divinity and of the humanity we accept what is said by them, we sin not; but if not, let us make use of that which is very plainly [affirmed], that is, of the Word of the Gospel: 'Christ was born'[44] and 'the book of the generation of Jesus Christ.'[45] And by things such as these we confess that Christ is God and man, 'of them[46] was born in flesh Christ, who is God above all.'[47] When you call her the Mother of Christ, [Christ] by union and inseparable, you speak of the one [nature] and of the other in the Sonship. But make use of that against which there is no accusation in the Gospel and settle this dispute among you, making use of a word, which is useful toward agreement.[48]

Accordingly, the manner in which Nestorius conceives the union would be in such a fashion that the Word passed through Blessed Mary inasmuch as he did not receive a beginning by birth from her, as is the case with the body, which was born of her. For this reason Nestorius would say that God the Word 'passed' and not 'was born', because he did not receive a beginning from her. And, in such passing, Mary's role in the mystery of the Incarnation could be conceived as a *'Heaven'*, making the two natures in the union united, indeed, in one Christ. And so, he who was born of the Father as to the divinity, and from the Holy Virgin as to the humanity, is One. For of the two natures there was but one union. In order to understand Nestorius' thinking, it is important to know that the notion of birth necessarily connotes to him the concept of generation – the coming into being, the rising to existence. As a committed Antiochean, Nestorius cannot compromise the dignity of either nature in Christ in any manner whatsoever. For this reason, in numerous places in the *Bazaar*, he makes certain that he explains why he avoids the assertion that God the Word was born of the Blessed Virgin, and, instead he maintains that:

> He who is God the Word has surely passed through [the Virgin] but was surely not born, because he derived not his origin[49] from her. But there both exists and is named one Christ,[50] the two of them being united, he who was born of the Father in the divinity, [and] of the holy virgin in the humanity, for there was a union of the two natures[51] ... God the Word existed in the body, in that which took the beginning of its coming into being from the blessed Mary, [yet] he took not the beginning of his coming into being. *In the beginning was the Word*,[52] and God the Word exists eternally.[53]

Communicatio idiomatum

For the Antiocheans, to adhere to the term *Theotokos* without first providing safeguards which affirm adequately the full and authentic humanity of the Lord and his real consubstantiality with every other human being would lead to a fundamentally monophysite conception of the union in Christ.[54] If the doctrine of the *'Hypostatic Union'* means that the Blessed Virgin Mary is not the mother of the divine nature of Christ (i.e., that he did not receive a beginning from her), but only that the Divine Logos joined himself to the human nature of Jesus at the 'moment' of his conception inside the womb, and that because of the intimate and inseparable union between the divine and human natures in Christ, the holy Virgin is therefore called *'Theotokos'*, then it has been shown that Nestorius already accepts this doctrine.[55]

Furthermore, Nestorius did not intend to deny the legitimacy of the *'communicatio idiomatum'*. The following text illustrates his understanding of this important doctrine:

> For he who refers to the one *prosopon* of God the Word the [properties] of God the Word and those of the humanity, and gives not in return the *prosopon* of God the Word to the humanity, steals away the union of the orthodox and likens it to that of the heretics. For you have learned from the orthodox in the testimonies that they have written, that they give in compensation the [properties] of the humanity to the divinity and those of the divinity to the humanity, and that this is said of the one [nature] and that of the other, as concerning natures whole and united, united indeed without confusion and making use of the *prosopa* of one another.[56]

Nestorius' way of expressing the exchange of predicates between God the Word and the human nature in Christ is through their *prosopa* – *'the divinity makes use of the prosopon of the humanity and the humanity of that of the divinity'*. This is a vocabulary particular to him, through which he performs at his best in expressing his thought. It is a terminology which seeks to arrive at the same point as that which the doctrine of the *'hypostatic union'* attempts to achieve. A question then can be asked: What if Nestorius did intend to mean by the usage of the term *'prosopon'* what was altogether equal to what Cyril meant by the term *'hypostasis'*? This language that Nestorius utilizes to articulate his doctrine of the *'prosopon of the union'* allows him to express the sought-after unity of the two natures in Christ. Through the *'prosopon of the union'* Christ's divinity makes use of the *prosopon* of his humanity, and the humanity of that of the divinity. In Nestorius' words each *prosopon* becomes the *'eikon and prosopon'* of the other nature in such wise that in the final analysis there is only one coalesced *prosopon* of Jesus Christ, both God and man.[57]

III. A conclusion

This brief overview – presenting liturgical and patristic texts, which employ the specific Marian christological title *Second Heaven* – lends strength to the overall consistent christological approach of the Fathers of the Church of the East. This theological sense is demonstrated in that both of the 'Western' Fathers quoted – fathers who were pivotal in the development of christological doctrine in Antioch, Alexandria, Mesopotamia (including Western Persia) – maintain that the one *Prosopon* of the union in Christ is the same Divine Person of the Son of God – thus the significance of the title *Second Heaven* for the Blessed Mother.

Just as the central piece of the historic *'Common Christological Declaration'*, signed at the Vatican in 1994 by Pope John Paul II and Catholicos-Patriarch Mar Dinkha IV, was based on clarification of ancient Marian titles, namely, *Theotokos* and *Christotokos*, so, too, we hope that today further theological elaboration, which is coupled with prayer and devotion to the Blessed Mother, will bring the Assyrian Church of the East, and the Fathers she respects, closer to the rest of Christianity.

Both Theodore and Nestorius are among the theologians most respected by Church of the East Fathers and tradition, and their cases continue to be an ecumenically sensitive issue. They have significantly touched upon the christological titles involving the Blessed Mother, especially Nestorius. But, since this paper is read in an ecumenical context also touching on the role of the Blessed Mother in the history of salvation, it seemed appropriate to me to consider briefly the christological thought of Theodore and Nestorius through their discussion of Mary's relation to her Son. The dispute over the *'Theotokos'*, a controversy in which this church supported and defended Nestorius, led the rest of Christendom to misunderstand the Church of the East's attitude toward the Virgin and her Son. The One who was born of her according to the flesh was none other than the divine Word of God. To the question 'Who do men say that I am?' we in the East proclaim, *'You are the Christ, the Son of the living God'*, the *'Ancient Babe'* who made his dwelling-place in the Second Heaven.

During the past 1500 years we followers of Christ and venerators of his Blessed Mother have discovered many ways to disagree, and many causes to dispute. At the advent of the third Christian millennium, it is my hope and prayer that this misunderstanding may be done away and that our brothers and sisters in the churches of the West may know and appreciate the love and deep and abiding devotion which the Assyrians and other members of the Church of the East feel toward the Mother of Christ as the obedient and faithful *'Handmaid of the Lord'*, whose womb became the gateway for our deliverance and salvation. In her the Word of God dwelt as in a temple, and through her the Son of God revealed himself *'for us men and for our salvation'*. In her prayers we seek refuge, even as we seek life through her Son, to whom, with his Father and the Holy Spirit, be eternal glory. Amen.

Notes

1 Nevertheless, the necessity for Marian veneration to remain 'within the limits of orthodoxy' requires that no matter how or when she is venerated through her devotions, feasts and memorials, the Virgin Mother is never to be elevated above her Son, or even equated with him (1 Tim. 2.5–6). The Church of the East, in and through her liturgical celebrations, proclaims God's providence, as made known in the Gospel, so that the Person and works of Jesus Christ are ultimately made prominent and glorified. This emphasis is given to preserve and make clear a distinction between Mary as mediator between God and men in prayer for help and comfort, which is encouraged among the faithful, and the uniqueness of Christ's role in mediating our redemption.

2 For a similar concept in Catholic theology, see *Lumen Gentium* 66. Mary is singled out and set above all humanity, keeping in mind that Jesus Christ was human, but also God.

3 *The Book of Khodra*, 'Common Prayer for the Feast of our Lady', vol. 1 (Mar Narsai Press, Trichur, India 1962), pp. 608–9.

4 'Shekinah' is the Hebrew concept of divine presence; it is a word that is also used in the Aramaic Syriac literature.

5 *Khodra*, vol. 1, pp. 609, 593.

6 The seventh-century theologian, Mar Babai the Great, in his *Memras*, 'On the Union', stated the received tradition in the Church of Persia thus: '. . . he went out by the power of the Godhead which was united in him from within the womb through the bound and virginal gates of natural protection, while those natural seals, the keepers of holiness, were not destroyed, forever confirming by a token the testimony of chastity for ever.' *On the Union*, Babai the Great, ed. A. Vaschalde, (CSCO 1915), p. 188.

7 *Bride of Light: Hymns on Mary From the Syriac Churches*, trans. Sebastian Brock, (St Ephrem Ecumenical Research Institute, Kottayam, India 1994), 9–11.

8 Concerning Mary's virginity, unlike the Latin tradition, the Church of the East's liturgical literature does not have any significant mention of Joseph, the husband of Mary. This might well be due to this church's wish to emphasize Mary's virginity before and after the birth of her Son. The Latin tradition, as influenced by St Augustine, would agree strongly with the Assyrian Church's position but without excluding Joseph from the familial context of Mary and Jesus, for it attributes to him the role of guardian over Mary and Jesus, as the Father's instrument to protect his Son during his early years on this earth. St Augustine states the following: 'Every good of marriage was fulfilled in the parents of Christ: offspring, loyalty, and the sacrament. We recognize the offspring in our Lord Jesus Christ himself; loyalty, in that no adultery occurred; and the indissolubility because of no divorce. Only conjugal intercourse did not take place.' (*De nupt. et concup.* XI, 13, in *PL* 44, 421, cited in Michael O'Carroll CSSp, *Theotokos* p. 234.

9 Brock, op. cit. 99. Here in this hymn Mary is described as a mystery through whose ear Life enters in to provide healing for the fallen world.

10 ibid. 116. This hymn is based on Luke 1.34.

11 ibid. 140.

12 ibid. 144.

13 By 'monophysite' we mean the strict sense of the word, i.e. Apollinarianism.

14 Also see Theodore of Mopsuestia, *Commentary on the Nicene Creed*, ed. Alphonse Mingana (Heffer & Son Limited, Cambridge 1932), Prefatory Note, 16–17.

15 ibid. VI, 63–4.

16 Cf. Gal. 4.4–5.

17 Theodore, op. cit. VI, 67–8.

18 *Catechetical Homilies*, 6:3, cited by Johannes Quasten, *Patrology*, vol. 3 (Christian Classics, Maryland 1983), p. 416.

19 Theodore, VI, 65.

20 J. L. McKenzie SJ, 'Annotation on the Christology of Theodore of Mopsuestia', *Theological Studies* 19, vol. 3 (1958), p. 364.

21 Francis A. Sullivan SJ, 'The Christology of Theodore of Mopsuestia', *Analecta Gregoriana*, (Rome 1949). In his conclusion, Sullivan maintains that 'Theodore of Mopsuestia, despite his orthodox intentions, was indeed what he has so long been called: the "Father of Nestorianism"', p. 288.

22 By *'theandric composite'* is meant that the union of natures results in that which is not the same as the Word of God, but in a new reality, called the Person of Christ.

23 McKenzie, pp. 364–6.

24 In reference to Philippians 2.8–11.

25 Theodore, VI, 66.

26 *Catechetical Homilies*, 8:1, as cited by J. Quasten in *Patrology*, vol. 3, pp. 415–16. See also Theodore, VIII, 87.

27 Theodore states 'that He is not God alone, and not man alone; but He is truly in the two by nature, both God and man.' (Raymond Tonneau, *Les homilies catéchetiques de Théodore de Mopsuestia*, Biblioteca Apostolica Vaticana, Vatican City 1949), p. 187, cited in McKenzie, p. 368). 'He is not God alone nor man alone, but He is truly both by nature, that is to say God and man.' Theodore, VIII, 82.

28 Theodore, VI, 66.

29 McKenzie, p. 366.

30 Ps. 18.9.

31 Theodore, V, 52.

32 Phil. 2.7.

33 Theodore, V, 53.

34 Acts 1.11.

35 Lit. 'did', or 'worked'. Mingana's text has 'manifested' here.

36 i.e. for the first time.

37 i.e. at his incarnation.

38 Theodore, VII, 81.

39 Moffett, p. 173.

40 ibid.

41 At Alexandria a mystic and allegorical tendency prevailed, at Antioch the practical and historical, and these tendencies showed themselves in different

methods of study, exegesis, presentation of doctrine and everyday piety.

42 Letters of the archdeacon Epiphanius to the patriarch Maximianus (Migne, *PG* lxxxiv. 826).

43 i.e. Paul of Samosata.

44 Matt. 1.16.

45 Matt. 1.1.

46 i.e. the Jews.

47 Rom. 9.5.

48 Nestorius, *The Bazaar of Heracleides*, G. R. Driver and Leonard Hodgson, eds. (Clarendon Press, Oxford 1925), p. 99.

49 Note the relation for Nestorius between birth and origination (or generation).

50 Christ is the subject of the verbs here. The 'both' does not refer to the natures. The clause in translation may read 'But one Christ both exists and is named'.

51 *Bazaar*, p. 296.

52 John 1.1.

53 *Bazaar*, p. 193.

54 Luigi I. Scipioni, *Nestorio e il concilio di Efeso* (Università Cattolica del Sacro Cuore, Milano 1974), p. 427.

55 *Anastos*, 122.

56 *Bazaar*, p. 241.

57 *Bazaar*, pp. 58, 81, 174, 182f, 191, 233, 240f.

(This paper was given at the ESBVM Oxford Congress
in August 2000)

29

Theotokos: Mary and the pattern of Fall and Redemption in the theology of Cyril of Alexandria

Frances Young

I. Fall and Redemption as the proper context for Mariology

As I read the Fathers, or indeed the principal sources of my own Methodist tradition, it seems more and more obvious that the overarching narrative that constitutes the core of the Christian tradition is one of fall and redemption. Exemplified in this paper in the work of Cyril of Alexandria, this could just as well have been illustrated from Fathers of both Western and Eastern traditions, Chalcedonian and non-Chalcedonian. All were shaped in their thinking by the typology of Adam and Christ, and integral to the development of that pattern was also the parallel and reversal found in Eve's sin and Mary's purity.

Irenaeus, of course, had pioneered this approach in the late second century by developing the hints in the epistles of St Paul and giving it a fundamentally biblical shape. In some patristic versions of fall and redemption there is undoubtedly a Neoplatonic flavour – I think of the Cappadocians and Augustine, and there may be an element of this in Cyril, too. But Cyril's focus on this pattern is found primarily in his biblical exegesis. This overarching story was a way of reading the Bible. Elsewhere this observation might open a discussion of the extent to which we all find ourselves adrift because of modernity's challenge to this 'grand narrative' about the human condition. But here I want to argue that this, and this alone, is the appropriate context for the honouring of Mary, the Mother of the Saviour.

So this paper, despite its title, points beyond Cyril. For a variety of reasons, as we shall see, Cyril provides a useful resource, but I hope through dialogue with him to reach a common ecumenical understanding of the faith within which Protestants, and women, may be enriched by taking Mary more seriously. The overarching theme of fall and redemption, made concrete in human lives both individual and corporate, is the setting in which such a convergence may be traced and, as already asserted, the right context for mariological doctrine.

The need to argue such a point perhaps requires some prior justification. My first contact with ESBVM was in the late 1970s when the Birmingham branch asked me to contribute to a series of seminars. Like most Protestants I had given little thought to Mary except at Christmas, and had grown up hearing the occasional Freudian remark about Marian devotion being natural for a celibate priesthood. My experience of worship was focused in word and music rather than image, and deeply imbued with the biblical and Reformation critique of idolatry. With such a background I responded to the challenge to look at patristic material on Mary for ESBVM. The paper I gave was, inevitably back then, in the historico-critical tradition, looking at issues of development: it need not detain us. What is important here, however, is my recollection of my own reactions. For this provides the justification sought.

It was then that I discovered what Quasten calls 'the most famous Marian sermon of antiquity',[1] the homily on *Theotokos* that Cyril is purported to have preached at Ephesus.[2] This homily hails Mary as the source of salvation. It is largely an incantation of honorific epithets – let me share some of it: Mary is

> the sacred treasury of all the world
> the unquenchable light
> the garland of virginity
> the mirror of orthodoxy
> the indestructible temple
> the container of the uncontainable
> mother and virgin.

Moreover, she is the one

> through whom the Trinity is sanctified
> through whom the Cross is called precious and is worshipped throughout
>   the world
> through whom heaven rejoices
> through whom angels and archangels are glad
> through whom demons are made to flee
> through whom the tempting devil falls from heaven
> through whom the fallen creature is received into the heavens
> through whom all creation, held back from idolmania, comes to
>   knowledge of truth
> through whom holy baptism came for those who believe
> through whom came the oil of gladness
> through whom churches were founded in all the world
> through whom the Gentiles came to repentance
> through whom the only-begotten Son of God gave light to those in
>   darkness and the shadow of death
> through whom the prophets prophesied

through whom the apostles preached salvation to the Gentiles
through whom the dead are raised
through whom kings rule through the Holy Trinity
The Virgin Mother – O marvel!

I confess that my reaction to this was not very favourable. Marginal notes to my notes show that I saw this as allowing Mary to usurp the roles of both Logos and Spirit. In the paper I suggested that 'the Nicene formula had had the effect of making Jesus Christ so transcendent, so much part of the unchangeable Godhead, that a new human mediator had become psychologically necessary. Mary becomes the instrument of salvation, the vehicle whereby God comes to Man.' I may not have articulated the thought then, but to my mind it seemed idolatrous, and had I come across Hilda Graef's remarks[3] linking the popular response to previous crowd enthusiasm for Diana of the Ephesians, I would have endorsed that view from a *Religionsgeschichtliche* standpoint.

I should add that I acknowledged at the time that it was possible to 'play it down and say – all that Cyril meant is that none of the saving events could have happened if Mary had not given birth to Jesus', even that 'if pressed I dare say that Cyril would have agreed that that was what he meant'. But my point here is that long-standing suspicions of mariological doctrines have to be met if she is to become a focus of ecumenical understanding. This is the justification of my argument in this paper. The authenticity of this homily is disputed. But whether genuine or not, Cyril fought for the title *Theotokos*. For Cyril, I shall argue, the urgency of this lay in its vital necessity to the overarching narrative that made sense of human life, corporate and individual, namely the story of fall and redemption.

But it is not just anxieties about the apotheosis of Mary that need to be met: many schooled by modernity find claims to perpetual virginity, or even the virginal conception, beyond belief; other post-Freudian thinkers regard the emphasis on virginity as deeply damaging to the human psyche; and feminists find oppressive the impossible ideal of virgin and mother. I hope that this study will indirectly bear on some of those issues, too. But it is time to move beyond the introduction.

II. The significance of Cyril of Alexandria

Some further introductory material is probably needed, however. My argument is to be exemplified by Cyril of Alexandria. Some may want to know why; others may need to know a little more about a figure they know little about. I will endeavour to sketch an answer to both questions with a few words about Cyril's significance.

Cyril was patriarch of Alexandria from 412 to 444. At the Council of Chalcedon certain of his letters were canonized: he is therefore significant for both Western and Eastern traditions. He is also the significant theologian for those churches of the East which eventually rejected Chalcedon. It would be hard to find a more important figure for ecumenical consideration – perhaps only Athanasius could challenge his position in this regard.

For our purposes, however, he is important as the defender of the title *Theotokos* for Mary. It is universally acknowledged that the Nestorian controversy was fundamentally christological, but because of the occasion which originated it, Mary figured large in the dispute. Nestorius, recently appointed Bishop of Constantinople, had reacted to a sermon in which Mary was celebrated as *Theotokos* (i.e. the one who gave birth to God) by saying that such a designation had to be balanced by the term *Anthropotokos* (i.e. the one who gave birth to man): in fact, strictly speaking, God did not take origin from a creaturely human being, and *Christotokos* would be better all round. Hearing of this Cyril leapt into action with letters all over the place, to the Bishop of Rome, to the monks, to Nestorius himself. The controversy had begun. It was the year 429.

One of the more notorious things Cyril did was to draw up twelve Anathemas, and the first provides another indication of how *Theotokos* was core to the debate:

> If anyone does not acknowledge Emmanuel to be truly God and therefore the holy Virgin to be *Theotokos* (for she gave birth according to the flesh to the Word of God made flesh), let him be anathema.

These Anathemas formed the basis of treatise and counter-treatise as the battle developed. But we need not follow through the details; suffice it to say that in 431 an Ecumenical Council was held in Ephesus which Cyril contrived to dominate, but it failed to achieve unity since large numbers of bishops from the Orient were excluded from the deliberations. A few years later, however, Cyril agreed a Formulary of Reunion with the leader of the Orientals. Even so, after his death, dispute broke out again, and this led to the Council of Chalcedon in 451, which amongst other things canonized some of his epistles as statements of christological orthodoxy, as we have already noted.

Cyril's position as evidenced in the literature associated with the controversy has been well worked over. What I propose to do is to look at some of his biblical exegesis, material which pre-dates the controversy. It is here, I believe, that we can see the fundamental patterns of thought which stimulated his responses during the subsequent doctrinal conflict.

III. Cyril's overall theological perspective

The text I wish to focus on is Cyril's massive treatment of the Pentateuch known under the title, *On Worship in Spirit and in Truth*.[4] Again introductory material is doubtless needed, but we are getting nearer to the heart of the matter. The work is a dialogue, Cyril responding to an interlocutor called Palladius. The opening question is this: how is the statement in Matthew's Gospel that not a jot or tittle of the law will pass away, to be reconciled with that in John's Gospel that the Father will be worshipped not in Jerusalem but in spirit and in truth? This becomes an occasion for working through the law to show that it is a *typos*, a foreshadowing of the proper shaping of devotion to God: the beauty of truth is hidden within it.

The law is a pedagogue – leading infants to maturity, using metaphors and types, delivering truth through stories and pictures which we need to understand spiritually. This general approach becomes specific as the story of Adam's fall provides the clue to one subsequent narrative after another. It is not just that in later books Cyril will turn Leviticus into spiritual sacrifices and passages on the priesthood into types of Christ and the Church, seeing the bloodless sacrifice of the eucharist and the roles of bishops and presbyters prefigured in the law, but also that the movement from fall into sin, through repentance, to renewal through God's grace becomes a universal paradigm, traced out in particular in one narrative after another and applied to 'us'; for each of us is an instance of the universal story of the human race. It is not hard to see that what happened to Adam, happens to each of us, Cyril suggests.[5]

Abraham becomes the first exemplar. Cyril wanders back and forth over the narrative a little so as to construct the fall and redemption pattern. He begins with the way Abraham was caught in Egypt by Pharaoh because of Sarah's beauty. The whole story is a paradigm of spiritual enslavement, the physical representing the spiritual, Pharaoh representing the father of sin, who treats us well as long as he can distract us with pleasure. Only God and the divine grace could rescue Abraham. Like Abraham those with Jacob went to Egypt because of famine and suffered God's anger through the yoke of slavery – they were tempted by worldly food when they should have been hungry for God's Word. All through the discussion is a profound intertextuality with allusions and quotations from across the prophets and the New Testament.

The point Cyril leads to is that we, like Abraham, are called to follow God, to leave behind everything in which we take pleasure, homeland, kindred – after all, Jesus spoke of leaving father and mother to follow him. Abraham leaves what is worldly to build an altar in the Promised Land. So we receive no grace as long as we are wedded to world; but we are called too, and if obedient will journey to the high country, to knowledge of God, and will stand before God as a living sacrifice well-pleasing to God. Yet the story of Sodom and Lot demonstrates the problem for us all of falling from this state of grace. With immense detail Cyril traces the symbols in the Lot story which point to the progress of the soul and its gradual ascent back to where it was.

Cyril now returns to Abraham in Egypt: he escapes rich to build an altar and call on the name of the Lord. Here is a changed life. Enigmatically, or in riddles, his journey shows the importance of changing wholeheartedly, of loving the desert, that is, the purity of mind and heart which humanity enjoyed in the beginning. And the same basic idea is to be traced in the story of the Exodus.

So now, from Abraham, Cyril moves to this second great exemplary story. Both descents into Egypt are seen as the result of a free choice, but the consequent enslavement is oppression from Pharaohs who stand for the devil. Human souls are oppressed and put to hard and useless labours, just like the Israelites. But God took pity on those harassed by Egyptian excesses, and he lavishes grace on those dragged into sin. For the Israelites he appointed Moses, and now writes the law on the heart through the mediator who brings free life to us. Enough said, I think, for you to see how Cyril works, and I need not proceed with all the detail. The thrust of his treatment is that God is the Liberator and Saviour, but we need to go out into the desert to prepare a holy feast for God apart from the Egyptians, removed from worldly darkness.

> We are all called to freedom through faith in Christ and ransomed from the tyranny of the devil, ... this being prefigured (*proanatupoumenou*) in those of old, especially Moses and Aaron, so that by reason of God's gracious arrangements (*oikonomikos*) you may discern that Emmanuel is in similar fashion, lawgiver, high priest and apostle.[6]

Cyril means us to understand, then, that not a jot or tittle of the law is taken away, but the whole matter concerns worship in spirit and in truth. God's intentions are graciously set out in Scripture if we only read the Scriptures aright. But that reading is shaped by a universal paradigm of fall and redemption. We have reached the end of Book 1, and Books 2 and 3 follow a similar pattern, developing Moses as type of Christ, the law as pedagogue, and so on. Let me share with you one passage to show how Cyril plays with the symbolic connections.

In Exodus 4, Moses expresses his fear that the Israelites will not believe him. He is told to throw his staff on the ground, and it became a snake. He ran from it. But God then told him to catch it by its tail, and it reverted to a stick. Cyril comments that God provides a 'wonder' to counter disbelief, but the form of the 'wonder' is a figure of salvation in Christ, of our transformation from the condition in which we were in Adam.

Pressed to explain by Palladius, he elucidates. The staff, or sceptre, is a symbol of kingship. Adam was to rule the earth, but through the snake was deprived of kingship and of his original glory, falling from paradise. Moses fled from the snake, and Cyril quotes from the Book of Wisdom 1.5: the Holy Spirit of wisdom will flee from deceit and back off from foolish thoughts. Holiness and impurity, light and darkness, righteousness and unrighteousness are incompatible, he comments. The fact that the staff fell from the hand of Moses would signify this: that in the beginning there was a sprig of paradise made in God's image, in the glory of kingship, in the hand of the Creator, but he fell to the ground and in the eyes of God was like a snake. But the result of Moses catching him by the tail was reversion into a sceptre, a sprig of paradise. When God was pleased to recapitulate everything in Christ, and create anew what he had made in the beginning, he sent to us the Only-Begotten, his right-hand, the Creator and Saviour of all, Cyril proclaims. He took our humanity, transformed our wildness, our sin, and through sanctification, brought us to royal honour and the tameness that leads to virtue.

Cyril expands the theme with many intertextual references, insisting on finding significance in the tail and the head. But his focus is on the transformation through grace of the whole human race, including the head, Adam. Christ died and rose so that he might rule over the living and the dead.

The temptation is to go on with this exploration, noting how the traditional types are woven into Cyril's treatment – thus the crossing of the Red Sea signifies baptism, Moses' arms raised in the battle with Amalek signifies the cross, and so on. But for the purposes of this paper I must proceed to link this with Cyril's understanding of the incarnation and of Mary *Theotokos*.

IV. Cyril and the importance of *Theotokos*

Two features of Cyril's theology in the conflict with Nestorius are worth recalling: The first is his appeal to *kenosis* – how to interpret Philippians 2.5–11 was much debated during the controversy, the Antiochenes emphasizing the phrase 'he *took* the form of a servant' as a way of avoiding the implication of change when 'he became flesh', Cyril focusing on the fact that it was the Word, the one in the form of God, who emptied himself. *Kenosis* became a keynote of his theology. The second noticeable feature of his argumentation is his refusal to assign different phrases of the Nicene creed to different subjects: it was the same one who was eternally begotten of the Father who came down from heaven and was crucified. Cyril is determined to hold on to a narrative of descent by keeping the unity of subject. My argument is that this is both vital for defending the title *Theotokos* for Mary, and for holding together in a single pattern the divine story of incarnation and the human story of fall and redemption.

That incarnation and redemption together lie at the root of Cyril's theology can be shown, I believe, by again turning back to his pre-controversy biblical exegesis. Already in his commentary on John's Gospel Cyril was speaking of the 'deep mystery' by which we are all in Christ:[7] 'the Word dwelt in all of us by dwelling in a single human being.' For

> the common element of humanity is summed up in his person, which is also why he was called the last Adam: he enriched our common nature with everything conducive to joy and glory just as the first Adam impoverished it with everything bringing corruption and gloom.

With a battery of scriptural quotations and allusions, Cyril shows that

> 'in Christ' that which is enslaved is liberated in a real sense and ascends to a mystical union with him who put on the form of a servant, while 'in us' it is liberated by an imitation of the union with the One through our kinship according to the flesh.

That was why Christ had to be made like his brethren in every respect (Heb. 2.16–17). Cyril speaks of him 'giving us himself as a gift, "so that we by his poverty might become rich"' (2 Cor. 8.9). The ascent of redeemed humanity depends upon the descent, the emptying, of the one who is full of grace and truth.

Later in the Commentary,[8] Cyril speaks of 'the blending of two elements into a single reality'.

> For his ineffable generation from God the Father raises him up, in that he is Word and Only-begotten, to the divine essence and to the glory that naturally accompanies it, while his self-emptying draws him down somewhat to our world.

He hastens to say that this self-emptying is not sufficient to overwhelm his divinity – indeed it was self-chosen out of his love for us: he humiliated himself voluntarily. It is only because he humbled himself willingly that we may become sons of God by grace. Though Cyril would have shied away from expressing it quite that way, we may almost speak of a chosen 'fall' to our level. He does dare to speak of him 'appearing to fall short of God's majesty by becoming a fully human being', while insisting that the Godhead is in no way diminished by this chosen path of humiliation. 'He brought himself down to that which he was not for our sake'.

These thoughts are perhaps most sharply expressed in the Commentary on Isaiah.[9] Cyril is sure that it is a property of human nature to have no trace of the heavenly graces of its own will or nature. Rather humanity was enriched from outside. So it was necessary

> that the only-begotten Word of God who brought himself down to the level of self-emptying, should not repudiate the low estate arising from that self-emptying, but should accept what is full by nature on account of the humanity, not for his sake but for ours, who lack every good thing.

I take that to mean that although full of the Spirit by nature, he had to empty himself in order to receive the Spirit for our sake. So, according to Cyril, he received the Spirit while being the supplier of the Spirit, and that receiving was proportionate to the self-emptying. In the beginning the Spirit was given to Adam; but he was careless and sank into sin. So the Spirit had no resting place among human beings, until the Word of God became man.

> Since he was not consumed by sin even though he became as we are, the Holy Spirit rested once again on human nature ... That grace was not bestowed upon him as a particular gift, in the way that the Spirit is said to have rested on the saints, but that it was the fullness of the Godhead which took up residence in his own flesh as if in his own temple ... the prophet makes clear when he says, 'the spirit of the fear of the Lord shall fill him' (Isa. 11.3).

Already in this commentary Cyril is insisting that it is the 'Lord of all' who was born of the Virgin when he 'made the limitations of humanity his own'.

The pattern of fall and redemption is mirrored in Christ's descent and ascent. Disobedience is reversed through obedience. Self-indulgence is reversed through self-humiliation. For Cyril this narrative movement is fundamental, and he will defend it through thick and thin against the apparently fragmenting analysis of a Nestorius. Our human destiny depends on the truth of the universal pattern whereby Christ redeems Adam, whereby God liberates from enslavement to the world, the flesh and the devil. Willing submission to God is the converse of that *hybris* which brought about the fall, and is supremely played out in the *kenosis* whereby the Word was made human that we might be made divine.

Now if humility is the key to our redemption, the receptivity of Mary as she becomes *Theotokos* is crucial. She is the one through whom God is formed within humanity. She is the 'type' of the Church, of the humanity which is God-receptive and therefore redeemable. Cyril would, of course, acknowledge that the Word pre-existed the birth of Christ from Mary – this birth was not, as he puts it, 'the beginning of his being'.[10] But if he is Emmanuel, God with us, then Mary must properly be called *Theotokos*. Mary is the vehicle of the new creation.

Of course, the Lord could have just created a body for himself, just as he did for Adam. But Cyril knows that that would easily encourage docetism. So in his work *Against Nestorius*[11] he comments thus:

> He therefore necessarily observed the laws of human nature, and since his aim was to assure everybody that he had truly become man, he took to himself the seed of Abraham (cf. Heb. 2.16) and with the blessed Virgin acting as a mediator to this end, partook of flesh and blood in the way we do (cf. Heb. 2.14). For this was the only way in which he could become 'God with us'.

He goes on to emphasize the fact that 'if he had not partaken of the same elements as we do, he would not have delivered human nature from the fault we incurred in Adam', and proceeds to rehearse the story of the fall once again. The Holy Virgin is blessed along with the fruit of her womb because 'in Christ we see human nature, as if experiencing a new beginning of the race, enjoying freedom of access to God'.

At the same time Cyril is adamant that it is 'God the Word who was with his Father before all ages' that we are talking about, claiming that he came 'to be with us according to the flesh'. 'Emmanuel, the second Adam, did not come forth for us from the earth like the first, but from heaven', he asserts, basing his point on Paul (cf. 1 Cor. 15.47). Nor did he simply descend on some human individual. Rather he 'recapitulated human birth in himself', having 'made his own the body which was from a woman, and having been born from her according to the flesh'. This is why Mary is *Theotokos*. He berates Nestorius: just because you are scared stiff that people will think 'the Word brought forth from God had the beginning of existence from earthly flesh', he charges, 'you destroy utterly the mystery of the economy of the flesh by saying the Holy Virgin should not be called *Theotokos* by us'.

I have argued, then, that Cyril's concern to defend the title *Theotokos* for the holy Virgin Mary is deeply founded on her role in the overarching story of fall and redemption. Whatever the popular influences that generated devotion to her as Queen of Heaven, there is a doctrinal logic specific to the whole ecology of the Christian faith, ecumenically shared by us all, which undergirds the core Marian dogmas. That she was the one providentially prepared to receive the divine Word, contain the Incontainable, and give birth to Christ is encapsulated in her purity and virginity. This makes her both unique and a 'type' or model for believers who seek to become 'Christophers' by denying themselves and submitting to the will of God. Thus the humble are lifted up and the hungry fed.

V. Confessions of a Protestant Woman

There are only certain circumstances in which I allow myself to mix the genre of scholarship with that of personal testimony. On this occasion, however, I find myself drawn to do so – not least so as to explain my willingness to be a Patron of this society despite my earlier apparently prejudicial statements; but also, I hope, in order to explore convergences and substantiate the doctrinal argument which I have built upon Cyril's theology. My own tradition, historically, fostered the giving of testimonies and the writing of obituaries which linked individual lives into the pattern of fall and redemption, of wandering away and being called back through God's amazing grace. In the spirit of that tradition. I intend to share three moments which have been for me profound experiences bringing alive the dramatic importance of Mary as type or symbol. Two of these moments are captured in poems, whose occasion will each be sketched but which otherwise will be left to speak for themselves.

The first moment must surely post-date that paper for the Birmingham branch of ESBVM, though not by much. In response to an invitation from our local convent, I went to share with neighbours in a carol service, taking my brain-damaged son with me. My hold on faith was tenuous, despite my outward persona as theologian. The severe disabilities of my first-born had been the last straw – the camel often staggered under the weight of doubt and despair. Mostly my soul wandered in a Godless wilderness.

   During the service I was deeply aware of two things: the statue of Mary which dominated the chapel, something I was not used to, and Arthur, in his wheelchair and all too evident since it is impossible to keep him quiet. As I walked the short distance home, I was given this poem:

> Mary, my child's lovely.
> Is yours lovely too?
> Little hands, little feet.
> Curly hair, smiles sweet.

Mary, my child's broken.
Is yours broken too?
Crushed by affliction,
Hurt by rejection,
Disfigured, stricken,
Silent submission.

Mary, my heart's bursting
Is yours bursting too?
Bursting with labour, travail and pain.
Bursting with agony, ecstasy, gain.
Bursting with sympathy, anger, compassion.
Bursting with praising Love's transfiguration.

Mary, my heart's joyful
Is yours joyful too?

The second experience I would mention is not captured in a poem, but has been described in a couple of articles published in several places, including an ESBVM pamphlet. For that reason I shall be brief. The occasion was Easter 1991, the Twentieth Anniversary pilgrimage to Lourdes of 'Faith and Light', the sister organization to the L'Arche communities, founded by Jean Vanier. I accepted Jean's invitation with many misgivings – I feared Lourdes would raise all my Liberal Protestant hackles. But I found that the place was about purification, not so much miraculous cures as deeper levels of healing and acceptance. Traffic gave way to wheelchairs, and the strong received ministry from the weak. In that context I found myself travelling through the Passion with Mary, and preaching at her feet on Easter morning at the Anglican eucharist in the Upper Basilica. That Easter it became profoundly important to me that she was the vehicle of purification and blessing through her Son.

The third moment I would share with you probably pre-dated this, but it matters not precisely when it happened. As a Methodist minister I was in the vestry preparing to lead midnight communion one Christmas Eve. I admit that my rational self had remained perplexed about miracles, including the virginal conception. As a teacher I was used to helping students weigh up arguments on all sides of a question, and I suppose I remained agnostic about the historical fact and ambivalent about the doctrinal consequences: after all if the Virgin Birth, as it is popularly referred to, implied a hybrid like a centaur, half human half divine, then it was most certainly inconsistent with the Chalcedonian Definition and nearer to ancient pagan myths than a robust doctrine of the incarnation.

But on that night a whole range of things picked up from many sources seemed to explode into a fresh vision and I knew that my mind and heart were convinced. This is captured in a poem which I entitled 'Breakthrough':

The womb of the earth is as good as dead
like the barren womb of Sarah
and the barren womb of Hannah
and Elizabeth's aged womb.
Each one stretched forth her hand
to touch the hem of his garment
like the one with the flow of blood;
and each one laughed or sang
at birth in the realm of death:
'The Lord kills and brings to life
He brings low, he also exalts.'

The womb of the earth is flowing with blood;
the womb of the earth is as good as dead;
the earth is on the waiting-list
for a hysterectomy.
No garment to touch,
no laugh, no song,
as the cruel raping goes on
and the womb of the earth is ripped out
and death mocks the source of life:
'The Lord makes poor, the Lord makes rich,
He brings low, he also exalts.'

The womb of the virgin conceives life.
Instead of an ancient barren womb,
instead of the bleeding womb of the earth,
he chooses a spring of freshness and youth,
a girl who's known no blood.
Instead of birth from the bowels of death,
a resurrection out of death,
instead of renewing, instead of healing,
God starts afresh
with a germ of new vitality,
a young untouched creation,
as the Spirit overshadows
the womb of the virgin earth:
'He who is mighty has done great things
and holy is his name.'

Now the womb of the heart receives the Spirit,
the chaste womb of the mind
laughs,
and then breaks forth in song:
'Glory to God in the highest,
Peace on earth, goodwill to men.'

Conclusion

Maybe I should leave it there, and let what I have shared speak for itself. Yet I find it hard not to conclude by briefly making a few things explicit.

First, I believe my testimony potentially points to the same key typological dynamics as we found in Cyril, and justifies the claim that mariology belongs to the overarching narrative of fall and redemption which constitutes the common Christian understanding of human existence.

Secondly, it emphasizes the same need for purity and humble receptivity if by grace the new creation is to be effected. It was years after that last poem was written that I came across the fascinating material in Gregory of Nyssa which likens the soul to Mary, urging the kind of receptivity that can give birth to Christ in our lives. Let me conclude by quoting from an article by Verna Harrison.[12] This, I believe, may provide an antidote to post-Freudian and feminist suspicions.

Notice that an essential feature of Mary's virginity and also that of the Christian soul is receptivity to God. Her purity and integrity open a place within her where God can enter, where Christ can be formed, and from which he can come forth ... [Mary's] receptivity is intrinsic to her creaturehood; like all human persons, as Gregory understands them, she lives by participation in God and is not the source of her own life ... For Gregory the virginal soul, like Mary, receives the entrance of God and brings forth Christ, though spiritually, not physically.

Notes

1 J. Quasten, *Patrology*, vol. 3, p. 131.
2 Homily 4, text in Migne, *PG* 77.
3 Hilda Graef, *Mary, A History of Doctrine and Devotion* (Sheed & Ward, London 1963–1965), p. 109.
4 Text in Migne, *PG* 68.
5 *PG* 68. 148.
6 *PG* 68. 200.
7 Quotations in the ET by Norman Russell, *Cyril of Alexandria* (Routledge, 2000), pp. 106ff.
8 Russell, pp. 125ff.

9 Russell, pp. 83ff.
10 *Explanation of the Twelve Anathemas 7*, Russell, p. 179.
11 Russell, pp. 131ff.
12 Verna Harrison, 'Gender, Generation and Virginity in Cappadocian Theology' in *JTS* NS 47 (1996), pp. 36–68.

(This paper was given at the ESBVM Oxford Congress
in August 2000)

30

'The Earthly Heaven': The Mother of God in the Teaching of St John of Damascus

Kallistos Ware

> The title *Theotokos* safeguards the entire mystery of the divine Economy.
>
> *St John of Damascus*

Doctor Marianus, the title assigned in the West to Duns Scotus, may also be fittingly applied within the Greek Patristic tradition to St John of Damascus (*c.* 675 – *c.* 749).[1] His three sermons on the Dormition of the Mother of God remain until today the most authoritative single account of the Orthodox understanding of the Holy Virgin.[2] Simple yet powerful in their style, they are distinguished not only by the richness of their imagery but equally by their warm and loving tenderness towards the person of Mary. 'What can be more sweet than the Mother of my God!' John exclaims. 'She has taken captive my intellect, she has made my tongue a prisoner, her image is before me waking or sleeping.'[3] 'To you we dedicate intellect, soul and body, the whole of ourselves', he says to the Theotokos. '... Loving Mistress (*despoina*), Mother of our loving Master, direct and guide our lives wherever you will. Subdue the onslaughts of our shameful passions, still the tempest, guide us to the safe harbour of the divine will, and count us worthy of the blessedness to come.'[4]

Little is known for certain about the life of St John of Damascus. According to the generally accepted account, he was born in Damascus, within a wealthy family of Christian Arabs, the Mansūr. His father held the office of 'logothete', that is to say, the chief representative of the Christian community before the Caliph, and in due course John succeeded to his father's position. In later life he abandoned his career in the civil service, and became a monk in the Lavra of St Sabas outside Jerusalem in the Judaean wilderness; here he was ordained priest. His three sermons on the Dormition of the Mother of God were delivered at the vigil of the Feast during the night of 14–15 August, most probably at Gethsemane, when he was already in his old age.[5]

John's three sermons are not an abstract treatise on mariology but homilies delivered to an actual congregation at a particular liturgical service. They are carefully planned but not systematic. Perhaps, then, the best way of approaching John's teaching on the Holy Virgin is to consider the different images and titles that he applies to her. Let us first survey fourteen images taken from the Old Testament, and then discuss eight titles or phrases of more general scope, defining Mary's role from a theological standpoint. We shall end by looking at his understanding of the bodily assumption.

Faithful to the patristic principle that the whole of Scripture forms a single, undivided unity, St John sees Mary foreshadowed throughout the Old Testament. Here, as almost always in his writing, he makes no attempt to innovate, but draws upon the many types and images already familiar in earlier authors.

1. Mary is 'the noetic *Eden*, more sacred and more divine than the Eden of old'. In the first Eden dwelt Adam, who was 'formed from the earth'; but in Mary there dwelt the second Adam who 'came from heaven' (1 Cor. 15.47).[6] She is the 'logical *paradise*' in which the tree of life is planted (Gen. 2.9).[7]

2. Mary is *Noah's ark* (Gen. 6.14), for she kept safe within her womb 'the seed of the second world ... Christ the world's salvation'.[8]

3. Mary is the *tent of Abraham*: just as Abraham and Sarah prepared food within their tent at the oak of Mamre for the three angelic visitors (Gen. 18.6), so the human nature of Christ was made ready within the 'tent' of the Virgin's womb.[9]

4. Mary is the *ladder of Jacob* (Gen. 28.12): 'Just as Jacob saw heaven united to the earth by the two extremities of the ladder and the angels ascending and descending upon it', so Mary has brought together that which was divided, 'becoming through her mediation the ladder whereby God has descended to us'.[10]

5. Mary is *Bethel*, 'the house of God' (Gen. 28.18–19): just as Jacob anointed with oil the pillar that he set up in Bethel, so within Mary – the 'new Bethel', the true house of God – the human nature of Christ is anointed with the unction of his divinity.[11]

6. Mary is the *burning bush* (Exod. 3.2), from whom is born 'the flame of the Godhead',[12] 'the consuming fire of the divinity' (Deut. 4.24; Heb. 12.29).[13]

7. Mary is 'Aaron's staff that budded' (Heb. 9.4: cf. Num. 17.8), who has borne as flower Christ the Saviour.[14]

8. Mary is prefigured likewise by the *tabernacle* and its furnishings: she is the *ark of the covenant*, the *tablets of the law* inscribed by God's hand, the *golden jar* that contained 'the most sweet and heavenly manna', the *candlestick* from which there shines 'the infinite light that no one can approach', the *table of the shewbread* (Exod. 16.33; 25.10, 23, 31;

32.15–16; Heb. 9.2, 4; 1 Tim. 6.16).[15]

9. Mary is the *fleece* upon which the heavenly rain has descended, as David affirms in the Psalms (Ps. 71 [72].6. LXX).[16]

10. Mary is the *City of God*, of which 'glorious things are spoken' (Ps. 86 [87]. 3);[17] she is *Jerusalem*.[18] Hence it was fitting that she, as the spiritual Jerusalem, should have died in the earthly Jerusalem before being translated to the Jerusalem on high.

11. Mary is the *closed gate* facing towards the east, seen by Ezekiel, through which none may pass except the Prince, the Lord God of Israel (Ezek. 44.1–3).[19]

12. Mary is the *mountain* seen by Daniel, from which was taken the rock not cut by human hand (Dan. 2.34, 45), Christ the Cornerstone (Isa. 28.16; Ps. 117 [118].22; Matt. 21.42; Acts 4.11; 1 Pet. 2.7).[20]

13. Mary is the *fiery furnace*, in which the burning flame was mingled with refreshing dew (The Song of the Three Children, verses 26–27; cf. Dan. 3.49–50. LXX).[21]

14. Mary is 'the *royal throne*, beside which stood the angels, gazing at their own Master and Creator who was seated on it' (probably a reference to Daniel's vision of the Ancient of Days: Dan. 7.9–10; but perhaps John is also thinking of Isa. 6.1 and Ezek. 1.26).[22]

It is noteworthy that all these Marian types and figures taken from the Old Testament have a christological significance. Each image points, not towards Mary in isolation, but towards the mystery of the incarnation. Nowhere is the Mother glorified apart from her Son. Here the approach of St John of Damascus clearly confirms the aim of the Ecumenical Society of the Blessed Virgin Mary, which is to understand and proclaim 'the place of the Blessed Virgin in the Church, *under Christ*'. John insists precisely upon this principle '... under Christ'. If we ask Mary to come and visit us, he says, then the whole purpose of our prayer is that 'she should bring with her Christ her Son, causing him to dwell in our hearts'.[23] Mary's role is to bring Christ to us, to bring us to Christ. Mariology is nothing else than a branch of christology.

Turning now from Old Testament types and figures to doctrinal titles, we find that there are eight words or phrases upon which John lays particular emphasis, and which sum up the master themes in his Marian theology.

First, Mary is the *New Eve*, an appellation which goes back to the second-century writers Justin Martyr and St Irenaeus of Lyons. Here John repeats the ideas which had long been customary among the Greek and Latin Fathers. Mary the second Eve 'corrects' and sets aright the error of the first Eve. Where Eve is disobedient, Mary is obedient. Where Eve is unguarded and inconsiderate, listening all too readily to the deceitful words of the serpent, Mary is watchful and prudent, only accepting the Archangel's message after she has carefully questioned him.[24] As Fr Pierre Voulet expresses it, 'Eve yielded to appearances, but Mary for her part consents to mystery.'[25] Eve brings the 'sleep of death' upon humankind, but Mary is 'initiator of life for the whole race'.[26] So John puts these words in the mouth of Adam and Eve:

> Blessed are you, daughter, for you have released us from the penalty of our transgression. You inherited from us a body that was subject to corruption, but for our sake you have conceived within your womb the garment of incorruption ... You have restored to us our ancient dwelling-place. We closed paradise, but you have opened once more the way of access to the tree of life. Through us blessings were changed into sorrows, but through you from these sorrows there have come to us yet greater blessings.[27]

'... yet greater blessings': through Christ's incarnation humankind is not simply restored to its original state of unfallen innocence, but it is raised to a new and more exalted level. The latter state is higher and more glorious than the former.

Second, Mary is *Bride* (*nymphē*). As Mother of God's Son, she is 'the bride whom the Father betrothed',[28] 'the bridal chamber of the divine incarnation of the Logos'.[29] Here John's language recalls the refrain, hard to translate, of that most celebrated among all the liturgical poems in Mary's honour, the Akathistos Hymn: *Chaire, Nymphē anymphevte*, 'Hail, Bride without bridegroom' (or 'Rejoice, unwedded Bride').[30]

Third, Mary is *Sovereign* over all the world. She is 'the queen mother',[31] 'the queen, the lady, the mistress';[32] 'The Son has subjected the whole creation to his Mother';[33] she is 'co-ruler' with her Son.[34] She 'blesses the world and sanctifies all things'.[35] Here then, the Holy Virgin is assigned a cosmic role; yet it is significant that, as the words quoted above indicate, this cosmic role is set within a christological context. It is Christ who is king of creation, but he has chosen to share this kingly role with his Mother. Her sovereignty is a direct consequence of the closeness and unity that exists between Mother and Son; it is only because Christ is king that Mary is queen. On this community and parallelism between Son and Mother we shall have more to say shortly. Her sovereignty, we may add, is shown above all in her power of intercession.

Fourth – and we come here to a more problematic title – Mary is *Reconciler* and *Mediatrix*. Developing the notion of the Mother of God as Jacob's ladder, John writes: 'You have become the intermediary and ladder whereby God comes down to us'.[36] As intermediary she is 'the mediatrix of all blessings for us'; here John uses the word *promnēstria*, meaning 'matchmaker', one who arranges a marriage.[37] Accordingly, she is 'forgiveness for those who sin';[38] and John is not afraid to say to her, 'Grant us salvation'.[39] The writer who – along with St John of Damascus – is *par excellence* the leading Marian theologian in the Greek East, St Nicolas Cabasilas (*c.* 1322 – *c.* 1391), uses yet more startling language: Mary, he says, is 'the purificatory sacrifice' offered on behalf of 'the whole human race'.[40]

Western readers, especially Protestants, will certainly find this kind of language excessive and disquieting. Does it not undermine the uniqueness of Christ as the sole Redeemer and Saviour, 'the one mediator between God and humankind' (1 Tim. 2.5)? In fairness to John and Nicolas, three points should be kept in mind:

1. They were not writing in the context of sixteenth-century Reformation controversies.
2. Their language reflects the worshipping practice of the Christian East, which in its liturgical prayers regularly uses such phrases as 'Most Holy Mother of God, save us' or 'You are the salvation of the Christian people'.
3. John and Nicolas, and the Orthodox Church in general, never envisage that the notions of the Blessed Virgin Mary as 'co-redemptrix' or 'mediatrix of all graces' should be defined as dogmas.

The next three of the eight titles applied by John to the Holy Virgin have a particular importance from the doctrinal point of view.

In the fifth place, John regards her as *Ever-Virgin* (*aeiparthenos*). Her virginity is threefold: 'A virgin before giving birth, she remains a virgin in giving birth and after giving birth.'[41] From another point of view her virginity is twofold: 'She kept safe the ship of a double virginity; for she watched over the virginity of her soul no less than over that of her body, and this is why her bodily virginity was preserved.'[42] In other words, Mary's virginity is not exclusively or even primarily a physical fact. Of course it includes the virginity of her body, but it is above all an inner and spiritual disposition; it signifies wholeness and integrity – in a word, an all-embracing sanctity.

This brings us to the sixth of John's titles: Mary is *All-holy*. This is a point on which he lays great emphasis. She is 'all-holy' (*panagia*),[43] 'pure' (*agnē*),[44] 'spotless' or 'immaculate' (*achrantos*),[45] 'blameless' (*amemptos*),[46] 'without blemish' (*amōmos*),[47] 'altogether without blemish' (*panamōmos*).[48] 'The immaculate Virgin had no converse with earthly passions', John states;[49] 'after God, she is truly holy above all others'.[50] '... after God': here again John confirms the basic principle of the Ecumenical Society of the Blessed Virgin Mary, that she is to be honoured always '*under Christ*'.

John believes that Mary underwent a special purification and hallowing at the moment of the annunciation, when 'the sanctifying power of the Spirit overshadowed, cleansed and consecrated her'.[51] But this does not signify that, in John's view, she was sinful prior to the annunciation; on the contrary, he clearly considers that she was *always* pure and guiltless. Moreover, he also states clearly that she was predestined from all eternity to be the Mother of God incarnate: 'She was chosen from ancient generations, through the preordained counsel and good pleasure of God the Father. ... The Father forechose her, the prophets through the Holy Spirit proclaimed her in advance';[52] 'Rejoice, preordained Mother of God; rejoice, for you were forechosen by God's counsel before the ages.'[53]

In view of such statements, it is not surprising that many Roman Catholic authors should regard John as anticipating the dogma of the immaculate conception. It would, however, be anachronistic to read back into John's words the technical precision of the doctrine as defined by Pope Pius IX in 1854. John is certainly convinced that the Holy Virgin was free from all *actual* sin, but he nowhere speaks explicitly of any exemption from the 'stain' of *original* sin. He does, however, specify that she bore Christ without enduring the pangs of childbirth due to the fall (Gen. 3.16), which suggests that she was indeed exempt from the effects of the fall.[54] But we must in any case allow for the fact that John's understanding of the fall and of original sin is not the same as that upheld by St Augustine and normally accepted in the Latin West.[55]

It is interesting that Nicolas Cabasilas, writing in the fourteenth century, is more specific than John had been six hundred years earlier, and definitely rejects the doctrine of the immaculate conception. 'The Virgin altogether without blemish', he writes, '... was born, not with a heavenly body, but with a body taken from the earth, in the same way as all other human beings'; she is sprung 'from this fallen human race'.[56] 'She did not come into being before all other human persons,' Nicolas continues, 'nor did she receive a nature free from all evil; equally she did not come into being after the New Man [Christ] and the power which humankind receives from him.'[57] This clearly implies that – contrary to the 1854 Roman Catholic dogma – Mary, although sinless as regards actual sin, was born under the Old Covenant and subject to the consequences of the fall. Whether Nicolas was aware of the thirteenth-century disagreement between Duns Scotus (who upheld the doctrine of the immaculate conception) and Thomas Aquinas (who denied it), we cannot say with certainty. But Nicolas was in fact well informed about Latin theology, and may indeed be making an oblique but deliberate comment on the teaching upheld by Scotus and the Franciscans.[58]

The seventh title applied by John to the Blessed Virgin is the most important of all from the doctrinal point of view: Mary is *Theotokos*,

'Godbirthgiver', Mother of God. It is this title *Theotokos*, John insists, that 'safeguards the entire mystery of the divine Economy'.[59] 'Since he who was born from her is truly God,' John states, 'she who gave birth to the true God that took flesh from her is the true *Theotokos*.'[60] Here John follows exactly the teaching of St Cyril of Alexandria, champion of the title *Theotokos* at the Council of Ephesus (431). Mary, that is to say, is not mother of a man who is united to the divine Logos; for that would be to posit in the incarnate Christ two distinct subjects of attribution, the Logos and 'the man'. There is on the contrary only one subject; Mary is mother of a single, undivided person, the eternal Son of God who has taken up into himself the fullness of our human nature. As Cyril puts it, 'The Holy Virgin is *Theotokos*, for she bore according to the flesh God the Word made flesh.'[61]

In this way, as John rightly appreciates, the designation *Theotokos* is not an optional title of devotion but an indispensable guarantee of the unity of Christ's person. Only God can save; a prophet or a holy person cannot be the Saviour of the world. If, then, it is not God himself who enters human life as our Redeemer – if it is not God himself, the second person of the Trinity, who is born from a human mother – then the whole scheme of our salvation breaks down. That is why the word *Theotokos* safeguards the entire mystery of God's saving Economy.

There is an eighth and final title used by John, which may be seen as summing up all that has been said so far: Mary is the *Earthly Heaven* (*epigeios ouranos*). This phrase, applied by John's contemporary St Germanos, Patriarch of Constantinople (d. *c.* 730), to the church during the celebration of the Divine Liturgy,[62] is employed by John to describe the Blessed Virgin. The *Theotokos*, by giving birth to God incarnate, has united heaven and earth, making heaven earthly and earth heavenly. Containing God within her womb, she is indeed 'heaven on earth':

> Without leaving the Father's bosom, the Logos descended into a virgin womb, being conceived and taking flesh; and following the path of voluntary suffering he underwent death. In his body born from the earth, through corruption he gained incorruption, and so he returned once more to the Father. And now, taking her who is his Mother according to the flesh, he has raised her up to his Father; he has exalted into the heavenly realm her who became truly an earthly heaven.[63]

Here we may recall what was said earlier about the Holy Virgin, that she is Jacob's ladder and mediatrix. Through her God has come down to earth, and humankind has been granted a way of ascent from earth to heaven; thus within herself she unites heaven and earth.

Interwoven within the complex tapestry of John's three homilies there are many other Marian threads, but it is not possible for me on this occasion to mention them all. At some other time it will be good to explore the special connection that he establishes between the Spirit and the Mother of God – 'the sacred Dove consecrated by the divine Spirit', as he calls her[64] – and also the way in which he sees Mary as a 'liturgist' of the Holy Trinity.[65] For the moment let us limit ourselves to just one further point: John's teaching on the bodily assumption of the Holy Virgin,[66] a theme implicit in the images of Mary as earthly heaven and ladder, which we have just been discussing. What, then, does he have to say about our Lady's death and resurrection?

First of all, John takes the fact of the bodily assumption as a matter beyond dispute; in this context Fr Antoine Wenger rightly speaks of John's 'certitude'.[67] John does not regard the bodily assumption as something that he has to prove, but he accepts it without question as part of the accepted tradition of the Church: 'From ancient times it has been transmitted to us from father to son'.[68] At no point does he express any doubts or hesitations because of the lack of explicit evidence in the New Testament or in the first four centuries of the Christian era.[69]

Yet, while entirely definite about the fact of the bodily assumption, John does not insist that the details in the various apocryphal narratives must all be taken literally. When recounting the events of Mary's death, he includes qualifying phrases such as 'so it seems to me' or 'so I would suppose'.[70] When he comes to the story about the Jew who tried to upset the bier on which Mary's body rested, and whose hands were then cut off by an angel, he is careful to introduce this merely as 'an account that circulates on the lips of many', 'they say ...', without adding that he himself gives credence to the story.[71] What interests him is not such (to us, at any rate) unedifying embroideries to the tale, but rather the basic theology of the Holy Virgin's resurrection.

So far as the facts go, John asserts with confidence simply that Mary underwent a genuine physical death, as did her Son; she was laid in the tomb, but after this on the third day her body was reunited with her soul and taken up by Christ into heaven.[72] In this way, as in the case of her Son, her body did not see corruption.[73] John is here more explicit than is the definition of the bodily assumption made by Pope Pius XII in 1950, which merely states that Mary was taken up bodily into heaven *expleto terrestris vitae cursu*, 'on the completion of the course of her earthly life', without specifying whether she underwent physical death or not. For John her experience of physical death is theologically important, for it shows that she is not a goddess but truly a human being: 'We do not call her a goddess – away with all such mythical drivel! – for we proclaim her death; but we acknowledge her as Mother of God incarnate.'[74]

When discussing the bodily assumption, John uses in particular the word *edei*, meaning literally 'it was needful'.[75] This could justifiably be translated 'it was necessary', but perhaps such a rendering involves a certain distortion. John is not speaking in terms of logical entailment, nor would he have considered that God is subject to our human notions of necessity. If Christ took up his Mother's body into heaven, it was because he freely chose to do so. It is better, then, to translate *edei* as 'it was right'. Yet to say merely 'it was appropriate' is altogether too weak. As Fr Martin Jugie urges, John is speaking here of a 'convenance' so powerful as to constitute almost an 'exigence'.[76] The word *edei* expresses the cohesion, the all-embracing unity, of the divine plan of salvation.

In explaining this 'exigence', John emphasizes four points in particular. First, Mary's bodily assumption follows from her *total purity*. John finds it strange, indeed almost incredible, that she who was sinless should be subject to mortality: 'And how could she who is immaculate taste of death?'[77] The paradox, however, is mitigated by the fact that, even though she did undergo physical death, yet this involved no bodily corruption: 'It was right (*edei*) that she who, when giving birth, preserved her virginity unimpaired should have her body preserved free from corruption also after death'.[78]

In the second place, the assumption of the Virgin's body into heaven follows from her *divine maternity*. As Mother of the Saviour she is the source of life to the whole human race: 'How then could she who caused the true life to spring up for all, be herself subject to the power of death?' Even though as a mortal she undergoes physical death, yet by virtue of her assumption this is then transformed into a 'lifegiving death'.[79]

This brings us to a third, more comprehensive point. Mary's bodily assumption follows from the fact that there should and can be *no separation* between the risen and ascended Son and her who gave him human birth. Christ took his human nature from her; and so it is right that the body in which he dwelt, and which formed his own body, should be raised up so as to be with him in heaven:

> Just as the holy and pure body, which the Divine Word took from her and united hypostatically with himself, was raised from the tomb on the third day, so it was right (*edei*) that she too should be snatched from the tomb and that the Mother should be united to the Son. Just as he came down to her, so it was right that she his beloved should be carried up ... to heaven itself.[80]

Between the lives of Christ and Mary there is in this manner a close parallel, a 'configuration', a constant correspondence: 'There is nothing between Mother and Son.'[81] In this context, the Damascene applies to Mary the words of Christ, 'Where I am, there will my servant be' (John 12.26).[82] Christ underwent genuine physical death; so also did Mary. Christ's body did not see corruption; nor did Mary's. Christ was raised on the third day; so also was Mary. Mary's life is modelled on Christ's; her bodily assumption is a consequence and corollary of his resurrection and ascension.[83]

Fourthly and finally, Christ's action in raising his Mother from the dead is to be seen above all as an expression of his *love*. The same 'tender compassion' which led the Logos to become incarnate leads him also to take up his Mother in his loving embrace after her death.[84] 'Into your hands, my Child, I commend my spirit', says the Mother to her Son as she dies; and her Son replies, 'Come, my blessed Mother, into my rest . . . Arise, come, my beloved, beautiful among women.'[85] The beauty of the Mother of God, we may note in passing, is another master-theme in John's Marian theology: 'She shines more brightly than the sun in the beauty of virginity.'[86]

There is, however, one theme which is not developed in John's three homilies on the Dormition as fully as we might have expected. Although eschatological imagery is by no means altogether absent from them, John does not lay any particular emphasis upon the way in which the assumption of the Mother of God is to be seen as an anticipation of our own resurrection at the Last Day.[87] Raised up into heaven, placed beyond death and judgement, dwelling already with both soul and body in the fullness of divine glory, she is our forerunner, the expression of our future hope. The bodily transfiguration which in her case is even now an accomplished fact, is something in which, by God's mercy, all of us are also called to share. In this way Mary shows us what it is to be, in the phrase of St Gregory of Nazianzus (*c.* 329 – *c.* 389), *zōon theoumenon*, 'a living creature deified'.[88] But if John does not draw especial attention to this aspect of the bodily assumption, there is nothing in his treatment that excludes it.

Let us in conclusion note two qualities which continually characterize St John Damascene's approach to the Blessed Virgin Mary: joy and wonder. She is 'the cause of joy',[89] 'to the angels and to all the supranatural powers ineffable gladness, to the patriarchs endless exultation, to the righteous unspeakable joy, to the prophets ceaseless rejoicing'.[90] 'Rejoice, inexhaustible ocean of joy; rejoice, our only remedy in grief.'[91] To express his astonishment in Mary's presence, John uses in particular the words 'wonder' or 'marvel' (*thauma*), 'mystery' (*mysterion*) and 'paradox' (*paradoxon*). 'O marvels truly divine! O mysteries surpassing nature and thought!' he exclaims.[92] 'What could be more paradoxical than this!' he says of the assumption. 'What could be more blessed? I grow dizzy with fear, I am filled with awe by my own words.'[93]

Let us make St John's joy and wonder our own.

Notes

1 Until recently we have lacked a satisfactory account of John of Damascus in the English language; but we now look forward eagerly to the new book by Professor Andrew Louth, *St John Damascene: Tradition and Originality in Byzantine Theology*, due to be published later in the present year (2002) by the Clarendon Press, Oxford. On John's Marian teaching, see C. Chevalier, *La Mariologie de saint Jean Damascène*, Orientalia Christiana Analecta 109 (Rome 1936); this is corrected and supplemented by V. Grumel in *Échos d'Orient* 36 (1937), pp. 318–46. For a brief treatment, see Hilda Graef, *Mary: A History of Doctrine and Devotion*, vol. 1 (London/New York 1963), pp. 153–9.

2 There is a critical edition of the Greek text by Bonifatius Kotter, *Die Schriften des Johannes von Damaskos*, vol. 5, Patristische Texte und Studien 29 (Berlin/New York 1988), pp. 461–555; for an earlier edition of the Greek text, with a French translation and a helpful introduction and notes, see Pierre Voulet, *S. Jean Damascène: Homélies sur la Nativité et la Dormition*, Sources Chrétienes 80 (Paris 1961). For an English translation of the second and third homilies on the Dormition, see Brian E. Daley (tr.), *On the Dormition of Mary: Early Patristic Homilies* (St Vladimir's Seminary Press, New York 1998), pp. 203–40. Also attributed to John of Damascus is a homily on the Nativity of the Mother of God, which Kotter includes in his edition (op. cit., pp. 147–82), but which he considers spurious. I am not altogether convinced by his arguments, but because of his doubts I refer to this homily only in my footnotes. I do not cite the abundant hymnographic material relating to Mary which is ascribed to John in the Greek service books, for here again there are often doubts about the authorship.

3 *Dorm.* [= Homily on the Dormition] 3:1.

4 *Dorm.* 1:14.

5 *Dorm.* 2:1.

6 *Dorm.* 1:8.

7 *Dorm.* 2:2.

8 *Dorm.* 1:8.

9 ibid.

10 *Dorm.* 1:8; cf. *Dorm.* 2:8; 3:2; also John of Damascus (?), *Nat.* [Homily on the Nativity] 3.

11 *Dorm.* 3:4.

12 *Dorm.* 1:8; cf. *Nat.* 10.

13 *Dorm.* 2:7.

14 *Dorm.* 1:8.

15 *Dorm.* 1:8; cf. *Dorm.* 1:12; 2:2, 12 and 16; 3:2; *Nat.* 6.

16 *Dorm.* 1:9; cf. *Nat.* 11. John may also have in mind the fleece of Gideon (Judg. 6.36–40).

17 *Dorm.* 1:1; 2:3; 3:2; cf. *Nat.* 9. On the eschatological significance of the symbolism here, see Pierre Voulet, introduction to Sources Chrétiennes 80, pp. 33–6.

18 *Dorm.* 1:9, 3:2.

19 *Dorm.* 1:9, 3:2; cf. *Nat.* 3, 4.

20 *Dorm.* 1:9; cf. 3:2 and 4; also 1:12, citing Ps. 67 [68]. 15–16; compare also *Nat.* 6, where the mountain is identified with Sinai.
21 *Dorm.* 1:8.
22 ibid.
23 *Dorm.* 2:19.
24 *Dorm.* 1:7. Compare *Dorm.* 3:2; also *Nat.* 1: 'Through her [Mary] the sorrow of Eve our first mother has been changed into joy'; *Nat.* 7: 'She is the correction of our first Mother Eve'. For a dramatic representation of Mary's doubts and their eventual resolution, see the dialogue between the Archangel and the Theotokos in the Canon at Matins on the Feast of the Annunciation, attributed in the service books to 'John the Monk' (is this John Damascene?) or to Theophanes: *The Festal Menaion*, translated by Mother Mary and Archimandrite Kallistos Ware (London 1969), pp. 448–57.
25 Sources Chrétiennes, p. 21.
26 *Dorm.* 2:3.
27 *Dorm.* 2:8.
28 *Dorm.* 2:14; cf. *Nat.* 7.
29 *Dorm.* 3:2; cf. *Nat.* 3 and 9.
30 See *The Lenten Triodion*, translated by Mother Mary and Archimandrite Kallistos Ware (London 1978), pp. 422–37; also available separately: *The Akathistos Hymn to the Most Holy Mother of God with the Office of Small Compline* (The Ecumenical Society of the Blessed Virgin Mary, 1987).
31 *Dorm.* 1:2.
32 *Dorm.* 1:12.
33 *Dorm.* 2:14; cf. 2:1: 'She rules over all created things, as Mother of God the Creator and Maker who rules over all.'
34 *Dorm.* 3:2.
35 *Dorm.* 1:11.
36 *Dorm.* 1:8.
37 *Dorm.* 2:16; cf. *Nat.* 11: Mary is our 'reconciler' (*diallaktēs*) with God.
38 *Dorm.* 1:11.
39 *Dorm.* 3:5.
40 *Homily on the Dormition* 6; cf. 13, where Cabasilas terms Mary 'the salvation of men'. Cabasilas' three Marian homilies, on the Birth of the Mother of God, on the Annunciation, and on the Dormition, were first edited by Martin Jugie in *Patrologia Orientalis* 19 (Paris 1925), pp. 465–510.
41 *Dorm.* 2:2; cf. *Nat.* 5: 'a virgin before giving birth, a virgin in giving birth, and a virgin after giving birth'. This threefold virginity is represented by the three stars which are depicted in Orthodox icons on Mary's *maphorion* or veil (but according to another explanation the three stars signify the grace of the Holy Trinity that rested upon Mary: see George Galavaris, 'The Stars of the Virgin: An ekphrasis of an ikon of the Mother of God', *Eastern Churches Review* 1:4 [1967–8], pp. 364–9).
42 *Dorm.* 1:7; cf. *Nat.* 5, which adopts a tripartite anthropology: 'She alone is ever a virgin alike in intellect, in soul, and in body.'
43 *Dorm.* 1:4, 2:11; cf. *Nat.* 2.
44 *Dorm.* 1:8; 2:16 and 19.

45 *Dorm.* 2:2 and 8; cf. *Dorm.* 1:3 and 12.
46 *Dorm.* 2:10.
47 *Dorm.* 2:10; cf. *Nat.* 7.
48 *Dorm.* 1:6; cf. *Nat.* 2. See also *Dorm.* 1:12 and 13; 3:4. It is amazing that, in Volume 5 of Kotter's critical edition, the 62-column 'analytical index' of Greeks words altogether omits the terms *panagia, achrantos, amemptos, amō-mos* and *panamōmos*. But they are all included in Voulet's much shorter index.
49 *Dorm.* 2:2.
50 *Dorm.* 2:16.
51 *Dorm.* 1:3.
52 ibid.
53 *Dorm.* 3:5; cf. *Nat.* 7, 9, 10.
54 *Dorm.* 2:3 and 14.
55 It is, however, a matter of dispute how far the Roman Catholic dogma of the immaculate conception, as defined in 1854, necessarily presupposes an Augustinian view of original sin. See the discussion between Fr Edward Yarnold and myself at the ESBVM Congress in Chichester in 1986, subsequently published as a pamphlet, *The Immaculate Conception: A Search for Convergence* (ESBVM, September 1987).
56 *Homily on the Nativity* 6.
57 op. cit. 7.
58 In his *Commentary on the Divine Liturgy* 29–30, Nicolas Cabasilas displays familiarity with the Canon of the Roman Mass and with the Latin Scholastic teaching about the moment of the consecration in the Eucharist. Also in his other major work, *The Life in Christ* 4:4, he shows knowledge of Anselm's theory of the Atonement.
59 *On the Orthodox Faith* 3:12; ed. Kotter, §56.
60 *Homily on the Nativity of Christ* 2 (ed. Kotter, vol. 5, p. 327). Compare *Nat.* 4: 'The child is God; how then can she who bore him not be *Theotokos*?'
61 *Letter 3 to Nestorius*, first anathema.
62 *Commentary on the Divine Liturgy* 1. There are some doubts whether the author is in fact Germanos.
63 *Dorm.* 3:1; cf. 2:2, 'a living heaven'. Compare *Nat.* 2: Mary is 'a living heaven, more spacious than the vastness of the heavens'; *Nat.* 3: she is 'heaven on earth'.
64 *Dorm.* 2:2.
65 *Dorm.* 3:5. Cf. the use made of the Trisagion in *Nat.* 10.
66 On the early development of the doctrine of the Assumption, see Martin Jugie, *La Mort et l'Assomption de la Sainte Vierge: étude historico-doctrinale*, Studi e Testi 114 (Rome 1944), Part 1 (pp. 245–50 refer to John of Damascus); Antoine Wenger, *L'Assomption de la T. S. Vierge dans la tradition byzantine de VIe au Xe siècle*, Archives de l'Orient Chrétien 5 (Paris 1955).
67 *L'Assomption de la T. S. Vierge*, p. 67.
68 *Dorm.* 2:4.
69 There is of course a famous passage in Dionysius the Areopagite (whom John of Damascus would presumably have regarded as an apostolic author): *The Divine Names* 3:2. John refers briefly to this in *Dorm.* 3:4.

70 *Dorm.* 2:9–10.
71 *Dorm.* 2:13.
72 *Dorm.* 1:10–12; 2:10–12, 14. See also *Dorm.* 2:18, where the story is recounted about the arrival of Thomas on the third day after Mary's death. Wishing to venerate her body, he had the tomb opened, but it was found to be empty. Almost certainly this chapter is a later interpolation, and not part of John's original text. (Cf. note 87.)
73 *Dorm.* 1:12; cf. Ps. 15 [16]: 10; Acts 2:31.
74 *Dorm.* 2:15. Here John is attacking the cult of Cybele: Mary, he insists, is altogether different from the mother-goddesses of paganism.
75 See in particular *Dorm.* 2:14; 3:3.
76 *La Mort et l'Assomption de la Sainte Vierge*, p. 248.
77 *Dorm.* 2:8.
78 *Dorm.* 2:14.
79 *Dorm.* 2:2.
80 *Dorm.* 2:14.
81 *Dorm.* 3:5; cf. *Dorm.* 2:10.
82 *Dorm.* 2:3.
83 For a similar line of thought, see Nicolas Cabasilas, *Homily on the Dormition* 11–12: Mary, supremely among all human beings, has been 'conformed' to the death of Christ, and so she, prior to all other human beings, has participated fully in his resurrection (cf. Rom. 6.4–5; Phil. 3.10).
84 *Dorm.* 1:4.
85 *Dorm.* 2:10; cf. Song of Songs 2.10.
86 *Dorm.* 3:4.
87 This is, however, emphasized in the extract from the 'Euthymiac History' which has been inserted into *Dorm.* 2:18, though it is not in fact by John.
88 *Oration* 38:11.
89 *Dorm.* 1:12; cf. *Nat.* 1 and 4.
90 *Dorm.* 1:11.
91 *Dorm.* 2:16.
92 *Dorm.* 1:8.
93 *Dorm.* 2:16; cf. *Nat.* 2: 'O marvel of marvels and paradox of paradoxes.'

*(This paper was given at the ESBVM Oxford Congress
in August 2000)*

31

Homily
'On the matter of forgiveness
among those of different expressions'
given in Oriel College, Oxford
by
The Reverend Dr Edward D. Garten
(Dean of Libraries, University of Dayton, Ohio)
17 August 2000

As an American Methodist, I was reared just outside of a small, rural town in a poor Southern state. There were a great many prejudices in that town – black vs. white, wealthier vs. poorer, educated vs. less-than-well educated – as well as prejudices within families themselves. One type of prejudice that, early on, affected me deeply as a child was, however, religious in nature. Prejudice – to prejudge ideas and people prior to having gained a discerning understanding and knowledge – is something we don't often like to face squarely. Prejudice, you see, is when we make a judgement before we give 'justice' to others as persons and before we give 'justice' to others' ideas.

Some of the prejudices held by some in that small Southern town were prejudices held religious denomination against religious denomination. These were often simple-minded – yet ignorant – prejudices, based on little fact or reality, but, more often, founded on emotion, anxiety, and fear. A true story (aren't they the best?): I had two aunts, one on my mother's side of the family and the other on my father's side – one a Baptist and the other a Roman Catholic. In our small town there were many churches but, interestingly to me, the large Baptist church was across the street from the very small Roman Catholic Church, St Patrick's. The Catholic Church was located right next door to the only grocery store in town – a Kroger store. On occasion, I would visit with Aunt Ruby Holland who lived in town and she would 'invite' me to go along with her grocery shopping. Aunt Ruby was the staunch Baptist in the family. Now, the Catholic Church was right next to the Kroger store with metered parking spaces in front of both. More times than I can recall, if there were no parking spaces directly in front of Kroger's and, yet, there were spaces available in front of St Patrick's, Aunt Ruby would drive around and around the block until someone would leave a parking space in front of the Kroger store. As probably only a twelve-year-old might do, I once asked Aunt Ruby why she wouldn't park in front of St Patrick's. Her reply: 'Those people (she emphasized *those*) worship statues and Mary and, besides, that stone statue of St Patrick in front of that church (she emphasized *that church*), with those snakes crawling around his feet was just plain creepy.' Now, Aunt Ruby has long passed to her reward and there's a good chance she's entered into some interesting conversations with some Roman Catholics she may have met already in heaven.

Then there was the other aunt in the family, Aunt Mae Ballengee, the staunch Roman Catholic. When she would occasionally come to our home for Sunday dinner she'd always find a way to let us know that we weren't quite 'right' in our religion. During grace her lips would purse and her forehead would wrinkle in uncomfortable fashion. Her typical story, told year after year – and in a way that would suggest it was the *first* time she'd ever told us the story – was that her church was like a Great Ship on the ocean and those of us who were Protestants were all huddled in a little boat behind, being pulled by the Great Ship. And, my aunt warned us sternly, *the captain of the Great Ship could set us adrift at any time and we'd drown.*

Both seem relatively harmless prejudices, from a distance, and several in this chapel may have heard such silliness growing up, as well. From a distance we can forgive these simple-minded prejudices. We know there is nothing particularly Christian about the practice of forgiveness since all religious traditions preach and practise it to some extent. We are forgiven and we forgive dozens of times a day. We bump into another person on the street by accident and we say *'I'm sorry'* and they say *'no problem!'* (in reality, you are forgiven). Most daily offences are trivial and unintentional. Forgiveness only becomes problematic when the trespasses are more serious, repeated, and systemic. Only a few years later – when I was seventeen – and my pastor invited me to travel with him to Selma, Alabama in the spring of 1965, did I begin to comprehend the difficulty of forgiveness in the face of hatred laid upon hatred. Even today I can hear in my head the vile and venomous taunts as 'good and righteous white folks' on the sidelines of that now historic march from Selma to Montgomery, lashed out at those of us who marched with Dr King.

Jesus is asked by Peter how many times one may forgive another. The rabbis generally agreed that you could forgive a repeated offence three times and then on the fourth time there would be punishment, or at minimum, simply long remembrance of the offence and, thus, no forgiveness. The response to Jesus by Peter makes Peter seem very generous – '*Can we forgive seven times?*' he asks. Perhaps Peter is think-ing: *Not just three times, but seven, look at how tolerant I am!* But in Matthew, we know, Jesus is seen as radically going beyond the law. 'You were told by your tradition of old, but I tell you!' Scholars disagree as to whether Jesus said '*7 times 7*' or '*7 times 70*' – nonetheless, the direc-tive is that we must forgive an unlimited number of times. Conduct in the community of disciples, known as the Church, is to be patterned after the mercy and grace of God's free forgiveness of sin – which is an important basis for the very existence of the community.

As God freely forgives those who have sinned against him, so are disciples to freely forgive those who have sinned against them. Jesus tells us that the failure to forgive one who is repentant casts doubt on the genuineness of the person's discipleship. If we fail to show grace to others who have repented, then this text promises us only to be handed over to the torturer. As Matthew suggests Jesus saying, '*And that is how my heavenly Father will deal with you unless you each forgive your brother from your heart.*' And, as James 2.13 reinforces for us: '*For judgement is without mercy to one who has shown no mercy.*' Divine and human forgive-ness go hand-in-hand. Nothing that we have to forgive can even faintly compare with what we have been forgiven already by God. Consider this: All of us have been forgiven more than we will ever forgive.

John Wesley was especially concerned, you know, with how we respect those of other traditions and perspectives. In his famous sermon 'on those who are Christian but practise their faith under different expressions' he tells us:

It is true, believers may not all speak alike – they may not all use the same language. It is not to be expected that they should – we cannot reasonably require it of them. A thousand circumstances may cause them to vary from each other, in the manner of expressing themselves, but a different expression does not necessarily imply a difference of sentiment. Different persons may use different expressions, and yet mean the same thing. Nothing is more common than this, although we seldom make sufficient allowance for it.

And in another context, Wesley observed that:

If there is a difference of opinion, where is our religion, if we cannot think and let think? What hinders but you may forgive me as easily as I may forgive you?

We Methodists – both on your side of the Atlantic and on my side – place great importance on the working of the Holy Spirit in the hearts of women and men. We believe that the Holy Spirit will aid our desire to forgive. And yet we continue to hurt one another, as Christian as we, while we pursue the truth of Christ along our several paths. Wesley, again:

> How dreadful and how innumerable are the contests, which have arisen about religion. And not only among the children of this world, among those who knew not what true religion was, but even among the children of God, those who had experienced the Kingdom of God within them, who had tasted of righteousness, and peace, and joy in the Holy Ghost. How many of these, in all ages, instead of joining together against the common enemy, have turned their weapons against each other, and so not only wasted their precious time, but hurt one another's spirits, weakened each other's hands, and so hindered the great work of their common Master.

I'm a devotee of the American humourist Garrison Keillor who often writes satire about the Lutherans of Minnesota – set against the fictional place called Lake Wobegon. Keillor talks about the 'Dark Lutherans' and the 'Happy Lutherans'. The two factions were divided over the role of women and the colour of the sky and how to make coleslaw, and they divided over the issue of '*Will we recognize each other in heaven, or will our spiritual forms not have our earthly features?*' The 'Dark Lutherans' were strict about dress – which should be modest – and after church one was to remain in a devotional mode for the rest of the day, sitting in a room with shades pulled, perusing a commentary on Obadiah or Habakkuk. The 'Happy Lutherans' said, '*Oh, what harm would it do to read David Copperfield on Sunday, or play baseball, or hear a Mozart sonata?*' And the 'Dark Lutherans' cried, '*Do you care so little for Him who shed His life's blood for you that you cannot spare one day out of seven to think of Him and of Him only? Is this too much to ask?*'

Keillor observes that it was generally a miserable argument and the 'Happy Lutherans' lost, of course – just how militant could you be, arguing for kindness and mercy? Could you scream and yell at the legalists, demand that they be tolerant, pound the table, threaten them with damnation if they didn't get themselves a sense of humour? One by one, most of the 'Happy Lutherans' migrated south or westward to California, where they prospered. They were polite, they were steady workers and cheerful, and they accepted the California climate as God's gentle blessing on them. The 'Dark Lutherans' throve in a cold climate, believing that adversity and suffering were given as moral instruction – and so was sickness. It was hard on the 'Darks', they didn't really believe in forgiveness, so if one of their numbers fell into worldliness, there was no way back. He or she had to move to Minneapolis or to California and attend a church where the sign in front didn't say '*Repent, O Wretched Man*', rather, it said, '*Mistakes make better artists of us all as we weave new patterns in the fabric of our lives.*'

Granted, this is only good humour, but there is a grain of uncomfortable truth here. Just as obviously, as Christians one to another, we are called to forgive each other those careless prejudices that stand in the way of sisterhood and brotherhood. But recall that Matthew goes one step further since this forgiveness to which we are called is meant not just for distribution among Christians (Anglican, Methodist, Lutheran, Roman Catholic, Baptist, and other stripes) it is meant for distribution among those whom the world considers unrighteous. The Good News incorporates the blemishes and disasters, the righteous and the unrighteous, in the line of Jesus Christ in whom God began a new and surprising work. Perhaps the strangest feature of the Matthean geneaology, which begins that Gospel, is the inclusion of those people in Jesus' lineage that the world might consider unrighteous – even his mother, Mary, a 'nobody', indeed, an unmarried mother, an ignorant peasant girl on the fringes of society. The British poet M. L. Goulder's verse captures some of those in Jesus' lineage in his poem:

The Women in the Matthean Genealogy

Exceedingly odd is the means by which God
Has provided our path to the heavenly shore –
Of the girls from whose line the true light was to shine
There was one an adulteress, one was a whore:
There was Tamar who bore – what we all should deplore –
A fine pair of twins to her father-in-law,
And Rahab the harlot, her sins were as scarlet,
As red as the thread that she hung from the door;
Yet alone of her nation she came to salvation
And lived to be mother of Boaz of yore –
And he married Ruth, a Gentile uncouth,
In a manner quite counter to biblical lore.
And of her there did spring blessed David the King,
Who walked in his palace one evening and saw
The wife of Uriah, from whom he did sire
A baby that died – oh, and princes a score:
And a mother unmarried it was too that carried
God's Son, and him laid in a manger of straw,
That the moral might wait at the heavenly gate
While sinners and publicans go in before,
Who have not earned their place, but received it by grace,
And have found them a righteousness not of the law.

M. L. Goulder, *Midrash and Lection*
in Matthew, SPCK, 1974, p. 232

This inclusion of that cast of characters in Matthew's opening genealogy reminded the Jewish and Gentile reader that God's great plan of salvation included Gentiles – even unrighteous Gentiles. Indeed, those whom the 'righteous and proper' may consider 'unrighteous and immoral' may – in God's plan – come first in the Kingdom. What is this thing strange to our ears – that the first shall be last and the last, first? Dear brothers and sisters in Christ, offences among us are to be confronted, yes, but only in the spirit of gentleness (Galatians 6.1). Even when dealing with the stubbornly unrepentant, we are asked to forsake vindictiveness and, by God's grace, give evidence that we are able to extend forgiveness because we ourselves are humbled by God's forgiving love. The stories in Matthew are often direct and simple. The more carefully we read them, the more searching we find them. Like the Sermon on the Mount, they require of us responsible decisions and fresh attitudes toward one another and they promise that these attitudes and decisions are of unimaginable significance in the here and now and for eternity.

In his parables, Jesus repeatedly taught the particular importance of remembering our own need for and experience of forgiveness when we ourselves are called upon to forgive. It was E. M. Forster who said it, but it could have easily have been Jesus – 'Only connect.' Connecting in this radically magnanimous way with the one who has offended is difficult, of course, but Jesus was right to make it the pivotal element of his teaching. Without radical forgiveness of one another, we condemn ourselves not only to the pain of our offences against one another, but to years of misery that deepen the original wound by the corrosions of bitterness and hatred. And this is true, as we well know, not only of our individual trespasses against one another as Christians, but of the sins of whole nations. Only connect with him or her who has offended us. Only forgive as we are forgiven.

May the Lord who knows our hearts beyond our several ways of expressing our desire for Him, be raised up and worshipped now and forever!

Amen.

Mary
in
literature

32

Mary and the saints
in early Scottish poetry

John Macquarrie

In the millennium before the birth of Christ, the Celts were, after the Greeks and Romans, probably the principal ethnic group in Europe. Unlike the Greeks and Romans, they never formed a single nation but were mainly tribal barbarians, in the eyes of the Mediterranean peoples. The Greeks called them Keltoi, a name similar to the modern term Celts, while the Roman called them Gauls. In those days, they probably occupied the heartlands of Europe north of the Alps, and some surviving place-names give an indication of the wide extent of their settlements. Galatia, nowadays in Turkey, was a Celtic area in the far south-east, and we may suppose it was to Celts that Paul wrote his Letter to the Galatians. They eventually merged into the surrounding cosmopolitan Hellenistic population. Still in the east, but much further north, there is an area called Galicia, on the borders of Poland and the Ukraine. At the very other end of Europe, in the north-west corner of Spain, there is another Galicia, the name of which probably dates from the time when the Celts or Gauls were being driven even further to the west by a kind of pincer movement, in which they were caught between the Roman Empire on the south and invading Germanic tribes on the north. Wales, also in the extreme west, is another example of the presence of the Gauls, for the names Wales and Welsh are variant forms of the terms Gaul and Gaulish – indeed, the French still refer to Wales as 'Pays de Galles'. France itself was known in ancient times as Gaul, and was in the main Celtic territory.

The earliest written reference to the Celts is probably one found in the writings of the Greek historian Herodotus. Writing about the middle of the fifth century BCE, he informs his readers that the River Danube rises in the land of the Celts. This seems good evidence that in his time the Celts were still living at the heart of Europe. About a century later, in his dialogue *The Laws*, Plato remarks that the Celts are much given to intoxication – a remark which, sadly, has still some truth in it. There were no Celtic historians in those days to record the history of their people, and we get glimpses of them only when they collided with the peoples of the south. In 390 BCE Celts from the north came down into Italy, where they captured and plundered the city of Rome itself. The violent events of that time are recorded by Livy, and for long afterwards the Romans remembered this barbarian visitation as one of the blackest days in their history. Just over a century later, in 279 BCE, another horde of Celts, this time from the Balkans, invaded Greece and raided the sacred precincts of Delphi.

Our particular interest is in that portion of the Celtic peoples called the Scots. Although nowadays we think of the Scots as the inhabitants of Scotland, the term was anciently used in a wider, more indefinite sense. The Scots were a Celtic people whose territory covered quite a large tract of land in both Scotland and Ireland. They spoke the same Gaelic language, and were linguistically different from the Welsh, who also spoke a Celtic language but one which was markedly divergent from Gaelic, and closer to the Celtic languages of Cornwall and Brittany. All of the Celtic languages belong to the Indo-European family, their closest neighbour being Latin. But the Celtic languages have lost the sound represented by the letter *p*, at the beginning of words and between vowels, except in late borrowings. For example, the Latin word for 'father' is *pater*, and we would expect to find a word similar to *pater* being used for 'father' in Gaelic, but the Gaelic word is actually *athair*, where the initial *p* has been completely lost, and even the *t* has been aspirated and in speech is reduced to an indistinct stop. In similar fashion, the Latin word *tepidus, 'hot'*, has for its Gaelic cognate *teth*.

The fact that the people called Scots might be geographically from either Scotland or Ireland has sometimes been cause for confusion. Two great medieval theologians were both known as John the Scot (*Ioannes Scotus*). One was Ioannes Scotus Eriugena in the ninth century, the other Ioannes Duns Scotus in the fourteenth century. The former was obviously Irish, since the title Eriugena means 'Irish-born', while the second was Scottish, taking the name Duns from his birthplace, a market-town in Berwickshire in the south-east of Scotland. But both might be called simply John the Scot. An amusing story about Scots and Scottishness is told concerning Eriugena. At one point in his life, he was teaching in the University of Paris and was invited to dine with the king, Charles the Bald. The two were sitting facing one another across the table when the king, in an attempt to be witty, propounded a question to the philosopher. *'Quid distat inter Scotum et sotum?'* 'What is the difference between a Scot and a sot?' Eriugena thought for a moment, and came back with the riposte, *'Tabula tantum'* 'Only this table'. The king, no doubt mellowed by wine, appears to have taken the reply in good part.

By the beginning of the Christian era, the Scots, Welsh and other Celtic peoples had been pushed to the very fringes of Europe, and occupied the inhospitable regions bordering on the Atlantic. There they gained a frugal living from farming and fishing. They continued to preserve their languages, and these have survived to the present. Strangely, the Welsh, in spite of their proximity to England, have been most successful in keeping the old language alive as a tongue of everyday discourse. Attempts have been made in both Ireland and Scotland to revive the Gaelic but not much progress has been made, except among scholars and those who have an attachment to Gaelic literature. After all, nobody writes textbooks of nuclear physics or computer science in Gaelic.

Something must be said here about the ancient Celtic religion or religions, since some of the old attitudes and beliefs persisted into the Christian period. Like the religions of many early peoples, Celtic religion played a very large part in daily life. There were many gods and goddesses, of whom about four hundred names are known. Many of these were local deities and perhaps they would be better described as spirits, usually associated with some natural feature, a well or a rock or a hill. This should be remembered when we come to consider the role of the saints in Celtic Christianity, for many local saints took over the numinous traits of pre-Christian godlings. But there were also some high gods, notably Lugh, the master of all skills. His name is preserved in place names, such as Lyon (Lugdunum) in France and Legnica in Silesia (now in Poland but formerly in Germany when it was called Liegnitz). There were also powerful goddesses, of whom perhaps the best-known was Brigit. Although this religion was polytheistic, it was tending toward a kind of pantheism, understood to mean that although there was no single universally-recognized supreme God, there was a deep sense of the immanence of the divine in all nature and also in all human activity.

A peculiarity of Celtic religion was that its devotees did not build temples for their gods. Caesar, who spent ten years of his life in Gaul, mentions this fact, and tells us that nevertheless the Celts set aside particular areas to serve as 'holy places' (*loci consecrati*), usually in the form of groves of oak trees. There are indeed some ancient pre-Christian structures in the former Celtic domains of Scotland (sometimes called the Gaelteachd) but it is quite likely that these are so ancient that they were already there when the Celts came to Scotland and had been erected by some still earlier and unknown people. For example, in the extreme north-west of Scotland, on the island of Lewis, at a place called Callanish, there is a circle of standing stones so impressive that, if it were not so remote, it might be a rival tourist attraction to Stonehenge. Some archaeologists believe that it is older than Stonehenge, and its stones may have been standing there for as long as 5000 years. It may have been associated with sun-worship, but its precise nature is unknown. But although they did not build temples, the Celts did construct tombs for the departed, and many of these have been excavated and explored in various parts of Europe. Some of them have been found to contain arte-facts, some of very high artistic quality, showing that these Celts were not quite the barbarians that the Greeks and Romans supposed them to be. If their exploits at the Battle of Alia and the raid on Delphi, to say nothing of their own internecine clan warfare, suggest that they were a warlike people, there was another side to their nature. They had a sense of beauty, a love of the still-unspoiled world around them, a warmth of feeling for one another and even for their animals. These gentler aspects come into prominence after the coming of Christianity.

It is hard to believe, but it is the case, that when Christianity did come to these sturdy peoples, almost driven into the ocean but still clinging precariously to the barren Atlantic seaboard, they became a shining light to the rest of Europe. Exactly when the Christian faith first reached them is unknown. It was probably brought by Mediterranean traders or Roman soldiers, but it established itself and in the so-called 'Dark Age' preceding the end of the first millennium, the Celtic realms preserved not only a considerable level of culture and learning but maintained a strong tradition of Christian piety when much of Europe was still pagan. The Ireland of that time has been called the 'land of saints and scholars' and the description would apply equally to Scotland and Wales. Admittedly, that time is now long past, but it is not just a romantic figment of the imagination.

The transition from the old Celtic paganism to the Christian religion would seem to have been a smooth one. Just how smooth the transition was is strikingly symbolized at the old parish church of Govan, nowa-days within the city boundary of Glasgow. The church there, which goes back to Celtic times and is dedicated to St Constantine (no relation of the emperor), possesses a unique collection of ancient carved stones. An interesting feature is that the churchyard is circular in shape, suggesting that it may preserve the shape of an ancient stone circle which, like the one at Callanish, may even have been pre-Celtic. The standing stones themselves have long ago disappeared from their places, but it is possi-ble that some of them have survived in altered form among the carved stones.

I have mentioned above how a sense of the divine immanence was an important element in the Celtic religion, and this passed over into Celtic Christianity. God was conceived not so much as a distant power in the heavens as a circumambient and inescapable presence here on earth. I shall expand on this later, but here I would just mention that the sense of immanence can be traced even in modern Scottish theologians of Celtic background. A good example is John Baillie, a highly respected theologian of the Church of Scotland and one who was born and nurtured in the Highlands. In his book, *Our Knowledge of God*, he denies that such knowledge is primarily inferential and claims that 'Distant though God may be in his transcendence, he may yet be nearer to me than my best friend'; and to emphasize the point, he quotes the famous lines of St Patrick's Breastplate:

> Christ be with me, Christ within me,
> Christ behind me, Christ before me,
> Christ beside me, Christ to win me,
> Christ to comfort and restore me,
> Christ beneath me, Christ above me,
> Christ in quiet, Christ in danger,
> Christ in hearts of all that love me,
> Christ in mouth of friend and stranger.

A few years later he published his Gifford Lectures with the title, *The Sense of the Presence of God*, in which the immediate sense of the divine presence, as he had himself inherited it from his Celtic ancestry, was claimed to be the surest ground of our belief in the reality of God.

Baillie and the old Celtic Church before him did not, of course, deny the transcendence of God. They were not reverting to a pre-Christian pantheism, but they were seeking to balance the belief in transcendence with a due recognition of God's immanence in their midst. We remind ourselves of the imagery of the sun and its rays, much beloved of patristic theologians. The sun is not only 'up there' at a vast remove from our earthly habitat; the life-giving warmth of the sun is among us day by day as we go about our activities. So those Celts had a tremendous sense of intimacy with God. He was present with them all the time, from getting up in the morning to lying down at night. 'Christ within me, Christ behind me, Christ before me ...' For them, the universe is a holy place, for it is God's world. And when we reflect how we human beings have exploited and defaced and abused the creation, including our fellow creatures, we realize the wisdom of such a reverential attitude toward the works of God. The sense of intimacy and closeness with God and with his Christ is expressed in brief poems and prayers which were used in the course of each day. There was not a time of day or a particular duty that did not have its appropriate prayer.

> This morning I will kindle the fire upon my hearth
> Before the holy angels who stand upon my path.
> No envy, hatred, malice, no fear upon my face,
> But the holy Son of God, the Guardian of the place.

Or in the evening:

> With God will I lie down this night,
>   And God will be lying with me.
> With Christ will I lie down this night,
>   And Christ will be lying with me.
> With Spirit will I lie down this night,
>   The Spirit will lie down with me.
> God and Christ and Spirit, Three,
>   Be they all down-lying with me.

The intimacy with God expressed in these lines, and the simplicity of the poetry itself, show the kind of society in which these people lived, a society in which genuine warm human relations and a genuine piety flourished. There is no irreverence in the intimacy with God which they expressed. Even when a number of clans recognized a 'high king' over them, he was not so very high as to be out of touch with his people. The High King of Tara had his abode on the Hill of Tara, which is quite a low hill. Must not even God, sometimes called the 'High King of Heaven' be likewise close to his people?

The stress on divine immanence, as I have mentioned, was already present in pre-Christian Celtic religion, and it received a new impetus and a fuller significance from the Christian belief in incarnation. It must too have been an influence in gaining for the saints the important place which they held in Celtic Christian spirituality. People for whom an utterly transcendent God or a highly exalted Christ were difficult ideas and who had therefore come to think of God and Christ in ways which located them as closer to the earth and to the daily lives of men and women, saw their presence also in holy men and women who had exhibited in their lives the Christian virtues. Though the veneration accorded to the saints may reflect in part the polytheistic beliefs of earlier times, it was not understood in any idolatrous way. The saints were venerated only to the extent that they had been channels through which God had conveyed his grace. A French (Gaulish?) writer of the eighth century, Ermoldus Nigellus, expressed what the people of that time intended: 'It is God whom we adore in his dear servants, whose prayers help us to reach heaven'. We could say that the people whom he had in mind were firm believers in the communion of saints. The phrase 'communion of saints' appears in the Apostles' Creed, though it was not a part of the creed in its earliest form. It is, however, not just a repetition of the preceding article, 'the Holy Catholic Church'. According to the current *Catechism of the Catholic Church*, reminding us of the use of the words *Sancta sanctis!* ('God's holy gifts for God's holy people') in the Eastern liturgy, 'the term "communion of saints" has two closely linked meanings: communion "in holy things (*sancta*)" and communion "among holy persons (*sancti*)".' At the fraction in the Anglican eucharist, the priest says, 'We break this bread to share in the Body of Christ', and the people reply, 'Though we are many, we are all one Body, because we all share in the one Bread'. Communion in the holy things signifies and effects a spiritual communion of the believers with Christ and with one another.

The Celtic Christian of the first millennium therefore thought of himself as a member of Christ's Church, but this did not mean simply the local congregation or even the worldwide Church. His Church extended through time as well as space. There was an unseen cloud of witnesses surrounding and supporting the Christians who were still on their earthly pilgrimage. At the head of this company was Mary, then the apostles and evangelists, then the teachers and missionaries of the Church, and soon some of the Celts themselves. In Scotland, Ireland and Wales the Celtic churches produced men and women of saintly stature from perhaps the fourth century onwards.[1] Some were shared among the three areas. Patrick became patron saint of Ireland and did his main work there, but he came originally from the British mainland, though whether from Wales or Scotland is a disputed – and even hotly disputed! – question. Columba, on the other hand, had his origin in Ireland, but moved over to Scotland to found his famous abbey on Iona and to labour among the people of Argyll and further afield. Kentigern is patron saint of Glasgow, but he had also close associations with Wales. One could mention also Ninian, Serf, Conval and many others, including many local saints who took over sacred sites from the old pagan deities. Among women saints, St Brigid acquired a special reputation, and it seems probable that she inherited something of the aura that had attached to the old goddess Brigit. But these saints were as much alive in the feelings and affections of the people as were their still-living neighbours. We could not even say that the saints were invisible, for visions seem to have been a common experience among the Celts. I have myself spoken to an islander from Lewis who claimed to have had a vision, and it certainly had been a reality, indeed, quite a formative reality for his own life. The vividness with which these people experienced the saints may be illustrated from the following short poem:

> Who are these in my fishing-boat today?[2]
> Peter and Paul and John Baptist are they.
> At my helm the Christ is sitting to steer,
> The wind from the south making our way.
> Who makes the voice of the wind to grow faint?
> And who makes calm the kyle and the sea?
> It is Jesus Christ, the Head of each saint.

The situation described in this poem makes it clear that for the Celts of that time, the 'communion of saints' was not just an article in the creed but a daily lived experience.

Poems like the one just quoted have been transmitted for centuries in Scotland, but only in relatively recent times has the extent and the value of this treasure been appreciated. In the nineteenth century, Gaelic scholars toured round the Highlands and Islands collecting these poems from the mouths of the people, especially the older people. Many of these poems appear to have remained unchanged over long periods. It has been said that they are more durable than even the ancient stones, and they are imbued with a deeply religious feeling. Chief among the collectors was Dr Alexander Carmichael, who published in 1900 two substantial volumes of poems, the *Carmina Gadelica*,[3] supplying English translations as well as the Gaelic texts. He died in 1912, leaving behind him a large quantity of unpublished material, some of which has since seen the light of day.

Mary had her special place in that spirituality. One of the earliest hymns from those days is in fact a hymn to Mary.[4] It was composed by a monk of Iona Abbey and has been dated with a high degee of probability to about the year 700, little more than a century after the death of Columba. The monk had a name that sounds strangely to us. He was Cu Chuimne, which means in Gaelic 'Hound of Memory'. The hymn was written in Latin, as it was intended for use in church, whilst the popular hymns and poems were in Gaelic. The rhyming Latin of this hymn is very elegant and attests to the learning of the monastic author and explains the reputation of the Gaelteachd as a 'land of saints and scholars'. The hymn is a long one, thirteen stanzas, and the second stanza indicates that it was sung antiphonally. I shall quote only the first six stanzas, first in Latin, then in English:

Cantemus in omni die	Let us sing every day
concinentes varie	harmonizing in turn
conclamantes Deo dignum	together proclaiming to God
ymnum sanctae Mariae.	a hymn worthy of holy Mary.
Bis per chorum hinc et inde	In twofold chorus, from side to side,
collaudemus Mariam	let us praise Mary
et vox pulset omnem aurem	so that the voice strikes every ear
per lauden victoriam.	with alternating praise.
Maria de tribu Iudae	Mary of the tribe of Judah
summi Mater Domini	Mother of the Most High Lord
opportunam dedit curam	gave fitting care
egrotanti homini.	to languishing mankind.

Gabriel advexit verbum	Gabriel first brought the word
sinu prius paterno	from the Father's bosom
quod conceptum et susceptum	which was conceived and received
in utero materno.	in the Mother's womb.
Haec est summa haec est sancta	She is most high, she is holy,
Virgo venerabilis	the venerable Virgin
quae ex fide non recessit	who by faith did not draw back
sed exstetit stabilis.	but stood forth firmly.
Huic Matri nec inventa	None has been found, before or since,
ante nec post similis	like this Mother,
nec de prole fuit plane	not out of all the descendants
humanae originis.	of the human race.

As I have said, this Latin poem is elegant and beautiful, a splendid tribute to our Lady. Yet it is also ecclesiastical and therefore somewhat formal. The Gaelic poems from the people are, by contrast, warm, and, though not lacking in literary merit, they are relatively artless. But they make up for any literary shortcomings by their obvious sincerity. They are speaking of Mary out of the communion of saints. I remarked earlier that the veneration of the saints is justified because this veneration arose among simple peoples for whom the notions of God and even of Christ so far transcended their ordinary lives that they looked for the divine as it manifests itself in the grace-filled lives of human beings like themselves. So in these vernacular poems, Mary does not appear as she does in church, in a statue, let us say, or in a stained-glass window. She is one of the community, sharing the home and the work-place, like those apostles whom we have already seen on the fishing-boat, not as passengers but as companions and helpmates. So Mary is in the kitchen, at the bedside of the sick, among the farm animals, comforting the dying. The mariology of the Celts has something to teach us. If veneration for Mary did indeed arise out of her being fully a fellow human being, then if we exalt her too much in the liturgy or in dogma, we push her to a distance and turn her into a demi-goddess. But the Celt spoke of her with an affectionate intimacy. Her care is for the family and even for the animals:

> Who keeps the night-watch now and over mine?
> Who but the Lord Christ of the poor is there,
> And the milk-white Bride, the Maiden of the kine,
> The milk-white Mary of the curling hair.[5]

This Mary is close to us in the communion of saints.

In the journal of Mundelein Seminary, I came across a piece by the

American poet, Alice Tarnowski, which, I think, sums up in a modern idiom the understanding of Mary found in the Celtic tradition. Addressing Mary, the poet says;

> O Lady of Guadalupe,
> Madonna of Czestochowa,
> Queen of Patriarchs,
> Mystical Rose,
> Do you sometimes long to cry out
> [To devout Christians]
> Stop! Be silent, listen to me!
> I'm Miriam, the Jewish girl of Nazareth
> Who said Yes to life.

Notes

1   For the early Scottish saints, see Alan Macquarrie, *The Saints of Scotland* (John Donald, Edinburgh 1997).
2   Two stanzas (conflated and slightly altered) from G. R. D. McLean, *Poems of the Western Highlanders* (SPCK, London 1961). The verse 'This morning will I kindle the fire' (p. 381) and the poem 'With God will I lie down' (p. 382) are taken from the same source. All reproduced with the permission of SPCK.
3   The two original volumes were reprinted by Scottish Academic Press, Edinburgh, in 1971. Further volumes have been published since then at various dates.
4   T. O. Clancy and G. Markus OP, *Iona: The Earliest Poetry of a Celtic Monastery* (Edinburgh University Press, 1995). Reproduced with the permission of Polygon.
5   McLean, op. cit. p. 414.

*(This paper was given at the ESBVM Oxford Congress
in August 2000)*